Norbert Elliot

On a Scale

A Social History of Writing Assessment in America

PETER LANG
New York • Washington, D.C./Baltimore • Bern
Frankfurt am Main • Berlin • Brussels • Vienna • Oxford

Library of Congress Cataloging-in-Publication Data

Elliot, Norbert.
On a scale: a social history of writing assessment in America / Norbert Elliot.
p. cm. — (Studies in composition and rhetoric; vol. 3).
Includes bibliographical references and index.
1. English language—Rhetoric—Study and teaching—Social aspects.
2. English language—Composition and exercises—Social aspects.
3. Report writing—Study and teaching—Social aspects.
4. English language—Ability testing—Social aspects.
5. College prose—Evaluation—Social Aspects.
6. School prose—Evaluation—Social Aspects. I. Title.
PE1404 .E447 808'.042'071073—dc21 99-051684
ISBN 0-8204-2778-0
ISSN 1080-5397

Bibliographic information published by Die Deutsche Bibliothek.
Die Deutsche Bibliothek lists this publication in the "Deutsche Nationalbibliografie"; detailed bibliographic data is available on the Internet at http://dnb.ddb.de/.

Cover design by Lisa Barfield

The paper in this book meets the guidelines for permanence and durability of the Committee on Production Guidelines for Book Longevity of the Council of Library Resources.

275 Seventh Avenue, 28th Floor, New York, NY 10001
www.peterlangusa.com

Printed in the United States of America

ADVANCE PRAISE FOR

On a Scale

"*On a Scale* will stand as a landmark study of writing assessment in the United States. Norbert Elliot combines thorough research with extraordinary insight into the people who shaped literacy instruction and the contexts in which they worked. Elliot's book changes our thinking about how and why we judge writing."

Lester Faigley, Robert Adger Law and Thos. H. Law Professor in Humanities, University of Texas at Austin; Author of Fragments of Rationality: Postmodernity and the Subject of Composition

"Norbert Elliot's *On A Scale* is a timely treatment of one of today's hottest educational issues—writing assessment. Elliot provides superb historical background, demonstrating how the testing of writing has always been fraught with difficulty in attaining reliability and validity. Today's teachers and scholars will benefit from Elliot's careful examination of all the sources, including his valuable look at the ETS archives. In an impressively researched volume, Elliot presents the best single overview of the topic, a book that is sure to become the definitive work on its subject."

John Brereton, Director, Calderwood Writing Initiative, The Boston Athenæum; Editor of The Origins of Composition Studies in the American College, 1875–1925: A Documentary History

On a Scale

Studies in Composition and Rhetoric

Leonard Podis
General Editor

Vol. 3

PETER LANG
New York • Washington, D.C./Baltimore • Bern
Frankfurt am Main • Berlin • Brussels • Vienna • Oxford

For Fran

Grace: An Acknowledgment

The numinous, Rudolph Otto believed, evokes three impulses: the sense that there is something wholly other in our lives (*mysterium*), that this otherness evokes a kind of awe (*tremendum*) and that this awe is mitigated with captivating grace (*fascinans*). Such has been the presence of this book in my life. The grace of others has moderated the fearful presence of an elusive topic.

Capturing the construct of writing and the techniques used to assess it is a process. Sometimes, the events emerging are familiar; other times, they recede into fog. Documentation involved time in the stacks at Princeton's Firestone Library and the archives at the Educational Testing Service. It involved structured interviews with specialists and a forest's worth of drafts. As a product, *On a Scale: A Social History of Writing Assessment in America* traces the ways that student writing has been viewed in educational settings. Cases are drawn from the freshman class of 1874, when Harvard University first required applicants to submit an English composition, to the freshman class of 2006, when the College Entrance Examination Board required an essay as part of the SAT®: Reasoning Test. Harvard's essay was designed to be taken by some 300 students; the SAT essay was taken in its first 2005 administration by approximately 330,000 students. Often regarded as an allegory of oppression and protest, the history of writing assessment should also be understood as a narrative of community. In 1874 teachers came together in oak-lined rooms to read student essays resting on mahogany tables; in 2005, with essays floating on pixels, others log into rooms without walls to read student compositions. As Alan C. Purves, perhaps the twentieth century's most subtle assessment practitioner, found in his last book, the basis of community is respect for individuality; even as modern consensus has eroded, the counterpoint of community—in this case, a writing assessment community—exists as an index of hope.

What was the United States like on the eastern seaboard when Harvard University elected to require each candidate to write a short composition on works of standard authors selected from a list that would be announced from time to time? What did the sponsors of that assessment hope to find? What did those who read those compositions think of them, and what definitions and expectations of ability did those readers hold? What were the actions of the communities involved, and how did those actions reveal dissatisfaction with both the rigidity of author lists and the flux of occasional announcement? How was disagreement—on committee strategy and essay worth—resolved among sponsors? How did educators, embedded within a demographically exploding national system of commerce, comprehend their responsibilities? What was the impact of the new laboratory psychology on writing assessment at the century's beginning? What was the impact of the First World War? The Second? Of the fear of communism? Of the rise of long-silenced voices? What changes did those new voices inspire—or demand—as dialect blossomed and cities burned? Did the singular Harvard fathers understand writing ability in the same way as those thousands who designed and staffed assessment programs across the nation during the 1970s and 1980s? How can we tell? What premises remained, and what disappeared? What is the relationship between the technology of the computer (a world lit by lightning) and the technology of writing (a thought reified by chirography) in the assessment community of the early 21st century?

And how, within this enterprise, does one get out of the way of the narrative while knowing full well that the choice of narrative detail is itself an autobiographical act?

With help from one's friends. The composition of this book may have been an isolating process, but the product is the result of many whose desire was my success. That desire, of course, often took odd forms. Miriam Levin, Senior Examiner at ETS, was the first to find me out. "Ugh, ugh, ugh," she typed in a May 30, 1984, review of my wretched attempt to write an item for the Graduate Management Admission Test. "This is real gobbledygook. Hard to understand what in heaven's name is being talked about. This really makes no sense. The problem is a real nothing, too, so junk this, fast." Since I was reported to have some skill as a teacher of freshman composition, she sent me off to the archives to see what I could find about the history of writing assessment and, no doubt, to get me out from underfoot. Twenty years later, I am still on that errand.

I have benefited greatly from the good (though often strong) will of my ETS colleagues over the years. The late Gertrude Conlan spent time explaining the premises of holistic scoring during the summer I had worked as an ETS temp to cover vacations, and both Paul Ramsey and Jill Burstein provided recent interviews for this book. Julie Duminiak worked tirelessly in the archives to help me find studies and photos; she made this project her own. At the College Board, Wayne Camara answered detailed questions and generously provided recent reports and studies; Brian Bremen of the University of Texas at Austin, a William Carlos Williams specialist helping to design the 2005 essay for the SAT, also provided an interview. Within the university community, Lee Odell of Rensselaer Polytechnic Institute was generous with his time and his intellect. Leonard Podis of Oberlin College was a prince among series editors, always and everywhere a critical, encouraging reader. At New Jersey Institute of Technology, Robert Lynch and Burt Kimmelman read the manuscript, provided support generally associated with social services, and never once muttered a single ugh. At the Robert W. Van Houten Library at NJIT, Rhonda Greene-Carter filled every imaginable interlibrary loan request. The following folks also helped to find images and secure permissions: Margaret Aldrich (Princeton University Press), Erin Burkert (the National Academy of Sciences), Margaret J. Kimball (Stanford University), Robin McElheny (Harvard University), Meriwether Schas (the College Board), and Jennifer Ulrich (Columbia University Archives-Columbiana Library). Thanks also to the NJIT Committee on Sabbaticals for giving me time to begin the book.

The subtleties of quantitative measurement, the dangerous edge of things, were explained first to me at Texas A&M University-Commerce by Paul F. Zelhart and Maximino Plata and, later, by Margaret Kilduff, Marian Passannante, Bart K. Holland, Joesph Holtzman, and Frances Ward at the University of Medicine of Dentistry of New Jersey. Most recently, W. Patrick Beaton and Vladimir Briller at NJIT have taken up the job of helping someone trained only to follow the trails of hounds, bay houses, and turtle-doves. Yet, to listen to Vlad (and to Paul, Max, Meg, Marianne, Bart, Joe, Fran, and Pat) you would think that scientific logic and humanistic understanding were practiced, at their best, by those who had equally heard the hound, the tramp of the horse, and even seen the dove disappear behind a cloud and were anxious to recover them. At Peter Lang, Phyllis Korper, Sophie Appel, and Bernadette Shade have been the best of editors and production coordinators, and Tom Bechtle was a meticulous copyeditor. Mary Salerno remains a patient impresario of the computer and its products.

My wife, Frances Ward, gave me a place to come to, and the children in our combined family—Christian, Kathryn, James, Luke, Sarah, Jesse, Nicholas and Sophia—were, at once, both curious and amused that a grown man could become excited about something as dull as writing assessment. But they knew, as children always do, that by turning and turning we come round right.

Contents

Prologue: Katherine, December 1913

I should pin the Hillegas scale, Katherine thought, at their eye level. But then she remembered that these were high-school juniors, not the elementary-school children she was used to teaching. Her students were nearly as tall as she.

I could take one of their essays in hand, read it to the class, and then compare it with the posted specimens—the term used by Edward L. Thorndike and his student, Milo Hillegas, to describe these samples of student writing. The students could then walk to the poster one at a time and try to judge the relative merit of their individual essays to those posted on the wall. The scale would be, she thought, the center of attention in class and break up the deadening recitation. That time in elementary school was not badly spent after all. Her work with younger children had allowed her to learn more techniques than her dull, rule-driven colleagues would ever be able to implement in their dreadful classes. Indeed, it would be nice to have the students work in groups, to talk together about their essays and how they compared to the specimens. But the forty desks were bolted to the floor.

"It is obvious that specimen 294 has more merit as English writing than specimen 519," Thorndike had written last month in the *English Journal.* In the library at Columbia University, Katherine had read Professor Thorndike's account of the scale when it had first been announced in the September 1911 issue of the *Journal of Educational Psychology*. She kept up with the journals so that she would be ready next fall to begin graduate studies at Teachers College. Reading Thorndike and Hillegas, she had become excited by the science of it, by the German-inspired laboratory spirit of the design of the scale. (But then again she smiled as she realized she had also been excited by Marcel Duchamp's *Nude Descending a Staircase* when she had seen it at the Armory Show last February. Yet there were commonalities, she realized, a search for something new to be invented by each in his own way. As was the case with many of her friends, she admired Europe's science and art but was uncomfortable about influence. Different as they were, there was something distinctly revolutionary about Duchamp and Thorndike, something that was not bound to tradition, something that hinted of vitality. In any case, her taste was not with Gallery

I, the chamber of horrors, as everyone called it, that held Duchamp's painting. She had spent most of her time in Galleries E and F and was taken with Childe Hassam's *The Spanish Stairs*. Its elegant steps captured her heart. She wanted a chance to see where those curved lines led.)

In an "appeal to experts," Hillegas had asked 160 English teachers to judge the relative merit of the writing specimens. With Thorndike, he had inductively developed a scale of merit that could be used to objectify the judgment of an essay's worth.

Professor Thorndike was very hard on Hillegas, Katherine thought, in the *English Journal*. She was looking forward to studying with Thorndike, to learning about the application of psychological and statistical methods to educational theory. Yet she wondered, with dread, if he were this critical of all his students. There was, it appeared, a hard edge to the man. The Hillegas scale (but wasn't the scale developed by both of them?) failed to differentiate, Thorndike had found, between samples of student writing (selections were taken from the unimaginable to the eloquent) and samples from world masters (selections were taken from Washington Irving and William Makepeace Thackeray). Thorndike was scathing: "Consequently, in the judgment of high-school teachers of English, the worst tenth of paragraph-writing of high-school pupils is still nearly half way from zero through the best the world knows." The scale had failed because it did not capture the phenomenon under investigation. (But what, she thought, is that phenomenon?)

Thorndike followed with an analogy—cutting indeed—describing how the scale would work if used to evaluate track performance: "Teachers of athletes would disagree very widely in the 'marks' that they gave to the same feat of running; and we should quarrel bitterly over the respective merits of A and B!" He had concluded that the scale did not measure the quality of the essays at all but only "the errors made in using such a scale." The scale doubly failed because it measured only the unstable judgment of the readers. (Perhaps, she thought, we should be studying the readers.)

Nevertheless, even Thorndike had to agree that the scale was better than nothing, that "at present a teacher, in grading a composition of general merit, uses a subjective, personal scale of values which, in the nature of the case, cannot, on the average, be as correct as one due to the combined opinions of a hundred or more judges who are on the average as competent as he is." (How Jeffersonian, she thought.)

So she had purchased it, the *Preliminary Extension of the Hillegas Scale for the Measurement of Quality in English Composition by Young People*, for eight cents. Twenty-three inches across and eighteen inches down, she had ironed it out (it had come folded like a passport) and pinned it flat on the wall next to the blackboard. Professor Thorndike's calculated quarrels aside, the specimens gave her something to work with.

In and of themselves, the specimens were interesting. She agreed with Thorndike that specimen 519 was an example of weak writing:

Specimen 519

First, De Quinceys mother was a beautiful woman and through her De Quincey inhereted much of his genius.

His running away from school enfluenced him much as he roamed through the woods, valleys and his mind became very meditative.

The greatest enfluence of De Quincey's life was the opium habit. If it was not for this habit it is doubtful whether we would now be reading his writings.

His companions during his college course and even before that time were great enfluences. The surroundings of De Quincey were enfluences. Not only De Quincey's habit of opium but other habits which were peculiar to this life.

His marriage to the woman which he did not especially care for.

The many well educated and noteworthy friends of De Quincey.

The student had started to categorize the reasons for De Quincey's fame but then became lost. There were spelling problems ("inhereted," "enfluences"). And opium was more memorable, or at least of more interest to this student, than the prose of the eminent Victorian.

She agreed with Professor Thorndike that specimen 294 did, in fact, have more merit than specimen 519:

Specimen 294

Among the beautiful islands on the Canadian side of the St. Lawrence River, there is a deep and narrow channel which separates three small wooded islands from a large fertile one. Of the three islands the largest is rocky and covered with a growth of stately pines and waving hemlocks, and a carpet of moss and ferns. On the second there is quite an assortment of trees, whose foliage during the fall turns to many shades of gold and red, which colors are greatly enhanced by the dark green background of its neighbor. On the third there is a thick growth of brush, with an occasional small tree. These three islands are so close together, that fallen trees and logs make it possible to walk from one to another.

Here was a vivid description combined with principles of classification. No wonder those 160 English teachers rated this essay higher than 519. Maybe the student's instructor, she imagined, had been a reader of Barrett Wendell's *English Composition*. In fact, perhaps the pupil's instructor had been educated at Harvard under Wendell himself. The paragraph certainly produced an effect, and Wendell's book was filled with advice to "know what effects to produce" and "by every means" to strive to produce them. Where the composition on De Quincey had failed, the description of islands had succeeded. This student had been trained, carefully, to please.

Although Thorndike had not found it obvious why the descriptive specimen, 294, had more merit than specimen 225, she realized that the answer was not in the writer but in the readers:

> Specimen 225
>
> Before the Renaissance, artists and sculptors made their statues and pictures thin, and weak looking figures. They saw absolutely no beauty in the human body. At the time of the Renaissance, artists began to see beauty in muscular and strong bodies, and consequently many took warriors as subjects for their statues. Two of the statues that Michel Angelo, the greatest sculptor and artist, made, Perseus with the head of Medusa, and David with Goliath's head, are very similar. They show minutely and with wonderful exactness every muscle of the body. Michel Angelo was a great student of the body, especially when it was in a strained position. The position of the figures on the tomb of Lorenzo the Great is so wonderful that one can almost see the tension of the muscles.

Specimen 225 was interesting, but the effect of the word choice, the combination of denotation and connotation, as Wendell would term it, had failed. (Or, she smiled, was that talk about straining positions a bit too forceful?) There was no clear sense of classification, as was evident in specimen 294. And the idea that pre-Renaissance art was full of "thin, and weak looking" figures would have offended at least some of those five medieval-loving English teachers who had built the scale through their rankings. (The older teachers may, in fact, have been students of George Lyman Kittredge at Harvard—she had met some of these, devotees of the bibliography of Icelandic mythology—while the younger teachers may have been trained by John Matthew Manly, student of Kittredge and Chaucer scholar, at the University of Chicago. Old or young, though, these philologists would have found the specimen offensive.)

It was specimen 580, with its score of zero, that most fascinated her:

> Specimen 580
>
> Letter
>
> Dear Sir: I write to say that it ain't a square deal. Schools is I say they is I went to a school. red and gree green and brown aint it hito but I say he don't know his business not today nor yeaterday and you know it and I want Jennie to get me out.

"Aint it hito?" she thought. Who speaks, or writes, like that? Why would the child correct "gree" to "green" and then stop revising? Why would the researchers add specimens that did not exist to the scale? A visit to almost any New York City school would have yielded weak specimens. Perhaps the researchers didn't leave campus much? A weak writer may have jumbled ideas, but no one's ideas are scattered in that fashion. And the tone so pleading, the desire to run away, to have Jenny—his sister?—help him escape. The letter would have been seen by the judges as an illustration not only of illiteracy but also of weakness. The deck was stacked. Weakness, as she had come to learn, gets a zero.

Yet, she thought, the Hillegas scale would be useful for its defined writing specimens and for its implicit lessons: classify and follow through; describe vividly; avoid error; and offend no one. (Science, she mused, tells us that subjectivity is to be avoided. Politics tell us that the voice of the many is superior in judgment to the few. And never, ever, show weakness in navigating these two worlds. There were lessons here for all.)

It was 1913, and Katherine knew what there was to know as she prepared to pin the scale on the wall of her classroom.

Chapter 1
A World Where Something Was A-Doing, 1874–1917

During the nineteenth century America witnessed a fundamental cultural change: the republic as a reflection of language was receding, and the nation as a construct of science was taking its place. As Americans struggled with their cultural identity throughout the nineteenth century, the nature of the emerging American character, molded by education and expressed in writing, was an ever-present debate.

Seventeen years before Abraham Lincoln signed the Land Grant College Act, Henry David Thoreau had set about to define American cultural identity at Walden Pond. Educated at the nation's great private school (Harvard University, class of 1837), Thoreau had studied under Edward Tyrrell Channing, the Boylston Professor of Rhetoric and Oratory, and had used Richard Whately's *Elements of Rhetoric* as his textbook. Relying on his journal—a laboratory notebook that captured nature when he was absent from it—Thoreau wrote and rewrote his testimony from the colony, publishing it at last in 1854. Desiring his countrymen to know what it was to live deliberately, Thoreau documented his experiences, teaching us how to live without our European kinsmen and their authority.

What was to be gained by reading and writing in America in the mid-nineteenth century? Why, everything, Thoreau reported: "A written word is the choicest of relics. It is something at once more intimate with us and more universal than any other work of art. It is the work of art nearest to life itself. It may be translated into every language, and not only be read but actually breathed from all human lips;—not be represented on canvas or in marble only, but be carved out of the breath of life itself."[1] Language was a timeless way for us to find our better selves, to carve out our place in the world.

That world was changing, though. The Fitchburg Railroad had touched the Pond:

> When I meet the engine with its train of cars moving with planetary motion,—or, rather, like a comet, for the beholder knows not if with that velocity and with that direction it will ever revisit this system, since its orbit does not look like a returning curve,—with its steam cloud like a banner streaming behind in golden and silver wreaths, like many a downy cloud which I have seen, high in the heavens, unfolding its masses to the light,—as if this traveling demigod, this cloud-compeller, would ere long take the sunset sky for the livery of his train; when I hear the iron horse make the hills echo with his snort like thunder, shaking the earth with his feet, and breathing fire and smoke from his nostrils, (what kind of winged horse or fiery dragon they will put into the new Mythology I don't know,) it seems as if the earth had got a race now worthy to inhabit it.[2]

Among the original pre-Revolutionary American universities, Thoreau's would respond most ardently to this brave new world during the last quarter of the nineteenth century. From Channing, Thoreau had learned to profit by the circumstances in which he was placed; from Whately, he had learned perspicuity, energy, and elegance.[3] If Thoreau was the product of such a rhetorical education, the more of it that could be obtained, the better. By 1874 Harvard had created a university-sponsored program of composition and, with it, a written examination required for admission.

As was the case with the train, the enterprise was value laden. Language, the American educator had realized, was an organizing system, one that could be harnessed both for eloquence and for persuasion. By turning to the rhetorical texts of Scottish theologian George Campbell during the American Revolution, then to those of the Presbyterian author Hugh Blair and British theologian and political philosopher Richard Whately, educators at universities such as Harvard could instill a frame of reference in students that urged them to see language as a vehicle for action. Reflective of mental processes themselves, language had a purpose beyond ornamentation in the new republic of industry.[4]

Useful to the emerging American consciousness was the desire for inductive reasoning and objectivity, the essence of science and its application in technology. To throw off the manacles of deduction, to discard the syllogism's major premise—this was the ideology fostered by Francis Bacon in Renaissance England, embedded into the textbooks of Whately and the lectures of Channing, and incorporated into the industrial America of Jay Gould's railways, Carnegie's steel mills, and Rockefeller's oil refineries.[5] The 1862 Land Grant College Act spectacularly grafted the mechanical arts of industry onto the agricultural interests of the Union. Each established before 1766, the original colleges—Harvard, William and Mary, Yale, New Jersey (later Princeton), Rhode Island, Queen's, and Dartmouth—were by 1900 a few (albeit an influential few) among many. The state colleges had arrived, evoking democratic agrarian values, cardinal among these the possibility of achievement. "I am a farmer's boy," a young man wrote to the college at East Lansing, Michigan, "And as soon as the wheat is sown, I am at liberty to go to school."[6]

The founding of Cornell University in 1865 was a symbol of American enterprise itself and reflected the decline of the classics and the free election of courses, the encouragement of scientific studies by which practical and liberal studies would be united, and the presence of nonsectarian control. Here was the very model of the land grant ideal by which youth would be prepared for a useful role in society.[7] Concurrent with the founding of Cornell University was that of Johns Hopkins University. Opening in 1876, Johns Hopkins, fueled by dollars from the Baltimore and Ohio Railroad, met the growing American impulse for advanced training.[8] Johns Hopkins was designed to foster the creation rather than the dissemination of knowledge. The school's influence was profound: any college engaging in advanced studies had to transform itself into a university, was obliged to recruit graduate students for the purpose of stimulating an excellent faculty ready to advance their careers in pursuit of the next best offer, and was to adopt, tacitly, a model in which advanced studies were equated with rigor, rigor with science, and science with truth. As Daniel Coit Gilman, the first president of Johns Hopkins, framed the enterprise in 1885: "No truth which has once been discovered is allowed to perish but the incrustations which cover it are removed. It is the universities which edit, interpret, translate and reiterate the acquisitions of former generations both of literature and science. Their revelation of error is sometimes welcomed but it is generally opposed; nevertheless the process goes on, indifferent alike to plaudits or reproaches."[9]

In perpetual motion, scientifically based scholarship existed in a pure domain within the university, a system in which theories and empirical observation complemented each other. When Louis Agassiz sought to demonstrate polygenism at Harvard University in 1846, theorizing that black people had different origins than white people, his findings were based on the skull measurements of Samuel Morton. The theory of polygenism was thus supported by the empirical measurements of craniometry. The more the scientific process continued, the more theory was tested by observation, the more truths would be revealed. (Even Thoreau had collected specimens for Agassiz in 1847.)[10] Induction was the way to knowledge, empiricism was equated with proof, and invention was demonstrated by application. The founding of the American Society for Civil Engineers in 1852, the American Society of Mechanical Engineers in 1880, and the American Institute for Electrical Engineers in 1884 responded to the same national impulse toward reform through systemization.[11]

This national call to action would drive the physician Joseph Mayer Rice to leave medicine, study pedagogy in Germany, survey the American school system in 1893, find it mindless, and propose its reform in 1914 under the title *Scientific Management in Education.* "The plan of application is very simple," he wrote. "It lies in subjecting children taught under different systems to one and the same test—which must be fair and practical—and comparing the results."[12] Testing—with its origin in the European science of psychological measurement—would become America's unique contribution to education.

The Idea of a University

The difficulty of establishing cultural identity is the most enduring legacy of colonialism. Throughout the nineteenth century, Americans struggled with their European masters. For some, the voice of authority was England; for others, it was Germany.

The Grand Tour became a quintessential right of passage. Beginning, perhaps, in London with trips to Italy, Switzerland, and France, the chaperoned young saw those things that America did not have. Such was the case with Henry James. Taken to Europe at age twelve (with his brother William)—his father had written to Emerson, telling him that he wanted his sons to "get a better sensuous education than they are likely to get here [in New York]"[13]—Henry James made a career of writing about Americans in Europe, of exploring the damp corridors and social stratifications he was first to experience in 1855.

With the leisure class, students of the humanities and science also went to Europe. Literally hundreds of American students traveled to Germany in the first half of the nineteenth century. Some, such as Francis James Child, studied philology; others, such as G. Stanley Hall, studied philosophy and physiology. But what they all uniformly absorbed was the form of the German university.

In his 1878 reminiscence of his time in Germany, James Morgan Hart defined the German university:

To the German mind the collective idea of a university implies a *Zweck,* an object of study, and two *Bedingungen*, or conditions. The object is *Wissenschaft*; the conditions are *Lehrfreiheit* and *Lernfreheit*. By *Wissenschaft* the Germans mean knowledge in the most exalted sense of that term, namely, the ardent, methodical, independent search after truth in any and all of its forms, but wholly irrespective of utilitarian application. *Lehrfreiheit* means that the one who teaches, the professor or *Privat-docent*, is free to teach what he chooses, as he chooses. *Lernfreiheit*, or the freedom of learning, denotes the emancipation of the student from *Schulzwang*, compulsory drill by recitation.

If the object of an institution is anything else than knowledge as above defined, or if either freedom of teaching or freedom of learning is wanting, that institution, no matter how richly endowed, no matter how numerous its students, no matter how imposing its buildings, is not, in the eye of a German, a *university*.[14]

What of the professors?

The character of the German Professor will be best understood by first disposing of the preliminary question: What is he not?

The professor is not a teacher, in the English sense of the term; he is a specialist. He is not responsible for the success of his hearers. He is responsible only for the quality of his instruction. His duty begins and ends with himself.

No man can become a professor in a German university without having given evidence, in one way or another, that he has pursued a certain line of study, and produced results worthy to be called novel or important. In other words, to become a professor, he must first have been a special investigator. Professional chairs are not conferred "on general principles," or because the candidate is "a good teacher," or "well qualified to govern the young…" Each of the two thousand professors now lecturing in Germany has risen from the ranks, first as gymnasiast, then as student, then as *Privat-docent* in a special branch. As *Privat-docent*, he makes some discovery in botany, or in chemistry, or in anatomy, or publishes some treatise on historical, philological, or theological topics, that attracts attention and elicits favorable comment. The discoverer or the author becomes at once a man of mark, a candidate for the next vacant chair. Living at Bonn, perhaps, or Wurzburg, he continues his work. In the course of a year or two, a vacancy occurs at Heidelberg. The Heidelberg faculty, every one of whom had probably read his publications and recognize in him a valuable co-worker, give him a call. This he accepts, removes to his new field of labor, and continues there his investigations. Probably he is at Heidelberg only *ausserordentlicher*. But his fame spreads more and more. A full professorship becomes vacant at Berlin; he is called once more, as *ordentlicher*. During these successive stages, as student, *Privat-docent*, *ausserordentlicher*, *ordentlicher Professor*, he has not made a single change in his line of study. He has been throughout an orientalist, a classical philologist, a mathematician, a chemist, an historian, or a theologian. His time and energies have been devoted exclusively to one limited branch of investigation, with a view to make discoveries. He has not *taught* a single hour.[15]

And the American university? How does it compare with the German?

> The [American] College, unlike the German University, rests upon nothing and ends in nothing.[16]

How does the American professor measure up to his German counterpart?

> How many of our college professors have been professors, and nothing else? How many have qualified themselves directly for the respective chairs which they occupy, by a life of special study? How many of them formed the resolve while still students, to lead a college life forever, to devote themselves exclusively to instructing others in turn, either at their own Alma Mater or at some other college? I do not have in view such institutions as Yale and Harvard, old, well endowed, fed from the rich soil of New England culture. I mean the typical American college as it exists in the Middle, Southern, and Western States. How many of the professors have been in business or tried their skill at farming, engineering, journalism? Has or has not the professor of Latin served an apprenticeship as mathematical tutor, or kept a boarding-school for young ladies? How few of the hundreds and thousands of men, from New York to San Francisco, calling themselves professors, can say with a comfortable degree of pride: I selected my specialty in youth, I have pursued it without intermission, and I have produced such and such tangible evidences of my industry as a specialist?[17]

Hart, a Columbia University professor of philology and the 1895 president of the Modern Language Association, was not alone—either in his first visit to Germany in 1861 or in his observations of American flaws. American students in Germany brought back something much more powerful than did their Grand-Tour contemporaries, laden with nostalgia and museum pieces: these young men brought back visions of specimens, systems, and science.

At Harvard, there were prophets of the vision from the Mecca of scholarship, as Herbert Weir Smyth, the Eliot Professor of Greek Literature, termed Germany.[18] In traditional humanistic scholarship, there was Francis James Child,[19] the Boylston Professor of Rhetoric and Oratory, who held a German Ph.D., as did Edward Everett, who had taken his doctorate at Göttingen in 1817 and would become Harvard's president in 1846. G. Stanley Hall, who had taken his doctorate at Harvard in 1878, traveled to Leipzig to study under Wilhelm Wundt, the founder of experimental psychology who had established the world's first formal psychological laboratory.[20] Hall had then established a psychological laboratory of his own in 1883 at the quintessential American university based on the new German model, Johns Hopkins.[21] Beyond Harvard there were others in the new field of psychology who exerted an equally important influence on the

American university.[22] James McKeen Cattell, who would direct the animal intelligence research of the young Edward L. Thorndike, studied at both Leipzig and Göttingen and brought a German-inspired sense of rigor to psychology, seeking to make it as valid and reliable as the study of the natural and physical sciences.

Written with the philosopher G. S. Fullerton, Cattell's *On the Perception of Small Differences* provided a method of understanding the differential limen, the "just noticeable difference" in perception, as the error created by humans judging that difference—a radical functional departure that dismissed human unreliability and emphasized human capacity.[23]

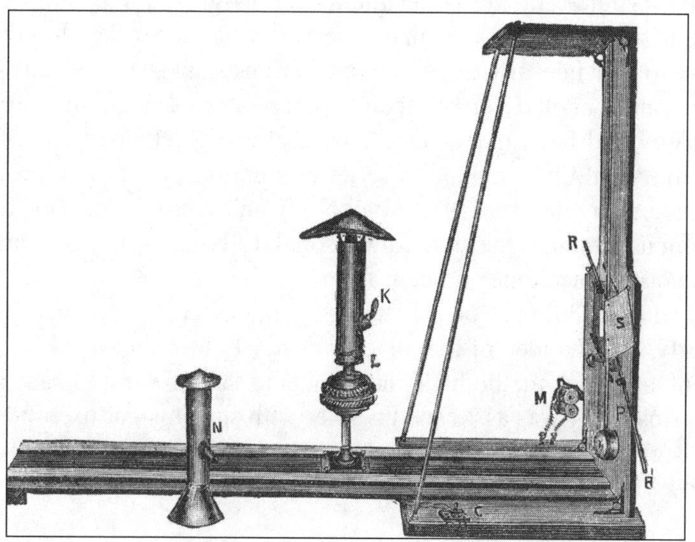

"The experiments were made as follows: —The observer having placed himself in position, the recorder gave him a signal to secure attention, and then, turning the key, allowed the pendulum to swing away from the magnet. The lamp being, say, at what we may call the normal distance [250 cm. from the paper at ten-candle power], the observer was thus given the standard sensation of light. With the return swing of the pendulum, and while the light was cut off by the screen, the lamp was moved nearer to the paper by certain distances marked on the slide, so that the second light seen by the observer should be more intense that the first.... The observer was required to state whether the second light in each pair seemed brighter or fainter than the first, and to express his degree of confidence by *a* [certainty of the correctness of the decision}, *b* [less certain] or *c* [uncertain]. [If an observer could discern no difference whatever, he was allowed to say 'doubtful' or *d*.] A record was made after each experiment." In discussing the results of their experiment with luminosity—they found that the *a* and *b* answers increased as the difference in luminosity increased and as the percentage of correct judgments increased—Fullerton and Cattell noted the following: "The confidence of the observer is, hence, a fair measure of the correctness of his judgment, but it is evident that *a* and *b* have a widely different meaning in the case of the several observers" (144). (Apparatus from George Stuart Fullerton and James McKeen Cattell, *On the Perception of Small Differences* [Philadelphia: U of Pennsylvania P, 1892]: 137.)

The method of the just noticeable difference—in which an observer identified a difference which could just be perceived—was not a satisfactory method of judging difference, the authors claimed, because the results are without objective criteria. In their study, therefore, Fullerton and Cattell designed a series of experiments to establish a new technique for identifying differences. In that new technique—the method of right and wrong cases—two stimuli nearly alike were presented to an individual who was then required to say which seemed the greater. By using different types of apparatus for measuring the force of movement, the time of movement, lifted weights, and intensity of light, the experimenters could establish exact objective criteria. In the experiments with lights, for example, 4000 experiments were made with nine observers who were asked to give their response to light intensity, an objective criterion established in candle power. Fullerton and Cattell described their experiments as successful, noting that psychology had been indebted to physics for its methods but, soon, the obligation would be mutual. "The determination of the relation of one magnitude to another makes of psychology an exact science," the authors had written, "whereas the study of personal differences may find practical applications in medicine and education."[24]

Whether philologist or psychologist, the place for practice was the university, and the idea of that place was newly forming: it was to be the center of an ardent, methodical, independent search for truth in any and all of its forms. Duty was associated neither with students nor usefulness but, rather, began and ended with the perfection of the intellect. Time and energy were to be devoted only to discovery.

Harvard, 1874

The teaching of modern languages at Harvard between 1870 and 1900 was in transition. For two centuries Harvard had demanded classical languages for its entering students. President Charles W. Eliot saw things differently.

In his inaugural address, delivered on October 19, 1869, he had set a new agenda:

> The endless controversies whether language, philosophy, mathematics, or science supplies the best mental training, whether general education should be chiefly literary or chiefly scientific, have no practical lesson for us to-day. This University recognizes no real antagonism between literature and science, and consents to no such narrow alternatives as mathematics or classics, science or metaphysics. We would have them all, and at their best. To observe keenly, to reason soundly, and to imagine vividly are operations as essential as that of clear and forcible expression; and to develop one of these faculties, it is not necessary to repress and

> dwarf the others. A university is not closely connected with the applications of knowledge until its general education branches into professional. Poetry and philosophy and science do indeed conspire to promote the material welfare of mankind; but science no more than poetry finds its best warrant in its utility. Truth and right are above utility in all realms of thought and action.[25]

Eliot's address was a précis for scientific orientation. While the statement advocated dispassionate observation that would have pleased any *ordentlicher Professor*, it was (as was Thoreau's description of the train) resplendent with allusion and values. Eliot was a devotee of Herbert Spencer, the civil engineer trained to run railways, perhaps the major social theorist of post-Civil War America.[26] Spencer's *Social Statics, or the Conditions Essential to Human Happiness Specified* was published in 1851 and became a guide for progress based on evolution. His *Education: Intellectual, Moral, and Physical*, published in 1860, proposed a set of preconditions essential for complete living, the most essential of which, as far as education was concerned, was science. He had even written a rhetorical text, *Philosophy of Style: An Essay*. In 1882, Spencer toured America, giving a series of lectures. His Social Darwinism centered the individual within the historical drama of survival. The basis of proof rested in the laws of nature; and the best way to train individuals to adapt was to train them in science.

The shift that occurred at Harvard under Eliot's presidency—indicative of the national shift toward dispassionate scientific systematization—is nowhere more apparent than in a comparison between the Harvard University catalogues of 1872–1873 and 1873–1874. At first glance, they were both the same. Both began with the calendar of the year, the classes beginning the fourth week of September. Both included the names, permanent residence, and room numbers of the senior, junior, sophomore, and freshmen classes, with 635 undergraduates in attendance for 1872–

Charles William Eliot, president of Harvard University, 1869–1907. "The President of the University is Primarily an Executive Officer....The President's first duty is that of supervision." Inaugural Address, October 19, 1869. [Call # HUP Eliot, Charles W. (27), Courtesy of the Harvard University Archives]

1873 and 706 undergraduates for 1873–1874. Even the expenses were identical, ranging from $353.00 to $581.00 for instruction, rent, thirty-eight weeks of board, and textbooks.

The difference was in the entrance examinations. Eliot was a great believer in admission to higher education on the basis of examinations. As he had declared in his inaugural address:

> The increasing weight, range, and thoroughness of the examination for admission to college may strike some observers with dismay. The increase of real requisitions is hardly perceptible from year to year; but on looking back ten or twenty years, the changes are marked, and all in one direction. The dignity and importance of this examination have been rising steadily, and this rise measures the improvement of the preparatory schools. When the gradual improvement of American schools has lifted them to a level with the German gymnasia, we may expect to see the American college bearing a nearer resemblance to the German faculties of philosophy than it now does.... The rigorous examination for admission has one good effect throughout the college course: it prevents a waste of instruction upon incompetent persons.[27]

In the 1872–1873 catalogue, members of the freshmen class were told that they would be examined in Latin, Greek, and mathematics. In subsequent examinations taken as early as possible after admission, they were to be examined in reading aloud English prose. "Prizes will be awarded for excellence," and students could prepare themselves by reading Goldsmith's *Vicar of Wakefield*.[28] The catalogue for 1873–1874, however, signaled a distinct shift. While students would continue to be examined in Latin, Greek, and mathematics, the change was in the new examination in English composition:

> *English Composition.* (Each candidate will be required to write a short English Composition, correct in spelling, punctuation, grammar, and expression, the subject to be taken from such works of standard authors as shall be announced from time to time. The subject for 1874 will be taken from one of the following works: Shakespeare's Tempest, Julius Caesar, and Merchant of Venice; Goldsmith's Vicar of Wakefield; Scott's Ivanhoe, and Lay of the Last Minstrel.[29]

Within one year, the orally based examination—and all that it implied—had vanished. Receding were the orations of Daniel Webster, voices from a time in which the day was carried by the persuasive presence of the speaker. By 1873 elocution ceased to be a required subject.[30] In his report of 1879–1880, President Eliot announced that "the recitation, considered as an opportunity of examining a student to see whether he has learned the lesson of the day, and to give him a mark...has well-nigh disappeared."[31] Present now was the silent world of the composition. Persuasion here was carried, voiceless, by proof presented logically and scientifically in print. Now, the day would be carried by the page.

Adams Sherman Hill had been the chief agent in ushering in this new world. He had graduated from Harvard with Eliot in 1853, was appointed by the new president in 1872, and had ushered in the required English composition and its assessment.[32] Hill, "a recruit from journalism,"[33] would become the Boylston Professor of Rhetoric and Oratory in 1876 when the former holder, Francis James Child, was promoted to professor of English. (The "one bitter note" to the "grand zest and sunny disposition" of Child was aroused "by the remembrance of the great proportion of his life that had been spent on theme-correcting."[34]) Hill published rapidly: his *Principles of Rhetoric and Their Application* in 1878 would become a classic textbook, and his *Our English* in 1889 would also be widely read.[35]

A view on student performance on the examination during this period was given by Hill in an analysis of the examination given in 1879. His was a reformer's message, a call issued to remind readers that literary skill is not an easy acquisition. "If the movement in favor of those things which make for good English is to be of much practical utility," he reminded his readers, "it must spread widely and penetrate deeply; every school-committee must insist that, whatever else is done or is left undone, a serious effort shall be made to teach boys and girls to use their native tongue correctly and intelligently; all our colleges must put English upon a par, at least, with Latin and Greek, and must provide their students with ample opportunities for practice in writing and speaking the language they will have to use all their lives." The mission was indeed a social one and, as such, the object of cost-benefit analysis: "If the schools and colleges do this work thoroughly, a short time will suffice to bring parents to a sense of the paramount importance to every one of knowing how to read and write, and to show them how much labor that knowledge costs."[36]

Hill began his analysis by providing the one-hour examination question for that year, a question similar to that asked of the first candidates to take the English composition essay of 1874:

> Write a short composition upon one of the subjects given below.
>
> Before beginning to write, consider what you have to say on the subject selected, and arrange your thoughts in logical order.
>
> Aim at quality rather than quantity of work.
>
> Carefully revise your composition, correcting all errors in punctuation, spelling, grammar, division by paragraphs, and expression, and making each sentence as clear and forcible as possible. If time permits, make a clean copy of the revised work.
>
> I. The Character of Sir Richard Steele.

II. The Duke of Marlborough as portrayed by Thackeray.
III. The Style of "Henry Esmond."
IV. Thackeray's account of the Pretender's visit to England.
V. Duelling in the Age of Queen Anne.[37]

A single examiner read the essays; 316 students took the examination, 157 failed, and only 14 passed with distinction. The reasons for failure: spelling (*champaign* instead of champagne); confounding of Steele with Sir Roger de Coverley; or confusing the style of *Henry Esmond*, the novel, with the manners of Henry Esmond, the hero of the novel. There were punctuation errors as well: "Some—a smaller number, however, than in previous years—showed such utter ignorance of punctuation as to put commas at the end of complete sentences, or between words that no rational being would separate from one another; and a few began sentences with small letters, or began every long word with a capital letter." Many books, Hill wrote, "were deformed by grossly ungrammatical or profoundly obscure sentences, and some by absolute illiteracy."[38] Nevertheless, "If the examiner erred, it was in giving the candidate the benefit of too many doubts, in tempering justice with too much mercy."[39] On the whole, Hill concluded, the examination made a poor showing for the schools. If Harvard does not succeed in giving graduates "the one mental acquisition deemed by her president the essential part of education, the fault is not altogether or mainly hers."[40]

There were other reasons for an essay's failure, as we find in the analysis of themes presented by Hill's student Le Baron Russell Briggs, later dean of Harvard College. There was "the fancied necessity of infusing morality somewhere," mere "schoolgirls' sentiments."[41] There was "gush"—a condition we should pity. Such writers will find at Harvard "agony,"—"the lashing that he must endure before he finds his true place in that hard-hearted little world."[42] An additional editing exercise was added to the required essay in 1882, and every candidate was now required to correct "specimens of bad English" given with the essay question.[43] Among the specimens of bad English for 1889 we find "Milton was too busy to much miss his wife" and "She confessed to having struck her husband with the axe, and plead self-defense."[44] Such errors must be purged, Briggs noted, because "scientific education is gaining ground and whole schools of scientific men are enthusiastically ignorant of English."[45]

Literacy, instrumental in the new capital of science and industry, had taken its place at Harvard. There, the new men of science were to be made literate, their messages improved through sentences balanced to just the right degree. After all, as Hill himself had explained in his 1878 textbook

The Principles of Rhetoric and Their Applications, "when not carried to excess, the balanced structure is agreeable to the ear, is a help to the memory, and gives emphasis to each of the balanced expressions; when carried to excess, it makes a writer the slave of sound; it produces upon the reader the monotonous effect without the charm of rhythm; and it leads to a sacrifice of strict truth."[46] On a scale, precision was most important in matters concerning balance.

Advertisements for Themselves

By 1900, those who taught at Harvard continued to publicize the program in English. Developments in this new arena, Charles T. Copeland and Henry Milner Rideout imagined, would have applications to other institutions. In their 1901 publication of *Freshman English and Theme-Correcting in Harvard College*, the co-authors (one a lecturer in English literature and the other an instructor in English at Harvard) set forth, complete with edited themes, the daily regimen in Cambridge. Their book-length outline of English A, the course in English composition begun in 1885 and required of all admitted students, concluded with the reflections of three students. Two praise the good that had come from the course, while the third observed that not much was gained. "In an endeavor (and not a very successful one) to conform to certain rules, I have lost all originality,—everything has a sort of labored rehashing, which makes whatever I have to say, dull and uninteresting." Undaunted, Copeland and Rideout note that, compared to the writer's earlier work, the specimen shows a gain in structure. "If he has got nothing else from his practice," they note, "he has learned to complain more effectively."[47] Everything included in the slim volume, then, could be considered a worthwhile means to a desired end.

Chief among the features of English A were the daily themes. Students were "under pretty definite orders" concerning their choice of topics.[48] For four days a week, the freshmen had to produce one-page narrative and descriptive sketches; on the other two days, they had to translate a passage from Latin, Greek, French, German, or some other language, and they had to comment—in a meditative and reflective fashion—on a lecture they had heard. The daily themes thus covered "narrative, descriptive, and expository work."[49] The presence of these daily themes in the curriculum was due to Barrett Wendell.

Wendell was a former student of Hill's, an 1877 graduate of Harvard who had studied law but found that it "was both detestable and depressing." He had encountered Hill in a chance meeting in Boston, their first meeting

Barrett Wendell, member of the Harvard University faculty, 1880–1917, in his office at Grays Hall during the publication year of *English Composition: Eight Lectures Given at the Lowell Institute*. "For he who scrawls ribaldry, just as truly as he who writes for all time, does that most wonderful of things, —gives a material body to some reality which till that moment was immaterial, executes, all unconscious of the power for which divine is not too grand a word, a lasting act of creative imagination." *English Composition* 40. [Call # HUP Wendell, Barrett (7b), Courtesy of the Harvard University Archives]

since his graduation. The Bolyston Professor asked Wendell what he was doing. "I told him I was reading law," Wendell recollected in a memoir written years later. "He asked whether I liked it; I said no. And on his duly inquiring what kind of job I should prefer, I am said to have answered, 'Even yours.' Somehow the incident stuck in his memory."[50] In October, Hill had proposed Wendell's name to President Eliot as someone who might be brought on to read sophomore themes. In that Eliot, as Wendell recalled, was "always fond of experiments with inexperienced teachers," a telegram was sent as an invitation to discuss an appointment. The telegram came at just the right time. Wendell had failed the bar.

Wendell's appointment reflected a Harvard tradition in which talented sons returned to the fold. Henry Adams (class of 1858) had accepted a similar offer to teach medieval history a decade before from President Eliot, and George Lyman Kittredge (class of 1882) would be listed as an instructor of English in the 1888–1889 catalogue. For all of what may be considered Wendell's Brahmin background—including Wendell's study in the Boston law office of Shattuck, Holmes (the son of Professor Holmes and the future justice of the United States Supreme Court)—the course that Wendell built with Hill at Harvard was the very model of engineered efficiency. The instructors were not to make the themes interesting but, rather, to make them correct. Common marks of error identification were devised: Cst. was the abbreviation for faulty construction; K. for awkward, stiff or harsh phrases; P. for faulty punctuation; R. for redundancy or repetition; and S. for sentences that were objectionable in form. These and other marks were provided on an English Composition Card, and students were required additionally to purchase Hill's *Rhetoric* and to have a good supply of regular theme paper.

Wendell was to prosper at Harvard, remaining there for thirty-seven years. While he wrote novels (*The Duchess Emilia*), biography (*Cotton Mather*), and literary criticism (*A Literary History of America*), it was his *English Composition* that memorialized him to generations of composition instructors. Written as a popular treatment of the subject, *English Composition* brought a practicing writer's sense to the teaching of composition. To organize an essay, for example, Wendell advised that a pack of cards with headings written on them would do nicely. "A few minutes' shuffling of these little cards," he wrote, "has often revealed to me more than I should have learned by hours of unaided pondering."[51] And as for words and style, their use was a matter of context. The name of Jefferson Davis would arouse one set of emotions in a citizen of the state of Massachusetts and quite another in Mississippi. The divergent connotative power of that name, he cautioned his readers to believe, is true, "in greater or less degree, of every word we use."[52] After all, writing was more about individualism and context than about rules. There are no two human beings "who tread the same road from cradle to grave," and this is a great, sad reality about the act of writing itself that style must express. The task of the writer was thus "a far more subtle and wonderful thing than we are apt to think it: nothing less than to create a material body, that all men may see, for an eternally immaterial reality that only through this imperfect symbol can ever reveal itself to any but the one human being who knows it he knows not how."[53]

Despite the methodological way he conducted the review of the daily themes and the practical advice about the composing process, there was a certain sadness in Barrett's view of composition. In 1894 he wrote to Robert Herrick, a former student, that he thought of himself as shut up in New England, wishing to goodness that as a youth he had "at once the luck and the pluck to give and take in a world where something was a-doing." He despised crude material and coeducation, but, nevertheless, couldn't help but think that "this is the stuff whereof—if of anything—our future is to me be made."[54] For "the old systems," as he had written in *English Composition*, strove to bring wisdom by reverent study. But there were new systems at work, those which asked, humbly, for each of us to do our best. Perhaps that was enough to bring us to the realization that what we sought was, ultimately, "beyond human ken."[55] Perhaps, as he told Robert Herrick, the best thing to do was to play our parts metaphorically. "God knows," Wendell advised, "what may become of the seed thoughtlessly sown."[56]

The Dial, 1894

The subject of English composition that had so captivated Harvard was becoming part of the national educational agenda. In 1894, *The Dial*, one of America's leading popular journals of literary criticism, discussion, and information published in Chicago, asked the chairs of English departments across the nation—the eastern institutions, the state-supported institutions of the New West, and the institutions of private philanthropy—to describe their writing programs.[57] Among these essays was one by Barrett Wendell, who had told Herrick to keep an eye out for it as an account, worthy of a John-shopkeeper, of the teaching of English at Harvard. For we are, Wendell noted, "above all else, a nation of shopkeepers, to some variable and expansive degree ennobled by lack of corruptions and standards of autocracy, it is subtle, and a beautiful tribute to the broadly rational excellence of the ideals so admirably embodied in the whiskers and the utterances of President Gilman."[58]

Not all shopkeepers conducted business, however, as did Harvard—even in the "venerable Eastern institutions," as William Morton Payne, the associate editor of *The Dial*, termed them.[59] As Albert S. Cook of Yale noted, there was no methodical instruction in rhetoric, and composition was systematically taught in but one course in the junior year. (A twelve-week course in English for freshmen had been planned in 1894, but the instructor had died during the summer vacation.) In that required junior class, the work was based on writing appreciative summaries of well-known authors, such as Irving, De Quincey, and Macaulay. At Yale, English was devoted to fostering love of literature and development of critical sensibility, "a most effective instrument of spiritual discipline."[60] At the University of Pennsylvania, Felix F. Schelling reported that the Department of English "set before the student one simple aim—the plain and unaffected use of his mother tongue." Each freshman in the university wrote two or three themes a week that were then corrected for further revision. A similar process continued through each year for all students, "except those hopelessly given over to technology."[61] (As had been the case with elocution at Harvard twenty-one years before, little use was made of forensics in the curriculum.)

Along with the Harvard program described by Wendell—those seriously interested would find a visit instructive, Wendell wrote[62]—Amherst College had developed its own solutions to teaching English composition. John

Franklin Genung of Amherst had taken his Ph.D. from Leipzig in 1881 and was influenced by the new science he had seen in Germany after Wundt had established the first psychological laboratory in Leipzig in 1875.[63] Rather than ranking composition instruction as the Ishmael among university studies, Genung wrote, the solution at Amherst was to develop "*laboratory work*" in which each of the courses was a "veritable workshop, wherein, by systematized daily drill, details are mastered one by one, and that unity of result is obtained which is more for practical use than for show."[64] At Amherst, however, extensive work in oral presentation was retained and combined with written work. In the freshman and sophomore years, there were essays and elocutionary drills; in the junior year, there were more declamations; and in the senior year, there were debates. Among the most profitable techniques for instruction, Genung noted, was the process of setting the student essays into type and proofreading them.

In the state-supported institutions of the New West, the State University of Iowa employed one professor of English and one instructor, offering eight courses to approximately 250 students. In the required courses, Edward E. Hale, Jr., reported, "We try to habituate the student to writing (as well as possible, of course, but without insistence on critical work), to give him practice in thinking over his material and putting it into good form, to give him exercise in the different modes of presentation." There were a good many students, and thus the basis of the method was "the cutting of our coat according to our cloth."[65] At the University of Indiana , "the work is as completely practical as we can make it. Writing is learned by writing papers, each one of which is corrected and rewritten. There are no recitations in 'rhetoric.' The bugbear known generally in our colleges as Freshman English is now part of our general requirements, and university instruction in composition begins with those fortunate students who have some little control of their native language when a pen is between their fingers." Yet the department was still responsible for teaching basic English to conditionally admitted students, and these classes made the "heaviest drain" upon the instructors' time.[66] In his review of English at Indiana, Martin W. Sampson described the widespread belief in Indiana that style was unworthy of serious consideration. The first-year courses, however, were working to correct that peculiar local condition. The University of Minnesota also had its regional complexities. There, George E. MacLean noted, "so large a proportion of the population consists of foreigners who are ambitious and capable, the University must be content to do a part of this drill. A boy may lead his class in mathematics and Latin and chemistry, and still be unable to free his tongue from the Scandinavian accent, or his written page from foreign idioms. The high schools are year by year doing better work, but with a foreign population so intelligent as ours, the fundamental work of the University must be a struggle for correctness."[67] The University of California's English Department refused to "content itself with requiring a satisfactory test-composition of students at matriculation; for, although that would be an easy way of shifting the burden from the University to that of the schools, it is but a poor substitute for the pedagogical assistance due the schools."[68] Instead, each school was required to send samples of compositions, and the school was then visited by one of the professors of English to review the work of the teachers and students. The schools were thus accredited by the university in English, and only those applying from non-accredited schools were examined.

Among these institutions of the New West, at the University of Michigan Fred Newton Scott, then a young faculty member who would later become president of both the Modern Language Association and the National Council of Teachers of English, had developed the most fully articulated program of instruction.[69] At Michigan, there were twenty-one courses in English and rhetoric: ten courses in literature, five in linguistics, and six in rhetoric and composition. For freshmen, there was a two-hour course in paragraph writing. "The big classes are about as heterogeneous as they well can be, most of the students writing crudely, some execrably, and only a few as well as could be wished." The second course in theme writing was required for all except engineering, chemistry, and biology majors. "The aim," Scott wrote, "is not to inspire students to produce pure literature, if there be any such thing, or even to help them to acquire a beautiful style. If we can get them first to think straight-forwardly about subjects in which they are genuinely interested, and then, after such fashion as nature has fitted them for, to express themselves clearly and connectedly, we have done about all we can hope to do. Perhaps the other things will then come of themselves." First and foremost, Scott wrote, the work in composition was to be practical, and to these ends the curriculum was to give "continuity and regularity of written exercises," consultation with the instructor (here the model was Thoreau's Harvard teacher, Edward Channing), and adaptation of the method to the needs of the student.[70]

Of the private institutions—whose "suddenly acquired wealth and mushroom-like rate of development, already threaten to overshadow the ancient fame of the New England Institutions"[71]—the new Stanford University had 150 applicants, but only 40 wrote satisfactory papers. The English Department faculty "were worn out with the drudgery of correcting Freshman themes,—work really secondary and preparatory, and in no sense forming a proper subject for collegiate instruction." The freshman English course was thus eliminated.[72] There was no mention of English composition at Cornell University.[73] Only at the University of Chicago was a required course in rhetoric and composition taken at the beginning of undergraduate work. Voluntary rhetorical practice, necessary to ensure that graduates could prove they could express their thoughts with grace and skill, would be maintained through newly formed literary societies such as the English Club. In a system of merit appropriate to a university funded by John D. Rockefeller, a student chosen to represent his club at the quarterly public meeting of the University Union would receive fifty dollars.[74]

In *The Dial* of November 1, 1895, the series concluded. Associate Editor William Morton Payne provided a summary of what he declared had been "the most elaborate comparative showing ever made of the methods pursued in this important branch of the higher instruction" at the nation's colleges and universities. University teaching in literature, as the articles had made clear, had become more than just "chatter about Shelley." Indeed, as the seventeen articles had demonstrated, there was proof that literature should be taught in its own specialized department. "If literature, linguistics, and rhetoric are grouped together as constituting a single department, it becomes almost impossible to provide that department with a suitable head. One can no longer be a specialist in so many fields." English, the editors concluded, was "alert, progressive, and eager in its outlook for higher things than have as yet been attained, however far it may yet be from the fulfillment of its whole ambition."[75] The teaching of literature, now an absolute location on the new map of American education, had appeared. Rhetoric—and with it the teaching of English composition—may have had a relative location to literature, but it had no place of its own.

A Vanished Frontier Line

Accompanying Albert S. Cook's article on English at Yale University in *The Dial* was a book review by a young historian at the University of Wisconsin. A new reprint of the history of the Lewis and Clark expedition of 1804–1806 had been published, it seemed, at just the right historical moment. "The most influential as well as the most picturesque factor in American history has been the steady march of civilization across the continent," the review began. Lewis and Clark had recorded that march in their expedition to the sources of the Missouri, across the Rocky Mountains, and down the Columbia River to the Pacific Ocean. However, the review revealed, a bulletin of the superintendent of the census for 1890 had included a significant statement, and Frederick Jackson Turner—always one to influence the reader in techniques mastered as an instructor of rhetoric—quoted the statement in full: "Up to and including 1880 the country had a frontier settlement; but at present the unsettled area has been so broken into by isolated bodies of settlement that there can hardly be said to be a frontier line." The quotation was critical, and the sentence crafted by Turner that followed contained a significantly vague pronoun reference, one that encompassed both the literal statement of the superintendent and the symbolic manifestation of the limits of westward expansion on the continent. "This," Frederick Jackson Turner wrote, "marks the close of the first period of American history, and inaugurates a new era. The continent is crossed by settlement."[76]

The lead paragraph was, in fact, quite similar to that which Turner had delivered some six months before at the World Columbian Exposition at Chicago. On July 12, 1893, Turner had read a paper entitled "The Significance of the Frontier in American History." He had begun by noting the census statement and claiming that the "existence of an area of free land, its continuous recession, and the advance of American settlement westward, explain American development. Behind institutions, behind constitutional forms and modifications, lie the vital forces that call these organs into life and shape them to meet changing conditions."[77] American institutions have been compelled to "adapt themselves" to the changes in crossing a continent. The language of the argument—talk of vital forces and of adaptation—indicated the influence of his Wisconsin colleague, the geologist Charles R. Van Hise, author of *Principles of North American Pre-Cambrian Geology* (1896) and later president of the university. Van Hise, along with many others, had been influenced by genetic interpretations of survival. The language of those committed to the preservation of inherited favorable characteristics had, no doubt, influenced the language of Turner's thesis.[78]

In America, the case was a complex one whenever vital forces (or trains or written entrance examinations for college) were noted. "American social development," Turner postulated, "has been continually beginning over again on the frontier." True, the "germ theory" of politics—that all people show development within a Social Darwinist framework—had been emphasized before, but an American character that was unique had emerged in the vast frontier encounter, a battle between the primitive forces of the Indians and the cartographic technology of Lewis and Clark. Simple colonial government had grown into "complex organs." Even manufacturing had progressed from "primitive industrial society" to "manufacturing civilizations." The "process of evolution" began again in each encounter and was reified in each expansion. Now that the frontier had closed, however, America had to adjust to its fate. The implications for Turner's audience were clear: standards had to be put in place, mechanisms by which vital forces of intelligence would be preserved now that America had reached its geographic limits. Intellectual resources were precious, and there was no use in frittering away time on those who were unfit.

Within American education, a mechanism had emerged to ensure that a prudent use of resources would result in the preservation of favorable inherited characteristics. While entrance examinations in English at Yale had not been in force, as Albert S. Cook had noted, "the requirement goes into effect with the beginning of the next academic year."[79] What Charles W. Eliot had proposed in his inaugural address a quarter century before had come to pass: "The rigorous examination for admission had one good effect through the college course: it prevents a waste of instruction upon incompetent persons."[80]

There was thus little doubt that the question of English—no less than the creation of a material body through written language, as Barrett Wendell understood it, a demonstration bearing witnesses to the worth of John Winthrop's new city on the hill—was tied to the question of competence. When William Morton Payne collected *The Dial* essays in *English in American Universities* in 1895, he added a new introduction in which he noted that the 1892 *Report of the Committee on Composition and Rhetoric to the Board of Overseers of Harvard College* had "made a burning 'question of the day' out of a matter previously little more than academic in its interest." The nation had witnessed in that report an "exhibit" of the writing of the young men and women who were products of the best preparatory education in America. "The report," Payne recalled, "was more than a discussion of the evils of bad training; it was an object lesson of the most effective sort, for it printed many specimen papers *literatim et verbatim*, and was even cruel enough to facsimile some of them by photographic process."[81] The Harvard *Report* had, in fact, even more influence, Payne noted, than the 1893 *Report of the Committee on Secondary School Studies*, popularly called Report of the Committee of Ten. Chaired by Charles W. Eliot, that 249-page analysis had summarized a process sponsored by the National Education Association in which committees examined secondary school subject areas so that entrance requirements could be systematized for college admission.[82] But the Harvard *Report* had something more than bland analysis, more than a discussion of "the evils of bad training." It had visual evidence of evil embodied in the specimen papers themselves. The "seed of discontent," Payne noted, had been sown.[83]

Particular Little Fads

By the time of the publication of Payne's volume, over 977 colleges and universities had been founded. The recorded growth was remarkable. Two years before the Land Grant College Act was signed into law by the Republican Congress during the Civil War, there had been only 381 institutions of higher education. (When Thoreau had studied rhetoric with Channing, there had been only 66.) While only 2.3 percent of the nation's students age eighteen to twenty-one attended post-secondary institutions in 1900, this represented a gain: in 1870, only 1.3 percent had attended institutions of higher learning.[84]

If there were now emerging two American populations, as Harvard expatriot George Santayana would hold—"polite America" (those sons of the eastern seaboard, ailing from "in-breeding and anæmia") and "crude but vital America" (the self-made men)[85]—then the public elementary and secondary school had certainly witnessed America's vitality. During the 1870s, public school enrollment had grown 44 percent. By 1900, there were over 16 million children in the nation's elementary and secondary schools. In 1870, the year data collection began, 57 percent of the nation's students age five to seventeen were in school; by 1900, that percentage had risen to nearly 72 percent. College enrollment had experienced a modest growth from 1870 to 1900, but the growth of public education was rampant.[86]

A keen observer of policy trends in school enrollment and the transition of students from secondary school to college was Wilson Farrand. He was the headmaster of Newark Academy and the newly elected 1895 president of The Schoolmasters' Association of New York and Vicinity. In his inaugural address, he began by noting that, while fellowship among teachers had been a worthy goal in the Association's eight-year history, "securing uniformity in college requirements" was the efficient reason for the existence of the organization.[87] Recognizing that the schools sent most of their pupils to Harvard, Yale, Princeton, and Columbia, Farrand realized the limits of the Association. Yet he also realized that the time was ripe for a movement toward uniform national admission standards. "In the last few years the schools and colleges have come to a better understanding and into closer relations than ever before," he told his audience. "New England and the Middle States are learning that it is possible and wise to act in harmony, and the West, whose educational progress and standing we of the East do not fully realize, stands ready to unite in every forward movement."[88] After reviewing the entrance requirements for the four schools—a limited review but sufficient for his purposes—Farrand concluded that "unreasonable diversity" existed, that each college called "for its own particular little fad."[89] The examiners themselves were, in addition, idiosyncratic. The examinations emphasized certain points arbitrarily, and the exams appeared to be designed to entrap students. As a result, grave distrust existed.

The remedy? First, each candidate should submit, before entering an examination, a certificate from the principal instructor stating the work done and the quality of that work. Second, the examinations should be made general with an eye toward determining the thoroughness and understanding of the student. With the certificate in hand showing what the candidate had done, there would be no need to test the details of past work; rather, the object of the examination would turn to the student's depth of understanding. The combined wise use of the certificate and the general nature of the examination would thus "rob the examinations of much of their terror for pupils and teachers."[90] Third, the judgment of admission should thus be made based on the evidence of the certificate and the results of the examination. Fourth, the colleges should administer the examinations accurately, fairly, and wisely. "The preparation of the papers should be in the hands of capable men, under such supervision and so restricted that the absurd travesties now sometimes inflicted upon us would be impossible."[91] If a student should fail to be admitted, the schoolmaster could obtain a statement of the grounds for the decision. The fifth remedy was critical: the requirements should be uniform across the colleges.

The means by which these five suggestions would be achieved? Agitation and legislation. A central committee, Farrand thought, might be formed, similar to that of the Committee of Ten. "This committee, when it is appointed, will have before it a magnificent opportunity, and its composition and its work will be watched with the keenest interest by every preparatory teacher in the land."[92] But that, of course, was legislation. As he reminded his readers in his closing sentence, "Agitation will compel legislation, and through agitation and legislation, we shall attain the desired end."[93]

Farrand found particularly keen allies in Eliot and in a promising dean at Columbia, Nicholas Murray Butler. Despite their differences—Butler was some twenty-eight years Eliot's junior and a student of philosophy, a contrast to the elder Eliot's position as a university president and trained chemist—both had been involved in the work of the Committee of Ten and

"The aim of Wilson Farrand was simple: to prepare every senior to take and pass the College Board Examinations which he had helped to found and to enter Princeton. Wilson Farrand could not conceal from [Newark] Academy students that there were other colleges and universities in the United States, but he did nothing to publicize such facts. At the beginning of senior year we were summoned to his office. On his desk were applications forms for Princeton already filled out, to which were attached transcripts of our grades and his recommendation. We were merely told to take one form home to be signed by our fathers and to obtain the reference signatures of three persons of our acquaintance, preferably Princeton graduates. I ended up with the signatures of the eye specialist who had examined me for my first set of glasses and two business friends of my father who would not have recognized me if they had encountered me on the street. But they were Princeton graduates. It was naturally quite a shock, after all those forms has been sent in, to return to the Headmaster's office, to tell him that I had changed my mind and that I wanted to apply to Williams College. When he recovered from his incredulity that I should presume to exercise any individual preference in the choice of a college, he made a most deathless Farrand remark. 'If you are sure that you do not want to go to Princeton, at least you have the good sense to select Williams.'" (Newark Academy Archives, qtd. in Suzanne Geissler, *A Widening Sphere of Usefulness: Newark Academy, 1744-1993* [West Kennebunk, ME: Phoenix Publishing, 1993] 181. Photo of Wilson Farrand by permission of Blackwood Parlin, Newark Academy)

considered each other allies in the struggle for rational enforcement of uniform standards. In 1899, Butler chose the annual meeting of the Association of Colleges and Preparatory Schools of the Middle States and Maryland, an organization he had helped to establish, to propose the establishment of an entrance examination board. Eliot took the train from Boston to attend the December 2 meeting in Trenton. At that meeting, it was resolved that a joint College Admission Examination Board should be formed by members of colleges and secondary schools in the Middle States and Maryland, that uniform statements of each subject required by two or more colleges be formed, and that a series of college admission examinations, with uniform tests in each subject, be given in June of each year. An invitation was extended to each college in the Association to send a representative to the next meeting at Columbia University on December 22, 1899, at 10:00 a.m.

At that meeting, Seth Low—a former Brooklyn mayor who had implemented a successful merit-based civil service system and was then serving as president of Columbia University—was elected chairman. Wilson Farrand was elected secretary. Representatives attended from Colgate University, the University of Pennsylvania, New York University, Barnard College, Union University, Rutgers College, Vassar College, Bryn Mawr College, Woman's College of Baltimore, Princeton University, Cornell University, Mixed High School of New York, and Collegiate Institute of New York. The group voted to move forward by drafting a constitution and taking a name: the College Entrance Examination Board. On May 12, representatives from the colleges and schools again met at Columbia University (again at 10:00 a.m.) and adopted the plan of organization that had been proposed by President Low and Professors Butler of Columbia, West of Princeton, White of Cornell, Dr. Goodwin of Mixed High School, and Headmaster Farrand. The plan was subsequently printed and distributed.[94]

The organizational plan of the new College Board was a realization of Farrand's inaugural address five years before. The unreasonable diversity and little fads were to end, and twenty-four detailed pages specified content of the examination requirements in English, history, Latin, Greek, French, German, mathematics, physics, chemistry, botany, and zoology. Here was proof of the presence of a uniform system. The requirements had their origins in authoritative bodies: those in English were taken from the Conference on Uniform Entrance Requirements in English, a plan originating at Harvard and evident in its 1874 catalogue.[95] An eye would be lent to determining the thoughtfulness and understanding of the student each December when a college teacher would act as chief examiner, and one additional college teacher and one secondary school teacher would act as associate examiners to prepare questions to be used at the annual examinations. The examinations would be administered accurately, fairly, and wisely in printed forms distributed by the board's secretary, and they would be evaluated fairly by a staff of readers, appointed no later than May. A reader would receive the examination and score it on the following scale of 100: 100 to 90 as Excellent; 90 to 75 as Good; 75 to 60 as Fair; 60 to 50 as Poor, and below 50 as Very Poor. No answer book was to be marked below 60 until it had been reviewed by two readers, and no revision of any examination was to be made after it was marked. Within one week after their receipt, the marked books were to be returned to the secretary, who would then issue a certificate of the name, residence, and age of the candidate, the name of the last school the candidate attended (or, if privately taught, the name of the tutor), the subjects in which the examination was taken, and the rating given to each subject. Only a single remedy for uniformity that Farrand had identified—the certificate from each candidate's principal instructor stating the work done and the quality of that work, a certificate that would be submitted before the examination—was absent from the board's plan. Each of the other measures had been adopted. Agitation and legislation had succeeded.

Definition of Requirements

1. ENGLISH

The requirement in English is that recommended by the Conference on Uniform Entrance Requirements in English

NOTE. — No candidate will be accepted in English whose work is notably defective in point of spelling, punctuation, idiom, or division into paragraphs.

a. READING. — A certain number of books will be set for reading. The candidate will be required to present evidence of a general knowledge of the subject-matter, and to answer simple questions on the lives of the authors. The form of examination will usually be the writing of a paragraph or two on each of several topics, to be chosen by the candidate from a considerable number — perhaps ten or fifteen — set before him in the examination paper. The treatment of these topics is designed to test the candidate's power of clear and accurate expression, and will call for only a general knowledge of the substance of the books. The candidate is expected to read intelligently all the books prescribed. He is expected not to know them minutely, but to have fresh in mind their most important parts. **In every case knowledge of the book will be regarded as less important than the ability to write good English.** In preparation for this part of the requirement, it is important that the candidate shall have been instructed in the fundamental principles of rhetoric.

The books set for this part of the examination will be:

1901 and 1902: Shakespeare's *Merchant of Venice;* Pope's *Iliad,* Books I, VI, XXII, and XXIV; The *Sir Roger De Coverley Papers* in The Spectator; Goldsmith's *The Vicar of Wakefield;* Coleridge's *The Ancient Mariner;* Scott's *Ivanhoe;* Cooper's *The Last of the Mohicans;* Tennyson's *The Princess;* Lowell's *The Vision of Sir Launfal;* George Eliot's *Silas Marner.*

1903, 1904, 1905: Shakespeare's *The Merchant of Venice* and *Julius Cæsar;* The *Sir Roger De Coverley Papers* in The Spectator; Goldsmith's *The Vicar of Wakefield;* Coleridge's *The Ancient Mariner;* Scott's *Ivanhoe;* Carlyle's *Essay on Burns;* Tennyson's *The Princess;* Lowell's *The Vision of Sir Launfal;* George Eliot's *Silas Marner.*

b. STUDY AND PRACTICE. — This part of the examination presupposes the thorough study of each of the works named below. The examination will be upon subject-matter, form, and structure. In addition, the candidate may be required to answer questions involving the essentials of English grammar, and questions on the leading facts in those periods of English literary history to which the prescribed works belong.

The books set for this part of the examination will be:

1901 to 1905: Shakespeare's *Macbeth;* Milton's *Lycidas, Comus, L'Allegro,* and *Il Penseroso;* Burke's *Speech on Conciliation with America;* Macaulay's *Essays on Milton and Addison.*

Either part of the examination may be taken separately.

Attention is called to the following recommendations of the Conference on Uniform Entrance Requirements in English:

1. That English be studied throughout the elementary and secondary school courses, and, when possible, for at least three periods a week during the four years of the high school course.

2. That the prescribed books be regarded as a basis for such wider courses of English study as the schools may arrange for themselves.

3. That, where careful instruction in idiomatic English translation is not given, supplementary work to secure an equivalent training in diction and in sentence-structure be offered throughout the high school course.

4. That a certain amount of outside reading, chiefly of poetry, fiction, biography, and history, be encouraged throughout the entire school course.

5. That definite instruction be given in the choice of words, in the structure of sentences and of paragraphs, and in the simple forms of narration, description, exposition, and argument. Such instruction should begin early in the high school course.

6. That systematic training in speaking and writing English be given throughout the entire school course. That, in the high school, subjects for composition be taken, partly from the prescribed books, and partly from the student's own thought and experience.

7. That each of the books prescribed for study be taught with reference to

a. The language, including the meaning of words and sentences, the important qualities of style, and the important allusions;

b. The plan of the work, i.e. its structure and method;

c. The place of the work in literary history, the circumstances of its production, and the life of its author.

That all details be studied, not as ends in themselves, but as means to a comprehension of the whole.

Definition of the Requirements in English. *Plan of Organization of the College Entrance Examination Board for the Middle States and Maryland and a Statement of Subjects in Which Examinations Are Proposed.* New York: College Entrance Examination Board, Adopted May 12, 1900. 12–14.

Extraordinary Fairness and Good Judgment

"The College Entrance Examination Board of the Middle States and Maryland," the first secretary and executive officer Nicholas Murray Butler recorded in the First Annual Report of September 1, 1901, "was organized at a meeting held at Columbia University, New York, on November 17, 1900."[96] The chief examiners had been appointed a month earlier than the plan of organization had specified, and the associate examiners were in place by January 12 of the new year. The examiners in English were prestigious: Francis Hovey Stoddard of New York University, student of philology at Oxford and author of numerous literary studies; Edward Everett Hale, Jr., of Union College, son of the author of *The Man Without a Country* and a professor of rhetoric and logic; and Helen Josephine Robins, a teacher in Miss Baldwin's School for Girls, a preparatory school for Bryn Mawr. Similar teams of examiners and associate examiners were also set for French, German, Greek, history, Latin, mathematics, and physics. Examination dates were set for the week of June 17, and 973 candidates were examined.

In English, students wrote on *The Iliad* in order to answer this question: "The two sides of the character of Achilles as shown in *The Iliad*. Illustrate each and tell whether we find anything like this contrast in the character of Hector." Macbeth's "Come, seeling night" reply to Lady Macbeth was provided with directions to give the meaning of key words, to state the meter of the passage with apparent variations from the normal line, to provide the context of the lines, and to write about how the character of the language in the passage demonstrated a side of Macbeth's nature. Students were given a choice to write on the fifth act of *The Merchant of Venice* and describe the feeling between Jessica and Shylock, or to describe the feeling between Rebecca and Isaac of York in *The Vicar of Wakefield*. There were questions on the different stories which are worked together in the plot of *Silas Marner*, and there were questions covering *Ivanhoe* and *The Last of the Mohicans* regarding which historical period seemed to lend itself more naturally to romantic incident and setting. There were questions on the picture obtained of the eighteenth century from reading Addison's *Sir Roger de Coverley Papers* and how this picture connected itself with Addison's purpose in writing the papers, and there were more general questions on *The Spectator* and its authors. There were questions on the main lines of Macaulay's comparison of Milton with Dante and the part this comparison played in Macaulay's treatment of Milton. Students wrote on Tennyson's *The Princess* regarding the Princess Ida's possible comment on the words of Portia to Bassanio. And, with an eye on the new world, students wrote on the three methods of dealing with America suggested by Edmund Burke and the argument he employed to support the method he favored. There were also passages on words, phrases, clauses, and kinds of sentences in which the candidate was required to enclose the correct word between two choices given in brackets (and to give the reason for the choice in a footnote), to write two sentences using correlatives, and to describe (with an illustration) how an adverb should be placed in a sentence to modify the right word and at the same time give force to a sentence.[97]

A total of 7,889 answer books in all examination areas had been read once, and 3,211 had been read twice because the first reader had given a score below 60. Hence, 40.7 percent of the answer books had been read twice. In cases in which "a difference of opinion" between two readers was noted, a third reader was called in to decide, but these cases were so few, Butler assured his readers, "as to be a negligible quantity."[98] In English, 1,039 books had been received (Butler does not reveal how 973 candidates submitted 1,039 examinations), with 459 read twice. An average of 14.3 books had been read per hour, and 105 hours had been spent reading. Just as the questions had been uniformly prepared, so too had the reading process been systematized:

> In order that there might be all possible uniformity in the rating of answer-books, the several groups of readers spent some time in studying the question set in their subject and in reading aloud a specimen answer-book, in order to arrive at a common standard of marking. This done, the rating proceeded smoothly and rapidly, and I believe that it was done with extraordinary fairness and good judgment, each group or research working together and in constant reference.[99]

Regarding the results of the examinations, Butler noted that "the one criticism that the board could not afford to face, namely, that the questions set were too easy, had not been made."[100] Of those taking the examination in English, 44 percent had failed.

Nearly 60 percent of all the answer books were rated at 60 or above, Butler noted. He provided no further analysis of the scores.

"The work of the Board," Butler claimed in the final section of the report, "will promptly elevate the secondary-school work in English, in history, and in the natural sciences to a new plane of importance and of effectiveness. It will control the examination system in the interest of education, and resist the tendency to make it a mere machine-like performance. It will declare and enforce standards of attainment which represent, not the labors of a zealous individual, however wise, but the mature judgment of a group of mature scholars of different training and points of view." As for the secondary-school teachers themselves, Butler

TABLE VII

RATINGS ACCORDED THE CANDIDATES FOR EXAMINATION IN EACH SUBJECT

	College Entrance Examination Board	Columbia University	Barnard College		(Excellent—90-100) A	(Good—75-90) B	(Fair—60-75) C	(Above 60—Fair, Good, or Excellent) Total	(Poor—50-60) D	(Very Poor—40-50) E	(Failure—Below 40) F	(Below 60 — Poor, Very Poor, or Failure) Total	
Chemistry	75	106	9	190	1	27	42	70	24	31	65	120	190
English													
a. Reading.............	319	169	66	554	52	95	192	339	56	93	66	215	554
b. Study	259	153	73	485	25	78	138	241	45	81	118	244	485
	578	*322*	*139*	*1039*	*77*	*173*	*330*	*580*	*101*	*174*	*184*	*459*	*1039*

The ratings in chemistry and English. From *First Annual Report of the Secretary, 1901* (New York: College Entrance Examination Board, 1901) 21. "The examination in Chemistry had its defects," board historian Claude M. Fuess recalled in *The College Board: Its First Fifty Years*, "but that was the only one which was disappointing" (48). (Reproduced with permission of the College Board. All rights reserved. www.collegeboard.com)

suggested that they "may well be pardoned the unrestrained enthusiasm they have shown at the board's organization and early work. The experience of each year should enable that work to be improved beyond the risk of fair criticism."[101]

Surely Room for Improvement

Edward Thorndike shared no such enthusiasm. In 1903 he had defined the role of tested knowledge in his textbook *Educational Psychology*. "We conquer the facts of nature," he had written, "when we observe and experiment upon them. When we measure them we have made them our servants. A little statistical insight trains them for invaluable work."[102] Indebted to the new quantitatively oriented research methods of Francis Galton and Karl Pearson in Great Britain, Thorndike examined the academic careers of 253 Columbia University students who had taken the College Board's examinations from 1901 to 1903 for their power of prediction. In May 1906 Thorndike published his conclusion of the merit of the Board's examinations in two widely respected journals: *Educational Review* and *Science*. The examinations, he concluded, "do not prevent incompetents from getting into college; do not prevent students of excellent promise from being discouraged, improperly conditioned or barred out altogether; do not measure fitness for college well enough to earn the respect of students or teachers, and do intolerable injustice to individuals.... There is," he added, "surely room for improvement."[103] The investigation of the College Board's new examinations would allow Thorndike to employ innovative methods of analysis, invented in Europe, on the uniquely American institution of testing. It was a young professor's dream.

The son of a Methodist minister, Thorndike had entered Wesleyan University in 1891 as a student of classics. He wrote essays with titles such as such as "The Novel as a Moral Force" for competition, but his inclination ran toward empiricism. "As a matter of hard fact," he wrote in 1894, "the laws of social science are precisely not that. They are not deductions but inductions, not from general principles of any kind, last of all from such disputed principles as the freedom and dignity of men, but from particular cases of historical fact."[104] In his junior year, Thorndike took a course in psychology under Andrew C. Armstrong, who had himself studied the new science at its birthplace in Germany during 1885–1886. It was, Thorndike recalled, the first time he had heard or seen the word psychology.[105]

Upon graduation from Wesleyan in 1885, Thorndike applied to Harvard for financial aid in order to take a second bachelor's degree through a year's work in English "and then, if finances allow, the Masters's degree."[106] He told his Wesleyan professors that he intended to become a secondary-school teacher of English. At Harvard, Thorndike enrolled in Barrett Wendell's course but was more interested in William James's course "Philosophy 2A: Advanced Psychology," a seminar focusing on Wundt's work.[107] Thorndike began his experiments with chickens, and, ever helpful to students, James kept the chickens in the basement of his Cambridge home.

Edward L. Thorndike, ca. 1898. "The main duty of the high schools is to train boys and girls to be capable and intelligent men and women. They and the public which supports them are willing to accept also the responsibility of fitting for college the small minority of their students who will go on to an academic degree; but they ought not to be asked to fit students primarily for an arbitrary set of examinations. With such a task, they cannot be expected to resist the temptation to give up a large part of the last two years to specific coaching for the process of examination-taking." (Thorndike, "The Future of the College Entrance Examination Board," *Educational Review* 31 [1906]: 477) [Photo Courtesy of University Archives and Columbiana Library, Columbia University]

("The nuisance to Mrs. James was, I hope, somewhat mitigated by the entertainment to the two youngest children," he later recalled.[108])

At Columbia, Thorndike studied animal learning, writing a dissertation on animal intelligence under the direction of James McKeen Cattell, the great experimentalist and first researcher in the world to hold the title of Professor of Psychology. Thorndike found that animals learn in stimulus-response conditions. The idea of association—he would later term it connectionism—was a critical force in learning, he proposed. Drawing on the associationism of the Scottish Common Sense Realist Alexander Bain, Thorndike believed that an impulse to generalize was critical in establishing an environment for learning.[109]

Thorndike also had been trained at Columbia to use the new science of statistics. Whether it was the chicks and monkeys of his dissertation or the experiments in human mental function of his early papers, Thorndike relied on measures of association to establish the presence of a stimulus validated by its anticipated response. If context mattered in learning, then the method needed to assess the strength of an association within a context was to be found in the degree to which a stimulus, such as an examination, produced responses that correlated with the outcome, such as performance in English. Examinations, after all, could be designed not only to capture present knowledge but to predict future performance.

In a brief autobiography published in 1939, Thorndike recalled those authors who had meant the most to him in his own intellectual development. Among the authors he listed whose writings he had read in their entirety, he noted both William James and Francis Galton. Among those writers whose works served as a stimulus for the study of problems, he noted both Alexander Bain and Charles Spearman.[110] The combined influence of philosophy and psychology would soon be permanently separated by disciplinary specialization, but for Thorndike the fields had much in common in that both offered a rational basis for understanding the world. Nevertheless, Thorndike would ultimately align his career neither with Bain, part of a receding humanistic world in which proof could be reified through language, nor with James, whose brave new world of the psychological laboratory was illuminated with philosophy.[111] Francis Galton and Charles Spearman, on the other hand, believed in statistics as the chosen method of establishing proof. In a world filled with examinations, Thorndike would model his career on theirs.

Their new science was built on mathematics designed to yield association. While Karl Pearson, as Galton's biographer, lamented that the English school of psychology was "handicapped by German dominance,"

Sir Francis Galton in 1909, at age 87, with Professor Karl Pearson. "If my view be correct, Erasmus Darwin planted the seed of suggestion in questioning whether adaptation meant no more to man than illustration of creative ingenuity; the one grandson, Charles Darwin, collected the facts which had to be dealt with and linked them together by wide-reaching hypotheses; the other grandson, Frances Galton, provided the methods by which they could be tested, and saw with the enthusiasm of a prophet their application in the future to the directed and self-conscious evolution of the human race." (Karl Pearson, *The Life, Letters and Labors of Francis Galton*, vol. 1 [Cambridge: Cambridge UP, 1914] vii. (Source of photo: Helen M. Walker, *Studies in the History of Statistical Method* [Baltimore: Williams and Wilkins, 1929] facing 175.)

he assured his readers that "the chief superiority over German and French work lies in the adoption of Galton's correlational calculus."[112] In his 1869 *Hereditary Genius: An Inquiry into Its Laws and Consequences*, Galton had identified eminent families listed in the biographical dictionary *Men of Time* who were related by blood and concluded that heredity set the natural boundaries for achievement. Further, he had shown that intelligence in general was inherited by defining it as a quantity that was distributed, as were all functions in nature, in a curve that was bell shaped, a concept that had first been used by the mathematician Carl Friedrich Gauss to estimate planetary positions. The Gaussian distribution was useful to Galton in that he could mathematically identify an average intelligence—the true value—and deviations from that mean. Instead of the positions of planets, Galton could determine the degree to which a population deviated from the mean.[113] The eminence of intelligence, manifested in the names listed in *Men of Time*, could thus be demonstrated as a constant, distributed in one small part of the scale. Even though the precise definition of intelligence itself could not yet be known, its height on the curve could be taken. This place on the bell-shaped curve must be preserved, Galton argued, and in 1904 he offered a name for the new strategy in the *American Journal of Sociology*:

> EUGENICS is the science which deals with all influences that improve the inborn qualities of a race; also with those that develop them to the utmost advantage. The improvement of the inborn qualities, or stock, of some one human population will alone be discussed here.
>
> What is meant by improvement? What by the syllable *eu* in "eugenics," whose English equivalent is "good"? There is considerable difference between goodness in the several qualities and in that of the character as a whole. The

> character depends largely on the *proportion* between qualities, whose balance may be much influenced by education. We must therefore leave morals as far as possible out of the discussion, not entangling ourselves with the almost hopeless difficulties they raise as to whether a character as a whole is good or bad. Moreover, the goodness or badness of character is not absolute, but relative to the current form of civilization.[114]

In *Hereditary Genius*—and in his subsequent studies *English Men of Science* (1874) and *Natural Inheritance* (1889)—Galton inferred the existence of intelligence, its location on the curve, by identifying eminent men and tracing the contributions of their children. The direct measurement of intelligence, however, would result from the application of the product moment correlation, a statistical method invented by Charles Pearson and put to use by a former British army officer, Charles Spearman.

In 1904, Spearman would derive that method of correlation and demonstrate its power in two articles in the *American Journal of Psychology*. In "The Proof and Measurement of Association Between Two Things," Spearman had begun with the premise that "all knowledge—beyond that of bare isolated occurrence—deals with uniformities."[115] He thus strove not only for the measurement of quantity but also for the significance of that quantity, an estimate that sheer chance might have caused the association. In the application of his statistical method of correlation and probability in the second article—"'General Intelligence,' Objectively Determined and Measured"—Spearman had used a school in Berkshire located within 100 yards of his house. There, using mechanical devices similar to those used by Fullerton and Cattell, Spearman had tested children on their perceptions of light (to discriminate among shades of light and dark), weight (among a graduated series of weights), and sound (among tones), each believed to be preeminently intellective operations. The students were also ranked according to "Native Capacity" by taking the difference between each boy's rank in school in subjects (such as classics, French, English, and mathematics) and his rank in age. Teachers were asked, as well, to identify the brightest students, and the older children were also interviewed and asked to give judgments about the other children. Sex and age were removed as irrelevant factors for their failure to correlate with the ability to discriminate along physical lines—the perceptions of light and weight and sound. But factors such as talent in classics, French, English, and mathematics were so correlated that there was, Pearson found, a kind of "intellective saturation" driving sensory and academic powers of discernment toward the same end. Ability in classics correlated at a level of .99 with general intelligence, and abilities in English at .90.[116]

Activity.	Correlation with Gen. Intell.	Ratio of the common factor to the specific factor.
Classics,	0.99	99 to 1
Common Sense,	0.98	96 4
Pitch Dis.,	0.94	89 11
French,	0.92	84 16
Cleverness,[3]	0.90	81 19
English,	0.90	81 19
Mathematics,[4]	0.86	74 26
Pitch Dis. among the uncultured,[5]	0.72	52 48
Music,	0.70	49 51
Light Dis.,[5]	0.57	32 68
Weight Dis.,[5]	0.44	19 81

"In the above Hierarchy one of the most noticeable figures is the high position of language; to myself, at any rate, it was no small surprise to find Classics and even French placed unequivocally above English (note that this term does not refer to any study of the native tongue, but merely to the aggregate of all the lessons conducted therein, such as History, Geography, Dictation, Scripture, and Repetition." (Charles Spearman, "'General Intelligence,' Objectively Determined and Measured," *American Journal of Psychology* 15 [1904] 277.)

A strong connection—the correlation—between high levels of general intelligence and facility with language was thus established in a hierarchy. The formula that had identified "the same final amount of correlation" had led to the inference "wholly and solely [of] the common faculty."[117] Along with correlation statistics themselves—the Spearman rank-correlation coefficient and its predecessor, Pearson's *r*—the connection between intelligence and language would have profound influence. By 1904, the European and American intellectual community had a new way of understanding intelligence through the two articles of Spearman. There was a general factor of intelligence, *g*, whose existence had been established by its association with language. The presence of high levels of *g*—of inborn qualities that should be preserved eugenically—could, in fact, be inferred when facility with language was observed. The greater the facility with language, the greater the associated presence of general intelligence.

The conclusion was clear. Here would lie, Spearman wrote, "the long awaited general rational basis for public examinations. Instead of continuing ineffectively to protest that high marks in Greek syntax are no test as to the capacity of men to command troops or to administer provinces, we shall at last actually determine the precise accuracy of the various means of measuring General Intelligence.... Thus it is to be hoped, we shall eventually reach our pedagogical conclusions, not by easy subjective theories, nor by some catchpenny exceptional cases, but rather by an adequately represented array of established facts."[118] Because God knew, as Barrett Wendell had warned a decade before, what would become of seed thoughtlessly sown, examinations would reveal who had the most ability, and social engineering would allow the preservation of those traits.

For Thorndike, publishing in *Educational Review* and *Science* just two years after Spearman, the examinations used by the College Board were thus an opportunity to examine the utility of these uniquely American examinations by means of the new British techniques. With Galton, Pearson, and Spearman, Thorndike was committed to validating facts through measurement. He had devoted an entire chapter to relationships among mental traits in *Educational Psychology* and had proposed suggestions for investigations in educational science that included discovering units of mental measurement, establishing the distribution of mental traits, and estimating the influence of selection. "The result of a careful tracing of a thousand children from the last year of compulsory attendance up through the higher schools would to my mind be one of the most brilliant reports in educational literature," he had proposed.[119]

Careful tracing of longitudinal data was indeed needed. The evidence offered just fourteen years earlier in the *Report of the Committee on Composition and Rhetoric to the Board of Overseers of Harvard College* may have created the burning question of the day by its rhetoric and its photographically reproduced images of poor student papers. Those Harvard specimens no doubt had suggested that many of the 156,000 students enrolled in the nation's colleges may have been equally poor writers. But that method of establishing proof was now assigned to a quaint and unreliable past associated with Charles Francis Adams (Harvard, class of 1825), the author of the report and the son of the first Boylston Professor of Rhetoric, John Quincy Adams. Publishing in 1906, Thorndike recognized a new fact of modern American life that would have eluded both son and father in the Adams dynasty (though not, perhaps, Henry Adams, who knew something of the power of dynamos): proof rested not in language alone but rather in calculations that created inferences.

Thorndike also recognized a second fact of the twentieth century that did not concern the Adams family: there were now multiple audiences of readers. And so Thorndike produced two versions of his findings. The first version, reported in *Educational Review*, was directed toward school administrators and informed teachers who were concerned more with policy than with statistics in serving what would soon be their 17 million enrolled students. The second, reported in *Science*, was targeted for the statistically trained new breed of university professor working with what would soon be some 355,000 university students; and so here Thorndike had included the correlations.

The lines of argument were essentially the same in both articles. Thorndike had undertaken three studies. In the first, he had longitudinally correlated the College Board examination results (in English, Latin, Greek, French, and mathematics) with the Columbia University grades of students in those subjects earned over four years. The correlations between examinations and courses were .62, .50, .47, and .25. "The relationship is only moderate even in the case of the work of freshman year and dwindles steadily," Thorndike concluded.[120] The second study, a work in progress, sought to establish the validity of the College Board examinations by examining their "prophetic" qualities. The highest correlation here was with science (.55), and the lowest was with mathematics (.30). The correlation with English was .40. The correlation between the College Board examination in Virgil and a Columbia course in Latin was almost zero.[121] In the third study, Thorndike examined College Board examinations that had been repeated because of initial failure. In 140 cases of repeated examinations chosen at random, the average difference of precisely the same examination taken on two occasions was over twenty-two points—evidence of instability. "The whole matter of the means of selecting students for continued education," he concluded modestly, "is in great need of scientific study."[122]

The article in *Educational Review* held no such restraint, as its provocative title—"The Future of the College Entrance Examination Board"—revealed. "Letting incompetents into college is, perhaps, poor economy, although in a well-regulated college they do not stay long, or do more harm, than they get good," Thorndike had written. "But to make a college education an impossibility for the really capable boy, in whose case the education is an investment by society that will yield from a hundred to ten thousand per cent., is criminal."[123]

It was therefore "unprofitable" to seek a modification of the College Board examinations "along conventional lines."[124] Instead Thorndike proposed a system that would allow continued education for all those who deserve it, that would encourage cooperation with the secondary schools, that would be both rigorous and just, and that would directly measure fitness for college ("not the mere opinion of inspectors or the length and assiduity of study, or the ingenious art of parading knowledge in a form to beguile examiners"). He called for a system that would be a "natural development" of the administrative organization of the Middle States board.[125] The Middle States board, he proposed, would accredit high schools, certifying a student fit for college. The work of the college admissions committees would be to treat the certificates of fitness as precisely as they treated the scores issued from the College Board. "We would have, that is, neither the conventional admissions systems, but a rigorous, continuous, and absolutely impartial

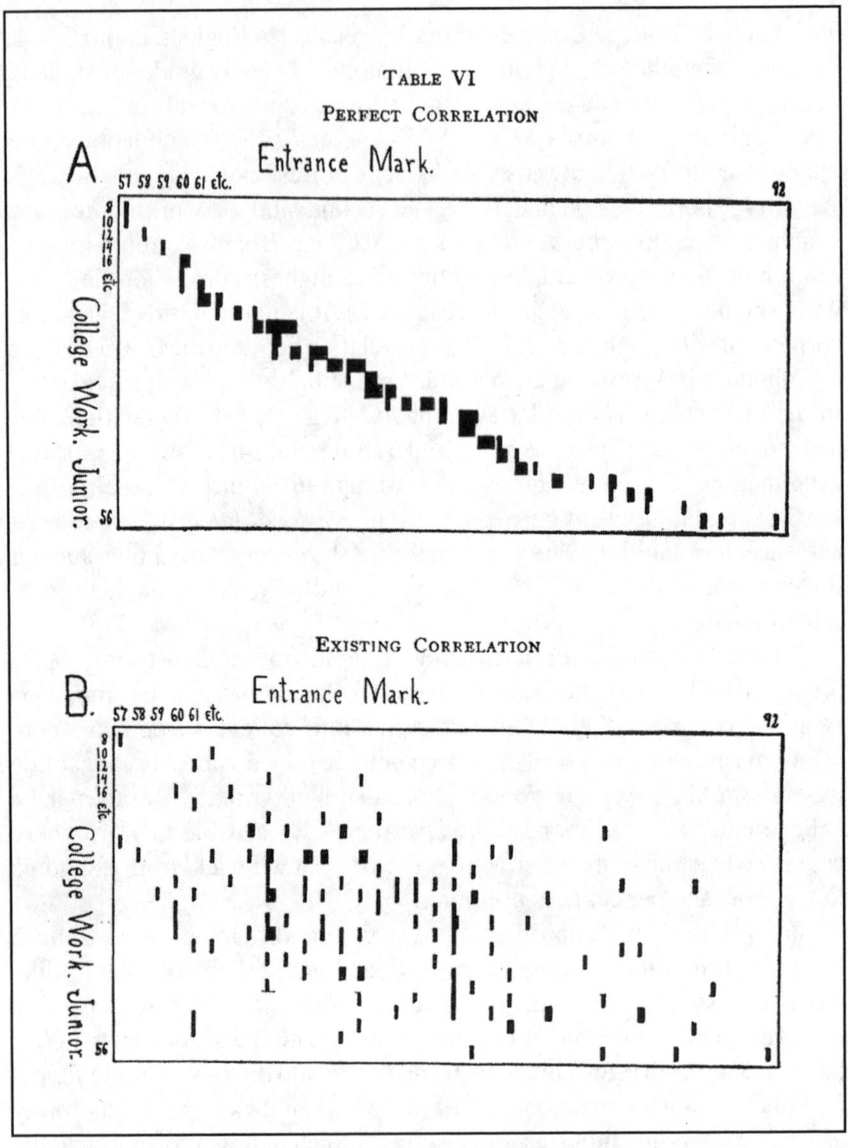

Thorndike included for his audience of administrators a visual model of ideal versus real correlations of the College Board examinations In these two figures he presented the ideal versus the existing relationship between entrance standing and college standing of junior-year students at Columbia University. "In these tables a black rectangle about 2.5 by .5 mm. equals one individual. The measures used were in this case the median of all entrance marks and the average of all the college marks of the given year." Table VIA shows "how the black rectangles would be arranged if each student's relative position in college work were the same as in entrance examinations." From Edward L. Thorndike, "The Future of the College Entrance Examination Board," *Educational Review* 31 (1906) 483.

examination of each school on the basis of its actual work in furnishing candidates who demonstrated their fitness for college by their work in college."[126]

It was a system nearly identical to that proposed by Wilson Farrand in 1895, a call for a certificate identifying the work done and the quality of that work. It was the one idea of Farrand's that had not survived the 1900 plan of organization for the board. And it was the one idea that could not compete against the growing American desire for economic efficiency and scientific objectivity. Faith rested neither in the secondary-school instructor nor in a certificate issued by such individuals. Faith now rested in the examination.

Scales Arranged Against a Wall

It was the impact of the Board's examinations, tested in the context of the Columbia curriculum, that so disturbed Thorndike. While Thorndike saw connectionism as behavioral, he also saw the metaphor behind the behavior: situations mattered a great deal.

But what if, instead of deductive and random acts of judgment made by the College Board examiners, a series of inductive and rational measurements could be made in the design of a scale? Thorndike had ventured such a project in his explanation in *Educational Psychology* of the normal distribution of mental traits—a type of distribution "found for most variable organs or functions in nature in the case of a single species when the organ or function in question is not subject to selection."[127] From the hypothesis of a normal distribution, it followed that measurements could be turned into "terms of amount."[128] His example: imagine that we could establish the rank order of 1,000 individuals in their excellence in English composition. That is, we could determine that one individual was better than anyone below in writing ability, that 999 are worse than the one above, and then, by incremental increases, demonstrate a range of ability. Then, if the group were divided in half, a scheme of distribution could be derived in which a measure could be determined for any individual whose position compared with the rest is known. Thus, "we make the hitherto arbitrary unit or amount a perfectly definite thing, as definite as an inch or an ohm or kilogram."[129]

In 1911, having demonstrated to his satisfaction that the examinations of the College Board lacked worth, Thorndike demonstrated the usefulness of a measurement plan based on distribution in the *Journal of Educational Psychology*. His scale for merit would be of great value to teachers, civil service examiners, college-entrance boards (in that there was only one such board, the reference was clear), scientific students of education, and others who needed to measure the merit of specimens of writing in order to estimate the abilities of individuals or changes in abilities as the result of mental maturity, educational effort, or other causes. In order to understand the derivation of the scale, readers were asked to perform an experiment. Eighteen samples were given, and readers were asked to rank the worst at 1, the next worse as 2, and so on. The readers were then asked to imagine a four-inch line, with the worst specimen placed at 1 and the best at 18. After providing this example of the scale construction method, Thorndike revealed that just such a scale had been constructed by nearly two hundred competent judges.

Thorndike also explained that a special team of twenty-eight individuals of literary ability, teaching excellence, and psychological training had been used to establish the point of zero merit on the scale, a critical point used to determine the "times as much merit" judgment.[130] The sample of zero merit read: "Dear Sir: I write to say that it ain't a square deal. Schools is I say they is I went to a school. red and gree green and brown aint it hito but I say he don't know his business not today nor yeaterday and you know it and I want Jennie to get me out."[131] The scale was, Thorndike announced, being extended, amplified, and refined so that more and better scales could be devised. The reader could not help but be engaged.

Assisting Thorndike in this project was a graduate student, Milo B. Hillegas. As one of the new school administrators Thorndike championed at Teachers College, Hillegas would become Vermont's Commissioner of Education from 1916 to 1920. Just as William James and James McKeen Cattell had supported his early research, so too did Thorndike support the work of his students. In the Preface to *Educational Psychology*, Thorndike had listed his debts to Galton and Pearson for the book's scientific and statistical precision, but he had also listed the names of ten students who had helped to collect material for analysis. In 1899 Teachers College had no Department of Administration, but Thorndike would change that. In 1901, just two years after coming to Teachers College, he had sent a plan for measuring student abilities to the superintendent of the Horace Mann School, and by 1916 educational administration had become the largest graduate group of students in the College.[132] Professional placements of graduates between 1900 and 1916 totaled nearly 1,000 in public-school central administration and supervision; an additional 1,300 graduates worked as school administrators.[133] In the hands of such trained individuals, scales would be invaluable.

"If there were standards or scales for the measurement of results in the various school subjects that would approximate the accuracy of the scales used in measuring extension, weight and time, educational administrators and investigators would be able to measure and express the efficiency of a school system in terms that would carry conviction. Such standards would also make it possible to define exactly the requirements of the college, high school, and civil service: and by them school superintendents could define requirements for promotions from one grade to the next." So Hillegas, echoing Thorndike, had written in the September 1912 issue of *Teachers College Record*.[134] It was Hillegas the student, not Thorndike the professor, who would introduce the scales to the American educational community in a project that would become so popular that, the following year, the research was reprinted by Teachers College itself and would be reprinted four times by 1917.

Hillegas explicated the theory of normal distribution used to derive the scale, essentially the same technique that Thorndike had described in *Educational Psychology* and had used in the development of his scale for handwriting, published in 1910.[135] Hillegas additionally identified the theory of establishing the smallest perceptible perception of difference—a central concept of the English composition study, an assumption that small differences (the limens) were, in fact, possible to measure—as belonging to G. S Fullerton and James McKeen Cattell.[136] If small differences could be established, the functionalist theory of Cattell and Fullerton had held, then it was error that had to be measured, not the failure to differentiate in the first place. Hence, to the extent that discrete choices were forced among writing specimens, differences could be noted and set on the bell curve that had proven so useful to Galton. The theory expressed in *On the Perception of Small Differences* was ideal for the study in its emphasis on the human capacity for discrete perception, a capacity that would be needed to build the English Composition scale. With the theory in hand, the critical decision-making point was set by Hillegas: if 75 percent of the judges agreed that one sample was better than the other, then the difference was used to set a unit of difference on the scale.

Essentially, there were four stages used to build the scale through the establishment of difference. In stage one, about seven thousand English compositions by young people had been collected in order to obtain the very poorest and the best work that is done in the schools. After the samples were collected, Hillegas and an assistant graded them into roughly ten classes, and from these seventy-five samples were selected. So that extremes of the scales might be established, artificial samples were included: The best samples were obtained from youthful writings of Jane Austen and the Brontës. The works of some college freshmen were also used. The set was thus expanded to eighty-three samples. The samples used in the first stage had been handwritten, but they were now typewritten and mimeographed so that penmanship would not influence the judges during the second stage of scale building. In stage two, sets of these eighty-three samples were given to about one hundred individuals with the following printed request: "Please arrange these in order of merit as specimens of English composition by young people. If there are two or more of them which seem to you to be absolutely equal in merit, give them the same number as a score. Score your results on the accompanying sheet calling the worst specimen 1, the next worst 2, the next worst 3, and so on."[137] Some of the readers, however, did not understand the directions, and thus only seventy-three of the readers' observations could be used. In stage three, a table was constructed to compare the position assigned each sample, but Hillegas discovered that there were great variations in the positions assigned to the samples. A final set of twenty-seven samples was finally derived by including samples on which there had been nearly universal agreement, by adding artificial samples, and by having judges place them on the scale. ("Dear Sir: I write to say that it ain't a square deal" is identified as an added artificial sample.) In stage four, more than one hundred of the sets consisting of twenty-seven samples were mailed to individuals whose positions as teachers, authors, and literary workers implied that they were competent judges of English writing. New directions accompanied each set: "Please arrange these samples in order of merit as specimens of English composition by young people. After determining your arrangement, pile all the specimens so that the best is in the bottom and the poorest on the top, and securely fasten them. Do not consult with anyone."[138] When seventy-five replies had been received, the results were tabulated in the same manner as they had been in stage three. Meanwhile, Thorndike himself secured the judgments of forty-one individuals who were especially competent to judge merit in English writing. These results were used as a check on the others.

The end result was a series of specimens arranged on a poster measuring twenty-three inches across and eighteen inches down that could, as Thorndike had said of his handwriting scale, be arranged "against a wall."[139] The existence of the poster, priced at eight cents, validated a claim that "the scale is accurate enough to be of very great practical value in measuring the merit of English compositions written in the upper grades of the elementary school and in the high school."[140] The scale was a manifestation of the love of systems, a passion that vastly overshadowed problems in its design. If more resources were added—in this case, more readers and samples—reader reliability issues would, no doubt, be solved in the future. Problems didn't matter if utility was present. A great future lay before these researchers, one in which most everything could be refined and perfected by methodically applied intelligence.

As the nineteenth century receded, the values of the new twentieth century were manifested in the scientific design of the scale as well as in the specimens. The artificial sample, Specimen 580, demonstrated that the writer was not only thoroughly illiterate ("it ain't a square deal") but, by means of the new association established by Spearman, completely lacking  in intelligence. Character defects were also manifested. The writer wants Jenny (his sister?) to get him out, evidence of effeminacy. He refers to the sacred world of commerce ("but I say he don't know his business") but has no idea of its meaning, nor of the valuable world of education in which he is to be prepared for a useful life. While literacy is an intrinsic good, its absence suggests both intellectual and moral flaws.

Conversely, the ideal republic is within sight, as the inclusion of Specimen 95 demonstrated in its command of language:

> If we finally ask what are the limitations of Aristotle, we find none save the limitations of the age and city in which he lived. He lived in a city-state where thirty thousand full male citizens, with some seventy thousand women and children dependent upon them, were supported by the labor of some hundred thousand slaves. The rights of man, whether native or alien, male or female, free or slave, had not yet been affirmed. That crowning proclamation of universal emancipation was reserved for Christianity three centuries and a half later. Without this Christian element no principle of personality is complete. Not until the city-state of Plato and Aristotle is widened to include the humblest man, the lowliest woman, the most defenseless little child, does their doctrine become final and universal. Yet with this single limitation of its range, the form of Aristotle's teaching is complete and ultimate. Deeper, saner, stronger, wiser statement of the principles of personality the world has never heard.[141]

A Methodist minister's son, Thorndike promoted the doctrine of improvement through systematic application, and so he had merged form and content in the specimens themselves as evidence of prudence. Trains and entrance examinations and vital forces aside, literacy, it seemed, was the very vehicle for America's salvation. While Greece had formulated the model of civilization under Aristotle's wise teaching, it would take America to incorporate it. All that had to be done was for the disciples to broaden the vision a bit to include the humblest man, the lowliest woman, and the most defenseless little child.

Endnotes

1 Henry David Thoreau, *Walden*, ed. J. Lyndon Shanley (1854; Princeton: Princeton UP, 2004) 102. In a statement that recalls Thoreau's emphasis on the universal quality of the written word, Adams Sherman Hill of Harvard wrote in 1879 that "the best talent in each school—it is not too much to say—cannot be better employed than in teaching the use of the great instrument of communication between man and man, between books and men, the possession without which learning is mere pedantry, and thought an aimless amusement." "An Answer to the Cry for More English," *Twenty Years of School and College English* (1879; Cambridge: Harvard University, 1896) 12. Hill, Briggs, and Hurlbut state in the Introduction to the volume that the article was first published in *Good Company* 4.3 (1879). For more on Thoreau's use of his journal, see Robert Sattelmeyer, "The Remaking of Walden," *Writing the American Classics*, eds. James Barbour and Tom Quirk (Chapel Hill: U of North Carolina P, 1990) 53–78.

2 Thoreau 116. For more on the American pastoral vision, see Leo Marx, *The Machine in the Garden: Technology and the Pastoral Ideal in America* (1970; New York: Oxford UP, 2000).

3 "Strange as it may seem to us, after hearing so much lofty declamation about the power of great speakers, whom nations listened to and obeyed," Channing had written, "it is nevertheless true, that the orator is the creature of the circumstances in which he is placed." *Lectures Read to the Seniors in Harvard College* (1856; Carbondale: Southern Illinois UP, 1968) 13-14. For Whately's approach to style—the triad of perspicuity, energy, and elegance—see Nan Johnson, *Nineteenth-Century Rhetoric in North America* (Carbondale: Southern Illinois UP, 1968) 59–60. See also Annette M. Woodlief, "The Influences of Theories of Rhetoric on Thoreau," *Thoreau Journal Quarterly* 7 (1975):13–22. *American Transcendentalism Web*, 16 Jan. 2005 <http://www.vcu.edu/engweb/transcendentalism/>. For more on Thoreau's education in Harvard's Department of Rhetoric and Oratory, see Robert Sattelmeyer, *Thoreau's Reading: A Study in Intellectual History with Bibliographic Catalogue* (Princeton: Princeton UP, 1988) 11–18.

4 James Berlin has analyzed the significance of Scottish Common Sense Realism—the philosophical orientation of Campbell, Blair, and Whately—in *Writing Instruction in Nineteenth-Century American Colleges* (Carbondale: Southern Illinois UP, 1984). Berlin writes: "The dominant philosophy in America in the first half of the nineteenth century was Scottish Common Sense Realism…The large number of Scottish immigrants in America had something to do with this preference. More important, this philosophy offered the Protestant clergymen who dominated American colleges during this time an antidote to the atheism and materialism of Hume and Voltaire, on the one hand, and a refuge from the philosophical perplexities of Berkeley and his German counterparts, on the other. It further offered a bland Christian doctrine that did not upset the delicate balance of competing religious sects. And while it served God, it also provided adequately for mammon. Its empiricism did not interfere with

a free economy which relied on scientific technology. Finally, the emphasis on common sense seemed to support the democratic glorification of the common person, endowed by God with faculties that gave him freedom and dignity. In other words, Common Sense Realism was safe, politically and religiously" (33). Campbell, Blair, and Whately could become "overwhelmingly dominant" in American colleges, Berlin found, because their ideas matched the social and intellectual climate (32). For more on these authors and their rhetorical philosophies, see Johnson, *Nineteenth-Century Rhetoric in North America.* Johnson identifies four assumptions of the rhetoric of Blair and Campbell: a link between affective intention and rhetorical techniques; an understanding that the study of rhetoric is to be considered as a scientific endeavor; an understanding that, as well, rhetoric is an art associated with taste; and that the faculty of taste can be enhanced to the benefit of "the intellectual and moral health of individuals and of society in general" (46).

5 Bacon had written in his *First Book of Aphorisms* (1620) this famous passage: "There are and can only be two ways of searching into and discovering truth. The one flies from the senses and particulars to the most general axioms, and from these principles, the truth of which it takes for settled and immovable, proceeds to judgment and the discovery of middle axioms. And this way is not in fashion. The other derives axioms from the senses and particulars, rising by a gradual and unbroken ascent, so that it arrives at the most general axioms last of all. This is the true way, but as yet untried." (Qtd. in Martin Hollis, *The Philosophy of Social Science: An Introduction* [Cambridge: Cambridge UP, 1994] 23.) Hollis reminds us of the traditions identified in Bacon's passage: "The one [deep dispute] which Bacon mentions is between those who start from 'the most general axioms', now known as rationalists, and those who start from 'the senses and particulars', now known as empiricists" (25). The traditions of rationalism and empiricism are manifested across researchers and historical periods in the assessment of writing.

6 Qtd. in Frederick Rudolph, *The American College and University: A History* (New York: Vintage, 1962) 265.

7 Rudolph 268.

8 Rudolph 270. See John C. French, *A History of the University Founded by Johns Hopkins* (Baltimore: Johns Hopkins UP, 1946).

9 See Daniel Coit Gilman, *The Benefits Which Society Derives from Universities: An Address* (Baltimore: Johns Hopkins UP, 1885) 15–16. The address was first delivered at a commemoration ceremony at Johns Hopkins on Feb. 23, 1885, then before the Literary Societies of Rutgers College, and at a convocation at the University of the State of New York at Albany. The text of the pamphlet, Gilman tells us, was the same as those delivered at the three addresses. Before coming to Hopkins, Gilman had become president of the University of California. In his Nov. 7, 1872, inaugural address, he also defined the purpose of higher education: "What is the University for? It is to fit young men for high and noble careers, satisfactory to themselves, and useful to mankind; it is to bring before the society of today, the failures and successes of societies in the past; it is to discover and make known how the forces of nature

may be subverted to mankind; it is to hand down to the generations which come after us, the torch of experience by which we have been enlightened" (*Inaugural Address* [San Francisco: John H. Carmany, 1872] 27)

10 See Sattelmeyer "The Remaking of Walden" 57.

11 A look at the history of the formation of engineering organizations yields a unique perspective on what Alan I. Marcus and Howard P. Segal have termed systematizing America (*Technology in America: A Brief History*, 2nd ed. [New York: Wadsworth, 1999]). The case of chemical engineering is especially revealing. In 1908, the discipline formed itself as the American Institute of Chemical Engineering. There remained, however, a lack of educational uniformity. The catalyst that gave the discipline both its foundation and its force came in 1915 in the form of Arthur D. Little's concept of "unit operations." Founder of an industrial consulting firm, Little wrote the following to the president of MIT:

> Any chemical process, on whatever scale conducted, may be resolved into a coordinate series of what may be termed "Unit Operations," as pulverizing, dyeing, roasting, crystallizing, filtering, evaporation, electrolyzing, and so on. The number of these basic unit operations is not large and relatively few of them are involved in any particular process. The complexity of chemical engineering results from the variety of conditions as to temperature, pressure, etc., under which the unit operation must be carried out in different processes, and from the limitations as to material of construction and design of apparatus imposed by the physical and chemical character of the reacting substances. (Qtd. in Terry S. Reynolds, *75 Years of Progress: A History of the American Institute of Chemical Engineers* [New York: AIChE, 1983] 10.)

This approach has had a significant impact on the nature of the chemical engineering profession, setting it apart from other engineering professions. In many ways, the concept of unit operations is the engineering equivalent of the writing scales that would be constructed by Thorndike and Hillegas. Richard Braddock would employ a metaphor from this field of the physical sciences in *Research in Written Composition* in 1963. See Chapter 5, note 59 and Chapter 7, note 12.

12 Joseph Mayer Rice, *Scientific Management in Education* (1914; New York: Arno P, 1969) 7. Chapter 10 presents the account of a study in which Rice designed a system in which he marked 8,300 papers. The papers were divided into five classes—excellent, good, fair, poor, and failure—and marked on that five-point scale. The judgment rendered by an individual examiner was "comparatively insignificant" because the class average, he claimed, would not vary sufficiently (183). See also Rice's earlier study, *The Public-School System in the United States* (1893; New York: Arno P, 1969). For more on Rice's place as a social efficiency educator, see Herbert M. Kliebard, *The Struggle for the American Curriculum, 1893–1958*, 2nd ed. (New York: Routledge, 1995) 17–21.

13 In *Henry James: A Life* (New York: Harper, 1985), Leon Edel provides part of the letter that Henry James, Sr., had written to Emerson (38).

14 James Morgan Hart, *German Universities: A Narrative of Personal Experience* (New York: G. P. Putnam's Sons, 1878) 249–250.

15 Hart, *German Universities* 264–265.

16 Hart, *German Universities* 341.

17 Hart, *German Universities* 255.

18 Herbert Weir Smyth, "The Classics: 1867–1929," *The Development of Harvard University Since the Inauguration of President Eliot, 1869–1929*, ed. Samuel Eliot Morison (Cambridge: Harvard UP, 1930) 37.

19 For more on Child at Harvard, see Charles H. Grandgent, "The Modern Languages, 1869–1929," *The Development of Harvard University*, ed. Morison 66–67, 73–75. For a contemporary interpretation of Child's career, see Patricia Harkin, "Child's Ballads: Narrating Histories of Composition and Literary Studies." *Disciplining English: Alternative Histories, Critical Perspectives*, eds. David R. Shumway and Craig Dionne (Albany: SUNY P, 2002) 19–37.

20 For more on this first experimental laboratory, see Edwin G. Boring, *A History of Experimental Psychology*, 2nd ed. (New York: Appleton, 1950) 323–328.

21 Just as Grandgent provided an invaluable guide to the modern languages at Harvard, Ralph Barton Perry provided an equally detailed guide to psychology. See "Psychology, 1876–1929," *The Development of Harvard University,* ed. Morison 216–230. Boring notes that Hall traveled twice to Germany, once to study philosophy and physiology before taking his doctorate (1868–1871) and a second time (1878–1880) after taking his doctorate with James in order to study with Wundt (518–519).

22 See Boring, *A History of Experimental Psychology* 505–583.

23 George Stuart Fullerton, and James McKeen Cattell, *On the Perception of Small Differences, with Special Reference to the Extent, Force, and Time of Movement* (Philadelphia: U of Pennsylvania P, 1892). In *A History of Experimental Psychology,* Boring noted that Cattell and Fullerton's 1892 monograph introduced a functional perspective to the idea of the limen, the smallest perceptible difference that could be measured. Fullerton and Cattell concentrated on the size of the average error instead of the just-noticeable difference. The key assumption in their functionalist perspective is that individuals attempt to achieve perfect discrimination. While orthodox psychophysics, Boring recalled, taught that observers could not make certain perceptions, Fullerton and Cattell maintained that small differences could indeed be identified, and the observational error could be measured by the method of right and wrong cases (534).

24 Fullerton and Cattell 9.

25 Charles William Eliot, "President Eliot's Inaugural Address," *The Development of Harvard University*, ed. Morison lvix.

26 For more on Spencer's influence on Eliot, see Lawrence A. Cremin, *The Transformation of the School: Progressivism in American Education, 1876–1957* (New York: Knopf, 1961) 92–94. See also Henry James (son of William James), *Charles W. Eliot: President of Harvard University, 1869–1909*, vol. 1 (London: Constable and Company, 1930). While Eliot did not totally agree with Spencer that "science should be the universal staple of education in childhood," James wrote, there was no doubt that Spencer helped Eliot "to clarify and formulate his ideas" (349–350).

27 Eliot, "President Eliot's Inaugural Address" lxiii.

28 *The Harvard University Catalogue, 1872–73* (Cambridge: Charles W. Sever, 1873) 53: "Members of the Freshman Class are examined, as early as possible after their admission, in reading aloud English prose. Prizes will be awarded for excellence. For 1873 students may prepare themselves in Goldsmith's *Vicar of Wakefield*."

29 *The Harvard University Catalogue, 1873–74* (Cambridge: Charles W. Sever, 1874). Examination questions from 1860 to 1877 were collected by R. F. Leighton, *Harvard Examination Papers*, 9th ed. (Boston: Ginn, 1883). Questions were included on all examination areas required for admission into Harvard: history and geography, modern and physical geography, Greek composition, Greek grammar, Greek prose, Greek poetry, Latin composition, Latin grammar, Latin, French, German, arithmetic, algebra, advanced algebra, plane geometry, analytic geometry, solid geometry, logarithms and trigonometry, physics, chemistry and physics, physics and astronomy, mechanics, ancient history and geography, English composition (beginning in June 1874), plane trigonometry, and botany. The June 1874 question in English composition was stated as follows: "A short English composition is required, correct in spelling, punctuation, grammar, and expression. Thirty lines will be sufficient. Make at least two paragraphs. SUBJECT:—The story of the Caskets, in the Merchant of Venice; Or, The story of Shakespeare's Tempest; Or, The Story of Rebecca, in Scott's Ivanhoe" (215). English entrance examinations from 1895 to 1899 were collected by Arthur Wentworth Eaton, *College Requirements in English Examinations* (Boston: Ginn, 1900). The Eaton collection included the June examination papers of Harvard, Yale, the Sheffield Scientific School, Princeton, and Columbia. In 1906 Wilson Farrand would protest the quantity of the requirements for admissions. See "Are College Entrance Requirements Too Great in Quantity?" *Educational Review* Jan. 1906 1–17. In *Tradition and Reform in the Teaching of English: A History* (Urbana: NCTE, 1974), Arthur N. Applebee wrote that the requirement in English "institutionalized the study of standard authors and set in motion a process which eventually forced English to consolidate its position within the schools" (30). The Harvard entrance examination contributed both to the systematization of English instruction and to the assessment of writing. See also Mary Trachsel, *Institutionalizing Literacy: The Historical Role of College Entrance Examinations in English* (Carbondale: Southern Illinois UP, 1992), especially her chapter on standardizing literacy 50–74. As well, see Linda Kay Mizell, "Major Shifts in Writing Assessment for College Admission, 1874-1964," diss., East Texas State U, 1994.

30 Grandgent, "The Modern Languages, 1869–1929" 76.

31 Qtd. in Morison, "College Studies, 1869–1929," *The Development of Harvard University*, ed. Morison xliii.

32 For more on the connection between Hill and Eliot, see *The Origins of Composition Studies in the American College, 1875–1925*, ed. John C. Brereton (Pittsburgh: U of Pittsburgh P, 1995) 45.

33 Grandgent, "The Modern Languages, 1869–1929" 67.

34 Grandgent, "The Modern Languages, 1869–1929" 67.

35 In the Harvard Catalogue of courses of instruction for 1873–1874, Assistant Professor Hill's course was listed under the section on philosophy. In the sophomore year, students were to read selections from George Campbell's *Philosophy of Rhetoric*, Richard Whately's *Elements of Rhetoric*, and Herbert Spencer's *Philosophy of Style*; in the junior year, there was more of Whately. Professor Child's courses, on the other hand, were listed under modern languages; he taught history and grammar of the English language, Anglo-Saxon and Early English; and English literature: Chaucer. The split between composition and literature, recorded by Peter Elbow in 2002 as involving "A vexed tangle of misunderstanding and hurt" was present from the beginning. See "Opinion: The Cultures of Literature and Composition: What Could Each Learn from the Other?" *College English* 64.5 (2002): 533–546.

36 Adams Sherman Hill, "An Answer to the Cry for More English" 7. The essay may conveniently be found in Brereton, *Origins* 45–57.

37 Hill, "An Answer" 9.

38 Hill, "An Answer" 10.

39 Hill, "An Answer" 11.

40 Hill, "An Answer" 11.

41 Le Baron Russell Briggs, "The Harvard Admission Examination in English," *Twenty Years of School and College English* (1888; Cambridge: Harvard University, 1896) 26–27.

42 Briggs, "The Harvard Admission Examination in English" 28.

43 Appendix, "History of the Requirement in English for Admission to Harvard College," *Twenty Years of School and College English* 56.

44 Le Baron Russell Briggs, "The Correction of Bad English, as a Requirement for Admission to Harvard College," *Twenty Years of School and College English* (1890; Cambridge: Harvard University, 1896) 34.

45 Briggs, "The Correction of Bad English" 38.

46 Adams Sherman Hill, *The Principles of Rhetoric and Their Application* (New York: Harper, 1878) 132.

47 Charles. T. Copeland and Henry Milner Rideout, *Freshman English and Theme-Correcting in Harvard College* (New York: Silver, 1901) 80.

48 Copeland and Rideout 7.

49 Copeland and Rideout 36. It was, Grandgent claimed in writing his history of modern languages at Harvard, these daily themes which drove Robert Frost out of Harvard. "Daily or weekly themes may be written by an army of pupils, and corrected and criticized by assistants of various degrees of competence," Grandgent wrote. "Yet this forced cultivation, however strenuous, does not, apparently, produce the growth desired" (70).

50 M. A. deWolfe Howe, ed., *Barrett Wendell and His Letters* (Boston: Atlantic Monthly P, 1924) 37. For more on Wendell, see Robert T. Self, *Barrett Wendell* (Boston: Twayne, 1975). See also Wallace Douglass, "Barrett Wendell," *Traditions*, ed. Brereton 3–25.

51 Barrett Wendell, *English Composition: Eight Lectures Given at the Lowell Institute* (New York: Scribner's 1891) 165.

52 Wendell, *English Composition* 74.

53 Wendell, *English Composition* 6–7.

54 Howe, *Barrett Wendell and His Letters* 109.

55 Wendell, *English Composition* 307.

56 Howe, *Barrett Wendell and His Letters* 110.

57 The first article was published on Feb. 1, 1894. Preceding the first article in the series by Albert S. Cook of Yale University, the editors introduced the series: "The article printed below is the first of a series to be devoted to the subject of English in the more important American colleges and universities. This series of papers will form a conspicuous feature of *The Dial: A Semi-Monthly Journal of Literary Criticism, Discussion, and Information* during 1894. An article, prepared by some member of the faculty concerned, will be devoted to each of a considerable number of institutions, and opportunity will thus be afforded for a comparison, that cannot fail to be instructive, of the methods pursued and the results aimed at. The article now offered by Professor Cook will be followed by articles from Professor Brander Matthews, of Columbia College; Professor Barrett Wendell, of Harvard University; Professor Melville B. Anderson, of the Leland Stanford, Junior, University; and many others that we shall have the pleasure of announcing at a later date." The articles were collected in *English in American Universities*, ed. William Morton Payne (Boston: Heath, 1895).

58 Howe, *Barrett Wendell and His Letters* 110.

59 "College and University English. A Summary," *The Dial* 1 Nov. 1894: 242. Payne is not listed as the author of the article, but in that much of the same text used in the summary in *The Dial* is used in the edited volume *English in American Universities*, it seems reasonable to attribute the summary to Payne.

60 Albert S. Cook, "English at Yale University," *The Dial* 1 Feb. 1894: 71.

61 Felix F. Schelling, "The University of Pennsylvania," *The Dial* 16 Sept. 1894: 146.

62 Barrett Wendell, "English at Harvard," *The Dial* 1 Mar. 1894: 133.

63 See Boring, *A History of Experimental Psychology* 323.

64 John F. Genung, "English at Amherst College," *The Dial* 1 Aug. 1894: 55.

65 Edward E. Hale, Jr., "English at the State University of Iowa," *The Dial* 1 June 1894: 328.

66 Martin W. Sampson, "The University of Indiana," *The Dial* 1 July 1894: 5.

67 George E. MacLean, "The University of Minnesota," *English in American Universities*, ed. William Morton Payne (Boston: Heath, 1895) 159. The article on English at Minnesota appears to have been added by Payne in his collection of 1895. The article is not part of the original collection of articles begun on Feb. 1, 1894, and concluded on Nov. 1, 1894.

68 Charles Mills Gayley "English at the University of California," *The Dial* 16 July 1894: 29.

69 For more on Scott, see Donald C. Stewart, "Fred Newton Scott," *Traditions*, ed. Brereton 26–49

70 Fred Newton Scott, "English at the University of Michigan," *The Dial* 16 Aug. 1894: 83.

71 "College and University English. A Summary," *The Dial* 1 Nov. 1894: 249.

72 Melville B. Anderson, "English at Stanford University," *The Dial* 16 Mar. 1894: 168.

73 Hiram Corson, "English Literature at Cornell University," *The Dial* 1 Apr. 1894: 201–202.

74 Albert H. Tolman, "English at the University of Chicago," *The Dial* 16 June 1894: 357.

75 "College and University English. A Summary," *The Dial* 1 Nov. 1894: 251.

76 Frederick Jackson Turner, "Crossing the Continent," *The Dial* 1 Feb. 1894: 80.

77 Frederick Jackson Turner, *History, Frontier, and Section: Three Essays* (Albuquerque: U of New Mexico P, 1993) 59.

78 The genesis of the frontier thesis is given in Ray Allen Billington, *Frederick Jackson Turner: Historian, Scholar, Teacher* (New York: Oxford UP, 1973) 108–131. The influence of Van Hise and the language of selection are noted on 114–115. In his important book, *In the Name of Eugenics: Genetics and the Uses of Human Heredity* (New York: Knopf, 1985), Daniel J. Kevles notes Charles Van Hise, along with Charles W. Eliot, as a leading progressive eugenicist (64). For a 1914 celebratory view of the history and popularity of eugenics, see A. E. Hamilton, "Eugenics," *Pedagogical Seminary* 21 (1914): 28–61.

79 Cook, "English at Yale University" 69.

80 Eliot, "President Eliot's Inaugural Address" lxiv.

81 Payne, "Introduction," *English in American Universities* 12–13. Charles F. Adams, E. L Godkin, and Josiah Quincy, *Report of the Committee on Composition and Rhetoric* (Cambridge: Harvard College Library, 26 Oct. 1892) 117–163, plus facsimiles. For an analysis of these reports and their impact, see Anne Ruggles Gere, "Empirical Research in Composition," *Perspectives on Research and Scholarship in Composition*, eds. Ben W. McClelland and Timothy R. Donovan (New York: MLA, 1985) 110–124.

82 National Education Association of the United States, *Report of the Committee of Ten on Secondary School Studies, with the Reports of the Conferences Arranged by the Committee* (New York: American Book Company, 1894).

83 Payne, "Introduction" 13.

84 Thomas D. Snyder, ed., *120 Years of American Education: A Statistical Portrait* (Washington: National Center for Educational Statistics, 1993). See especially the analysis on 64 and Tables 23, 24, and 27.

85 George Santayana, *Character and Opinion in the United States, with Reminiscences of William James and Josiah Royce and Academic Life in America* (New York: Scribner's, 1920) 140.

86 Snyder, *120 Years of American Education.* See especially the analysis on 25 and Tables 8 and 9.

87 Wilson Farrand, *The Reform of College Entrance Requirements. Inaugural Address* (Newark: Wm. A. Baker, Printer, 1895) 3. The year before, the authors of *The Report of the Committee of Ten on Secondary School Studies* had questioned "the wisdom of requiring, for admission to college, set essays" on lists of books. The Conference on English that prepared their set of recommendations—a group that included Harvard's George Lyman Kittredge—held that there were "serious theoretical and practical

objections to estimating a student's power to write a language on the basis of a theme composed not for the sake of expounding something that he knows or thinks, but merely for the sake of *showing his ability to write*" (94). The solution to written admission examinations? Questions should focus on "topics of literary, history or criticism, or on passages cited from prescribed works" in that these would bring out subject knowledge from the pupils and test the ability to "methodize knowledge" and to write "clearly and concisely" (94). Regarding corrections of poor English on admissions examinations, the members felt that such exercises should not constitute more than one-fifth of the examination. The members were also careful to articulate the relationship between the preparation for such examination and the examinations themselves. A course in elementary rhetoric could well serve such students by providing "unremitting practice," yet rhetoric was not to be studied for its own sake. "Its connection," the members warned, "with the pupil's actual written or spoken exercises should be kept constantly in view" (95).

88 Farrand, *Reform* 4.

89 Farrand, *Reform* 7.

90 Farrand, *Reform* 13.

91 Farrand, *Reform* 14.

92 Farrand, *Reform* 16.

93 Farrand, *Reform* 16.

94 The time line of the formation of the College Entrance Examination Board was scrupulously recorded in its *Plan of Organization of the College Entrance Examination Board for the Middle States and Maryland and a Statement of Subjects in Which Examinations Are Proposed* (New York: College Entrance Examination Board, Adopted May 12, 1900) 12–14. A narrative of the origin of the board is found in John A. Valentine's *The College Board and the School Curriculum: A History of the College Board's Influence on the Substance and Standards of American Education, 1900–1980* (New York: College Board, 1987) 3–16.

95 Eaton, *College Requirements in English Examinations* 3–4. Eaton provides the history through an excerpt taken from Eliot's Annual Report of 1886–1887.

96 *First Annual Report of the Secretary, 1901* (New York: College Entrance Examination Board, 1901) 1.

97 I have assembled the questions on the first examination from *Entrance English Questions Set by the College Entrance Examination Board, 1901–1923* (Boston: Ginn, 1924). The questions were compiled for the board by Winifred Quincy Norton.

98 *First Annual Report of the Secretary* 18.

99 *First Annual Report of the Secretary* 18.

100 *First Annual Report of the Secretary* 20.

101 *First Annual Report of the Secretary* 32.

102 Edward L. Thorndike, *Educational Psychology* (New York: Lemcke and Buechner, 1903) 164.

103 Edward L. Thorndike, "The Future of the College Entrance Examination Board," *Educational Review* 31 (1906): 474. Readers at the College Board took note of Thorndike's analysis. In the *Twenty-Second Annual Report* Clark S. Northup, a professor at Cornell University and a chief examiner in English, offered a written statement to the board in which he cited Thorndike's *Educational Review* article. The logic, Northup wrote, proved nothing. There are many influences on young men, and they are not the same in the junior year as they were in the freshman year. "They may have followed different paths; some may have joined fraternities, some may have gone in for athletics, some for study, etc." (5).

104 Qtd. in Geraldine Joncich, *The Sane Positivist: A Biography of Edward L. Thorndike* (Middletown: Wesleyan UP, 1968) 65. The traditions of rationalism and empiricism are evident here, as is the allusion to Bacon. See note 5 above.

105 "Edward Lee Thorndike," *A History of Psychology in Autobiography*, ed. Carl Murchison (1930; Worcester: Clark UP, 1961) 263.

106 Joncich, *The Sane Positivist* 78. His statement is taken from Thorndike's application for financial aid to Harvard.

107 Joncich, *The Sane Positivist* 86.

108 Murchison, ed., "Edward Lee Thorndike" 264.

109 For more on the influence of Bain on Thorndike, see Joncich, *The Sane Positivist* 338.

110 Murchison, ed., "Edward Lee Thorndike" 268.

111 The informal psychological laboratory at Harvard, Boring documented in *A History of Experimental Psychology*, was established first, but its aim was to enable graduate students to repeat experiments for themselves (509). Wundt's laboratory at Leipzig in 1879 was the first formal psychological laboratory (323–324).

112 Karl Pearson, *The Life, Letters and Labors of Francis Galton: Researches of Middle Life*, vol. 2 (Cambridge: Cambridge UP, 1924) 213.

113 Among the histories of standard error and correlation, see the following: Stephen J. Gould, *The Mismeasure of Man* (New York: Norton, 1981) 75–77 and 256–272; Stephen M. Stigler, *The History of Statistics: The Measurement of Uncertainty Before 1900* (Cambridge: Harvard UP, 1986) 140–143, 265–299, and 326–338 ; Kevles, *In the Name of Eugenics* 3–40; and Theodore M. Porter, *The Rise of Statistical Thinking,*

1820–1900 (Princeton: Princeton UP, 1986) 128–146. Invaluable for its proximity to the original studies and their relation to education is Helen M. Walker, *Studies in the History of Statistical Method, with Special Reference to Certain Educational Problems* (Baltimore: Williams and Wilkins, 1929).

114 Francis Galton, "Eugenics: Its Definition, Scope, and Aims," *American Journal of Sociology* 10.1 (1904) 1.

115 Charles Spearman, "The Proof and Measurement of Association Between Two Things," *American Journal of Psychology* 15 (1904): 73.

116 Charles Spearman, "'General Intelligence,' Objectively Determined and Measured," *American Journal of Psychology* 15 (1904) 276.

117 Spearman, "'General Intelligence,'" 255.

118 Spearman, "'General Intelligence,'" 277.

119 Thorndike, *Educational Psychology* 172. In Chapter 2, Thorndike cites Pearson's formula for correlation (26).

120 Edward L. Thorndike, "An Empirical Study of College Entrance Examinations," *Science*, 1 June 1906: 840–841. JSTOR 23 Jan. 2005 <http://www.jstor.org/search>.

121 Thorndike, "An Empirical Study" 843.

122 Thorndike, "An Empirical Study" 845.

123 Thorndike, "The Future" 475.

124 Thorndike, "The Future" 474.

125 Thorndike, "The Future" 475.

126 Thorndike, "The Future" 476.

127 Thorndike, *Educational Psychology* 16.

128 Thorndike, *Educational Psychology* 20.

129 Thorndike, *Educational Psychology* 22.

130 Thorndike, "Scale for Merit in English Writing by Young People," *Journal of Educational Psychology* 2 (1911): 367–368.

131 Thorndike, "Scale" 364.

132 Joncich 286.

133 Joncich observes that Thorndike was quite eager to advance training at Teachers College for "practical school men." She writes, "The principal reason why Thorndike pushed so eagerly, vigorously, and successfully for educational-measurement training at Teachers College," Joncich proposes, "was the favorable response from those first few students of his who were already school administrators" (296–297). The numbers for professional placement are provided by Joncich.

134 Milo B. Hillegas, "Scale for the Measurement of Quality in English Composition by Young People," *Teachers College Record* 13.4 (1912): 1–55. By 1917 four impressions had been issued. A reprint was published by Teachers College Press in 1919.

135 Edward L. Thorndike, "Handwriting," *Teachers College Record* 11.2 (1910); by 1917 there would be four impressions of the reprint study of handwriting published by Teachers College.

136 Hillegas cites the Fullerton and Cattell monograph in note 11 of the *Teachers College Record* study. The scale, he acknowledged, was derived from the method of right and wrong cases: "The theory of this method as applied to this study may be stated as follows: Differences that are equally often noticed are equal, unless the differences are either always or never noticed" (14).

137 Hillegas, "Scale" 22.

138 Hillegas, "Scale" 36.

139 Qtd. in Hillegas, "Scale" 10. It does seem that the idea of a poster came after the 1910 handwriting article. At first, it appears that Thorndike intended the scales to be distributed by having the individual samples printed on individual sheets.

140 Hillegas, "Scale" 50.

141 The sample appears in the chart—*The Preliminary Extension of the Hillegas Scale for the Measurement of Quality in English Composition by Young People* (New York: Teachers College, n.d.).

Chapter 2
Promiscuous Intermingling, 1917–1937

"This is not a day of triumph; it is a day of dedication," Woodrow Wilson, the former president of Princeton, had said in his first inaugural address as president of the United States on March 4, 1913. "Here muster, not the forces of party, but the forces of humanity. Men's hearts wait upon us; men's lives hang in the balance; men's hopes call upon us to say what we will do. Who shall live up to the great trust? Who dares fail to try? I summon all honest men, all patriotic, all forward-looking men, to my side."[1] On April 2, 1917, Wilson asked Congress to demonstrate that dedication by declaring war against Germany:

> It is a fearful thing to lead this great peaceful people into war, into the most terrible and disastrous of all wars, civilization itself seeming to be in the balance. But the right is more precious than peace, and we shall fight for the things which we have always carried nearest our hearts,—for democracy, for the right of those who submit to authority to have a voice in their own governments, for the rights and liberties of small nations, for a universal dominion of right by such a concert of free peoples as shall bring peace and safety to all nations and make the world itself at last free. To such a task we can dedicate our lives and our fortunes, everything that we are and everything that we have, with the pride of those who know that the day has come when America is privileged to spend her blood and her might for the principles that gave her birth and happiness and the peace which she has treasured. God helping her, she can do no other.[2]

A student of government and history who had served on the Conference for History, Civil Government, and Political Economy as part of the *Report of the Committee of Ten*, Wilson (Ph.D., Johns Hopkins, 1886) easily established the rhetoric for war.[3] The recruitment effort of the U.S. armed forces was not, however, so easily established. War, Wilson told Congress, "will involve the immediate addition to the armed forces of the United States already provided for by law in case of war at least five hundred thousand men who should, in my opinion, be chosen upon the principle of universal liability to service, and also the authorization of subsequent additional increments of equal force so soon as they may be needed and can be handled in training."[4] The regular army included 123,000 soldiers, and to that number 180,000 members of the National Guard were added. Led by army Chief of Staff Peyton C. Marsh and Secretary of War Newton D. Baker, the War Department followed Wilson's call and initiated the Selective Service Act in 1917. Under the act, all males between the ages of twenty-one and thirty were required to register for military service; in 1918, the age requirements for registration were expanded to males eighteen to forty-five. By November 1918, 24 million American men had registered, and 3 million of these were drafted. With the addition of volunteers and National Guardsmen, 4.3 million were now enlisted in the armed forces.[5]

The Selective Service Act provided the ideal opportunity for the largest formal psychological experiment in history. To identify America's emerging character—progressive in its idealism, systematic in its orientation, scientific in its proof, literate in its communication—and test its ability as a global power, America's leaders turned to their new belief, expressed so well by Thorndike: whatever exists does so in quantity and, thus, can be measured.[6] The recruits became subjects to be tested; after the Armistice was signed on November 11, 1918, the examiners claimed they had helped win the war. In placing men of equal liability into armed service so that they would be appropriately trained, the experimenters achieved far more than bragging rights: they had advanced the significance of mental measurement in the service of a nation forming definitions of national character. And in the process they would, as had Charles Spearman, again inextricably link literacy to intelligence.

Here and Over There

To manage placement of these recruits—between September, 1917, and March, 1918, over 600,000 men were drafted and sent to training camps across the nation[7]—the War Department turned to the American Psychological Association and its leader, Robert M. Yerkes. Educated at Harvard, Yerkes was a student of experimental psychologist Hugo Münsterberg, the author of *American Traits from the Point of View of a German*, who had taken over the psychological laboratory from William

James.[8] With many other social theorists of the period, Yerkes came to believe, as he wrote in 1915, that the "development of a serviceable method of measuring mental ability for use in hospitals, clinics, schools, reformatories, prisons, and wherever a rough estimate of mental status is demanded" was much needed.[9]

By the advent of World War I, the concept of mental tests had just become familiar in American culture. Lewis M. Terman of Stanford University had developed the Intelligence Quotient. Revising tests devised by Alfred Binet in France, Terman set the stage that would make the term "IQ" part of the texture of American life.[10] Yerkes was eager to advance mental tests. In 1917, he had been made president of the American Psychological Association and had gained access to the military through his chairmanship of the National Research Council, created in 1916 to mobilize America's scientific resources for defense.[11] The surgeon general of the army, William C. Gorgas, became interested in the potential of mental testing. In 1904, Gorgas had taken part in the Panama Canal Commission program against yellow fever as a sanitary officer and was aware of the potential of scientifically based measures to improve society. Gorgas had found skeptics in the army who had refused to use known scientific techniques to combat malaria and, hence, was sympathetic to the obstacles faced by Yerkes.[12]

On August 17, 1917, Yerkes became a major in the Sanitary Corps and began to develop an intelligence examination with sixteen psychologists who were commissioned as first lieutenants and twenty-four others who were given civil appointments.[13]

The test the psychologists were to design had to be able to measure the mental abilities of an enormous number of recruits. Yerkes and his colleagues developed two examinations: one for literates and one for illiterates. These examinations were then field tested on four thousand soldiers, and the results were analyzed at Columbia University. From the results of the field test, Yerkes found the test for literate subjects (Army Alpha) to be a sound assessment of intelligence and proposed the use of these tests to Surgeon General Gorgas. Gorgas established a psychological division in his office and recommended that Yerkes be promoted to major and put in charge of the effort. The tests were then to be further assessed after they had been given to over eighty thousand recruits. The results were found to be promising, and on December 5, 1917, the program of psychological testing was approved. In the *New York Times* of January 21, 1918, Yerkes stated that "psychology has achieved a position which will enable it to substantially help to win the war and shorten the necessary period of conflict."[14]

The First Company of Commissioned Psychologists. Major Yerkes is shown in the corner. In 1930, Yerkes recalled the following of his military service: "Often it seemed that my foremost duty and obligation—one for which I usually felt myself peculiarly unsuited—was to vanquish seemingly insuperable difficulties by overcoming the passive resistance of ignorance and the active opposition of jealousy, misinformation, and honest disagreement." (Carl Murchison, ed., *A History of Psychology in Autobiography*, vol. 2 [Worcester: Clark UP, 1930] 398.) (From Robert M. Yerkes, ed., *Psychological Examining in the United States Army* [Washington: GPO, 1921] facing 32. Reprinted with permission from the National Academy of Sciences, Courtesy of the National Academies Press, Washington, DC.)

Yerkes and his staff designed an alpha test (*a*) with eight sections: oral directions, arithmetical problems, practical judgment, synonym-antonym, disarranged sentences, number series completion, analogies, and information.[15] The beta tests (*b*) were composed of seven sections: maze, cube analysis, X-O series, digit-symbols, number checking, picture completion, and geometrical construction.[16] By May of 1918, twenty-four army camps were ready to send every draftee through the testing program. Examiners, trained at Fort Oglethorpe, Georgia, had been sent in advance to various camps to ensure unity in the test administration process.[17] The testing process was transformed into a large-scale effort. According to Yerkes, the approximate number of examinations prior to April 28, 1918, totaled 139,843. From April 28, 1918, to January 31, 1919, the number of examinations totaled 1,588,904.[18]

Yet the question of literacy haunted the testing process: how could mental capacity be evaluated if those taking the test could not read?[19] Yerkes and his colleagues had determined in the unofficial trail of examination alpha (*a*) that "a large proportion" of soldiers could not be given the group psychological examination because of their inability to read English.[20] In

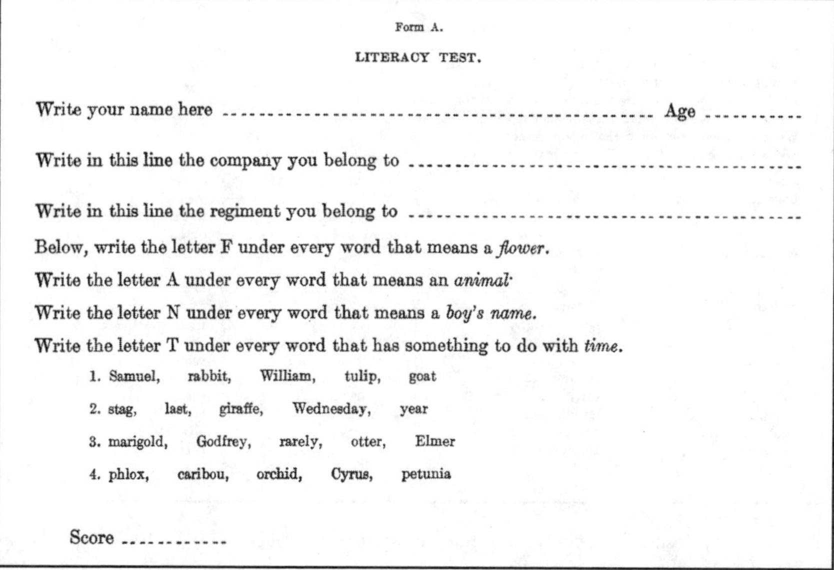

Form A.

LITERACY TEST.

Write your name here .... Age ....

Write in this line the company you belong to ....

Write in this line the regiment you belong to ....

Below, write the letter F under every word that means a *flower*.

Write the letter A under every word that means an *animal*.

Write the letter N under every word that means a *boy's name*.

Write the letter T under every word that has something to do with *time*.

1. Samuel, rabbit, William, tulip, goat
2. stag, last, giraffe, Wednesday, year
3. marigold, Godfrey, rarely, otter, Elmer
4. phlox, caribou, orchid, Cyrus, petunia

Score ....

Modification of Thorndike Reading Scale, Form A. This test was given to all men at the time they were assembled for group intelligence examinations. Those who had filled in the blanks and had made few or no errors in line 3 (regiment) remained for the group intelligence examination *a*. Those who could not write or who had made many errors in lines 1 (name) and 2 (company) were sent at once to the group skill tests, examinations devised for those who failed to pass the literacy test and who failed to make a satisfactory score in group examination *b*. (From Robert M. Yerkes, ed., *Psychological Examining in the United States Army* [Washington: GPO, 1921] 279. Reprinted with permission from the National Academy of Sciences, Courtesy of the National Academies Press, Washington, DC.)

order to segregate the literate from the illiterate, several solutions were attempted.

Lewis M. Terman of Stanford University (now Major Terman) prepared a modification of Thorndike's Reading Scale.[21] If the candidate correctly completed numbered line 4, the examiners assumed high-school literacy. For correct completion of line 3, the candidate was assumed to possess eighth-grade literacy. For line 2, the candidate was assumed to possess sixth-grade literacy. If line 1 and part of line 2 were correct, the candidate possessed fourth-grade literacy, but if only line 1 was completed, the examiners designated the candidate as literate at only the second grade level.

Another solution was the use of a second modification of Thorndike's literacy test designed by his pupil, T. L. Kelley. While a score of 47 or better on columns 2–4 constituted a pass, the Kelley literacy test set too high a standard and was discarded after preliminary trials. At Camp Devens in Ayer, Massachusetts, a test of literacy was developed and tested for its

KELLEY LITERACY TEST.

Name...Age...........................

What company do you belong to..

What regiment do you belong to..

In the columns below write a F after every word that means a *flower*.

Write a W after every word that means something about *war* or *fighting*.

Write a G after every word that means something *good to be* or *do*.

Write a T after every word like *now* or *then* that means something to do with *time*.

army..............( )	tulip..............( )	late..............( )	colonel..........( )
brave..............( )	violet..............( )	while..............( )	year..............( )
when..............( )	commander........( )	before..............( )	fortress..........( )
bullet..............( )	clean..............( )	guard..............( )	defend............( )
navy..............( )	fort..............( )	morning...........( )	carnation.........( )
at once............( )	buttercup..........( )	captive............( )	worthy............( )
black..............( )	gun..............( )	lilac..............( )	first..............( )
honest.............( )	clover..............( )	whenever..........( )	cavalry............( )
lily..............( )	hour..............( )	fair..............( )	wednesday........( )
camp..............( )	truthful............( )	evening...........( )	heroic.............( )
kind..............( )	captain............( )	worthy............( )	tuesday...........( )
flag..............( )	primrose...........( )	afterward..........( )	never..............( )
daisy..............( )	early..............( )	military...........( )	useful.............( )
early..............( )	minute.............( )	soon..............( )	conquer...........( )
fight..............( )	defeat..............( )	meantime..........( )	aster..............( )
general............( )	afternoon..........( )	last..............( )	battery............( )
troops.............( )	noble..............( )	generous...........( )	instant............( )

Kelley Literacy Test. Examiners were directed to use the first eight words in the first column as practice. The examiners were to pass around the room, giving individual help on these words. In this process, the examiners would discover who was "evidently illiterate." Those papers were to be marked with an "I" and the recruits sent to the group skills test. (From Robert M. Yerkes, ed., *Psychological Examining in the United States Army* [Washington: GPO, 1921] 280–281. Reprinted with permission from the National Academy of Sciences, Courtesy of the National Academies Press, Washington, DC.)

correlation power by E. A. Shaw of Tufts College, who arranged for the test to be given to students in grade and high school in Somerville, Massachusetts. Trials for the Devens Literacy Test were conducted in Trenton, New Jersey, and the scoring norms were derived from 947 children in the Medford, Massachusetts, school and 90 students at Cornell University. After it was found to correlate with the school grades of the recruits, the Devens literacy test was understood to test literacy as defined by the ability to read printed sentences.

At New Jersey's Camp Dix, as well as at several other camps, other less formal methods were used. It had been concluded by the examiners, for example, that basic segregation could be achieved by giving the subjects blank pieces of paper and having them write the dictated sentence: "We are in the army." Thirty seconds were allowed for an individual to write his name, and forty-five seconds were allowed for writing the sentence. "Orderlies then inspected the slips scoring the individual 'literate' or 'illiterate.'"[22] Those who wrote the sentence legibly with correct or phonetic spelling were held for the alpha examination. At Camp Lee in Petersburg, Virginia, the segregation procedure followed these lines: when all the men

282 MEMOIRS NATIONAL ACADEMY OF SCIENCES. [VOL. XV,

Form 1.]

Name.. Grade..

DEVENS LITERACY TEST.

Draw a line under *right* answer.

Do dogs bark?............ No. Yes.
Is coal white?............ No. Yes.

Can you see?............ No. Yes.
Do men eat stones?............ No. Yes.
Do boys like to play?............ No. Yes.
Can a bed run?............ No. Yes.
Do books have hands?............ No. Yes.
Is ice hot?............ No. Yes.
Do winds blow?............ No. Yes.

Have all girls the same name?............ No. Yes.
Is warm clothing good for winter?............ No. Yes.
Is this page of paper white?............ No. Yes.
Are railroad tickets free?............ No. Yes.
Is every young woman a teacher?............ No. Yes.
Is it always perfect weather?............ No. Yes.
Is the heart within the body?............ No. Yes.

Do clerks enjoy a vacation?............ No. Yes.
Is the President a public official?............ No. Yes.
Would you enjoy losing a fortune?............ No. Yes.
Does an auto sometimes need repair?............ No. Yes.
Is it important to remember commands?............ No. Yes.
Are avenues usually paved with oxygen?............ No. Yes.
Do we desire serious trouble?............ No. Yes.

Is practical judgment valuable?............ No. Yes.
Ought a man's career to be ruined by accidents?............ No. Yes.
Do you cordially recommend forgery?............ No. Yes.
Does an emergency require immediate decision?............ No. Yes.
Should honesty bring misfortune to its possessor?............ No. Yes.
Are gradual improvements worth while?............ No. Yes.
Is a punctual person continually tardy?............ No. Yes.

Are instantaneous effects invariably rapid?............ No. Yes.
Should preliminary disappointment discourage you?............ No. Yes.
Is hearsay testimony trustworthy evidence?............ No. Yes.
Is wisdom characteristic of the best authorities?............ No. Yes.
Is extremely athletic exercise surely necessary?............ No. Yes.
Is incessant discussion usually boresome?............ No. Yes.
Are algebraic symbols ever found in manuals?............ No. Yes.

Are tentative regulations ever advantageous?............ No. Yes.
Are "diminutive" and "Lilliputian" nearly identical?............ No. Yes.
Is an infinitesimal titanic bulk possible?............ No. Yes.
Do all connubial unions eventuate felicitously?............ No. Yes.
Is a "gelatinous exaltation" ridiculous?............ No. Yes.
Are "sedate" and "hilarious" similar in meaning?............ No. Yes.
Is avarice sometimes exhibited by cameos?............ No. Yes.

R..............................
W..............................
Score..............................

Devens Literacy Test, Form 1. A score below 6 indicated illiteracy. Scores from 6 to 20 were to be associated with primary literacy. Scores from 21 to 25 were to be associated with a level of literacy appropriate to grammar school. Scores from 26 to 30 were to be associated with junior high school, and from 31 to 35 with senior high school. Scores ranging from 36 to 42 were at a college level of literacy. (From Robert M. Yerkes, ed., *Psychological Examining in the United States Army* [Washington: GPO, 1921] 281–282. Reprinted with permission from the National Academy of Sciences, Courtesy of the National Academies Press, Washington, DC.)

"In the case of white recruits a high correlation has been found to exist between psychological rating and military value. The report from Camp Upton [in Yaphank, Long Island] indicates that the same is true in the case of negroes, and that just as they are inferior to the whites in intelligence, so also are they inferior in their value to the military service.... The question of the military value of the negro fighter when he gets actually into action may well be quite a separate one and it is at all events one which our present data do not enable us to discuss" (742). (From Robert M. Yerkes, ed., *Psychological Examining in the United States Army* [Washington: GPO, 1921] following 90. Reprinted with permission from the National Academy of Sciences, Courtesy of the National Academies Press, Washington, DC.)

were seated, the examiner said: "All those who do not read and write put down their books and come to the front of the room."[23]

Special attention was paid to the literacy of the "negro draft." As Yerkes writes, several different methods of segregation were used to divide the black men into literate and illiterate groups to be sent to alpha and beta respectively. In some cases all who could not read and write were told to step out. Usually a standard of proficiency was indicated, such as the ability to read a newspaper and write a letter home. In some cases an educational qualification was added—three, four, or even five years of schooling. In some cases the men were all sent in a body directly to examination beta.[24]

Ultimately, the modified Thorndike Reading Scale, the Kelley Literacy Test, and the Devens Literacy Test were all found to be wanting. The description of the shortcomings, both administrative and conceptual, of the Devens test applied to all three measurements:

> The necessity for speed and prompt and expeditious handling of groups was the first difficulty encountered that led to the shortening of the preliminary questioning.

Extra blanks were needed to give this [the Devens] test, and these had to be collected and scored; in the meantime the men would become restless, and green examiners feared losing control of their groups. No satisfactory scoring or inspection procedure was developed that hastened the manipulation of this test. In the second place, as the test was arranged, it proved difficult to standardize and gave results that seemed ambiguous. The standards set were too high. The test failed to "get over," frequently even in the case of men who made average scores or better on examination *a*. On the other hand several reports on the use of the literacy test indicated that it apparently operated as a rough intelligence test, thereby tending to remove men of low intelligence whatever their degree of literacy. It did not perform satisfactorily either of the operations intended.[25]

Significantly, it could only be concluded that the literacy testing was deeply flawed.

As Yerkes and his colleagues admitted, information on illiteracy in the drafted army was obtained only incidentally. The percentages of men taking the beta examination were available, but unfortunately the method of classification for beta in different camps and at different times differed greatly. Without a standard definition of literacy, statistics of illiteracy were meaningless. "The degree of adequacy with which the intended separation was made depended on chance conditions, such as the skill of a sergeant who separated the men, the presence of an interpreter, the time available for segregation, or even, perhaps, the immediate availability of space in the

TABLE 41.—*Basis of segregation, 1918.*

Station.	Literacy basis.	Number examined.	Number sent to beta.	Per cent beta.	Per cent Negro.
Bowie	Read and write,[1] finished fourth grade	27,464	5,497	20.0	10.7
Cody	Fourth grade	43,482	5,003	18.8	....
Custer	Read and write, Negroes, 5 years at school	54,354	10,004	18.4	9.9
Devens		50,031	11,370	22.7	1.7
Dix	Read and write	67,768	19,768	29.2	19.8
Dodge	Read easily, sixth grade	69,927	22,701	32.5	25.4
Funston	Read and write, finished fourth grade	75,678	21,967	29.0	25.5
Gordon	Read and write	63,648	16,119	25.3	10.8
Grant	Read and write rapidly, or seventh grade	83,229	24,218	29.1	18.8
Greene	Read and write, four years at school	27,807	10,512	37.8	38.6
Greenleaf	Read and write, fourth grade, and 5 years in United States	56,097	9,992	17.8	.8
Hancock	Read and write fairly, and reached sixth grade	44,433	12,714	28.6	5.1
Humphreys		13,981	1,957	14.0	....
Jackson	Read and write	98,996	19,587	19.8	17.5
Kearny	Read, write, and speak English, and over fifth grade	18,921	2,931	15.5	.005
Lee		82,441	23,104	28.0	8.8
Lewis	Read and write	75,519	10,209	13.5	2.2
Logan	....do	19,984	3,679	18.4	.3
Meade	Reached fifth grade	65,700	21,069	32.1	20.8
Pike	Read and write	75,942	21,891	28.8	16.1
Sevier	4 years at school (later 6 years at school)	24,139	6,567	27.2	18.7
Sheridan	Read and write (later 6 years at school)	55,165	11,985	21.7	10.0
Sherman	Sixth grade, Negroes, finished sixth grade	64,408	26,938	41.8	30.4
Taylor	Read and write, Negroes, finished sixth grade	53,336	10,672	20.0	16.9
Travis	Read and write	77,555	17,403	22.4	22.0
Upton	Read newspapers	61,559	14,486	23.5	15.4
Wadsworth	Northern recruits, third grade, southern recruits, fourth grade	67,704	13,442	19.9	6.0
Wheeler	Read and write, reached sixth grade (later seventh grade)	32,988	10,411	31.6	10.9
Total		1,552,256	386,196	24.9	14.2

[1] "Read and write" means "ability to read and understand newspapers and write letters home."

"From the standpoint of a comparison of groups in different camps this lack of a uniform process of segregation is certainly unfortunate." (From Robert M. Yerkes, ed., *Psychological Examining in the United States Army* [Washington: GPO, 1921] 354. Reprinted with permission from the National Academy of Sciences, Courtesy of the National Academies Press, Washington, DC.)

beta examination room. Camp conditions were rough and examining procedure was constantly being adapted to meet the ever-present emergency."[26]

These reservations notwithstanding, Yerkes and his colleagues nevertheless concluded that "measures, though rough and varied, do indicate conditions of serious public concern." The concern was identified in two groups: "negroes" and foreign-born soldiers. The extent of illiteracy of a group was dependent, Yerkes claimed, upon the proportion of black men in the group. From April 27, 1918, to the closing of the examinations on January 31, 1919, 1,552,256 men were examined. Nearly 30 percent—386,196—were sent to the beta test. Of this 30 percent, more than half were black men. Black recruits from the South were especially noted for high rates of illiteracy: "The records of all South Carolina men in one company were analyzed, with the result that of the 177 men in the company 109, or 61.6 percent, were illiterate."[27] "In view of the importance of Americanization," Yerkes provided evidence that immigrants from England, Scotland, and Ireland were usually literate. Immigrants from Italy, Poland, and Greece were illiterate.[28]

In summarizing the achievements of the psychological services, Yerkes and his team of psychologists focused on those found to be of low intelligence:

> Between April 28, 1918, and January 31, 1919, 7,800 men (0.5 per cent) were reported with recommendations for discharge by psychological examiners because of mental inferiority. The recommendations for assignment to labor battalions because of low grade intelligence number 10,012 (0.6 per cent). For assignment to development battalions, in order that they might be more carefully observed and given preliminary training to discover, if possible, ways of using them in the Army, 9,487 men (0.6 per cent) were recommended.
>
> During this same interval there were reported 4,780 men with mental age below 7 years; 7,875 between 7 and 8 years; 14,814 between 8 and 9 years; 18,878 between 9 and 10 years. This gives a total of 46,347 men under 10 years' mental age. It is extremely improbable that many of those individuals were worth what it cost the Government to maintain, equip, and train them for military service.[29]

The process of large-scale assessment dramatically shifted the testing movement in the United States. Prior to January 31, 1919, a total of 1,723,966 recruits—one third of all who had been drafted—had been examined by Yerkes and his colleagues.[30] "As could never otherwise have happened, military opportunities, demands, and achievements gave American psychology forward and directed impetus," Yerkes recalled.[31] After the war the Rockefeller Foundation's General Education Board allocated $25,000 to the National Research Council for the development of group examination in the schools, and both industry and the private sector became interested in the use of tests for placement purposes.[32] The quantification of intelligence, its existence established by the presence or absence of literacy, had now become more than a preoccupation of a few university researchers in Great Britain and America. As the College Board's new secretary, Thomas Scott Fiske, a professor of mathematics at Columbia University and founder of the American Mathematical Society, wrote just six months after the Armistice in reference to the Board's role in American post-secondary education:

> It should be the purpose of the College Entrance Examination Board not only to ascertain whether the candidates have acquired the information and methods of thought necessary for successful work in college, but also to determine whether they possess certain important intellectual qualities which are sometimes described as alertness, strength, and endurance, although these terms would seem to indicate excellences of the body rather than the mind. The Board's endeavors in this direction are exhibited most conspicuously in the comprehensive examinations. If these examinations continue to respond to the demands of the times they should eventually become the best possible tests combining the necessary elements of an informational and of a mental, or psychological, character.[33]

The Board's examinations, so very dependent on presence of literacy, could now be used to document the presence of intelligence in the 12,716 students examined in 1919.[34] The process of testing, the vehicle for the quantification of intelligence, was rapidly becoming part of the fabric of American life.

Yerkes and Brigham: Large-Scale Testing

While the process of psychological examination in the army established the place of large-scale testing in America, it was Carl Campbell Brigham who brought forward the test results compiled by Yerkes and his colleagues to a wider American audience in *A Study of American Intelligence*.

Brigham was among the army officers who field-tested the new psychological tests under Yerkes. Taking each of his three degrees in psychology from Princeton University, Brigham used Princeton and Trenton school children in order to investigate the validity of Alfred Binet's tests for his dissertation, a study of intelligence evaluation. Brigham defended his dissertation in May 1916 and the following year became involved with preparing the nation for war.

Brigham met Yerkes during that year. The young Princeton graduate had enlisted in the Canadian Military Hospitals Commission in March and

Carl Campbell Brigham, 1890–1943. "A movement launched by Francis Galton has eventually grown to encompass every description of man by man" (*The Reading of the Comprehensive Examination in English: An Analysis of the Procedures Followed During the Five Reading Periods from 1929–1933* [Princeton: Princeton UP, 1934] i). (Reprinted by Permission of Educational Testing Service. All Rights Reserved.)

had come to know Yerkes, who was then in Canada gathering information about the selection of military personnel. Yerkes was impressed by Brigham. After getting the information he needed, Yerkes returned to the United States, and Brigham stayed in Canada for four more months, returning in July 1917, to enlist in the Field Artillery.[35] When Yerkes became the "responsible head of psychological work" for the army[36] and requested sixteen psychologists for appointments as first lieutenants in the Sanitary Corps, Brigham was among them. He was commissioned in September 1917 and stationed at Camp Dix.[37]

The psychological staff had reported for duty to Camp Dix in late September, but the work did not begin smoothly; indeed, the work of examination of the entire camp did not begin until November. The commanding general apparently delayed the examinations, at least in part because the hospital wards in which the examinations were to be conducted were not completed. So, during November, the psychological staff "busied itself with individual examining, with efforts to perfect methods, and with intensive study of a single regiment—the Three hundred and third Engineers. Nine days were devoted to this organization alone, and, as a result, exceptionally detailed and valuable reports were made to the Surgeon General."[38] By December, arrangements were made to expand the examinations to include 1,115 officers and 5,462 enlisted men of the 19,000 soldiers stationed at the camp. Between December 10 and December 22, the number of examinations grew—"rushed" in Yerkes' terms—to 1,500 examinations per day.[39] By January 1, approximately 14,000 men had been examined.

In April 1918, Brigham left the psychological staff at his own request to serve with the Tank Corps at Camp Colt, Pennsylvania.[40] When it was found that Brigham was a psychologist, however, he was given yet another desk job and spent the remainder of the war selecting other men for overseas duty.[41] After the war, Brigham joined the Federal Board for Vocational Education in Washington. With his previous experience in the Canadian Military Hospitals Commission and his work processing men during the war, Brigham was appointed assistant to the Director of the Rehabilitation Division.[42] Under this federal system, veterans applied for occupational training to district boards that would judge the eligibility of the candidates and refer the cases to Brigham's board in Washington for final approval. Harold V. Stirling, who was to become head of the Vocational Rehabilitation and Education Division, later noted that suggestions made to him by Brigham regarding vocational advisement helped him to fashion an assessment system for the Veterans Administration.[43] In 1920, Brigham left government employment and returned to Princeton University as an assistant professor of psychology.

The Superiority of Our Nordic Group

In his role as assistant professor, Brigham furthered his career by capitalizing on his assignment with the Canadian Military Hospitals Commission, his war experiences, and his federal work with veteran placement. His knowledge of test design, large-scale administration, data analysis, and report-writing afforded him a valuable set of highly unique skills that he would use to launch his career.

In his first major publication, Brigham summarized those aspects of race and culture that supported a eugenic orientation toward society. Working with data from Yerkes' *Memoirs of the National Academy of Sciences*, Brigham published *A Study of American Intelligence* in 1923. Yerkes wrote in the foreword that

> Mr. Brigham has rendered a notable service to psychologists, to sociology, and above all to our law-makers by carefully re-examining and re-presenting the data relative to intelligence and nativity first published in the official report of psychological examining in the United States army.... The author presents not theories or opinions but facts. It behooves us to consider their reliability and their

> meaning, for no one of us as a citizen can afford to ignore the menace of race deterioration or the evident relations of immigration to our national progress and welfare.[44]

Brigham himself claimed no less: "These army data constitute the first really significant contribution to the study of race differences in mental traits. They give us a scientific basis for our conclusions."[45]

Brigham began his study by recalling the key role of literacy in the army examination processes, with tests for "separating the English speaking and the literate from the non-English speaking or illiterate."[46] In Part I of the book, Brigham gave samples of the examinations used in the army tests, summarizing and interpreting the scores of recruits. He found the analogies test, for example, "the most effective test in the entire series in differentiating officers from men."[47] In Part II he focused on the eugenics implications of the army test results. "Comparing the foreign born with the negro draft," he wrote, "we find that 70.44% of the foreign born exceed the average of the negro draft."[48] Those from Holland, Germany, Denmark, Scotland, and Sweden performed quite well on the test, but recruits from Russia, Italy, and Poland did poorly. Brigham converted the army findings to mental ages of eight and concluded that few found to be at that mental level would be able "to manage their affairs with ordinary prudence. Many of them should be in custodial institutions."[49]

Brigham ended his book with an argument supporting the race hypothesis—that the Nordic race has the most to offer in genetic terms and that intermarriage with other groups led to debilitation—offered by Madison Grant's popular *The Passing of the Great Race*. "The results of the examination of the nativity groups," Brigham wrote, "suggest immediately that the race factor may underlie the large differences found."[50] To demonstrate the significance of the race factor, Brigham separated English-speaking recruits (born in England, Scotland, Ireland, and Canada) from non-English-speaking recruits (born in Holland, Denmark, Germany, Sweden, Norway, Belgium, Austria, Russia, and Poland) to demonstrate the inferiority of the non-English-speaking Nordic group; indeed, even the non-English-speaking Nordics were superior to the Alpine and Mediterranean groups. There was "a marked intellectual inferiority of the negro," and the data also disproved that the "Jew is highly intelligent."[51] The "purity of the white race"[52] was vanishing, and Brigham urged his readers to "frankly admit the undesirable results which would ensue from a cross between the Nordic in this country with the Alpine Slav, with the degenerated hybrid Mediterranean, or with the negro, or from the promiscuous intermingling of all four types."[53] The "really important" policy steps, he concluded, were those "looking toward the prevention of the continued propagation of defective strains in the present population."[54]

Such sentiments would have struck a familiar cord with many readers. The Immigration Act of 1917, often referred to as the Literacy Act, banned immigrants who were illiterate either in English or in their native language. Excluded were:

> All aliens over sixteen years of age, physically capable of reading, who cannot read the English language, or some other language or dialect, including Hebrew of Yiddish.... That for the purpose of ascertaining whether aliens can read the immigrant inspectors shall be furnished with slips of uniform size, prepared under the direction of the Attorney General, each containing not less than thirty nor more than forty words in ordinary use, printed plainly in legible type in some one of the various languages or dialects of immigrants. Each alien may designate the particular language or dialect in which he desires the examination to be made, and shall be required to read the words printed on the slip in such language or dialect....[55]

The impact of the 1917 act had been enormous. While nearly 4.5 million immigrants entered the United States between 1911 and 1915, from 1916 to 1920 immigrant entries plummeted to 1.3 million.[56] And after World War I, literacy continued to assume an important role. Idaho and Utah required their non-English-speaking aliens to take Americanization classes, and in 1919 fifteen states passed laws requiring classroom education to take place only in English. Brigham had such immigration statistics in mind when providing a table of arrivals of alien passengers from 1820 to 1920 and showed that the immigrant population of "Russia, including Poland" grew from a mere 91 immigrants in 1820 to 921,957 in the years 1911 to 1920.[57] He reminded his readers that 6.8 percent of the tested Polish group had mental ages below that of eight-year-olds (just above the 10.0 percent of the "Negro draft," the very bottom of the scale). "The Fourth of July orator can convincingly raise the popular belief in the intellectual level of Poland by shouting the name of Kosciusko from a high platform," Brigham wrote, "but he can not alter the distribution of the intelligence of the Polish immigrant."[58]

When Brigham's study was released in 1923, it provided additional support to the efforts being taken by Congressman Albert Johnson, chair of the Committee on Selective Immigration. Johnson had appointed Harry H. Laughlin, a prominent eugenicist who believed that the lowest 10 percent of the American population should be sterilized, to the House Committee.[59] As early as 1922 the committee had drafted a bill to decrease the number of immigrants, particularly those from southern and eastern Europe, the very populations that Brigham would later target as mentally inferior in his study. The strategy of the bill was based on both reducing the quotas and moving the census base year from 1910 to 1880. Such an adjustment in the base year would drastically reduce immigrants from Russia and Poland. In 1910 immigrants from Poland numbered 1,597,306, but in 1880 the number had been only 265,088. Basing quotas on the 1880 number would therefore drastically restrict immigrants from Poland as well as from other eastern and southern European nations.[60]

The Immigration Act of 1924 instituted the national origins quota system. Congress thus established a system by which only 150,000 visas would be allowed annually. Immigrants from northern and western Europe received 83 percent of the visas, and southern and eastern Europeans received only 15 percent. Other groups received the remaining 2 percent. The army data that Brigham popularized, based on a command of English, helped to establish a system that barred up to six million southern, central, and eastern Europeans between 1924 and the outbreak of World War II.[61]

When *A Study of American Intelligence* was published, the significance of literacy was prominent in the minds of many Americans. Yerkes, Brigham, and their colleagues had designed measurement tools that rested upon literacy when they decided to measure mental ability by means of an understanding of synonym-antonym relationships, the revision of disarranged sentences, and the completion of analogies. Even the alpha test 2, arithmetic reasoning, was a series of word problems. At the close of the nineteenth century, literacy had been proof of the value of the city on the hill; in the new century, literacy was now equated with intelligence, a mental characteristic that could be measured, the race possessing it preserved according to appropriate social policy informed, always and everywhere, by science.

Brigham and the SAT: The Empirical Study of Signs

Brigham continued to pursue his interest in mental testing. His was a unique position in American education: he understood both psychometric design and large-scale administration, and *A Study of American Intelligence*—revealing his skills in analyzing data in order to persuade audiences—announced his ability and desire to work on a national scale.

Just before the publication of *A Study of American Intelligence*, Brigham had been asked to review a series of admissions tests developed by Thorndike and used at Cooper Union in New York.[62] At Princeton University, Brigham designed and executed the original Princeton Test in 1925, a two-hour assessment battery of verbal, mathematical, and spatial questions. His work so impressed his faculty colleagues that his tests were voted to be required of all applicants to Princeton.[63] Thus, Brigham ushered in intelligence testing as part of the admissions policy at one of the nation's leading universities.

So great was the growing popularity of the tests that the College Entrance Examination Board appointed Brigham to make a series of recommendations regarding the use of tests for post-secondary admission. To the College Board, Brigham and his methods were a welcome addition. In 1920 the Board had come under such sharp criticism for the "great fluctuations" in the examinations in elementary algebra and plane geometry that a conference had to be called.[64] The following year, a report by L. Thomas Hopkins of Harvard's Graduate School of Education had found in a study of the examinations from 1902 to 1920 that "only in rare instances" did the assignment of marks approximate the normal distribution of the now widely used Gaussian curve and that the "method of reading and scoring papers" was a "very natural factor in causing the existing conditions."[65]

The College Board's solution—a proposal that the fluctuations be "eliminated, or at least rendered innocuous, by the introduction of percentile grades"[66]—did not truly address the stability issues that the Board hoped Brigham could solve.

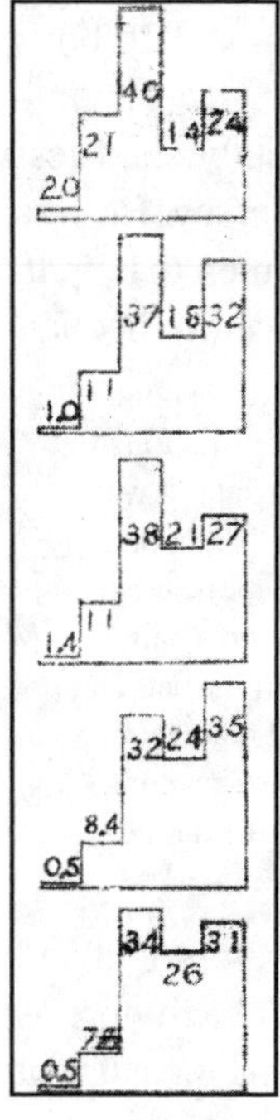

Graphs representing readings for the Examination in English. The different divisions in each column were as follows: 90–100, 75–89, 60–74, 50–59, 0–49. "Finally, in view of the large number of cases, no sufficient justification exists for the wide difference in the relative percentages assigned in the different subjects. Whether the distribution approximates the curve of error, or some other form, a certain uniformity in the different subjects may reasonably be expected. To accomplish this there must be co-operation between examiners and readers in the different subjects." (Source: L. Thomas Hopkins, *The Marking System of the College Entrance Examination Board*, Studies in Educational Psychology and Educational Measurement, Series 1, No. 2 [Cambridge: Harvard Graduate School of Education, 1921] 5.)

Brigham was to serve on an advisory committee with John E. Anderson of Yale and Harry T. Moore of Dartmouth.[67] On April 4, 1925, the College Board approved a plan for a new series of psychological tests. Just as Princeton had broken Ivy League ground under Brigham's direction in the intelligence testing movement, the College Entrance Examination Board—in the 1920s responsible for coordinating the admissions of 19,755 applicants from 1,691 secondary schools[68]—now gave the movement national authority.

The committee—Roswell P. Angier of Yale, Andrew H. MacPhail of Brown University, David C. Rogers of Smith College, and Charles L. Stone of Dartmouth College—worked with Brigham to build the final form of the test.[69] Each member of the committee had experience with these new types of academic aptitude tests. The test consisted of nine sections, all relying (as had the army tests) on verbal ability: definitions (9 minutes), arithmetical problems (8 minutes), classification (6 minutes), artificial language (9 minutes), antonyms (10 minutes), number series completion (9 minutes), analogies (6 minutes), logical inference (10 minutes), and paragraph reading (30 minutes). The test also included a 30-minute experimental section, a feature to aid in test refinement that was developed by Brigham in the original Princeton tests. The Scholastic Aptitude Test (SAT) was first given on June 23, 1926, to 8,040 candidates—4,829 boys and 3,211 girls.[70]

To coordinate the test development effort, Brigham established test development offices at 20 Nassau Street in Princeton, New Jersey. He was provided with a budget of $25,000. He recruited a staff of women to help in the work. The occasional visitor would have found laboratory life hectic:

> Inside was an array of apparatus—manually operated Monroe calculators, a punch card machine, and an old vertical sorter. By the early 1930s Brigham had also invented an automatic testing machine to add a new dimension to test data. It was an ingenious device designed to record the time required for a subject's response as well as his answer. The machine was a box-like affair with a projection screen and dials on the front, and a moving-picture camera, a film projector, and a pair of stop watches inside. At a flip of a switch the gears whirred, a test item flashed on the screen, and the first stop watch began. After the subject had dialed his answer, he flipped a second switch. The camera then recorded the time and the response on a 35mm film, and the second stop watch timed the rest period until the next question.[71]

As a designer, Brigham placed great emphasis upon development and refinement of the test, paying careful attention to the value of each item as judged by its ability to correlate with other items in the test—a measure of internal consistency. In the early administrations, it was impossible to establish the ability of the test to forecast grades in college—a predictive measure—so Brigham and his colleagues attempted to correlate the test scores with the age of the candidates and with a multiple regression analysis that yielded the candidate's hypothesized success (a "bogie-grade" based on the weighted average of the College Entrance Examination Board's regular examinations, school grades, and the SAT).[72] To ensure a process of continuous refinement—an innovative concept in testing—an experimental section was added to the SAT, as it had been added to the original Princeton test, thus allowing Brigham to evaluate new items that could be used more accurately on future tests.[73]

Administratively, the test process was highly systematized. The exams were administered under secure conditions, and the examination supervisor read instructions from a printed schedule. The test booklets were secured after each examination, valuable because of the items and their demonstrated power of evaluation. The test booklets were scored in New York City by Princeton and Columbia undergraduates who had done well on intelligence tests used at those universities.

Philosophically, Brigham placed great emphasis on the validity of the SAT, seeking to unify the emphasis that he placed on the statistical and administrative aspects of the test into a coherent approach to test development. Indeed, the first two chapters of *A Study of Error*—Brigham's most comprehensive treatment of the theory and practice of test development—are devoted to explications of meaning and the study of symbols. Quoting at length from the systems analysis offered by psychologist E. B. Titchener, the social framework described by educational pragmatist John Dewey, and the semiotic analysis made by literary theorists C. K. Ogden and I. A. Richards, Brigham argued for a theory of meaning based on a study of symbols.[74] The symbols—in effect, the test items themselves—may be studied, Brigham proposed, according to methods of correlation:

> We may take whatever we find—symbols as used—and trace out the origins of particular errors. This technique is diametrically opposed to the present method of advancing general explanations of how thought proceeds correctly. The proposal is to launch an enormous number of separate investigations to learn how thought proceeds incorrectly. Such investigations will produce a science of education which is akin to an experimental epistemology.[75]

Ultimately, what would this new science of item analysis, designed with the exam questions themselves as meaningful signifiers, reveal? "Detailed information concerning errors should provide the materials for explicit instruction devised to eradicate them. From this point of view, therefore, test findings would not be construed as necessarily revealing unalterable psychological characteristics of the individual, but merely as exposing what is happening to the individual in his culture."[76] The signification would therefore provide information, on one level, about students embedded in their schools and, on another level, about individuals surrounded by their environment.

And what of the national laboratory itself, the system that allowed such research? "The project," Brigham wrote of the SAT in 1932, "has coasted along on its accumulated stock of item material since 1929 and is presently largely an administrative matter."[77] The modern system of test development had begun, and with it the college admissions process, complete with its explicit administrative presence and its elaborate statistical premises.

Re-Thinking the Race Hypothesis

In *A Study of American Intelligence*, Brigham had acknowledged his debt to eugenics, a science, as A. E. Hamilton claimed, that "was bringing us nearer the time when we shall have a working criterion of worth for each human strain and stock."[78] As Tom Buchanan would put it in F. Scott Fitzgerald's *The Great Gatsby*, published two years after Brigham's book, "The idea is if we don't look out the white race will be—we'll be utterly submerged. It's all scientific stuff; it's been proved."[79]

In *A Study of Error*, Brigham wrote that his own tests identified only what was occurring in a subject's culture. Gone were claims about the intelligence of immigrants and black men. Present were arguments for the study of error as a better way to understand individual performance in the academy. Brigham had undergone a shift regarding the measurement of intelligence and had begun to think more carefully about intelligence, its measurement, and the claims that one made about knowledge of either. His reversal of position was recorded in 1930 in "Intelligence Tests of Immigrant Groups."[80]

Brigham began his article with a statement that he would address, in editorial form, research articles with the following formula: "The Blank test of intelligence was given to *n* children in *x* grades of a certain school system; the average test scores of children of nationality *A*, *B*, and *C* were as follows."[81] Brigham differentiated tests from the constructs they are said to measure, warning readers to beware of the "naming fallacy" of psychologists to "slide mysteriously from the score in the test to the hypothetical faculty suggested by the name given to the test."[82] He acknowledged that combining test scores produced an internal inconsistency because different tests measure different attributes: verbal intelligence, quantitative intelligence, and spatial intelligence.[83] Thus, combining test scores—as he had done in *A Study of American Intelligence*—caused the "entire hypothetical superstructure of racial differences" to collapse completely.[84] The final two paragraphs of his editorial were remorselessly logical:

> For purposes of comparing individuals or groups, it is apparent that tests in the vernacular must be used only with individuals having equal opportunities to acquire the vernacular of the test. This requirement precludes the use of such tests in making comparative studies of individuals brought up in homes in which the vernacular of the test is not used, or in which two vernaculars are used. The last condition is frequently violated here in studies of children born in this country whose parents speak another tongue. It is important, as the effects of bilingualism are not entirely known.
>
> This review has summarized some of the most recent test findings which show that comparative studies of various national and racial groups may not be made with existing tests, and which show, in particular, that one of the most pretentious of these comparative racial studies—the writer's own—was without foundation.[85]

In 1932, Brigham warned against "the hypostatization of *g*"—Charles Spearman's general factor thought to underlie performance on tests.[86] "We gain," Brigham wrote, "much from the study of individual performance—we gain nothing from the hypostatization of abilities, powers, faculties, and intelligences which 'explain' these performances."[87] Ascribing material existence to intelligence as Spearman had done in "'General Intelligence,' Objectively Determined and Measured" could no longer be valid if the plan was to associate the presence of intelligence with specific racial or ethnic identities. Philosophically, as Brigham had found, the systems analysis offered by Titchener, the social framework of pragmatist John Dewey, and the semiotic analysis of Ogden and Richards all led to one conclusion: the linguistic relationship between the signifier and signified was complex. When language was at play within an item, any number of results could occur. Analytically, the detailed attention required to perform error analysis on test questions—research intended to capture scholastic achievement—had led Brigham to realize that intelligence was a multi-faceted concept that could not be equated with native intelligence.[88] As Harvard psychologist Edwin G. Boring—Captain Boring when he worked with Yerkes and Brigham during the war—claimed in the *New Republic*, "Intelligence is what the tests test." There was, he had come to believe, no such thing as a test for pure intelligence. "Intelligence," he told his readers, "is not demonstrable except in connection with some special ability."[89]

Intelligence, Boring cautiously claimed, was only one factor among many in mental life. By 1930 Brigham was inclined to agree.

Brigham and the Comprehensive Examination in English

Brigham became the associate secretary of the College Board in 1930, following an April recommendation by the Executive Committee.[90] Now forty years old, he turned his attention to testing as its own independent entity. He spent less time in the Princeton Department of Psychology and more time with developing the new field of testing.[91] The testing movement, he had written in 1930, "has become ridiculous only when it has tried to maintain its pseudo-scientific contacts with laboratory psychology by borrowing its phantom formulae. It is now merely necessary to show that the data may be regarded from another viewpoint which is not psychological. It is the writer's expectation that a science independent of psychology will emerge from a closer scrutiny of test data."[92]

In his continuing effort to establish this new science of testing, Brigham undertook a formal study of the Comprehensive Examination in English. Although written examinations in English had been designed, administered, and scored since the organization of the College Entrance Examination Board was formally announced on November 17, 1900, there had been a shift away from topics that were restrictive in nature, a change evident in the new Comprehensive Examinations, first offered in 1916.[93] Throughout the 1920s, there had been a continuous shift in the design of the examinations away from topics that were restrictive in nature (questions designed to test knowledge about specific works of literature) to those that were more comprehensive in design (questions constructed to test academic aptitude). This movement toward a more valid test was delineated by Abbot Lawrence Lowell, Charles William Eliot's successor as the new president of Harvard, in his 1926 essay "The Art of Examination."[94] "We hear," wrote Lowell,

> much today of teaching by problems: and rightly, because bare facts are of little value unless one knows how to use them. The important thing is to understand their relation to one another; to be able to correlate them, as the current expression goes; not merely to grasp and retain the relations one has been taught, but to perceive new relations, for no teacher can cover more than a minute fraction of the combinations actually met in the pursuit of any subject. The pupil must learn to apply principles to new and unexpected conditions, and the extent to which he can do so will largely determine the degree of his future effectiveness.[95]

Operationally, the idea of a comprehensive examination meant a shift from very specific questions on the Restrictive Examination (such as

"Analyze either Macaulay's *Essay on Addison* or his *Essay on Milton* so as to show its construction, noting the development of the theme and the main transitions"[96]) to more general questions on the Comprehensive Examination (such as "What do you consider some of the important reasons for the reading and study of non-fiction prose? Illustrate your answer with specific references to three works of prose other than fiction which you have read or studied"[97]). The new examination questions were "a symbol of a shift in educational thought—an evolution from rigid flexibility, from narrowness of breadth, from emphasis on content to emphasis on choice," as the historian of the College Board and headmaster of Phillips Academy, Andover, Claude Fuess, defined the shift. Recollecting the impact of this new approach on his own classroom, he reminisced: "I can remember feeling a sense of liberation as I was left free to teach other Shakespearian plays besides *The Merchant of Venice* and *Macbeth*, free to talk about Robert Frost and Carl Sandburg as well as Milton and Whittier. Much the same relief was experienced by instructors in other subjects. For many schools it seemed like the opening of a marvelous era."[98]

The new examination afforded Brigham an opportunity for research into freedom and discipline. The balance between the validity of the examination in its creation and the possibility of error in its implementation informed the first pages of his 1934 study, *The Reading of the Comprehensive Examination in English: An Analysis of the Procedures Followed During the Five Reading Periods from 1929–1933*. In his introduction, Brigham agreed that the new examinations had given greater freedom and that "a new spirit has entered the classroom." But he also reminded his readers that "persistent queries and criticisms" have arisen from those trained in mental measurement: "a movement launched by Francis Galton has eventually grown to encompass every description of man by man. The use of the method of correlation has thrown the error of measurement into the foreground and this notion of error can no longer be obscured."[99]

It did not, however, follow for Brigham that all forms of testing were equally valid for all subjects. The testing practices that had been used during the war had, as Boring recalled, "reached into the remotest corner of the laboratory and swelled college classes...."[100] With the concept of testing had come a tidal wave of questions used in the tests—seemingly objective in nature and free from human errors of evaluation. Scored rapidly by trained evaluators, objective tests stood ready for what Boring called "the Galton-Pearson biometrical statistical methods [that were] ready for the run-of-the-mill mental tester."[101] Perhaps it was the 1928 editorial in the *English*

Journal advocating the limited use of "well constructed, correctly proportioned" objective tests in literature.[102] Perhaps it was the support for these tests voiced by Charles Swain Thomas in his 1932 *English Journal* article on examinations in English. (Reflecting on the need for student mastery of mechanical skills, he advocated that "no well prepared pupil could logically object to taking such an objective test as part of an examination."[103] After all, these were mere "automatisms," not to be confused with "creative thought and expression."[104]) Certainly it was the detailed study of the nuance of language embodied in *The Study of Error*. But whatever the reasons, Brigham objected to the "new blunders" arising to ensure error reduction. "The objective tests in English include vocabulary surveys, information tests in literature,—completely factual in type,—and various grammatical or proof-reading tests. As representative of a goal these new English tests are silly, and as descriptive of the individual the measures which have been found reliable cannot be related to what competent masters regard as 'English.'"[105]

With his unwillingness to sacrifice validity for reliability established, Brigham then got down to business and provided a sketch of the reading process used by the College Board:

> The unit of organization was the table consisting of about twelve readers under a table leader or supervisor. The readers were trained in a group conference which was followed by round-robin re-reading at each table for the first day. During the second and third days each reader was paired with another reader at the table under the direction of the group leader. These reader-colleague pairs were changed each day, or more frequently. By the fourth day readers were cross-paired from table to table and the pairs were changed daily to the end of the reading period. The group leaders also cross-paired themselves with other group leaders to check their own standards. Difficult cases were referred to a special re-read committee.
>
> Each reader kept a tally sheet showing the separate marks assigned to each question, the tentative rating, the rating assigned by the colleague who re-read the script, and the final rating reported to the college.[106]

Brigham then gave the bad news. From 1929 to 1932, the examinations failed to meet standards of reliability—readers disagreed, often wildly, on the scores of the essay booklets.[107] He also found that "some readers would erase the marks on their tally sheets and substitute other marks after conference with their colleagues."[108] The problem of reliability persisted in 1930, and only those readers who were known to have achieved agreement were asked back in 1931. But even the use of readers known to achieve agreement did not yield acceptable correlations—and it remained impossible to control erasures of scores so that disagreement would be recorded.

In 1932, a major shift was made in the procedure under Brigham's direction. Readers were selected whose scores on booklets were consistent (defined by Brigham as "a small sigma of the difference between their own tentative rating and the final rating"[109]). Only those who were most promising could be retained after the disaster of Black Tuesday. In 1929, just before the crash, the U.S. gross national product had been $104 billion, but by 1932 it had dropped to $59 billion. Nearly 13 million were jobless. As a result, there had been little or no growth in college enrollment. In the period from 1929 to 1930, enrollment as a percentage of the population aged eighteen to twenty-four had been 7.2 percent. In the period from 1933 to 1934 it would drop to 6.7 percent.[110]

Significantly, the economic stress of the Depression drove the need to ensure inter-reader reliability: "As the Board at this time was facing a very great decrease in the number of candidates and the resulting loss in income, it seemed unwise to spend large sums of money in re-reading the scripts of apparently highly qualified readers in order to correct occasional errors."[111] For economic reasons, the system of using two readers on all booklets was temporarily abandoned. In that a total score of 100 points on the examination was possible, the Committee on Examination Ratings decided that booklets receiving ratings below 60 points would be rechecked, but only one-sixth of the booklets receiving scores above 60 points, randomly chosen, would be checked. Books were read on an average of 1.8 times, and the cost of reading dropped from over three dollars per book to less than two dollars.[112]

Yet scoring issues persisted. One of the examination questions employed a 35-point rating scale, and the readers—as had been the case with the readings of 1929 to 1931—could not find agreement; Brigham described one distribution as "freakish."[113] In addition, even though the scale allowed 35 points, the readers seemed to use only 15 of these points. The same large differences in distribution were found for the 20-point rating scale, and some readers forgot that the scale had been reduced and awarded the booklets scores of 26, 27, and 28. And, in the 10-point scale, most readers used only 4 points. Brigham reached the only conclusion he could: that all readers should use the same scale in rating all questions; in fact, he argued that readers should not use numbers to score the booklets at all.

The plan for the reading of 1933—the final study described in *The Reading of the Comprehensive Examination in English*—was established using the best techniques known at that time, and Brigham tried to eliminate the sources of error that would potentially result in a failure of inter-reader reliability when the 6,970 answer books were examined. The marks from the first reader were concealed from the second, and the readers were randomized. A new eight-level scale was developed for the readers, from "A+: Exceptional work throughout," to X, a "Bad Failure."[114] Readers read six examination questions with Question 6 providing an opportunity for the candidates to write essays.

Page 5

(*Sixty minutes*)

For all candidates.

6. From one of the following suggestions select a subject and write upon it a composition of about three hundred and fifty words. Follow an orderly, consecutive plan. Prefix an appropriate title. Give the letter of the suggestion followed.

a) Should your school include in the last year of English study more contemporary literature?

b) "Have nothing in your house that you do not know to be useful, or believe to be beautiful."—WILLIAM MORRIS, *The Beauty of Life.*

c) Highways are flattened walls.

d) When you have a radio and a victrola in your home, is it worth while to learn to play a musical instrument?

e) Drama close-packed with life

f) It is impossible to study any subject without studying English; it is almost equally impossible to study English without studying something else.

g) "Our prevalent notion [about freedom] is that it is a most happy and important thing for a man to be able to do as he likes. On what he is to do when he is free to do as he likes, we do not lay so much stress."—MATTHEW ARNOLD, *Doing as One Likes.*

h) "Oh, a day in the city-square, there is no such pleasure in life."

i) Mountain, mist, and valley

j) Waste that we pay for when we buy

k) Working my way through the depression

l) If science has injured mankind, it is not because science has gone too far but because it has not as yet gone far enough.

Question 6, the essay section, of the 1933 Comprehensive Examination in English. Such new examination questions were "a symbol of a shift in educational thought—an evolution from rigid flexibility, from narrowness of breadth, from emphasis on content to emphasis on choice," as Claude Fuess described them. (Source: Carl Campbell Brigham, *The Reading of the Comprehensive Examination in English: An Analysis of the Procedures Followed During the Five Reading Periods from 1929–1933* [Princeton: Princeton UP, 1934] following 43. Reprinted by permission of Princeton University Press.)

TABLE VIII

CORRELATION PLOT OF FIRST READING AGAINST SECOND READING OF QUESTION SIX

FIRST READING	SECOND READING X	F	D	C	C+	B	A	A+	
A+			1		1	4	7	2	15
A		4	13	19	22	27	18	3	106
B		17	70	127	139	131	30		514
C+	1	55	194	269	198	121	23	2	863
C	5	170	524	562	285	164	24		1734
D	17	406	787	536	186	93	16	1	2042
F	63	542	393	176	64	28	1		1267
X	41	53	16	4	1	1			116
	127	1247	1998	1693	896	569	119	8	6657

Table VIII, Correlation Plot of the Essay Scoring for 1933. The inter-reader correlation for the essay was recorded as .49. (Source: Carl Campbell Brigham, *The Reading of the Comprehensive Examination in English: An Analysis of the Procedures Followed During the Five Reading Periods from 1929–1933* [Princeton: Princeton UP, 1934] 25. Reprinted by permission of Princeton University Press.)

The inter-reader reliability calculations were a disappointment to Brigham: "77 percent of the cases are found to be either in perfect agreement or one scale-interval off on either side. This is equivalent to saying that three scale steps included about 77 percent of the differences between the two ratings. About 94 percent of the differences are included within a distance of four scale steps. As the readers are using an 8-point scale and using X and A+ infrequently, it is apparent that the unreliability of the reading is very great."[115] The correlations of .52, .56, .56, .48, and .49 between the first and second readings on the six questions used in the examination were "too unreliable to be reported."[116] Brigham concluded that "the factors making for unreliability are now so great that the examination should be discontinued unless progress can be made in getting a single stable score which is descriptive of the candidate."[117]

Because the readers could not agree (and, it may be inferred, because scores could thus not be reported to those high-school students who had paid to have reports sent to their college admissions offices), a scale was constructed from the Board's frequency curve for 2,034 candidates who had previously taken the examination in English. A "grading committee of some of the most expert and experienced readers" then assigned each answer booklet a final grade.[118] Brigham recorded that resourceful, clever process:

> Each member of the grading committee had a conversion key showing the approximate grade which would be assigned if the weighted sum of the numerical

> grades were translated directly into Board marks. The members of the grading committee were instructed to look for discrepancies in ratings and to attempt to reconcile differences between widely divergent ratings of independent readers. The papers of all candidates were rated by the grading committee. The correlation between the ratings reported by the grading committee and the converted sum of numerical equivalents of the letter grades was .988 for 6,657 cases.[119]

The addition of the grading committee had allowed marks to be returned, evidence that scarce dollars had not been frittered away. But Brigham had come to realize that inter-reader reliability was an enduring problem. His solution was to select readers whose scores had, in past readings, correlated highly. "If one were able to select only those readers whose judgments correlated higher than .60 with the group judgment on questions one, three, and four, and higher than .50 with the group judgment on questions five and six, the general reliability of the readings would be greatly increased. A selection of superior readers only would give a more homogeneous and consistent group against which the reliability of the single reader could be tested."[120]

In his conclusion to the report, Brigham turned, characteristically, to metaphor to explain the need for selective standards in employing readers:

> The individual reader respects his own judgment and protests against the group judgment. One might almost say that there is a naïve theory of reading which holds that there is an absolute mark and only one mark which may be affixed to each single effort of each candidate. This theory regards the individual reader as a sort of refined micrometric microscope with exact powers of seeing and gauging, not *a* grade but *the* grade. The opposing theory regards the readers as more or less efficient cameras varying in the efficiency of the lens, focusing devices, and sensitivity of the film. This year the Board took four pictures of each candidate with this collection of cameras.

"It is now," he warned, "examining its cameras and is about to select the ones which were found most effective."[121]

Existing Evils and the Future of the College Board

The environment of American education was changing dramatically in the first three decades of the twentieth century. Driven by population growth, college enrollment had risen nearly 50 percent between 1899–1900 and 1909–1910. In the following decade, enrollment rose by 68 percent. Between 1919–1920 and 1929–1930, enrollment rose by 84 percent. During the eighteen years that Brigham had been in higher education (he was admitted to the Princeton class of 1912), the ratio of college students aged eighteen-to twenty-four years to all persons in that age group rose from 2 to 7 percent.[122] In addition, the Great Depression was at hand, and there was an increase in criticism aimed at the College Board's influence on secondary schools as college enrollments either declined or remained, at best, only stable.[123] While there were questions regarding the survival of the Board itself, the Scholastic Aptitude Test had become a major source of income.[124] The world of higher education was becoming a vastly different place, and Brigham urged the College Board to refashion itself.

As part of that refashioning, Brigham himself took the lead. In 1929, he urged that his Scholastic Aptitude Test be divided into two parts:

> The committee must now consider the possibility of adding a mathematical aptitude section to the present scholastic aptitude test to make the test more generally useful for engineering colleges or for the selection of scientific students in colleges of the more general type. The present scholastic aptitude test seems quite definitely related to English, Latin, History, and the more general reading courses in college. It may be pictured as measuring the varying degrees of literacy to be found in college applicant populations. It is limited in scope in that it seems to deal only with verbal symbolism, a type of symbolic thinking which is of prime importance if the student is expected to derive benefit from lectures and textbooks, but which is not of paramount importance in mathematics and science. A supplementary test of thinking in mathematical symbolism might serve the double function of revealing students who might profitably continue in the scientific fields, and of exposing those students whose proposed election of a scientific curriculum is the result of a verbal display rather than a high degree of mathematical and scientific aptitude.[125]

In equating the verbal section of the SAT with literacy and finding it to be a test to assess an individual's ability to deal with verbal symbolism, Brigham revealed his abandonment of the search for Spearman's factor of *g*, of a single characteristic defined as intelligence. Brigham thus expressed his willingness to embrace different tests as measuring different constructs. As well, if the Board embraced a role as an educational placement service, such willingness would deflect criticism aimed at its gate-keeping tests.[126]

Throughout the Depression, Brigham continued to serve as a consultant to the Board, often arguing vigorously for the establishment of a research agenda. The board, he noted in 1933, had developed a system of readers rather than of examiners, and during a twelve-year period it had spent more than $1 million for reading the written examinations and less than $43,000 for research.[127]

Brigham had come to fear the very consolidation he once sought. In a meeting held in New York on October 28, 1937, Harvard President James Bryant Conant, who had succeeded Lowell in 1933, supported the consolidation of several of the existing testing agencies. "Such a suggestion," Brigham wrote in the popular *School and Society*,

> brings to the fore the fundamental purposes of the proposed organization. A new organization solely for the dissemination of present knowledge concerning tests and the promotion of testing programs would be difficult to justify; an organization which advances knowledge, however, is to be desired. It is the writer's belief that the present testing movement carries the germs of its own destruction and that unless the proposed organization is set up to develop a cure for these afflictions it will retard rather than advance education.[128]

"The cure," he believed, "is found in research and more research. Fundamental research must become an integral part of any consolidation. From one-third to one-half of the total income of any testing organization should be ploughed into research. Because research is apt to become institutionalized, not more than one-half of the available funds should be allowed the organization itself, the remaining half being used to subsidize original investigations by outsiders. The provision for an extensive research program will prevent degeneration into a sales and propaganda group; provision for external investigations will prevent the research from becoming too narrow."[129] No doubt influenced by his army draft experiences, Brigham even had a plan regarding who would staff the organization.

> The projected organization must incorporate in such a manner that the evils of the existing situation must eventually be corrected. Since the testers of today are for the most part insensitive to the nature of the things they are trying to measure, a major function of the new organization must be the training and recruitment of better personnel. As it is probably simpler to teach cultured men testing than to give testers culture, the research wing should act as a training school for promising young men drafted from the major fields of learning.[130]

With an allusion to Plato, Brigham proposed a rotating system of testers in which enlightened researchers would return to their cave-like disciplines: "By some such method the organization could incorporate into itself the active minds of successive generations."[131]

Brigham's ideas continued to influence the College Board as America recovered from the Depression.[132] He continued to urge that research should become a mainstay of the testing system. While the nation's first educational research organization would eventually emerge with some, if not all, of the values Brigham desired, the time for that republic was not yet at hand.

It was 1937 and Franklin Delano Roosevelt had just emerged from a re-election campaign. While Americans were determined to stay out of another war, within two years the swastika would fly over Czechoslovakia and Poland. From 1933 to 1938 nearly sixty thousand refugees fled to

America, some part of the Jewish strain and stock that Hitler had found wanting. Because of America's immigration policy, many found wanting were barred. Sensing that he could be of use to the nation, Brigham wrote to the War Department offering his expertise for officer selection. He was appointed expert consultant to the secretary of war and worked to establish a central registry for the mobilization of American scientists who would soon be swept into the gathering storm.

Endnotes

1 Woodrow Wilson, "First Inaugural Address," *The Papers of Woodrow Wilson*, ed. Arthur S. Link, vol. 27 (Princeton: Princeton UP, 1978) 151–152.

2 Woodrow Wilson, "War Message," *The Papers of Woodrow Wilson*, vol. 27 (Princeton: Princeton UP, 1978) 526.

3 Wilson's name appears on page 10 of the report as a representative from the College of New Jersey.

4 Wilson, "War Message," *The Papers of Woodrow Wilson*, vol. 27 (Princeton: Princeton UP, 1978) 522.

5 Daniel R. Beaver, *Newton D. Baker and the American War Effort, 1917–1919* (Lincoln: U of Nebraska P, 1966). See also Neil M. Heyman, *World War I* (Westport: Greenwood P, 1997) 71–72.

6 For the origin of this phrase, see Geraldine Joncich, *The Sane Positivist: A Biography of Edward L. Thorndike* (Middletown: Wesleyan UP, 1968) 283.

7 Beaver 37.

8 Recalling the sentiments of James Morgan Hart, Münsterberg had claimed that a comparison of European and American scholarship could be "as easily as briefly stated: there is none." *American Traits from the Point of View of a German* (New York: Houghton, 1901) 81.

9 Robert Mearns Yerkes, "A Point Scale for Measuring Mental Ability," *Proceedings of the National Academy of Science* 1.2 (1915): 116.

10 In "Testing the Army's Intelligence: Psychologists and the Military in World War I," Daniel J. Kevles reminds us, however, that mental tests were not accepted without criticism. Kevles cites Justice John W. Goff of the New York State Supreme Court, who had refused to admit the results of a Binet test as evidence in a case. "Standardizing the mind," Justice Goff had said, "is as futile as standardizing electricity." See "Testing the Army's Intelligence," *Journal of American History* 55.3 (1968): 565–581.

11 Kevles, "Testing" 567.

12 See John M. Gibson, *Physician to the World: The Life of General William C. Gorgas* (Durham: Duke UP, 1950). According to Gibson, Gorgas had been denied an adequate supply of wire screen, cloth, disinfectants and other material necessary to combat malaria by Rear Admiral John G. Walker, the chairman of the Committee (103–104). For Gorgas' support of Yerkes, see Kevles, "Testing the Army's Intelligence" 567–568.

13 Yerkes, "Measuring the Mental Strength of an Army," *Proceedings of the National Academy of Sciences* 4.10 (1918): 295.

14 Qtd. in Kevles, "Testing" 571.

15 Yerkes, Robert Mearns, ed., *Psychological Examining in the United States Army*, Memoirs of the National Academy of Sciences, vol. 15 (Washington: GPO, 1921) 202–211.

16 A reproduction of the beta test is given in Yerkes, *Psychological Examining* 251–258. See also 363–377.

17 On January 20, 1918, the School of Military Psychology at Fort Oglethorpe, Georgia, was "authorized for the Surgeon General by the chief of the training division of his office." Yerkes, *Psychological Examining* 92.

18 Yerkes, *Psychological Examining* 100, Tables 3 and 4. The impact of the Armistice, signed November 11, 1918, is evident in Table 4. In October 1919, 105,729 recruits were examined. In November 1919, the number had fallen to 86,506. In December 1919, the number was recorded at 46,629, and in January—the end of the process—the number totaled 123. It is significant that no mention is made of the Armistice in the General Summary of the period 1917–1919 (91–95). The only note for the month of November 1918 is as follows: "Arrangements made with Surgeon General Oreland for the completion of psychological examining and the transfer of officers of this service to general hospitals for assistance with the work of physical and mental reconstruction" (95). The word "armistice" does not appear in the Subject Index. Yet obscure General Order No, 74, giving the psychologists credentials, is clearly set into the record of August 14, 1918. The suspicion of those in the army that "many novelties" (97) were being imposed upon the service by the psychologists may have some validity: the involvement of the United States in a world war does not immediately rise out of the pages of Yerkes' memoir.

19 As Yerkes wrote, "The task of separating the illiterate and semi-literate from the literate was recognized previous to the fall [1917] examining in the Army." *Psychological Examining* 472.

20 Yerkes, *Psychological Examining* 347.

21 Here is Terman's recollection of the War: "Then came the War, with service on the committee that devised the army mental tests; on Yerkes' staff, first, as Director of

Research on the army tests and later as collaborator with Yerkes, Boring, and others on the historical account of psychological work in the army; and as a member of Scott's Committee on Classification of Personnel. It would take us too far afield to enter into the new world of experiences which the war work opened up to me. Their most important aspect, so far as my personal development is concerned, was in the opportunity they gave me to become acquainted with nearly all of the leading psychologists of America. Among the war associations which meant most to me were those with Yerkes, Thorndike, Whipple, Scott, Woodworth, Kelley, Bingham, Yoakum, Mabel Fernald, Bridges, Boring, Dodge, Goddard, Strong, Wells, and May. Through them and others my information was extended and my interests broadened in many fields of psychology. My intimate contacts with Yerkes in particular, both in our daily work and during the long periods when I lived in his home, meant more to me than could easily be expressed. One result of the war experiences was to confirm and strengthen my earlier beliefs regarding the importance of mental tests as an integral part of scientific psychology. Whereas I had thought that only a handful of psychologists were of this opinion, I now learned that many were. I no longer felt isolated. I could return to my work with more confidence than ever that, in the long run, contributions in the field of mental tests would receive the recognition they deserved." "Robert Mearns Yerkes," Carl Murchison, ed., *A History of Psychology in Autobiography*, vol. 2 (Worcester, MA: Clark University Press, 1930) 297–331. The personnel roster of the Division of Psychology, given in Yerkes (*Psychological Examining in the United States Army*) 6–40, illustrates that the leaders of the field of psychology were actively involved in the examination process. Among the names most relevant to the present study are Carl Campbell Brigham, Marion R. Trabue, and E. G. Boring.

22 Yerkes, *Psychological Examining* 348.

23 Yerkes, *Psychological Examining* 473.

24 Yerkes, *Psychological Examining* 705.

25 Yerkes, *Psychological Examining* 473.

26 Yerkes, *Psychological Examining* 743.

27 Yerkes, *Psychological Examining* 746.

28 Yerkes, *Psychological Examining* 745 and 697. Illiteracy rates were established by the number of recruits assigned to the beta test.

29 Yerkes, *Psychological Examining* 99–100. The mental age of the recruits was determined from a calculation that combined the eight alpha tests, the Stanford-Binet scale, and tests 4, 5, 6, and 7 of the beta test. The process is described in detail in Yerkes, *Psychological Examining in the United States Army* (573–657). Table 163 shows how the frequencies of each class interval of a Stanford-Binet mental age distribution are to be interpreted on the combined scale. It is this combined scale upon which Brigham rests his analysis of the relationship of mental age to race in *A*

Study of American Intelligence (Princeton: Princeton UP, 1923). The invalidity both of the construct of mental intelligence and the statistical procedure used to validate its presence is described by Stephen J. Gould in *The Mismeasure of Man* (New York: Norton, 1981) 212–224.

30 Yerkes, *Psychological Examining* 99.

31 Yerkes, *Psychological Examining* 399.

32 Kevles, "Testing the Army's Intelligence" 580.

33 *Nineteenth Annual Report of the Secretary* (New York: College Entrance Examination Board, 1919) 2.

34 *Nineteenth Annual Report of the Secretary* 12.

35 Matthew T. Downey, *Carl Campbell Brigham: Scientist and Educator* (Princeton: Educational Testing Service, 1961) 8. See also Thomas F. Donlon, "Brigham's Book," *College Board Review* 113 (1979): 24–30, and Warren G. Findley, "Carl C. Brigham Revisited," *College Board Review* 119 (1981):6–9.

36 Yerkes, *Psychological Examining* 13.

37 In Yerkes' *Psychological Examining*, Brigham is listed as stationed at Camp Dix, reporting to "chief psychological examiner" Joseph W. Hayes (13), and Brigham is listed among the personnel of the Division of Psychology (36).

38 Yerkes, *Psychological Examining* 15.

39 Yerkes, *Psychological Examining* 15.

40 Yerkes lists Brigham's assignment as ending in April 1918 (*Psychological Examining in the United States Army* 31).

41 Downey 8.

42 Downey 9.

43 Downey 9.

44 Robert M. Yerkes, foreword, *A Study of American Intelligence*, by Carl Campbell Brigham (Princeton: Princeton UP, 1923) viii.

45 Brigham, *American Intelligence* xx.

46 Brigham, *American Intelligence* xxiii.

47 Brigham, *American Intelligence* 27.

48 Brigham, *American Intelligence* 88.

49 Brigham, *American Intelligence* 152.

50 Brigham, *American Intelligence* 137.

51 Brigham, *American Intelligence* 190.

52 Brigham, *American Intelligence* 206.

53 Brigham, *American Intelligence* 208.

54 Brigham, *American Intelligence* 210. For the impact of Brigham's ideas, see Gould 224–233. See also Gary D. Saretzky, "Carl Campbell Brigham, the Native Intelligence Hypothesis, and the Scholastic Aptitude Test," *Research Memorandum* RM-82-4 (Princeton: ETS, 1982).

55 *Encyclopedia of American Immigration*, ed. James Ciment, vol. 4 (Armonk, NY: M. E. Sharpe, 2001) 1290–1291.

56 Brian N. Frye, "Restrictive Legislation," *Encyclopedia of American Immigration*, ed. James Ciment, vol. 1 (Armonk, NY: M. E. Sharpe, 2001) 150.

57 Brigham, *American Intelligence*, Table 34, 160–161. In *Dividing Lines: The Politics of Immigration Control in America* (Princeton: Princeton UP, 2002), Daniel J. Tichenor has observed that the legislative achievements of immigration restrictionists in the 1920s were "staggering." The 1929 quota plan, which Brigham's book helped bring to fruition, "decisively ended the path national immigration had followed for more than a century. The 1920 quota plan set an annual ceiling for legal immigrant admissions at 153, 714, a sharp decrease from the annual average of roughly 700,000 immigrants since the turn of the century. By design, the vast majority of these cherished immigration slots were reserved for northern and western Europeans; Greek, Hungarian, Italian, Polish, and Russian quotas soon produced ten-to-seventy-five-year waiting lists" (150).

58 Brigham, *American Intelligence* 202.

59 Daniel J. Kevles, *In the Name of Eugenics: Genetics and the Uses of Human Heredity* (New York: Knopf, 1985) 100–104.

60 My discussion of immigration policy is informed by the following: Daniel J. Tichenor, *Dividing Lines: The Politics of Immigration Control in America*; Robert A. Divine, *American Immigration Policy, 1924–1952* (New Haven: Yale UP, 1957); John Higham, *Send These to Me: Immigrants in Urban America* (Baltimore: Johns Hopkins UP, 1984). Also of interest is Sam McSeveney, "Immigrants, the Literacy Test, and Quotas: Selected American History College Textbooks' Coverage of the Congressional Restriction of European Immigrants, 1917–1929," *History Teacher* 21.1 (1987): 41–51. The link between Brigham's ideas and immigration policy is delineated in Gould 232–233.

61 The figure is given by Alan Chase, *The Legacy of Malthus: The Social Costs of the New Scientific Racism* (New York: Knopf, 1977). The figure is quoted in Gould 233.

62 Carl Campbell Brigham, *Preliminary Report of a Study of the Entrance Examination System at Cooper Union* (Princeton: Princeton University, 1923).

63 Carl Campbell Brigham, *A Study of Error* (New York: College Entrance Examination Board, 1932). Chapter 8 is devoted to the Princeton test. Similar tests, Brigham tells us, were undergoing experimentation at Yale, Smith, Brown, and Dartmouth.

64 *Twentieth Annual Report of the Secretary* (New York: College Entrance Examination Board, 1920) 9.

65 L. Thomas Hopkins, *The Marking System of the College Entrance Examination Board*, Studies in Educational Psychology and Educational Measurement, Series 1, No. 2. (Harvard: The Graduate School of Education, 1921) 14. It is interesting to note that Hopkins references E. G. Boring's review of I. E. Finkelstein's book, *The Marking System in Theory and Practice*, in which Boring refuted that author's claim that the ideal curve of high-school and college marks is not the probability curve but a skewed curve with the mode to the right of the middle of the abscissa. This claim, Boring concluded, "cannot be justified" and that if reforms are to depend on both practice and theory, then "a more careful induction than has hitherto been presented" would be needed ("The Marking System in Theory," *Pedagogical Seminary* 21 [1914]: 277). Hopkins, nevertheless, believed that the Board scores should follow a normal distribution.

66 *Twenty-First Annual Report of the Secretary* (New York: College Entrance Examination Board, 1920) 6.

67 Brigham, *Error* viii.

68 Claude M. Fuess, *The College Board: Its First Fifty Years* (New York: Columbia UP, 1950) 95.

69 Brigham, *Error* ix. These names appear as authors of the "First Annual Report of the Commission on Scholastic Aptitude Tests, 1926." The first six annual reports (1926–1931) are included in *A Study of Error.*

70 First Annual Report, in *Error* 331–339. See also Ida M. Lawrence, Gretchen W. Rigol, Thomas Van Essen, and Carol A. Jackson, *A Historical Perspective on the Content of the SAT*, College Board Research Report No. 2003–3, ETS-RR-03-10 (New York: College Board, 2003).

71 Downey 14.

72 Recognizing that "considerable interest attaches to the use of the scholastic aptitude test as a method of predicting college grades," Brigham correlated the SAT with freshman grades in 1927, the first year that such a relational study was possible. By 1931, it was possible to correlate the SAT with class standing during four years of

college. Cecil M. Broyler, Brigham's statistical colleague and author of the 1931 report, wrote of the validity of the SAT: "It is impossible to state the validity of any test as distinct from the situation in which the measure of validity is determined. This is particularly true of the scholastic aptitude test, which is used at institutions having different philosophies of education, different courses of study, different standards of grading, and different sorts of student bodies. A test which gives reliable and homogeneous scores may have to be used in different ways at different places." "Sixth Annual Report of the Commission on Scholastic Aptitude Tests, 1931," in *Error* 384.

73 Brigham claimed as his own the invention of an experimental section in test development: "the idea of using the last half-hour of an examination period for testing test items, of printing many of these experimental tests and of reporting scores on the basis of the core tests only…originated with the author" (viii).

74 Brigham carried forward key aspects of theory-building from each theorist. From Titchener, he advanced the idea of the scientific empiricism as a basis for knowledge: "In the light of what we have already said," Titchener wrote in *Systematic Psychology: Prolegomena*, "there can be but one task for science to perform. It must try, without distortion of the facts from which it starts, to work up observational knowledge-of-acquaintance into a body of knowledge-about that shall be manageable, compassable, available, communicable. If we turn, now, to recent discussions of the question, we find that they converge precisely upon this result. For a long time science was confused, and failed to realize its proper business; but there is general agreement at the present day that the problem of science may be summed up in the single word 'description.' When a qualification is added, the phrase runs 'the simplest possible description' or 'description in the simplest terms'" (qtd. in Brigham, *Error* 3.) From Dewey, Brigham embraced the pragmatist's love of the particular: "The problem of knowledge as conceived in the industry of epistemology is the problem of knowledge *in general*—of the possibility, extent, and validity of knowledge in general. What does this 'in general' mean? In ordinary life there are problems a-plenty of knowledge in particular; every conclusion we try to reach, theoretical or practical, affords such a problem. But there is no problem of knowledge in general.… The problem of knowledge *überhaupt* exists because it is assumed that there is a knower in general, who is outside of the world to be known, and who is defined in terms antithetical to the traits of the world" (from *A Recovery of Philosophy in Creative Intelligence*, qtd. in Brigham, *A Study of Error* 12). After evoking both a need for empirical observation and a call to pragmatism, Brigham reproduced a basic semiotic triangle—with the three corners representing thought, symbol, and referent—from *The Meaning of Meaning* by C. K. Odgen and I. A. Richards. As Odgen and Richards argue: "We are able largely by means of symbols defined in terms of one another to compound references, or in other words to abstract common parts of different references—to distinguish, to compare, and to connect references in, to, and at, various levels of generality. The compounding of all these diverse modes of adaptation into a specific judgment is the process generally alluded to as Thinking, this activity being commonly maintained through any long train by the use of symbols" (qtd. in Brigham, *A Study of Error* 14).

The systematic, empirical study of symbols thus became the theoretical basis of Brigham's item analysis.

75 Brigham, *Error* 45.

76 Brigham, *Error* 46.

77 Brigham, *Error* ix.

78 A. E. Hamilton, "Eugenics," *Pedagogical Seminary* 21 (1914): 57.

79 F. Scott Fitzgerald, *The Great Gatsby* (1925; New York: Collier, 1986) 13.

80 Carl Campbell Brigham, "Intelligence Tests of Immigrant Groups," *Psychological Review* 38 (1930): 158–165.

81 Brigham, "Intelligence Tests" 158.

82 Brigham, "Intelligence Tests" 159.

83 Brigham cites T. L. Kelley's *Interpretation of Educational Measurement* (Chicago: World Book, 1927) for his enumeration of different intellectual traits.

84 Brigham, "Intelligence Tests" 164.

85 Brigham, "Intelligence Tests" 165.

86 Brigham, *Error* 22. For more on Spearman's advocacy of a theory of general intelligence, see his *The Abilities of Man: Their Nature and Measurement* (New York: Macmillan, 1927). For an analysis of the flaws in the formulation of Spearman's *g*, see Gould 250–272.

87 Brigham, *Error* 28.

88 Saretzky's "Carl Campbell Brigham, the Native Intelligence Hypothesis, and the Scholastic Aptitude Test" carefully documents Brigham's rejection of the race hypothesis.

89 E. G. Boring, "Intelligence as the Tests Test It," *New Republic*, 6 June 1923: 35. For an examination of the relationship between Boring and Brigham, see Dale Stout and Sue Stuart, "E. G. Boring's Review of Brigham's *A Study of American Intelligence*: A Case Study in the Politics of Reviews," *Social Studies of Science* 21 (1991): 133-142.

90 Fuess 110.

91 Downey 30.

92 Brigham, *Error* 28.

93 Fuess 37. Examinations were given in chemistry, English, French, German, Greek, history, Latin, mathematics, and physics (40).

94 A. Lawrence Lowell, "The Art of Examination," *Atlantic Monthly*, Jan. 1926: 58–66; rpt. in *The Work of the College Entrance Examination Board, 1901–1925* (New York: Ginn, 1926) 31–43. That the College Board reprinted this article in its own volume suggests the importance of the movement away from restricted examinations toward comprehensive examinations. The first mention of a comprehensive examination was made in the *Fourteenth Annual Report of the Secretary*, September 1, 1914: "By this term [comprehensive examination] is implied an examination occupying a period of three or four hours designed to test the candidate's intelligence and maturity as well as his general mastery of a certain field of study. Such an examination should be so framed as to give the candidate opportunity to exhibit his power to think independently and to compare or correlate different parts of the field" (*Work of the College Entrance Examination Board* 130).

95 Lowell, "The Art of Examination" 63.

96 *Entrance English Questions Set by the College Entrance Examination Board, 1901–1923* (Boston: Ginn, 1924) 28–29.

97 Rpt. of the 1933 Comprehensive Examination in English as an appendix in Carl Campbell Brigham, *The Reading of the Comprehensive Examination in English: An Analysis of the Procedures Followed During the Five Reading Periods from 1929–1933* (Princeton: Princeton UP, 1934).

98 Fuess 85.

99 Brigham, *Comprehensive Examination* i.

100 Boring, *A History of Experimental Psychology*, 2nd ed. (New York: Appleton, 1950) 575.

101 Boring, *Experimental Psychology* 569.

102 "Objective Tests in Literature," Editorial, *English Journal* 17.3 (1928):252.

103 Charles Swain Thomas, "The Examinations in English," *English Journal* 21.6 (1932): 448.

104 Thomas, "The Examinations in English" 446.

105 Brigham, *Comprehensive Examination* i.

106 Brigham, *Comprehensive Examination* 1–2.

107 Brigham was in search of correlations between readers that would be nearly perfect (.9 and above), the kind of correlation found among multiple-choice items scored by clerks. It is interesting to note that Brigham, theorizing on what could be learned

from the 1933 study, set .6 as an acceptable correlation in the future (30). Perhaps he realized that clerical evaluation of multiple-choice responses and human scoring of essays are two very different matters. Perhaps the semiotic triangle had an impact on his view of the complexity of evaluating writing ability. In any case, Brigham had certainly come to recognize the role that context plays in evaluating an individual.

108 Brigham, *Comprehensive Examination* 4.

109 Brigham, *Comprehensive Examination* 6.

110 Thomas D. Snyder, ed., *120 Years of American Education: A Statistical Portrait* (Washington: National Center for Educational Statistics, 1993). See 65 and Table 24. For more on the economics of the Depression from a contemporary point of view, see Cornelius Daniel Bremmer, "American Bank Failures," diss., Columbia U, 1935.

111 Brigham, *Comprehensive Examination* 6.

112 Brigham, *Comprehensive Examination* 6.

113 Brigham, *Comprehensive Examination* 10.

114 Brigham, *Comprehensive Examination* 19.

115 Brigham, *Comprehensive Examination* 26.

116 Brigham, *Comprehensive Examination* 26.

117 Brigham, *Comprehensive Examination* 41.

118 Brigham, *Comprehensive Examination* 21.

119 Brigham, *Comprehensive Examination* 21–22.

120 Brigham, *Comprehensive Examination* 30.

121 Brigham, *Comprehensive Examination* 30.

122 Snyder, *120 Years of American Education* 65.

123 Fuess 111.

124 Downey 36.

125 Qtd. in Fuess 110.

126 Fuess 111. In response to the request to recommend "ways and means by which the examinations of the Board may be given greater prognostic value," Brigham replied: "The conflicting motives would be most easily brought to light by asking the Board to decide whether its examinations should measure *institutions* or *individuals*. The

Board's present high position in the educational world is the direct result of its efficacy as a form of *institutional* control. Its chief weakness lies in its somewhat inadequate descriptions of individuals seeking admission to college." (Qtd. in Fuess 112.)

127 From information provided in Fuess 112.

128 Carl Campbell Brigham, "The Place of Research in a Testing Organization," *School and Society*, 11 (1937): 756. In his 1937 article, Brigham consciously reflects back to his 1930 "Intelligence Tests of Immigrant Groups." "The writer, along with most of his friends," Brigham now wrote in 1937, "is guilty on all counts enumerated in the diatribe, and he requests, therefore, that the remarks be considered neither a personal accusation nor a confession" (756). Brigham, it seemed, did not wish his current statements to be received as yet another apology.

129 Brigham, "The Place of Research" 756.

130 Brigham, "The Place of Research" 758.

131 Brigham, "The Place of Research" 758.

132 This observation is made both by Fuess (110–119) and by Downey (31–38), and the evidence points to Brigham's lasting impact. With the threat of war growing, Brigham was appointed expert consultant to the secretary of war because of his earlier experiences with army testing. His work centered on tests for officer selection. In addition, Brigham was appointed to the Social Science Research Council to assemble a roster of scientific personnel; this central registry, Downey notes, was invaluable in mobilizing American scientists and technicians in World War II. An early heart attack in 1937 warned of failing health and, after a long illness, Brigham died in 1943.

Chapter 3
Irresistible Colored Beads, 1937–1947

The late morning air was chilly. The admissions director at Princeton University, Radcliffe Heermance, had called them together. Richard Mott Gummere and Edward Simpson Noyes sat in front of a wood fire in Dean Heermance's Princeton study. Gummere was the chairman of the Commission of Admissions at Harvard University; Noyes was an associate professor of English and chairman of the Board of Admissions at Yale University. Friends referred to them as The Three Musketeers.

Heermance had called his colleagues together on a Sunday morning in December 1941 to consider a new agenda for the College Board's schedule of admission tests. Heermance broached the subject: Princeton, he felt, might shortly turn to the April tests given by the College Board; the June tests, with their required written essays, simply did not serve Princeton's admission schedule as well as did the earlier April tests, which used the objective items found in the Scholastic Aptitude Test. Gummere and Noyes were in sympathy but thought the idea too radical a departure from tradition, even for 1941.

They sat smoking after lunch when the call came. "Well, I'll be damned," Heermance was heard to say. He returned with news of Pearl Harbor. "Then and there," Claude Fuess recalled in his account of that meeting, they agreed that "an entire change in the Board's program could not be avoided."[1]

The next morning Heermance met with his administrative colleagues at Princeton; Gummere phoned Harvard and Noyes phoned Yale. Together, the three men planned to shift the date of admissions to April to assist the war effort: year-round instruction would accelerate training of those deferred students who would, upon completion of their education, be called to active service.[2] With the help of George W. Mullins, the executive secretary of the College Board, the three men crafted a letter for national newspaper distribution. Entitled "Harvard, Princeton, and Yale Announce War-Time Changes in Curriculum and Plans for Admission," it began with a statement of unity:

> The three universities will move together to a war-time footing. Provision will be made for year-round instruction, so as to accelerate training for those students who may be called to service. In all three universities, studies will continue throughout the summer. Further announcements of details will be made separately by the three universities.
>
> In order to make possible early selection of the next entering class, so that Freshmen who wish to participate in the accelerated curriculum may be ready to start work in late June or early July, Harvard, Princeton, and Yale announce, for the duration of the emergency, a plan by which applicants may be notified of admission early in May. As before, chief weight will be laid on the applicants' records in secondary school. As validating tests, the three universities will use, for most applicants, the April series provided by the College Entrance Examination Board. These tests consist of the Scholastic Aptitude Test on the morning of Saturday, April 11, and a series of achievement tests in languages, sciences, and social sciences on that afternoon.[3]

Soon after, the women's colleges—Barnard, Bryn Mawr, Mount Holyoke, Radcliffe, Smith, Vassar, and Wellesley—joined the shift to the April examinations, as did Haverford, Wells, and Wheaton. Mullins wrote: "An analysis of the estimated 10,000 candidates who might have been expected to take the June essay examinations in 1942 indicated that 6,500 would be transferred to the April tests. Of the remaining 3,500 there was some doubt as to how many might be expected to take the June examinations."[4] The estimate was quite correct. In June 1941, 12,445 candidates provided essay answers on their admissions test; in June 1942, this number plummeted to 5,320. In April 1941, 10,799 students took the SAT; in April 1942, the number rose sharply to 16,626.[5] Expenditures for "Reading, Scoring, and Reporting" also dropped sharply. The 1942 cost for the multiple-choice examinations totaled only $7,659.86[6]; the 1941 cost for the same line item ("Reading and Scoring") had been $40,744.96.[7]

The three-hour Comprehensive Examination in English had been eliminated, thus ending the essay tests that had been the board's hallmark procedure since its founding in 1900. As suited to the efficiency of war as the army alpha and beta tests had been in the placement of recruits in 1917, the items of the SAT—seemingly objective in nature because their multiple-choice questions prompted a single correct answer—were now becoming established as the most efficient method for identifying those who should continue their education in order, later, to be called into active service. In place of writers and readers were now answer sheets "scored mechanically and expeditiously by clerks."[8]

John M. Stalnaker and Edward Simpson Noyes, 1937: Incorporating a New Tradition

When the Board asked for a memorandum analyzing the impact that the shift to the April tests would have for 1942 candidates, it turned to John M. Stalnaker. The protégé of Carl Campbell Brigham, Stalnaker had come to New Jersey in 1936 from the University of Chicago, where he had taken an M.A. degree in 1928. Stalnaker had taught at Purdue and had served on the examining staff at Chicago from 1931 to 1936 before taking his appointment as an assistant professor of psychology at Princeton University with his mentor.

Stalnaker had been interested in writing assessment from the start of his career. The University of Chicago had instituted a plan requiring students to pass six comprehensive examinations in order to receive a college certificate, a document certifying that two years' worth of college work had been completed. Included in these examinations was an additional requirement: that the student was to have "acceptable and reliable habits of writing." To demonstrate such habits, the student had to pass an "objective" or "short answer" section (with questions on spelling, word meaning, diction, coherence, wordiness, and paragraph division) and an essay section. In 1932 Stalnaker had described the wordiness test in an article in the *English Journal*. A year later, he analyzed 1,500 student scores on the writing requirement in the same journal. He had given the names of the those students to their composition instructors and asked them to comment on the performance of the students, a measure of the validity of the test. After classifying and qualitatively analyzing the instructors' comments, Stalnaker reported that the objective section of the test was the more valid estimate of student skills. Students who received high essay scores and low objective scores tended to be "an inferior group."[9]

This was just the kind of researcher Brigham was seeking: Stalnaker had experience in large-scale testing, a desire to conduct validity checks on instruments, and an ability to publish and thus carry forward findings to a national audience in order to advance the scientific understanding of human ability. While Brigham may have dismissed the 1928 *English Journal* article advocating objective tests and its 1932 counterpart written by Charles Swain Thomas as artless,[10] it is likely that he was pleased to see the reasoned treatment of the reliable reading of essay tests by John Stalnaker and his wife, Ruth, in the *School Review*. "The significant criterion of a test item, whether the item is in essay or objective form," the husband and wife co-authors had written, "is not its reliability but its validity—the fidelity with which it measures what it was intended to measure."[11] Indeed, the line of argument was identical to that offered by Brigham in his analysis that year of the Comprehensive Examination in English.

John and Ruth Stalnaker. "If care is taken to formulate essay-test questions in such a way that a restricted form of answer is required and if readers will judge papers on the basis of specific predetermined criteria which trial has shown can be consistently evaluated, there is no reason why reliability of reading cannot be measurably improved" (John M. Stalnaker and Ruth C. Stalnaker, "Reliable Reading of Essay Tests," *The School Review* 42.8 [1934]: 605). (Photo Reprinted by Permission of Educational Testing Service. All Rights Reserved.)

Brigham had gone to Chicago and asked Stalnaker to meet with him for dinner in the Stevens Hotel. Stalnaker has been won over by the charm, wit, and insistence on data integrity that were characteristic of the older researcher. Brigham had warned Stalnaker that, as a young midwesterner, he would encounter the self-satisfied superiority of the eastern establishment. But Brigham had also shown Stalnaker his charts and item analyses. "I felt if he were willing to take the risk that I represented," Stalnaker recalled, "I could not resist the opportunity of working with the man who had the evidence from his research and plans for future developments."[12] With Brigham, Stalnaker worked on assessment among his very first projects and made good on his potential to publish his findings in two articles in 1937.

The first, published again in the *English Journal*, dealt with the 1936 comprehensive English examination. Stalnaker took his time in the article, writing in a statesmanlike yet urbane voice that represented the College Board, his new employer. There were, he acknowledged, "antagonistic feelings" between those interested in the demands of test construction (the psychologists) and those interested in the teaching of English (the humanists), but these positions need not have been seen as mutually exclusive:

> If, in his effort to reduce the error in measurement, the technician resorts to indirect devices which the teacher finds unsuitable, the teacher objects strenuously. The technician speaks with equal vigor in opposition to unsound measuring devices proposed or used by the teacher. The intensity of these protests at times makes the groups forget that they are both working toward the same end—an English examination which is sound from every point of view.[13]

This conflict, and its potential resolution, was evident in the College Board's English examination. Consistency of the reading is critical, Stalnaker told his readers, but from 1933 to 1936 that consistency was lacking: no reader-reliability coefficient above .60 was recorded; indeed, a reader reliability of around .90 was desirable. Why did the reliability problem exist? First, the psychology of the readers was a problem. When 81 percent of 6,834 examinations were marked at scores of "C" or below, the scale itself was not achieving its purpose of differentiation. "English readers by and large," he concluded, "do not care to commit themselves by saying a paper is excellent."[14] Indeed, if the papers had not been read a second time and an arbitrary grade of "D" had been assigned, agreement could have been recorded at 37 percent. The actual agreement, obtained "at great expense"—the readers were, after all, paid—was 41 percent. The second readings were hardly worth the effort.

But there was more to the story. The topics themselves were the second problem; there were just too many. The seven topics given in 1936 did not offer "equal opportunity" to the student. The wise student, the English teachers who set the topics predicted, would choose topics such as "Something in contemporary music, sculpture, painting, or architecture that you have tried to understand." The less able students, it was predicted, would select "Some forms of athletics develop character better than others." The predictions held true: only one student in one hundred who wrote on athletics obtained a score of "B" or better. Seventeen students in one hundred, conversely, achieved a grade of "B" or better who wrote on art. Perhaps the poor students selected the topic on athletics, the better ones the topic on art? "Perhaps, perhaps, perhaps," Stalnaker lamented. "But no one can say definitely. No one knows what happened. The student is the scapegoat, for he does not get the grade which represents his ability." The topic formula described by Sir Philip Hartog—"Write anything about something for anybody"—was flawed. "In time, the options must go because the examination cannot become a sound instrument until they do."[15]

But it was Stalnaker's second 1937 article that proclaimed a victory over reliability. In the November 20 issue of *School and Society*, "Essay Examinations Reliably Read" noted a landmark finding that had been achieved by the College Board. Stalnaker had realized the reforms identified in his analysis of Question 6, and the reliability coefficients indicated success—indeed, a greater success than that achieved by Brigham himself.

In his detailed study, *The Reading of the Comprehensive Examination in English: An Analysis of the Procedures Followed During the Five Reading Periods from 1929–1933*, Brigham had used the very best methods to ensure reliability during the 1933 reading. The results were not satisfactory, and he had concluded that "the factors making for unreliability are now so great that the examination should be discontinued unless progress can be made in getting a single stable score which is descriptive of the candidate."[16] Three years later, however, Stalnaker declared in *School and Society* that essays were reliably read at organizations such as the College Entrance Examination Board.

The tone of his two-page article is, indeed, quite matter-of-fact, despite the eye-grabbing title declaring victory on the reliability front. Stalnaker began by reminding readers of early studies demonstrating conclusively that ordinary essay-type examinations were not reliably or consistently evaluated; however, ensuring reliability in objective examinations was merely a matter of "clerical proficiency."[17] While such proficiency ensures "reader" reliabilities of over .99 on objective tests, there are, he claimed, assurances regarding the reliability of essay examinations:

> Essay tests, too, can be so constructed so that they can be reliably read, and if the essay test serves a worth-while function, then means can be devised for reading the papers consistently. The essence of measurement is objectivity and it should, therefore, be no surprise to learn that, if highly consistent reading is to be done, the reading process must be objectified and handled in a quite thoroughly rigorous fashion.[18]

To support his claim, Stalnaker provided data from Table XIII, taken from the 1937 College Board report, demonstrating reliability of the readings in the following examinations: biology, chemistry, English, German, history, Latin, mathematics, physics, and Spanish.[19] "With a single exception [.84 was reported for English], all the papers were read with reliabilities of over .98," he claimed, "and several with reliabilities over .98." He then declared victory:

> Many means are available to improve the reliability of reading, but the results suggest that accurate reading is already being obtained. Cooperation between technician and reader will result in improved procedures which should raise all these reliabilities to even higher figures. However, the present figures indicate consistent reading and should dispel the notion that essay papers can not be read reliably.[20]

In his 1934 study, Brigham had called for greater uniformity both in procedure and in reader selection. In November 1937, Stalnaker had announced the benefits of this uniformity.

A year later, Stalnaker provided a detailed description of his methods (techniques that had yielded that .84 reliability coefficient reported in *School and Society*) in a monograph written with Edward Simpson Noyes, *Report on the English Examination of June 1937: A Description of the Procedures Used in Preparing and Reading the Examination in English and an Analysis of the Results of the Reading*. Noyes was the ideal co-author. As an associate professor of English with a Ph.D. from Yale (class of 1913), Noyes had collected and edited the letters of Tobias Smollett in 1926 and had, in 1933, edited a volume of readings in the modern essay. In 1938 he was serving as chairman of the Board of Admissions at Yale, and he had served as a chief reader in English for the College Board. Noyes was also an admirer of Carl Campbell Brigham.

Edward Simpson Noyes at the Dedication Ceremony of the Carl Campbell Brigham Library, Educational Testing Service. "From the time of that first meeting, I became one of Carl Brigham's ardent admirers. I cherish the memory of his friendship, and the perspective of time has given me a far broader comprehension of the importance of his work. To that work, no one connected with the College Board can be anything but enthusiastic in paying tribute, as no one who knew him can help recalling his sympathy, his humor" (Dedication Ceremony [ETS Archives: November 12, 1961] 14) (Photo Reprinted by Permission of Educational Testing Service. All Rights Reserved.)

Noyes had met Brigham in the 1930s and had been pleased to find that the psychologist, statistician, and creator of objective tests, "then an anathema to practically every teacher of English in the country," was in reality a humanist well read in literature.[21] The co-authorship of Noyes, an associate professor of English At Yale, and Stalnaker, an associate professor of psychology at Princeton (he had been promoted in 1937, only a year after his arrival), was the very incorporation of humanistic and psychometric traditions.

The tone of this 1938 volume, published by the College Board, is quite different from the experimental tone of Brigham's 1934 analysis, published by Princeton University Press. Brigham's report of research was of trial and error, of an experiment as yet unproven in worth. Noyes and Stalnaker are writing to certify that the four intervening years had been used at the Board to define a process that was now effective, so much so that a description of the process was in order:

> The purpose of this bulletin is to describe the methods of preparing, holding, and reading the comprehensive English examination of June 1937. Teachers in the colleges and the secondary schools are rightfully curious about the procedures of the College Entrance Examination Board, and the Board, in turn, is anxious to have its procedures known by all persons interested.[22]

Referring to the 1931 report of the Commission on English, a committee appointed by the College Board and chaired by Charles Swain Thomas,[23] Noyes and Brigham recalled that committee's definition of the requirements in English, designed to "develop in the student (1) the ability to read with understanding, (2) knowledge and judgment of literature, and (3) accurate thinking and power in oral and written expression." But the examination developed by the College Board was additionally significant: the skills learned in English were able to be transferred to other subjects; indeed, it was this notion of transferability that had formed the basis for using the Comprehensive Examination as an admissions examination since 1916: "This training is to be viewed not merely in its bearing upon the student's work in courses in English, but in its relation to his work in all other subjects."[24] With the definition and significance of the examination established, Noyes and Stalnaker recalled Thorndike's famous assertion that whatever exists at all exists in some quantity. Such was the case for the essay. "A student's attainment can be measured," they assure their audience.[25] And since that measurement needed to have "significance as an index either of past attainment or of future promise"—there was an increasing need to demonstrate the validity of these examinations as they related to high-school performance and college success—"it must be assumed further that the ability being measured is one of reasonable stability from day to day for a given person."[26]

With the validity of the requirements in English defined and the potential of predictive power of the examination noted, Noyes and Stalnaker turned to the procedures themselves. The former eight-level scale used by Brigham (a scale from A+ to X) had been abandoned. In its place, a new method had been developed to score the examinations. Instead of the pass-fail system used by Brigham, resting on the pre-determined "D" grade of 60 percent, the new method would be based on the answers the candidates actually presented. These answers would be analyzed and then categorized, and the scales would thus be inductively developed. As the authors reminded their audience, even the instruction sheet was "not prepared a priori, but [rather] the categories were based on a study of the actual answers."[27] Then followed thirty pages of questions asked at the examination, instructions that had been given to the readers, and sample answers with points awarded and comment provided. The scoring scales varied according to the six questions that had been asked. The answer to Question 1 below, for example, was to be composed in 30 minutes:

> Besides the main characters in a novel or plan, there are relatively unimportant persons who contribute to its total effect by serving as instruments in the plot, providing humor, giving local color, or commenting on the action and theme of the story.
>
> Directions: From each of three novels and three plays that you have read, name one minor character such as this quotation describes, and, by using specific illustrations, show in a few sentences what each character contributes to the work in which he appears. The question calls for six brief answers.[28]

Readers were then to score answers to Question 1 on a four-point scale. Answers to Question 2 were to be composed in 25 minutes, to Question 3 in 20 minutes, to Question 4 in 25 minutes, and to Question 5 in 20 minutes. Question 6, the essay, was to be written in 60 minutes:

> Directions: Write a composition of about 350 words, entitled "the Ruling Passion." In your composition develop and illustrate ideas found in the following passage. As illustrations choose three characters from your reading in history or biography, or three from your reading in other literature, or three from contemporary life.
>
> "In every life there is a ruling passion. People are ruled by such passions as the love of honor, money, children, friends, art, or nature; by the love of a man for a woman; or if a woman for a man; by ambition or by pride; by a sense of duty or a sense of loyalty; by the desire for revenge, or the desire to stir up strife. With some people this single passion seems to rule throughout life; with others the rule is shorter lived. Some people recognize that their lives are controlled by a ruling passion; some do not. When circumstances operate to prevent a person from finding expression of, or satisfaction in, his ruling passion, then character emerges...."
>
> —Henry Van Dyke, *The Ruling Passion* (adapted)[29]

Readers were to score Question 6 using three evaluation categories: organization, paragraphing, and sentences—each of which included a four-point scoring scale:

I. Organization

Points	
1	*Following Directions*: Three illustrations chosen from proper categories.
1	*Simple Unity*: Three ruling passions, expressly or implicitly described.
2	*Qualifying Ideas*: These ideas are:
	(a) Length of rule of passion
	(b) Character's consciousness of rule
	(c) Effect on character of passion when checked
	Points are to be given under the following conditions:
	(1) Partial recognition of *c*—1 point
	(2) Threefold recognition of *a* or *b*—1 point
	(3) Threefold recognition of *c*—2 points
	(4) Partial recognition of *c* and partial recognition of either *a* or *b*—2 points

II. Paragraphing

Points	
1	*Paragraphing*: To show structure
1	*Coherence*: Logical relation of sentences; transition
2	*Relevance*: Points given as follows:
	(1) Thin *or* irrelevant material—no points
	(2) Average relevant material—1 point
	(3) Well chosen, well developed material—2 points

III. Sentences

Points	
2	*Mechanics*: Spelling, punctuation, grammar, loose or unidiomatic construction
1	*Diction*: Good vocabulary, *consistently* employed
1	*Sentences*: Distinguished by variety, strength, or some special quality[30]

The new system, developed by William Merritt Sale, Jr., of Cornell University, with the assistance of H. E. Joyce of Dartmouth, was designed to substitute a more careful analysis of the essays. "It is certain," the authors felt, "that the reading of the theme was done with a closer approach to uniform standards than ever before."[31]

On June 21, 1937, over 7,000 candidates sat down in the morning "from Maine to California in the United States, and in such foreign cities as London, Paris, Berlin, Geneva, and Shanghai" to write for 190 minutes.[32] Their papers would be graded by this scheme. As had been the case with Brigham's 1934 study, Noyes and Stalnaker used the best assessment methods known. The a priori scale had been developed from pre-testing.

As the completed examinations arrived, the answers were classified according to their merit, and descriptions were developed of the categories. Typical answers were selected and mimeographed. "This process requires much time and thought, but it is essential if uniform grading standards are to be approached," Noyes and Stalnaker reminded their audience. "It is one

ENGLISH 1937 T=

	I READER NO.	II	III	IV	V	VI READER NO.
		READER NO.		READER NO		
	4 POINTS EACH	4 POINTS EACH	3 POINTS EACH	4 POINTS EACH	2 POINTS EACH	4 POINTS EACH
NOVELS	1	a	a	a	a	Organ.
	2	b	b	b	b	Para.
	3			c	c	Sent.
PLAYS	1			d	d	
	2				e	
	3				f	

"The method of reading, once approximate standardization had been effected, was simple. Aides distributed to each Table the answer books on which booksheets, like the facsimile given [above], had been stapled. Thus a Reader simply opened the book to the answer for which he was responsible, studied it with the instruction sheet and sample answers, and set down the grade in the proper box on the book-sheet, beneath his own number, which he had been given on the first day. At stated intervals the aides removed books which had been graded at one Table and transferred them, to a Table in a different Group, until the booksheets had been completely filled in. The book was then ready for the tabulators. Thus each book received the entirely independent judgment of four different Readers, on its four separate sections. If, in the tabulating of these four grades, serious discrepancies became apparent, the book was taken out for re-reading" (Edward Simpson Noyes and John Marshall Stalnaker, *Report on the English Examination of June 1937* [New York: College Entrance Examination Board, 1938] 47–48). (Reproduced with permission of the College Board. All rights reserved. www.collegeboard.com)

of the most important parts of the reading of the paper, and the fourteen experienced readers spent two days and a half of exhaustive work before it was completed."[33] At the end of the process, instruction sheets covering each question—as well as illustrative answers—had been prepared in order to train the main group of readers.

The process had begun while the candidates were writing their answers. The categories of answers and sample sets had been prepared between June 21 and June 23. On June 24, a Thursday, the main group of readers arrived; their work was completed on the next Thursday, July 1.

Had the process achieved uniformity among the readers? The first check was to select 1,149 books at random, remove the scoring sheets, replace them with fresh sheets, and send them back for scoring. If wide variations were discovered between the first and second set of grades, more books were re-read, while those on which "discrepancies" were noted were sent to Table Leaders (responsible for coordinating groups of readers) or the Chief Reader (responsible for the reading process in its entirety) for decision. Nearly one-sixth of the total number of answer books for Questions 1 through 6 were thus read with a reliability of .84. "It was then found that the standardization, while by no means perfect (in grading English papers, absolute uniformity has never been attained and undoubtedly never can be), was superior to that achieved on previous papers, and the other books were therefore not re-read."[34] In analyzing the interrelations among the six questions asked on the examination, the sixth question, the essay, had "the most in common" with the other questions, drawing the highest correlation of .46 with Question 1.[35] Indeed, the correlation of the readers judging the essay, Question 6, had been raised from .55 in 1936 to .68 in 1937.[36]

The report concluded with a brief study of the correlation of the total English grade and the Scholastic Aptitude Test. The use of English, as defined by the 1931 Commission on English, was similar to that measured by the SAT: precision, range of vocabulary, accuracy in the use of connectives, clarity in perceiving the relevance of a figure of speech, and the internal logic consistency of a short paragraph were "clearly tested by the Scholastic Aptitude Test."[37] Noyes and Stalnaker then listed, without elaborative comment, the "pertinence" of the correlations of the Comprehensive Examination in English (that is, of all of the written answers) and the SAT (consisting only of objective items): .57 for 1937; .63 for 1936; .59 for 1935; .61 for 1934; .60 for 1933; and .53 for 1932.

A set of comments by the readers was then provided, the majority of which praise the new process of reading the essay: "Both the Question 6 itself and the system of reading have proved more satisfactory than I expected," one reader noted. "And doubts I had have been largely removed."[38] Suggestions for improving the examination, the authors wrote, would be welcomed.

While the reading had yielded correlations lower that that found in other board examinations—the reliability in history was .93 for 1937, and the science papers yielded reader reliabilities of .96 to .99—English was "fundamentally a more difficult paper to read, possibly primarily because of factual content on which to base a grade, and reliabilities as high as .84 are rare." The authors nevertheless hoped "that the new method of reading will, when it is perfected, yield Reader reliabilities approximating those obtained in other subjects."[39]

When Noyes and Stalnaker published their 1937 study, they claimed to do no more than "explain the goals set by the Examiners and Readers."[40] Yet they were clearly proud of the method of assessment of Question 6, the essay. They had discovered a way of scoring the theme in detail according to organization, paragraphing, and sentences. The new method Sale had devised avoided the markings of "A" to "F" and their associated notions of passing or failing and, rather, substituted a more discrete judgment of the essay according to the three main scoring categories. "It is fair to say," Noyes and Stalnaker had noted, "that this radical departure aroused much comment among the Readers of Group IV [Sale's group] and that at first this comment was not entirely favorable. It is also fair to say that before the reading ended, practically all the Readers had become enthusiastic in their approval of the system. It is certain that the reading of the theme was done with a closer approach to uniform standards than ever before."[41] So great was the enthusiasm for this new scoring method—"an important step in the effort to attain reasonable uniformity of judgments in the answers to the essay question"[42]—that it was employed by the College Board and reported by Noyes, Stalnaker, and their new co-author, Sale, in their 1945 publication, *Report on the First Six Tests in English Composition*. The new method, however, would pose more problems than anyone had anticipated.

Noyes, Sale, Stalnaker, and the Failure of Reliability, 1944

There were similarities between the *Report on the First Six Tests in English Composition, with Sample Answers from the Tests of April and June 1944* and the earlier *Report of the English Examinations of June 1937*. The 1945 report, the authors stated, had been written for reasons similar to that of the 1937 report: so that "a useful document for many people" would be available.[43] As well, the new team of Noyes, Sale, and Stalnaker included fifty-two pages covering the questions that had been asked, the instructions given to the readers, and the sample answers, with points awarded and comments. But the confidence of the 1937 report was absent. In 1945, the authors revealed that "The Board is eager to have teachers and administrators in school and college understand the special problems presented by a one-hour test in composition, and the efforts that have been made and are still being made by Examiners and Readers alike towards the solution of these problems."[44] Where there had been confidence in 1937, in 1945 there were now special problems that needed elaboration.

The shift in tone toward the essay examination was apparent in Stalnaker's position on reliability. In his 1937 *School and Society* proclamation, Stalnaker had declared that the empirical evidence of consistent reading should "dispel the notion that essay papers can not be read reliably."[45] By 1943 (a testing period covered in the 1945 report) his position had been reversed, and he had adopted a new rhetoric in the College Board's *Forty-Third Annual Report of the Executive Secretary*:

> The type of test so highly valued by teachers of English, which requires the candidate to write a theme or essay, is not a worth-while testing device. Whether or not the writing of essays as a means of teaching writing deserves the place it has in the secondary school classroom may be equally questioned. Eventually, it is hoped, sufficient evidence will be accumulated to outlaw forever the "write-a-theme-on…" type of examination.[46]

Stalnaker's shift in position was due to the reinstatement of the essay examination in 1943. What he found on second glance was an expensive assessment process that, with a war on, was not worth the effort.

After the Board discontinued the three-hour June comprehensive examination following Pearl Harbor, no candidate had written an essay on any of the College Board tests—the achievement tests that had been offered were given using limited-response, objective items. "Little wonder," Orville Palmer noted some sixteen years later, "the immediately forthcoming protests of English teachers were vehement and bitter."[47] And so in April 1943 the Board included a one-hour test in English composition to be included in the achievement tests. The SAT during this period had remained in place, drawing the largest number of candidates: 22,467 in 1942; 1,735 in January 1943; and 14,000 in April 1943. The English achievement test, however, proved very much in demand. When it was offered again in April 1943, 10,574 candidates wrote essays. English proved to be the most popular of the achievement tests.[48]

In that Question 6, the essay question, had proven so viable in the 1937 study, it must have seemed a natural candidate for the 1943 reinstated essay test. The essay, after all, had correlated best with the other questions in the 1937 analysis; the readers themselves had "become enthusiastic in their approval" of the scoring system devised by Sale; and Stalnaker himself had gone on record six years earlier in the *English Journal* in favor of eliminating essay question options and asking all candidates to "run the same race." As Noyes, Sale, and Stalnaker wrote regarding the aim of the test:

> Obviously, this test cannot be directly one of literary knowledge or background, although the Examiners and Readers alike would probably agree that thorough training in reading is one of the best fundamental preparations for it. Nor is it a test of ability in so-called creative writing, or of writing the *belles-lettres* tradition. The artist can scarcely be required to create on demand, and in a brief time. In college, students must constantly express in writing their ideas and the results of their study, not in English courses alone, but in all courses. The English composition test, therefore, should provide candidates with an opportunity to demonstrate their normal skill in written expression, and should measure that skill.
>
> A problem at once arose regarding the form which the test should take. A theme question, for which one hour had been allowed, had traditionally formed Part III of the previous comprehensive English examinations [Question 6]. Hence it was natural for the Examiners, faced with a mandate to provide a one-hour test in composition, to select the theme or essay type of test. Since previous experience had shown the impossibility of grading themes on different topics according to a common standard, one topic only was given.[49]

The co-authors had, thus, distanced themselves from any lingering tradition of the old Restricted Examinations, criticized by Charles Swain Thomas' Commission on English in 1931 and formally abandoned in 1935 by the College Board. Gone was any question which, in the Commission's words, "throws such stress on details, both in questions on the nomenclature of theoretical grammar and in questions on literature, that it tends to lose sight of the broader, more essential aspects in training in composition and literary study, or, at least, does not give these aspects the attention they deserve."[50]

In place of the singular text-based world of Barrett Wendell and linguistically oriented world of George Lyman Kittredge was a new, more democratic approach in which expression of normal skills would be measured. The vehicle of this expression had also shifted. Gone were questions on the performance of Pyramus and Thisbe before Duke Theseus.[51] Present instead were questions concerning media and its influence on American life. Radio had brought the news of December 7, and the nation had listened as Roosevelt recalled that infamous date and asked Congress to declare war on Japan. Two years later, the nation was listening to *The Kate Smith Hour* and Jack Benny's *The Jello-Program*. Bob Hope's *The Pepsodent Show* was broadcast from military bases around the country. Ovaltine sponsored *Captain Midnight*; there were burnished bronze medals of membership for the faithful and secret codes worked into the story line that only members would know. There was Edward R. Murrow reporting from London during the blitz, but by 1943 there was also *Terry and the Pirates* with Nazi and fascist villians. Curiosity about the war in Europe could be satisfied by listening to the CBS European broadcast boys of Murrow, but curiosity about the Far East could just as easily, by the turn of a dial, be satisfied by listening to The Dragon Lady—a former enemy of Terry, listeners knew, who was now working with him to destroy a Japanese plantation run by Baron Von Krell.[52]

Clearly, a discerning analysis was needed, and the College Board rose to the occasion with its 1943 question for the April examination:

> *Directions*: The following paragraphs state three criticisms of the radio.
>
> In a theme of from 400 to 500 words discuss each of these criticisms. In your discussion of each criticism you may support or attack it, or adopt a middle ground. In all three cases, however, illustrate by description of a specific program the position you adopt and the point you are making.
>
> Your theme will be graded on
> 1. Material: your use of specific and pertinent evidence;
> 2. Organization: of the theme as a whole and of the separate paragraphs;
> 3. Style: the clarity and accuracy of your writing.
>
> *Note*: You will be given a special answer booklet in which to write your theme.
>
> Critics of the radio allege that the tendency of radio programs is to lull listeners into a state of unquestioning receptivity, thereby preventing them from using their reasoning powers. The kind of entertainment offered by the radio must make its appeal to thousands; it is therefore pitched at a relatively low level and, proving successful, is monotonously repeated. It is fatally easy to sit back and listen uncritically to such programs. The state of mind encouraged by this attitude is undiscriminating; the taste of the audience becomes standardized.
>
> Further, these critics maintain that under the ceaseless barrage of advertising broadcasts the American way of life is becoming stereotyped. People are coming more and more to eat, drink, wear, buy, believe, think, and live alike; they thus become standardized as consumers of goods as well as of entertainment.
>
> Finally, the critics charge that the picture of life presented by radio fiction in serials or drama is hackneyed and sentimental. In its stock of characters and situations, in its over-simplified or romantic solutions for the problems with which it deals, it is like bad fiction of any kind, but more dangerous, since it reaches a public larger than the reading public.[53]

Other questions focused on the shocks of war in communities (June 1943), the revolt of an individual against restrictions (December 1943), and misinterpretation of a given situation (June 1944). Each question reflected the fundamental importance of language as a basic instrument in maintaining a democratic way of life, as expressed in "Basic Aims for English Instruction in American Schools" (1942).[54] Such themes could be found in popular textbooks such as S. I. Hayakawa's 1941 *Language in Thought and Action.* Building on the work of semanticist Alfred Korzybski, Hayakawa encouraged his students to see beyond a "two-valued orientation ("I am right and everybody else is wrong") and value, rather, a "multi-valued orientation" ("I don't know—let's see").[55] There was nothing wrong with the categorical, value laden system of Aristotelian logic, Hayakawa told his students; it was just that "anyone whose knowledge and thinking are limited to Aristotle's can hardly behave sanely in *our* time."[56]

In 1937, the essay had been scored on organization, paragraphing, and sentences. Now, in the scoring sessions from April 1943 until June 1944, the essays were scored on the following scale: I. Material (subdivided into categories of experience, character, change, illustrations); II: Organization (subdivided into proportion, movement of thought, paragraphing, and transitions); and III: Style (subdivided into spelling, punctuation, vocabulary, and sentence structure). Thus, twelve judgments were made about each theme, a slight increase from the nine judgments that had been required in 1937. In 1937, the inter-reader reliability for the entire test had been .84; the essay reliability (Question 6) had been .68. For the readings of April 1943, the reliability had been .67; for June 1943, .66. In the six examination periods covered by the *Report of the First Six Tests of English Composition*, the inter-reader correlations ranged from .58 to .83 with an average of .67 during the period.

While similar correlations had been declared satisfactory in 1937, they were now a cause of distress in 1945 in the absence of supporting correlations from Questions 1 through 5, parts of the examination that had been abandoned when the single essay had been adopted. "The figures," Noyes, Sale, and Stalnaker admit, "are about the same as those for the theme question, taken by itself, of previous comprehensive examinations." Yet in the absence of answers to the other five questions, the inter-reader correlation coefficients from the essay alone were just too low to be satisfactory. The authors appeared to be at the ends of their wits. An adjustment in the reading procedure of June 1944—undertaken to correct these unsatisfactory correlations and utilizing a 37-point scale—made the reliability correlation even lower, yielding a .59 level of agreement. The authors confessed that "no noteworthy improvement in the reliability of reading has been shown."[57]

The number of readers and essays read had remained similar. Roughly the same number of papers had been read in 1937 (1,149) as in April 1943 (1,051). Roughly one-sixth of the total books had been read twice in 1937; roughly one-tenth of the total books had been read twice in 1943. There were approximately twenty-eight readers in the 1937 study; for the April 1944 test—the test singled out for the most in-depth analysis by Noyes and his colleagues—forty-nine readers were used. Overall, the evaluation conditions were the same. The correlations were similar. What had changed was the critical decision-making point of acceptable reliability when the essay alone (Question 6) was used. In 1937, a correlation of .85 was "unusually high."[58] In 1945, however, the standard had shifted when consideration was made of the essay viewed as a one-item test. As such, this declaration appeared: "Reliabilities of reading should be of the order of .85 or higher before the reading can be deemed satisfactory."[59] Thus, the authors found, the reliability of the scoring system was unsatisfactory for the essay tests given from April 1943 to June 1944. They concluded:

> Much time and thought have been spent in the constant endeavor to improve the reading. With the limits of time allowed both for writing the test and for scoring it, it is not easy to see how more can be done in this respect.[60]

Gone were the assurances made in 1937. Now there were claims of a failure of reliability of essay scoring. Stalnaker hoped that the "write-a-theme-on" essay—the single-item test—would be forever outlawed. Indeed, the few studies made of the 1943 English test, he claimed, do not show the test to be of "significant value" as a means of predicting grades in freshman English. "As was true when the three-hour comprehensive examination in English was offered," he wrote in the 1943 annual report, "the Scholastic Aptitude Test is again found to do a better job in this one respect."[61] If the idea was to place students accurately into the college curriculum, the SAT yielded superior performance.

In a period in which performance was critical, there were larger issues, after all, at stake. Between 1943 and 1944, the United States Navy had turned the tide in the Atlantic by using advanced sonar and radar, as well as new types of torpedoes to defeat Hitler's submarines. Bombardment of Germany had begun. In 1943 General Douglas MacArthur and Admiral Chester Nimitz had battled their way across the Pacific, defeating the imperial fleet and capturing islands close enough to launch bombers that would incinerate Japanese cities. The tests being used to review the potential of recruits to contribute to the science of the war effort—multiple-choice, objective items derived from the SAT format—were fulfilling their reliability duties splendidly and providing information at a much lower cost to an audience more competitive for precious Board resources than English teachers: the Department of the Navy.

The College Board in World War II

When Stalnaker prepared his 1942 memorandum detailing the effect of shifting the examinations to April, an act that removed the essay examination from the College Board tests, he was quick to establish that this shift may have taken place in any event. The three largest users of the College Board tests—Harvard, Princeton, and Yale—were already seriously considering the shift. So, Stalnaker wrote, it would be "wise to look at once toward developing for April 1943 and thereafter a series which will continue to be used after the emergency."[62] Pearl Harbor aside, the time for objective testing had arrived.

The College Board had been involved throughout the 1930s in psychological testing of the armed forces. In 1930 officers at the Bureau of Navigation who were interested in training and selection issues had given College Board tests at the San Diego and Hampton Roads training schools to candidates for admission, and Brigham continued his interest in the development of officer-selection tests during the 1930s.[63] In 1940, Brigham had served as a consultant to the government to help the army design a test battery to identify those with special talents for further training.

When Franklin Roosevelt proclaimed a "date that would live in infamy" to Congress on December 8, 1941, his audience of young radio listeners realized that their lives would now be radically different. During the next four years, the government would put 16,354,000 million men in uniform, and almost 10 million would enter through the draft.[64] While only those setting their sights on college would have been touched by the visible hand of the College Board, now many more of the nation's youth would have their fates determined by testing. The Board itself had acknowledged this fact in its 1942 annual report:

> No narrow view should be taken at the present time of the Board's work and function; useful and practical consideration should be the determining factor in shaping its policies. Broad plans for greater co-operation in the future between school and college need not be discarded, but these should be put in the background. Every effort must now be centered on the present with help for the war effort as the paramount concern.[65]

To this end, the Executive Committee approved plans for national service work. Five projects for the government were underway at the Board's Research and Statistical Laboratory in Princeton. It was "a deep satisfaction that the type and quality of the work the Board has been doing, its adequate modern equipment, and the talents of its personnel have found a useful place in the important work related to the war effort and the nation."[66] The

Executive Committee also released the associate secretary of the Board to work on the war effort. John Stalnaker was now chairman of the Committee on Service Personnel—Selection and Training.

By 1943, the Board had felt the full impact of dedicating itself to the war effort. The Qualifying Test for Civilians had been instituted, a nationwide screening program that would measure and assess students for the Navy College Training Program. On April 2, 1943, the test was given at more than 13,000 centers in high schools and colleges to approximately 316,000 young men. Stalnaker directed the program with the help of his new assistant, Henry Chauncey. The two men also coordinated tests given on April 20, 1943, to all men enrolled in the Navy Reserve, Class V-1, who had completed three or more semesters of college work; and on September 28, 1943, the men coordinated an achievement test given to Navy V-12 students at 150 colleges. All tests were scored at the Princeton laboratory and sent to the navy.

When the Executive Committee reviewed its financial statement for the period ending September 30, 1944, Claude Fuess, a member of the very first board of trustees and now a custodian of the Board, recalled that the members were startled.[67] While the total operating income for examination fees was $179,033 (a slight rise from the previous year's income of $163,261), the income from special government projects had soared to $337,422 (a dramatic jump from the 1943 total of $202,758). In 1941, the excess of operating income over expenditures had been $18,788; now, in the heat of World War II, the excess was noted at $37,581. In 1941 the Board's main income was from examination fees; in 1944, over 60 percent of its operating income was from special government projects.[68]

When the last of the Qualifying Tests for the armed services was given on April 12, 1945, the total number of young men tested had reached 600,000.[69] Each had been tested on such items as the following:

> "..........is an opinion held in opposition to the established ....: (1) belief .. doctrine (2) stubbornness .. doctrine (3) heresy .. doctrine (4) heresy .. government (5) fascism .. government"[70]

These items were called double definitions, but there were also opposites and analogies, item types taken directly from the SAT. In all, the recruits had been tested on 150 multiple-choice questions that were designed to test verbal, scientific, reading, and mathematical ability. Similar questions were included in the Basic Test Battery, administered to over 2,000,000 recruits, as well as the Officer Qualification and Officer Classification Tests, administered to over 100,000 officers.[71]

In the 1945 *Forty-Fifth Annual Report of the Executive Secretary*, Stalnaker reported on each of these activities, but he also included information on further developments on assessment work in composition conducted subsequent to the report that he, Noyes, and Sale had submitted. In September 1944, four compositions were required in place of the single one formerly required. The reader reliability increased to .89.[72] During the year 1944–1945, the number of questions was lowered to three to allow the candidates more time to write. The reliability ranged from .94 to .97. The data, Stalnaker concluded, were encouraging.[73] While he acknowledged that the objective type of test "has much to be said for it"—it permitted, he noted, wide sampling, economy of time of the person being tested, and quick, cheap, and accurate scoring—such tests had their limitations. "In a field like English composition," he wrote, "the objective test is a feeble instrument. One can but urge that more effort and attention be given to the many problems of improving the preparation and evaluation of the discursive type of test which now seems so essential in a field like English."[74]

The ETS Consolidation

Hitler would commit suicide in a bunker on April 30, 1945, and on September 2 General MacArthur accepted the Japanese surrender on the battleship *Missouri*. The war was over, and in the process questions such as

> WATER is to sponge as INK is to ....
>
> (1) pen (2) bottle (3) write (4) blotter (5) desk[75]

were becoming part of American educational life. In 1948 Willy Loman, messenger from a dying world, had assumed that all tests were the same. Willy was sure that the hard-studying Bernard would give his son, Biff, the answers to the New York State Regents Examination, just as he had done in high school. "You'll give him the answers," Willy says with great agitation. "I do," the misunderstood Bernard yells back, "but I can't on a Regents! That's a state exam! They're liable to arrest me."[76] When Willy tells Biff in *Death of a Salesman* that "Bernard can get the best marks in school, y'understand, but when he gets out in the business world, y'understand, you are going to be five times ahead of him," the audience understood well enough that this was an American tragedy in the making.[77]

That the Board had experienced a radical shift during the war was clear, and it soon became even clearer that the time for a radical change was at hand if it wanted to maintain its dedicated mission to the academy. Its 1946 post-war report noted that "the process of 'turning swords into ploughshares' has not been solely responsible for changes in the scope of the Board's activities."[78] The volume of testing had increased "even beyond generous advanced estimates," and shifts were being made within the organization to accommodate the growing demands for tests. In June 1944 Congress had enacted the Serviceman's Readjustment Act—popularly known as the G.I. Bill—to offer living allowances and tuition to the 15 million soldiers who had gone to war. The College Board had begun to offer a Special Aptitude Test for veterans that could be taken in lieu of the regular Board tests. In support of America's role as a global force was a new foreign student English examination that would "assist the Department of State in eliminating at the source foreign students desirous of federal or other support for study in this country, whose command of English is inadequate."[79] Peacetime work for the Bureau of Navy Personnel continued, and the College Board was now administering the Navy College Aptitude Test for candidates to the Naval Reserve Officers' Training Corps and the Naval Aviation College Program. While the operating income for special government projects had fallen to $184,188.71 (it had been $254,446.85 the previous year), the testing fees had soared to $373,117.00 (from $214,200.00 the previous year).

And the English Composition Test? The 1946 *Annual Report* concluded that the examination "continues to be the major problem of the present series of Achievement Tests. Despite the continued efforts of the examiners and of the readers, the results are still unsatisfactory. The problems involved in developing a reliable essay examination are, if not unsolvable, at least far from being solved at the present time."[80] A possible way of improving the test? A half-hour essay question could be read in all cases by two readers, and in cases of discrepant readings, by a third; and a half-hour objective test could be used to measure qualities such as punctuation, grammar, and usage. Influenced by the success of objective testing and the realization that the essay should be maintained, a new pattern of writing assessment—the objective test combined with the essay test—appeared to have potential.

Yet this new pattern was not the result of policy established by Stalnaker. The death of Brigham in 1943 had left a vacancy in the position of research secretary to the Board, and Stalnaker had resigned on July 1, 1945, to become professor of psychology and dean of students at Stanford University.[81] The strongest, most informed advocates of the assessment of composition abilities were no longer with the Board. Harold O. Gulliksen, professor of psychology at Princeton, was appointed to the position of research secretary, and the position of associate secretary fell to Stalnaker's assistant during the war, Henry Chauncey.[82]

Chauncey had been an assistant dean at Harvard from 1929 to 1943 when he had come to the College Board. He had taken a B.A. from Harvard in 1928 but held no graduate degrees. He played professional baseball and was the traveling companion of the son of Gifford Pinchot, the first head of the U.S Forest Service appointed by Theodore Roosevelt and the famous opponent of John Muir in the 1913 battle for Hetch Hetchy Valley within Yosemite National Park. At the College Board Chauncey had risen rapidly from an associate director of the Army-Navy Qualifying Tests to the associate secretary of the board.

It was Chauncey who worked with the Carnegie Corporation and James Conant, successor to Abbot Lawrence Lowell in 1933 as president of Harvard University, to create the new Educational Testing Service (ETS), a merger of the College Board, the American Council on Education (ACE, a national association of universities, colleges, teachers' colleges, and junior colleges founded in 1918 and directed by George Zook), and the Cooperative Test Service (CTS, the major supplier of tests for the ACE, directed at its founding by Benjamin Wood).[83] When the plan for the merger was put into place on January 1, 1948, Chauncey became the first president.

In 1948, the *College Board Review*, the College Board's glossy new magazine, included a reprint of a speech by Chauncey. The speech was clearly an introduction to the new president of ETS. (The lead to the article notes, almost as an aside, that the College Board "has delegated the technical aspects of its testing activities to the Educational Testing Service.") Chauncey's address, significantly, was given in Highland Park, Illinois—a

Henry Chauncey. "The ETS is a unique organization with a rare opportunity for great service to American education. A year or so ago Dr. Conant, President of Harvard University, whom we are very fortunate to have as Chairman of our Board of Trustees, said that in his opinion the development and application of testing would be the most important factor in education in the years ahead. The challenge to this new organization is tremendous. I know that all of you have devotedly served the agency with which you have been connected and I am confident that the same spirit will give the ETS strength to accomplish the tasks that lie ahead" (Memorandum to Members of the Staff of the Cooperative Test Service, the National Teacher Examinations, the Graduate Record Office, and the College Entrance Examination Board, Dec. 22, 1947 [ETS Archive, Chauncey Merger File, Folder 1-9, 1947]) (Photo Reprinted by Permission of Educational Testing Service. All Rights Reserved.)

new testing market. The visit was a signal that the eastern seaboard educational focus was evaporating in postwar America. Chauncey's address was historical in nature, respectful of the stability of the Board's goals "of conserving and enriching the human resources of this country by helping ensure that the best students get to college...." He reminded an audience just becoming attuned to the dangers of communism that "the star which guides our present course is the star of freedom." He recalled Nicholas Murray Butler and Charles William Eliot; he warned of misuse of test results; he reminded his audience of the need for constant research in testing.

But the end of the address took a new turn: attention was to be afforded not to the system alone but to the individual within the system. "I am no prophet," he concluded:

> My "predictions" are not probably "valid." But everywhere I go, I find increasing interest and new enterprises directed toward the tailoring of education to fit the individual. And I think that this increasing emphasis on the individual student, in the face of growing numbers of students, must mean that testing will play a larger and larger role in college admissions and guidance programs. Not, perhaps, testing as we have known it in the past—testing that measures only isolated hues or qualities of a student's talents—but testing which displays the full spectrum of his personality. Keeping pace with the developments in education, no less a development must take place in testing itself.[84]

The audience reading these remarks in the fall of 1948 was coming to realize America's new global role and its mission: to secure individual freedom through education. In March 1947 Harry S. Truman had declared a war against communism, and Executive Order 9835 had been issued establishing the Federal Employee Loyalty Program to ferret out subversives. During the November presidential election, Whittaker Chambers had identified Alger Hiss to the House Un-American Activities Committee. The domestic, eastern seaboard version of American education was vanishing, and the West was (Frederick Jackson Turner aside) a new frontier for ETS. College enrollment was booming as veterans poured into classrooms under the G.I. Bill. In the fall of 1949, a staggering 2.4 million students entered college—about 15 percent of those aged eighteen to twenty-four.

(When the College Board had been founded, only 2 percent of those aged eighteen to twenty-four were in college classrooms; by the end of Chauncey's presidency, college enrollment would rise by 120 percent, and 35 percent of the population aged eighteen to twenty-four would be enrolled in college.[85]) Among those demanding to see themselves in the American dream were the many black men who had served in the armed forces and who now demanded the right to vote. There were active voter-registration drives in 1945 and 1946 by the National Association for the Advancement of Colored People. Harry Truman established the first President's Committee on Civil Rights and won the 1948 election with a higher percentage of the black vote than Roosevelt had in his four victories. Students who had never before been seen in vast numbers —veterans of the war and refugees from discrimination—would soon appear in the nation's colleges. University researchers of Thorndike's generation had to imagine the writing of the disadvantaged: "I write to say it ain't a square deal" was a sentence that had to be imagined by Hillegas' team to establish a point of zero merit. The writing of the truly undereducated was unimaginable in 1917; soon, for Chauncey and his ETS staff, such writing would be commonplace in the answer books.

In 1937 Brigham, ever prescient, had warned of a market for tests and the dangers that were intrinsic to that market. Now, eleven years later, the consolidation of agencies had come about. Would the new Educational Testing Service advance knowledge, or would it seduce with "the lure of numbers, letters, and pictures—I.Q.'s and the paraphernalia of graphics and curves which are the salesman's standard devices"?[86] Because the "colored beads were irresistible," would those reluctant to use tests succumb and commit research treason by making the right choice for the wrong reason?

Whatever the answer, one fact was evident: the ambition and drive of the new organization. On December 12, 1947—just before consolidation of the testing offices of the ACE, CTS, and the Board came into effect on January 1, 1948—Henry Chauncey made a list entitled "ETS—Major Problems in Effecting the Merger of Constituent Agencies."[87] Some of the problems were logistical: "Would it be better to build an entirely new building in spite of present high costs [a venture that would result in a campus on Rosedale Road] or remodel 20 Nassau [the single-building, original Princeton home of ETS] and build additions?" Some were managerial: "What should ultimate organizational set up be?"

But one item stands out. If the College Entrance Examination Board, he mused, "alone was under scrutiny, what changes might be suggested to make it more effective and more economical?" Even if he had to create it himself, Henry Chauncey was ready for change.

Endnotes

1 Claude M. Fuess, *The College Board: Its First Fifty Years* (New York: Columbia UP, 1950) 154–155. In the 1942 report of the College Entrance Examination Board (*Forty-Second Annual Report of the Executive Secretary*), Fuess is listed as an officer for the 1941–1942 term; there is every reason to believe that his recollection of the events of December 7, 1942, is accurate.

2 The draft, administered by the Selective Service System, became law on Sept. 16, 1940. On October 29, 1940, the War Department arranged for the first drawing of numbers. The capsules carrying the numbers were placed into the same fishbowl used for selection during World War I. Henry Stimson, the Secretary of War, was blindfolded with a cloth taken from the room where the Declaration of Independence was signed. The numbers were stirred with a wooden ladle made from a rafter of Independence Hall (George Q. Flynn, *The Draft, 1940–1973* [Lawrence: UP of Kansas, 1993] 22). For an excellent treatment of the draft and its contradictions for education—the identification of all youth as subject to the draft while selecting for exclusion those in college—see especially Chapter 3 in Flynn.

3 Fuess, *The College Board* 155. In the *Forty-Second Annual Report of the Executive Secretary*, Mullins reported the following: "On December 17 the Executive Secretary was notified separately by Harvard, Yale, and Princeton, the three colleges making the greatest use of the June examinations, that they had decided as an emergency action to accelerate their program of studies and begin the college year in June or July. This early beginning of the academic year made it necessary for these colleges to direct their candidates to take the April tests in 1942 instead of the June examinations. It was evident that this shift of approximately 3,100 candidates from the June to the April series would have an important effect on the June examinations" (1). In that Fuess recalled that Mullins was present at the 1941 meeting in Heermance's study—"Dr. Mullins…gracefully played the part of D'Artagnan"—and that Mullins helped craft the newspaper release (154–155), it is clear that Executive Secretary Mullins played an active role in shifting the examination dates and was not merely "notified separately" by Harvard, Yale, and Princeton.

4 *Forty-Second Annual Report of the Executive Secretary* 2.

5 *Forty-Second Annual Report of the Executive Secretary* 18–19.

6 *Forty-Second Annual Report of the Executive Secretary* 22.

7 *Forty-First Annual Report of the Executive Secretary* (New York: College Entrance Examination Board, 1941) 19.

8 Writing of the SAT and the April achievement tests, Fuess, in *The College Board*, reminds us of the economy of the new "objective" (limited-response) tests: "All the tests were scored mechanically and expeditiously by clerks" (151).

9 John M. Stalnaker, "Essay and Objective Writing Tests," *English Journal* (College Edition) 22.3 (1933): 222, Microfilm Roll No. 10 (Green Files) (Princeton: ETS Archives).

10 Editorial, "Objective Tests in Literature," *The English Journal* 17.3 (1928): 251–252; Charles Swain Thomas, "The Examinations in English," *The English Journal* 21.6 (1932): 441–452.

11 John M. Stalnaker and Ruth C. Stalnaker, "Reliable Reading of Essay Tests," *School Review* 42.8 (1934): 599. JSTOR 23 Jan. 2005 <http://www.jstor.org/search>.

12 *Dedication Ceremony: Carl Campbell Brigham Library, Educational Testing Service, November 12, 1961* (Princeton: ETS Archives, 1961) 12.

13 John M. Stalnaker, "Question VI—The Essay," *English Journal* (College Edition) 26.2 (1937) 133, Microfilm Roll No. 10 (Green Files) (Princeton: ETS Archives).

14 Stalnaker, "Question VI—The Essay" 134.

15 Stalnaker, "Question VI—The Essay" 138.

16 Carl Campbell Brigham, *The Reading of the Comprehensive Examination in English: An Analysis of the Procedures Followed During the Five Reading Periods from 1929–1933* (Princeton: Princeton UP, 1934) 41.

17 John M. Stalnaker, "Essay Examinations Reliably Read," *School and Society* 46 (1937) 671.

18 Stalnaker, "Essay Examinations Reliably Read" 671.

19 College Entrance Examination Board, *Thirty-Seventh Annual Report of the Executive Secretary* (New York: College Entrance Examination Board, 1937). To make the table more dramatic for readers of *School and Society*, Stalnaker placed the reading reliability coefficients in the second column of his table; in the 1937 *Annual Report*, the correlations are in the final column. Significantly, Stalnaker graphically rearranged the reliability correlations, demonstrating that the long-standing issue of reliability had been solved at the College Board. Stalnaker had just been appointed consultant examiner at the April 1936 meeting of the Executive Committee (15), and he wasted no time in demonstrating to a national audience that concerns about inter-reader reliability were misplaced.

20 Stalnaker, "Essay Examinations Reliably Read" 672.

21 *Dedication Ceremony* 14.

22 Edward Simpson Noyes and John Marshall Stalnaker, *Report on the English Examination of June 1937: A Description of the Procedures Used in Preparing and Reading the Examination in English and an Analysis of the Results of the Reading* (New York: College Entrance Examination Board, 1938) 5.

23 Commission on English, *Examining the Examinations in English: A Report to the College Entrance Examination Board* (Cambridge: Harvard UP, 1931). Along with the bibliography found in Rollo L. Lyman's *Summary of Investigations Relating to Grammar, Language, and Composition* (Chicago: U of Chicago P, 1929), the bibliography in the Commission's volume provides a detailed picture of the enormous interest and extent of research that was given to the measurement of writing ability in the first three decades of the twentieth century.

24 Noyes and Stalnaker, *Report on the English Examination of June 1937* 7.

25 Noyes and Stalnaker, *Report on the English Examination of June 1937* 7.

26 Noyes and Stalnaker, *Report on the English Examination of June 1937* 7. The shadow of the 1931 report of the Commission on English was clearly upon Noyes and Stalnaker. In its "Specific Recommendations," the Commission had noted that there was "a low correlation between the College Entrance Examination Board's English grades and the grades in freshman English…" (212). The English examination had less "prognostic value" than the Scholastic Aptitude Test, the Commission noted (212). Indeed, the Commission recommended that admissions committees should take note of three factors before judging a candidate's qualifications in English: "(a) the Scholastic Aptitude Test scores; (b) the school English records; (c) the English Examination grades" (213–214).

27 Noyes and Stalnaker, *Report* 17.

28 Noyes and Stalnaker, *Report* 16.

29 Noyes and Stalnaker, *Report* 32.

30 Noyes and Stalnaker, *Report* 33–35.

31 Noyes and Stalnaker, *Report* 33.

32 Noyes and Stalnaker, *Report* 11.

33 Noyes and Stalnaker, *Report* 16.

34 Noyes and Stalnaker, *Report* 48.

35 Noyes and Stalnaker, *Report* 53.

36 Noyes and Stalnaker, *Report* 50.

37 Noyes and Stalnaker, *Report* 53–54.

38 Noyes and Stalnaker, *Report 1937* 56.

39 Noyes and Stalnaker, *Report 1937* 50.

40 Noyes and Stalnaker, *Report* 56.

41 Noyes and Stalnaker, *Report* 33.

42 Noyes and Stalnaker, *Report* 37.

43 Edward Simpson Noyes, William Merritt Sale, Jr., and John Marshall Stalnaker, *Report on the First Six Tests in English Composition, with Sample Answers from the Tests of April and June, 1944* (New York: College Entrance Examination Board, 1945) 5.

44 Noyes, Sale, and Stalnaker, *Report on the First Six Tests* 5.

45 Stalnaker, "Essay Examinations Reliably Read" 672.

46 *Forty-Third Annual Report of the Executive Secretary* (New York: College Entrance Examination Board, 1943) 24. Stalnaker's report to the Board as its associate secretary appears on 23–34.

47 Orville Palmer, "Sixty Years of English Testing," *College Board Review* 42 (1960) 12.

48 *Forty-Third Annual Report of the Executive Secretary* 25.

49 Noyes, Sale, and Stalnaker, *Report on the First Six Tests* 6.

50 Commission on English, *Examining the Examinations in English* 128.

51 Asked on June 16–21, 1913. *Questions Set at the Examinations, June 16–21, 1913* (Boston: Ginn, 1913) 22.

52 For more on these radio programs, see John Dunning, *On the Air: An Encyclopedia of Old Time Radio* (New York: Oxford UP, 1998). For *The Kate Smith Hour*, see 382–384; for the Jack Benny's *The Jello-Program*, see 355–363; for the Bob Hope's *The Pepsodent Show*, see 105–109; for *Captain Midnight*, see 137–138; for *Edward R. Murrow*, see 492–493; and for *Terry and the Pirates*, see 565–567.

53 Noyes, Sale, and Stalnaker, *Report on the First Six Tests* 14–15.

54 Basic Aims Committee, "Basic Aims for English Instruction in American Schools," *English Journal* 31.1 (1942): 40–55. For a treatment of the English curriculum during the 1940s, see Arthur N. Applebee, *Tradition and Reform in the Teaching of English: A History* (Urbana: NCTE, 1974) 139–183, esp. 156–160.

55 S. I. Hayakawa, *Language in Thought and Action*, 2nd ed. (New York: Harcourt, 1941) 239–241.

56 Hayakawa 242.

57 Noyes, Sale, and Stalnaker, *Report on the First Six Tests* 11.

58 Noyes and Stalnaker, *Report 1937* 52.

59 Noyes, Sale, and Stalnaker, *Report on the First Six Tests* 67.

60 Noyes, Sale, and Stalnaker, *Report on the First Six Tests*. In 1961, as the Acting President of the College Entrance Examination Board, Noyes reflected on this series of tests in "Teaching and Testing of English," *College Composition and Communication* 12.1 (1961): "Looking back," he wrote, "I can see clearly why the one-hour written tests failed. The single theme compelled a student to put all his eggs in one basket, a basket not of his choosing. The short paragraphs gave him only three or four baskets. One strength of an objective test is that they can have a great many items in a short time; the reliability of a test depends largely on the number of judgments the candidate has to make and on what he can, in turn, be judged. Even though we tried to break the themes up into various elements—style, diction, mechanics, content, or organization—and judge them on each of these separately, we found the elements fluid, very hard to measure independently. We came, regretfully but firmly, to the conclusion that one hour's work is just not time enough to provide Readers with a sample of an unknown candidate's normal ability to write" (36).

61 *Forty-Third Annual Report of the Executive Secretary* 23–24.

62 *Forty-Second Annual Report of the Executive Secretary* 43.

63 Jane B. Alderfer and Gary D. Zaredzky, "History," *Navy Papers Inventory* (Princeton: ETS Archives, 1971) 8. A list of all of the programs sponsored by the government in the war effort and administered by the College Board is given on 10–13.

64 George Q. Flynn, *Conscription and Democracy: The Draft in France, Great Britain, and the United States* (Westport: Greenwood P, 2001) 60. See also Flynn, *The Draft*.

65 *Forty-Second Annual Report of the Executive Secretary* 4.

66 *Forty-Second Annual Report of the Executive Secretary* 4.

67 Fuess, *The College Board* 168. Fuess would have been a very reliable narrator of the Executive Committee's startled reaction to its assets, now totaling a "book value not far from $300,000." Fuess, headmaster at Phillips Academy in Andover, Massachusetts, had been a member of the first board of trustees and named in the original charter for the Board in 1900. In the 1944 *Annual Report*, he was listed both as a committee member to the Board (ix) and as custodian to the Board (xi).

68 These financial statements of the Board appeared in the following: *Forty-First Annual Report of the Executive Secretary* 18–20; *Forty-Third Annual Report of the Executive Secretary* 19–22; and *Forty-Fourth Annual Report of the Executive Secretary* 18–21.

69 *Forty-Fifth Annual Report of the Executive Secretary* (New York: College Entrance Examination Board, 1945) 14.

70 Dewey B. Stuit, ed., *Personnel Research and Test Development in the Bureau of Naval Personnel* (Princeton: Princeton UP, 1947) 109.

71 Stuit, *Personnel Research and Test Development* x.

72 *Forty-Fourth Annual Report of the Executive Secretary* 24.

73 *Forty-Fifth Annual Report of the Executive Secretary* 38. For the reliability correlations, see Table 15.

74 *Forty-Fifth Annual Report of the Executive Secretary* 27. Edward S. Noyes took on the task of explaining the new type of tests in composition in April 1945 in the *English Leaflet*. In place of the single topic, he analyzed the impact of the new method of presenting four topics (e.g., "suppose you have been asked to write a theme comparing two applicants for the same position") for separate paragraphs (of about 75 to 125 words each). He noted that the use of single topics had yielded a reliability of .66, "too low for any comfort" (52). The new tests, however, had yielded a reliability of .80. Noyes concluded that the new tests allowed the candidates a better chance to exhibit their normal ability to write than allowed by a single essay, had afforded greater reliability, and were thus rewarding good students with high scores and detecting students with poor scores (57). "The New Type of Tests in Composition," *English Leaflet* 44.392 (Apr. 1945) 49–58. ETS Archives, Reel #5, Green File.

75 Stuit, *Personnel Research and Test Development* 56.

76 Arthur Miller, *Death of a Salesman: Certain Private Conversations in Two Acts and a Requiem* (New York: Viking, 1949) 33.

77 Arthur Miller 40. In *The Big Test: The Secret History of the American Meritocracy* (New York: Farrar, Straus and Giroux, 1999), Nicholas Lemann also notes the significance of this passage in Miller's play (111–112). Note also that Miller captures the significance of education for specific purposes. When Willy asks Bernard why "nothing good ever happened to Biff after the age of seventeen," Bernard's answer is delivered with deadly accuracy. "He never trained himself for anything," Bernard replies (92).

78 *Forty-Sixth Annual Report of the Executive Secretary* (New York: College Entrance Examination Board, 1946) 1.

79 *Forty-Sixth Annual Report of the Executive Secretary* 48.

80 *Forty-Sixth Annual Report of the Executive Secretary* 7.

81 While it is difficult to say exactly why Stalnaker left the Board, his remarks in a 1985 interview with Gary Saretzky are revealing. Asked if he had the sense in 1945 that "something like ETS [might] come into being," he replied that the knew the "Carnegie people who were the ones who were back of merging testing groups. It's a move Carl Brigham would have opposed." Asked if he approved of the idea of a testing organization, he said that "it would freeze things." Asked if he approved of the creation of ETS, he replied, "No, I was opposed to it, for which Henry [Chauncey] and some of the other people will never forgive me." Asked why he had voiced opposition, he replied, "I think, in general, it is never wise to have an organization which sells

products (whether it's non-profit or profit doesn't make a whit of difference) do research on their own products. They are concerned about selling a product and getting enough cash to keep their jobs and improve and expand. It doesn't make any difference whether profit or non-profit, they still have the objective of keeping the organization alive and enlarging it. That is their goal. Such an organization is not the kind that ought to deal with research" (*ETS Archives Oral History Program*, 12 June 1985 [Princeton: ETS Archives, 1985] 38–39). If these were the opinions voiced privately in 1945, there is no doubt that Stalnaker must have felt that an error was being made in the creation of ETS and that it was time for him to return to university life. He remained balanced, however, in his respectful yet reserved evaluation of the assistant he had hired. "Henry Chauncey made a series of decisions as ETS developed that many sound business people would have said were very risky—even dangerous. Most of his decisions paid off. What could you say?" (42).

82 Chauncey's role in the Educational Testing Service has been recalled by Lemann and by Robert L. Hampel in "The Origins of the Educational Testing Service," *A Faithful Mirror: Reflections on the College Board and Education in America*, ed. Michael C. Johanek (New York: College Board, 2001) 247–270.

83 Chauncey himself summarizes the consolidation in "Testing Offices of the Three Organizations Merge," *College Board Review* 1.3 (1947): 36–37. "The ETS," he summarizes, "unites in a single organization the testing functions hitherto performed by the Carnegie Foundation for the Advancement of Teaching (through the Graduate Record Office), the College Entrance Examination Board, and the American Council on Education (chiefly through the Cooperative Test Service, the Psychological Examination, and the National Committee on Teacher Examinations)" (36). For more on the merger, see also Ellen Condliffe Lagemann, *Private Power for the Public Good: A History of the Carnegie Foundation for the Advancement of Teaching* (Middletown: Wesleyan UP, 1983) esp. 115–121. For a history of the ACE, see Hugh Hawkins, *Banding Together: The Rise of National Associations in American Higher Education, 1887–1950* (Baltimore: Johns Hopkins UP, 1992).

84 Henry Chauncey, "The College Entrance Examination Board: Origins and Current Trends," *College Board Review* 1.5 (1948): 67.

85 Thomas D. Snyder, ed., *120 Years of American Education: A Statistical Portrait* (Washington: National Center for Educational Statistics, 1993) 65–66.

86 Carl Campbell Brigham, "The Place of Research in a Testing Organization," *School and Society* 46.1198 (1937): 757.

87 *Chauncey Merger File*, Folder 1, Box 9 (Princeton: ETS Archives).

Chapter 4
Off the Diving Board, 1947–1966

On June 24, 1950, North Korean troops breached the thirty-eighth parallel. Since Japan's surrender ended World War II, that line had come to be seen as the symbolic demarcation between the Soviet-sponsored government in the north and the American-supported government in the south. On June 27, President Truman released a statement that confirmed America's worst fears: "The attack upon Korea makes it plain beyond all doubt that Communism has passed beyond the use of subversion to conquer independent nations and will now use armed invasion and war."[1] Americans had been focused on Europe during the previous decade; the path to globalism now led through Asia. After the Soviet Union had exploded its own nuclear weapon in 1949, Americans expected bombs to fall; instead, they now found themselves locked in a ground war.

At first, General Douglas MacArthur, commanding the United Nations effort, thought he could push the North Korean troops back across the thirty-eighth parallel with the forces on hand. On November 15 he succeeded, but on November 23 thirty-three North Korean divisions (approximately 300,000 troops) counterattacked, and U.N. troops retreated below the thirty-eighth parallel. It was clear that more troops would be needed, and America's newest classification system—the peacetime draft—would supply 180,000 men in the first three months of the war.

The Selective Service Act of 1948 was a system that Carl Campbell Brigham would have admired, a government entity designed to ensure efficiency. The general conscription of the Selective Service Act of 1917 had required all men from twenty-one to thirty years of age to register for service, and in 1940 the Selective Service and Training Act required peacetime conscription. Now, in 1948, all men aged eighteen to twenty-six were eligible for registration, and men aged nineteen to twenty-six were eligible for a twenty-one-month tour of duty. The Selective Service operated through local boards that assigned classifications, inductions, and exemptions. After MacArthur's forces were driven back in November 1950, a subsequent draft bill was adopted to ensure universal military training, and the term of service was extended to twenty-four months. Nearly 80 percent of the one million men reaching eighteen years of age would be inducted annually; a small, select group of approximately 75,000, however, would be chosen for specialized training. On March 31, 1951, Truman reinforced the efficient use of manpower by issuing an executive order for student deferment, thus ensuring a pool of educated scientists and engineers for the armed forces. Deferment was gained after a student met a predetermined score on a new measure of ability, the Selective Service College Qualifying Test. The SSCQT was designed, administered, and scored by America's newest testing organization: Henry Chauncey's Educational Testing Service.

Sharply Critical

Chauncey recognized that his new organization, recently chartered in 1947, would come under fire for building the SSCQT. Anticipating publicity problems, he hired a consultant, Dr. Raymond H. Miller, a visiting lecturer at the Harvard Business School and a public relations consultant to the Food and Agricultural Organization of the United Nations. Chauncey also noted that A. Glenwood Walker of the ETS California office could work "through Nixon, a California Senator."[2] And ETS had worked with the Liberty Broadcast System in a series entitled "Youth and the Draft" for radio audiences. ETS was quickly emerging as a national force, a testing resource for the nation.

In his memorandum to his board of trustees dated April 20, 1951, Chauncey noted the complexities of the SSCQT program:

> Since the President's announcement, there has been a great deal of editorial comment on the program, much of it sharply critical. So far, ETS has pretty well escaped criticism, which has been directed toward the policies of Selective Service rather than toward the test or toward ETS as the organization responsible for its administration.
>
> Happily, the first outburst of negative criticism regarding the program seems to have been followed by expressions of opinion which have been on the whole

> somewhat more favorable. The college deferment program was vulnerable because of the apparent inequality of treatment of individuals in and out of college. And since in general students in college are from families of higher incomes, the plan seems to be undemocratic in favoring the sons of the rich.[3]

The criticisms of the program, Chauncey noted, were exaggerated by the "common misunderstanding" that deferment meant exemption instead of postponement of service.

Chauncey's strategies worked well. A Gallup survey released May 27–28, 1951, reported public approval of the deferment plan. "Despite sharp criticism from some quarters when it was first announced," George Gallup concluded, "the present selective service plan of deferring college students from the draft on the basis of their passing a test of general ability is supported by a majority opinion throughout the country. In a ratio of approximately 3-to-2, representative voters questioned by the Institute say they think students who can pass the test should be allowed to complete their college course before becoming subject to call."[4]

The Gallup survey was reported the day after candidates had taken the first test. In its initial administration, the Selective Service College Qualifying Test was given on May 26, 1951; June 16, 1951; June 30, 1951; and July 12, 1951. In the *Bulletin of Information*, candidates were told that the test "examines your ability to read with understanding and to solve new problems by using your general knowledge. These abilities are necessary for success in fields which require advanced training." Sample questions on reading comprehension, verbal relations, arithmetic reasoning, and data interpretation were provided in the bulletin: questions on a reading passage ("The passage is chiefly concerned with..."); questions on synonyms ("SOOTHE: 1-subjugate, 2-machinate, 3-compensate, 4-immo-late, 5-mollify"); questions on antonyms ("COMPATIBLE: 1-changeless, 2-definite, 3-cruel, 4-irreconcilable, 5-entire"); questions on analogies ("HAMMER:TOOL: 1-anger:insensibility, 2-emotion:insensibility, 3-plane:shavings, 4-chisel:plane, 5-anger:emotion"); questions on sentence completion ("There is a kind of superstitious____for office which leads us to____the merits and abilities of men in power and to suppose that they must be constituted differently from other men. 1-distaste..respect, 2-disrespect..emulate, 3-reverence..exaggerate, 4-disrespect..accept, 5-reverence..minimize"); questions on the interpretation of graphs ("In which year does the graph show farm income to have been the least?..."); questions on geometry ("Figure 1 represents a triangle sail, PQR, in which the edges PQ and QR are perpendicular to each other. If PQ is 16 feet long and QR is

8 feet long, what is the area [in square feet] of the sail?"); and questions on applied mathematics ("4 is 16% of what number?").[5]

During the first four testing dates, the SSCQT was administered to 339,042 candidates, a total of approximately 21 percent of the total male college-student population. Sixty-four percent achieved the cut score of 70 or better; in the second series, given on December 13, 1951; April 23, 1952; and May 22, 1952; 58 percent of the 74,327 students achieved the same cut score of 70. Geographic disparities, however, appeared in the data. Students in college in the New England, Middle Atlantic, and Pacific states performed much better than students enrolled in colleges in the East South Central region and the West South Central region. Candidates majoring in engineering, the physical sciences, and mathematics gained higher scores on the test than those majoring in education and business.

The results were similar to those obtained from older tests used to evaluate recruits during World War I: the geographic region and occupation of the candidate were related to test performance.[6] As early as June 13, 1951, Lyndon B. Johnson, chairman of the Preparedness Subcommittee of the United States Senate Committee on Armed Services, had sensed the potential for scores that captured not linguistic and quantitative ability but the geographic location of the student. Senator Johnson had written to Major General Lewis B. Hershey, director of the Selective Service System, expressing deep interest in the examination. He requested a copy of the test along with its key.

> I will also greatly appreciate it if, after final tabulation of the results of this test, you will supply me with a state-by-state total of the number of students who took the test and the number of students who passed it and were eligible for further deferment. I would also like you to supply me with a breakdown which will show the proportion of students who made satisfactory grades on the test in agricultural and mechanical schools, as compared with those who made satisfactory grades on the test in liberal arts schools.[7]

Johnson, intuitively, was anticipating problems; a testing insider, however, had seen the pre-test results from Lackland Air Force Base in San Antonio, Texas. On May 16, 1951, Paul B. Diederich had written to Henry Chauncey, adding his voice to those "sharply critical" editorial comments that Chauncey had noted in his April 20 memo.

Diederich, a classics scholar recruited by Chauncey to join ETS in 1949, was wary of the pre-test results: while 73 percent of New England students achieved the cut score of 70, only 42 percent of those attending southern colleges achieved the same score. "I doubt that the man in the street (who contributes to the local boards)," he wrote, "would be interested in or impressed by figures on the predictive efficiency of tests, especially when the only figures we could honestly quote would appear to him to be extremely unfavorable to the test." Diederich told Chauncey to stress to Hershey that colleges had always had to make choices regarding ability, that ETS had experience in these types of ability tests, and that the tests were carefully constructed. Diederich attached a five-page letter in which he "planted" these three ideas. ("I doubt that the average man can absorb more than three ideas about anything in one publication," he mused.) He told Chauncey he would do more: "If you think I should go further and tell more about tests, I shall have a shot at it but with the underlying conviction that, like almost everything else I have written about the SSCQT, it will never be used."[8]

Diederich was right. Across the top of the memo, Chauncey wrote "unused" and added his own initials, H.C., just for good measure.

ETS tested over 500,000 college students for deferment between 1951 and 1954. The total payment from the government contract was $1.2 million, and ETS had cleared over $900,000.[9] Clearly, ETS had done its part in protecting the academic brain trust that would be fundamental to winning the Cold War to come.

And come it did. In October 1957 Russia launched *Sputnik*, that great technological symbol of communism's threat to democracy embodied in a satellite. As John E. Burchard, dean of the School of Humanities and Social Sciences at Massachusetts Institute of Technology, wrote in the *College Board Review*, "By November 7, 1957, events have made it perfectly clear that Russian science and technology have done wonders and justify for Americans the most sober reconsideration of their programs and a determination to do everything that is democratically possible, short of panic."[10] The SSCQT, designed and monitored by ETS, had helped to prepare the country for a new world in which scientific training would be at a premium. Even the students agreed: a poll of fifteen thousand high school students in 1959 found that almost 80 percent favored military service for all, but 64 percent favored college deferments.[11] In light of *Sputnik*, as the president of the Society of American Military Engineers put it, "equality of sacrifice is incompatible with the demands of national security."[12] The SSCQT had not, after all, favored the sons of the rich; instead, it had helped preserve national security.

ETS was now part of a new world in which science was the preeminent value in American society; indeed, as part of the "conjunction of an immense military establishment and a large arms industry" in the American experience, ETS was now positioned to conduct tests that certified the abilities of those who would preserve democracy itself. Within this new military-industrial complex, the "total influence—economic, political, even spiritual—is felt in every city, every State house, every office of the Federal government"—just as Eisenhower had predicted.[13]

Within this national organization, the assessment of writing ability continued to be investigated, but the emphasis shifted to one in which the definition of writing ability was aligned with measures designed to secure an effective evaluation system.

During the 1950s, Diederich—who would become the best-known figure in writing assessment to emerge from the nation's most influential and successful testing agency—worked with Edith Huddleston, Earle G. Eley, William E. Coffman, Frances Swineford, John French and Fred I. Godshalk to transform the assessment of writing into a regularized process. By 1966 ETS researchers would claim to have established writing assessment methods that were as useful and predictable as the SSCQT itself.

Edith Huddleston: No More Than Verbal Ability

Edith Huddleston had come to the Social Studies group in Test Construction in the spring of 1942; by 1947 she was head of the Social Studies Section, reporting to William W. Turnbull. She had become involved with the English Composition Test (ECT), begun in 1943. In the spring 1948 issue of the *College Board Review*, Huddleston—now part of the newly formed ETS (chartered on January 1, 1948) and its Test Construction Department—launched her first volley into writing assessment with a question. "What," she asked, "is the ability to write? And however it is defined, how can this ability be measured?"[14] The traditional essay examination, despite all efforts, was declared an unreliable measurement device:

> The English essay test has profited from the years of painstaking effort devoted to it, but it has begun to appear doubtful that we can hope for any great additional improvement through further refinement of present techniques.[15]

What to do? How to think about writing and its assessment? She spent the next six years formulating answers.

Part of the answer, she knew, had been given in 1946. In its *Forty-Sixth Annual Report of the Executive Secretary*, the College Board had declared the ECT "the major problem of the present series of Achievement Tests."[16] Reliability was cited as the chief problem. The predictors of writing ability, assessed by checklists of material, organization, and style, performed well

Edith Huddleston (seated fourth from right, with William E. Coffman on her left). "The investigation," Huddleston concluded in her 1954 study, "points to the conclusion that in the light of present knowledge, measurable 'ability to write' is no more than verbal ability" ("Measurement of Writing Ability at the College-Entrance Level: Objective vs. Subjective Testing Techniques," *Journal of Experimental Education* 22.3 [1954] 204). (Photo Reprinted by Permission of Educational Testing Service. All Rights Reserved.)

only in the August and December reading periods, when there were fewer candidates. In the larger April and June administrations, the reliability dropped. The main cause of the unreliability of the reading, Henry Chauncey had written as the acting executive secretary, rested in the difficulty of making sure that thirty to seventy-five teachers were "'in tune' in their grading."[17] The essay, Chauncey reminded his readers, was not retained because of its questionable predictive value; it was retained, rather, because of its influence on teaching.

One possible way of improving the test would be to divide it into two parts: "a half-hour essay question that would be read *in all cases* by two readers, and in cases of discrepant grading by a third; and by a half-hour objective test. The latter section would be designed to measure certain qualities such as punctuation, grammar, usage, etc., which can be more effectively tested by an objective examination, while the former would measure sentence structure, organization, and style and would be carefully graded."[18] With the documented failure of the first six tests in English composition given after World War II in mind, a new series of experiments, Chauncey reported, had been approved for 1947.

Thus, when Huddleston summarized the series of 1947 experiments in her 1948 article, she was presenting a case in which the Board hoped to establish a possible set of solutions through ETS. (The report of Noyes, Sale, and Stalnaker was part of a dying College Board tradition of reporting—good or ill—adventures in assessment, but the new ETS could not afford to publicize tests resulting in questionable scores. The new ETS was not in the business of documenting gaffes.) It is, then, no wonder that Huddleston emphasized, first, the new question types tried—the instruments designed—rather than answer her own question: What is the ability to write? The answer, she believed, could be found in the devices used to measure it.

Three types of evaluation measures were used. The objective section of the experimental test contained forty-five multiple-choice questions. The item types contained sentences in which portions were underlined and numbered. The correct answer demonstrated the student's command of grammar, punctuation, sentence structure, and conciseness of expression. In the second measurement instrument, the essay, candidates were asked to discuss, in a single paragraph, a serious error that parents may make in rearing a child, and to indicate the possible consequences of the error. The third part of the test presented students with two paragraphs "to be rewritten in the interest of correctness and good style."[19]

Candidates assessed in the experiment, Huddleston explained, were those whose teachers themselves were in Princeton during the April 1947 reading. "The presence in Princeton of all the cooperating teachers made it possible for all to participate in the discussions of the criteria to be used in evaluating the various question types."[20] Two criteria were used in the study: course grades (the average course grades of all student final grades in English for the junior and senior years of secondary school) and teachers' ratings (a rank ordering of their students' ability to write expository prose). In this validity study, Huddleston wished to establish the criterion measure—course grades and the teachers' ratings of their own students—and to evaluate the extent to which the three types of measurements (objective, essay, and paragraph revision) corresponded with those criteria.

The results, Huddleston found, were "clear cut."[21] The objective questions yielded higher correlations with each criterion (.48 with teachers' ratings and .44 with average course grades) than did either the essay or the paragraph-revision section. To drive the point home, Huddleston provided a note that a similar earlier study yielded only a .34 correlation between a 60-minute essay examination and college instructors' ratings of their students' ability to write. The findings: "It is obvious that, given the tests are as they are, the essay and the paragraph revision sections have added nothing to the predictive validity of this particular examination."[22]

Huddleston's article concluded in the same fashion as the majority of the College Board-sponsored studies since Charles Swain Thomas' Commission on English had recommended in 1931 that "admission committees of colleges and universities, before deciding upon the candidates' qualifications in English, take note of three factors: (a) the Scholastic Aptitude Test scores; (b) the school English records; (c) the English Examination grades."[23] That is, Huddleston concluded that the SAT verbal, taken by the majority of the students in the study, provided the highest correlation with the criterion measures: .65 with the teachers' ratings and .46 with the average course grades. "Thus, *the S.A.T. Verbal has a higher correlation with each criterion than has any section of the English test, or even the English test as a whole.*"[24] Better questions, Huddleston believed, were needed to measure writing, item types that would add to the predictive ability of the SAT verbal.

Nevertheless, Huddleston had not answered her own question: What is the ability to write? In her 1952 dissertation, submitted to the Department of Psychology at New York University, she would answer that question because she now had identified item types to capture that ability. The 1954 publication of the dissertation in its entirety in the *Journal of Experimental Education* would make the case for a new definition of writing ability to a national audience.

"Measurement of Writing Ability at The College-Entrance Level: Objective vs. Subjective Testing Techniques" began with a review of the literature positioned to emphasize "the pitfall of unreliability" in direct writing assessment.[25] The section in which the literature on writing assessment is reviewed was an extended historical account designed to advance the opposition of techniques. The advantages of objective-type questions—emblematic of the scientific orientation that was beginning to serve as the emblem of Cold-War American education—were overpowering. These item types captured the ability to write (to be defined only at the conclusion of the article) because they required thought and organization. And these item types yielded to statistical analysis: they correlated with other desirable academic abilities, and they were remorselessly reliable. The disadvantages of subjective-type essays—symbolic of an antique American culture that seemed hopelessly primitive in the global world of Korean conflicts and Soviet escalation—were presented as being guilty of the sin (mortal, now, because of the precision required of all cold warriors) of unreliability. Stalnaker's old aphorism—essays that achieved a reader reliability of .55 suggested about the same as the relationship between height and weight—was added by Huddleston for good measure.[26]

The dissertation study design was inductive, one in which item types would derive a construct. The ability to write, Huddleston warned, "cannot be defined in great detail; it is a comprehensive ability, one which can be expected to vary in the same person from time to time and from task to task."[27] But perhaps, Huddleston hypothesized, objective items could be designed that would measure verbal ability. And, syllogistically, verbal ability could then be associated with writing ability: certain objective tests measure verbal ability; verbal ability is associated with writing ability; therefore, certain objective tests measure writing ability. "The hypothesis," she wrote, "was made that all of our tests of writing ability, both objective and subjective, are measuring verbal ability and are measuring it less well than the traditional test measures it." Therefore, it would follow that if the objective tests proved reliable and could correlate with other criterion measures such as grades and instructors' ratings—the technique that she had used in her 1948 article—Huddleston could claim that she had answered her own question: What is the ability to write? And, in the process, she would have designed item types to measure that ability.

Huddleston conducted two studies. In the first, her sampling plan was similar to her 1948 study. She selected sixteen college freshman English classes whose teachers were also accessible to her. The method was nearly identical: students took an objective test (the example from the 1948 study is used to illustrate the test), answered three 20-minute essay questions (one of the three was from the 1948 study), and revised a paragraph. Students also took the antonym section of the SAT. As a criterion measure, Huddleston used—as she had in 1948—the instructors' evaluation of their students' writing abilities; she also used, again, course grades in English.

The objective test and the verbal test (the antonym section of the SAT) were tested for their reliability using the Kuder-Richardson "Prophecy Formula," a technique for judging the reliability which would be obtained for individual item difficulties. (The objective tests, unlike the essay tests, were not read by two readers. The Kuder-Richardson formula was a mathematical calculation of prophesized item reliability.[28]) The formula yielded a reliability of .93 for the objective test and .85 for the verbal test. Huddleston concluded that the reader reliability of the essay test (.78 for the three essays combined) was too low for satisfactory measurement. The paragraph revision test yielded a reliability of .83 for Part A and .59 for Part B. For these items, she concluded, "The data indicate that there is a potentiality, at least, for satisfactory reader reliability in Paragraph-

Revision."[29] The correlation of the criterion variables (the instructors' ratings of their students' expository writing abilities and the English course grades) with the test items was profoundly low; among the highest was the correlation between the antonym section of the SAT and the instructors' ratings (.43). Nevertheless, Huddleston concluded the following: "The Objective English Test, the Verbal Test, and the Essay Test are measuring the verbal factors chiefly."[30]

The second study used was that reported in the spring 1948 issue of the *College Board Review*. Complete data were obtained on 420 students, and data for all test items except the SAT were obtained on 763 students. Huddleston's dissertation and journal article thus repeated, modified now by calculation, what was known in 1948: the verbal test (i.e., the SAT) had a higher correlation with instructors' ratings (.76) and course grades (.77) than any other variable. In addition, the new objective items that Huddleston had designed were reliable (.78) and had high correlations with the instructors' ratings (.73) and course grades (.75).

The first study was set aside, and the second study was advanced because it achieved the desired syllogistic logic: certain objective tests—now shown by Huddleston to be (a) the items she designed and (b) the verbal section of the SAT—measure verbal ability; verbal ability is associated with writing ability (as defined by instructors' ratings and course grades and as demonstrated by correlation of these criterion measures with the objective tests). Therefore, Huddleston's items and the verbal section of the SAT measured writing ability. "The investigation," she found, "points to the conclusion that in the light of present knowledge, measurable 'ability to write' is no more than verbal ability."[31]

The argument was set, the construct of writing demystified. Huddleston had answered the question she posed in 1948. All along, writing ability had been no more than verbal ability. And, as she had demonstrated, there were more efficient and scientific ways to assess this ability. ETS had captured both the construct and the items by which to assess it. The Cold-War logic seemed irrefutable.

Earle G. Eley and the Test of General Composition: Beyond the Bounds

The *Fiftieth Annual Report of the Director* noted the distinction between Huddleston's research orientation and the orientation of direct assessment. "Symptomatic tests"—Huddleston's work is included in this group—ask the candidate to "perform exercises which are related to competence in composition and which, therefore, could be judged on technical standards alone."[32] Since the Comprehensive English Examination had been abandoned in 1942 during World War II due to restrictions of test dates, the Board had devoted itself almost entirely to symptomatic testing.

Yet the call for direct tests "which require that the candidate write a composition which would be judged on both technical and literary standards" remained.[33] As a result of this demand among the Board's membership of 115 colleges, an invitation was issued to members to "join in the construction and administration of an experimental test which would be, in fact, a composition test, but which would be graded in a way designed to reduce the hazards of reader unreliability."[34] But a warning followed, one that made it clear that this was the last chance for the development of an essay test: "If the administration is successful, the test will be incorporated into the Board's battery, probably for the use of preliminary candidates. If unsuccessful, it will make an end, at least for the foreseeable future, of experimentation in direct testing."[35] An efficient new world was being constructed, and the essay would have to prove its scientific worth if it were to be part of the brave future.

The first trial of the test, reported by Frank D. Ashburn, president of the New England Association of Schools and Colleges, was unsuccessful. Questions were set on three topics—literature, science, and social studies—and were given to more than one thousand students in some twenty colleges and schools. The candidates, it was found, had not had enough work in science and social studies to answer the questions well, and few outstanding scores were awarded. The examiners did notice, however, that when a reader read with the purpose of assigning only a single score—outstanding, adequate, and inadequate—instead of a combination of gradations of the scores—such as awarding an outstanding/adequate score—there was a "striking reduction" in reading time: "The actual average reading time, although there were wide variations, astonishingly did not exceed ten minutes."[36] Although the trial run failed, there remained overwhelming support for an essay assessment. The name for this continued hope: the General Composition Test. The General Composition Test was led by the University of Chicago's Earle G. Eley, a researcher who had written a dissertation on writing competence in 1953.[37]

Eley summarized the General Composition Test as an attempt to reconstruct the very validity of writing itself. "Advocates of objective English tests," he noted,

> have been unable to produce convincing evidence that such tests constitute a

> valid measure of the ability to write creatively. The educational objectives which such tests might be said to measure can be stated somewhat like this: the ability to *recognize* grammatically incorrect constructions, the ability to *select* from several alternatives a correct construction to fit a context, the ability to rearrange previously concocted sentences into a well organized paragraph. It cannot be said that the *ability to write* is one of these objectives.[38]

The nine hundred candidates for the proposed General Composition Test wrote essays, but some were given background materials on the topic at hand. Eley believed that this experimental form of the test did not depend on specific subject matter in the curriculum but instead was "designed to minimize subject matter differences in educational background among candidates: we attempted to evaluate the general objectives which related to the ability to write rather than any content in the curriculum."[39] The essays were scored for five qualities: mechanics, style, organization, reasoning, and content; and each quality was given merit on a four-point

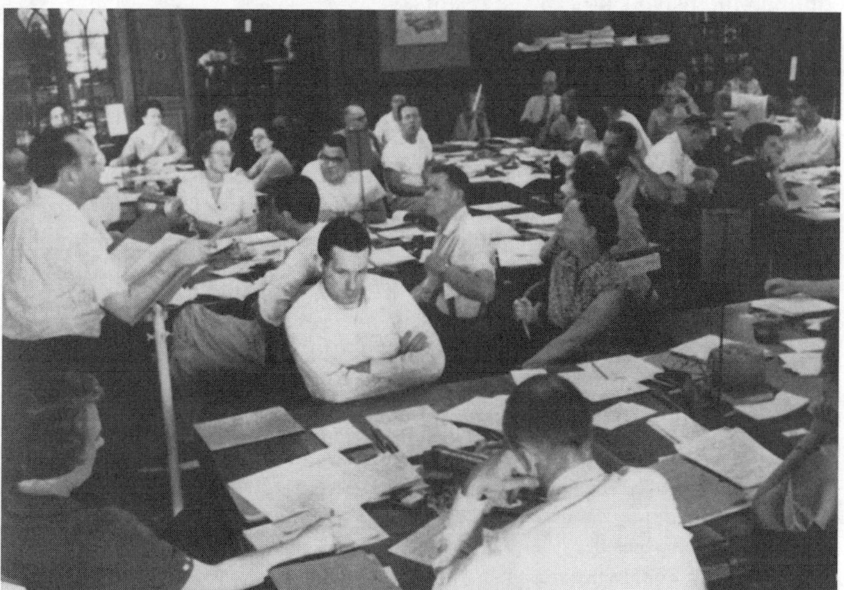

Earle G. Eley (standing at left) discusses the General Composition Test with fifty-eight readers at Hun School, Princeton, before scoring 4,122 essays. "Too often, we have achieved precision in the measurement of human behavior by mechanizing the elements of that behavior. Such a procedure is effective only part of the time: the creative or dynamic aspects of the human personality resist atomization. They must be assessed as wholes or not at all" ("The Test Satisfies an Educational Need," *College Board Review* 25 [1955] 13). (Source of Photo: *College Board Review* 27 [1955] 21. Copyright © 1955 by College Board. Reproduced with permission. All rights reserved. www.collegeboard.com)

scale from superior to inadequate. The result: the inter-reader correlation on all qualities in all 900 candidates was .88; those students who scored highest were those given the background readings. The experimental form of the test was successful. The experiment, Eley wrote, strongly suggested that "an improved essay test is feasible as a direct measure of the ability to write."[40]

Even the Board agreed. In its 1951 *Fifty-First Annual Report*, Director Frank H. Bowles reported a breakthrough: "The results of the experimental administration have made it clear that an essay test can be so constructed as to be read with reasonable reliability, and to produce results which give an appraisal of the candidate's writing skills and ability."[41] Nevertheless, an important question remained, which Bowles phrased as follows: "Assuming that the test per se is a good test, what then does it test, and how can the results be used?"[42] An additional hurdle now appeared, but there had, after all, been a warning the year before. And so it was decided to continue intensive study of the results.

Behind the scenes, Paul Diederich was arguing intensely against permanent adoption of the test. He advanced the type of analysis used by Stalnaker in "Question VI—The Essay." In 1937 Stalnaker found that "English readers by and large do not care to commit themselves by saying a paper is excellent."[43] Diederich found a similar explanation for the narrow dispersion of scores in Eley's study. A paper receiving a score of 4 suggested that a candidate was unprepared for college work; a score of 1 indicated that a candidate might be excused from introductory writing courses. "Of these categories," Diederich concluded, "1 and 4 are so drastic that English teachers are willing to apply them only rarely; and 2 is the category in which I should expect the great bulk of the papers to fall."[44] Diederich then told a breathtakingly candid story in his General Composition Test memo:

> I used such categories as these at the University of Chicago only when there had been a great turnover in the writing staff from the previous year, and I realized that their grades on the initial essay written during Orientation Week would not be worth the paper they were written on. Then, with an appearance of manly frankness, I would say to the staff: "I may as well tell you what I shall take your grades to mean. I shall regard a grade of either A or B as a recommendation for exemption from Freshman English. The only difference between them is that I shall regard A as a strong recommendation, B as a weak one. I shall take C as indicating that the student needs Freshman English. Either D or F will mean that you think this student should go into Remedial English, again with a difference only in the strength of the recommendation."
>
> With these instructions, the English staff would regularly give C's to about 90 per cent of the papers; they thought almost everyone needed Freshman English,

> and shrank from exemption as a privilege that should be accorded only to geniuses, from remediation as too harsh a penalty. I faithfully translated their grades into the scaled scores that were traditionally associated with those grades, added in the three objective scores in which I had some confidence, and took the average. It looked entirely open and above-board, but since the essay contributed almost nothing to the *variance* in scores, it had a negligible effect on placement; the objective scores made all the difference. In other words, I used this dodge to render the essay scores null and void. But, whenever I had confidence in the staff, we defined the letter grades precisely as we defined them in the final examination, and they had appropriate weight in determining placement.

"For this reason," Diederich concluded, "I should strongly recommend avoidance of the definitions of scores 1, 2, 3, and 4 as given above."[45] Diederich also took issue with Eley's system of resolving discrepant scores—that of considering adjacent scores as essentially in agreement. Diederich found the system "very persuasive," but "beyond the bounds" of traditional definitions of agreement in which papers must receive identical scores. Further, Diederich called for an expanded notion of writing reliability as measured within the abilities of the candidates: "What further needs to be done before we can report satisfactory reliability for a test of this sort is to find correlations between scores on two essays written by the same students."[46] Student reliability, he felt, would be far lower than reader reliability. He recognized that it would be virtually impossible to obtain two long essays from each student, and he also predicted that a parallel-form reliability would never exceed .60—a level "completely unsatisfactory for individual predictions."[47] He expressed doubts that this problem "can ever be solved within the time limits and reading costs of a national examination for admission to college."[48] Bowles had hung the sword with gossamer; Diederich was willing to let it fall.

In 1955, the General Composition Test was debated publicly in the pages of the *College Board Review*. The introduction to the debate between Richard Pearson, the ETS project director for the test and Eley, the "principal interpreter and spokesman" of the General Composition Test (now called the GCT), was framed as follows: "The positions are far apart, based on differences in theory which could have been advanced just as firmly five years ago before there was a GCT, and before the quest for 'a test of writing ability' could be expressed as a debate on specific testing procedures or statistical interpretations."[49] Pearson focused on inter-reader reliability and on validity. He found that the test failed on both counts: the system of reconciling disagreements among readers may have increased agreements, but papers read a second time by different readers did not produce high correlation rates: the score seemed to depend more on which reader read

A question of reliability

GRADING SHEET

No. of Paper______ No. of Reader______

Date______ Time Begun______ Time Finished______

	Mechanics	Style	Organization	Reasoning	Content
4	X				
BORDER	∧				
3					
BORDER					
2					
BORDER					
1					

Place papers in categories 1 to 4 with an X; border may be marked *only* ∧ or V.

GCT grading sheet illustrates case described below in which two readers assign different scores in Mechanics category. In practice, each reader uses a separate grading sheet and indicates scores in all five categories

The startling difference between the GCT reader reliability correlations reported in their articles by Mr. Pearson (page 5) and Dr. Eley (page 10) arises, among other things, from a difference between the authors as to what constitutes "agreement" between readers.

In the oversimplified illustration one reader scores the essay "4" in Mechanics and a second reader indicates by the carat (∧) in the borderline space that he considers it a "high 3" in Mechanics. Dr. Eley accepts this as agreement and *before* computing his correlation for Mechanics, plots it as an instance of reader agreement, as indicated by the cross mark in the shaded area below. Mr. Pearson considers the "4" and "high 3" scores to be a case of reader disagreement and plots his mark in the unshaded area to indicate this.

Since the correlations obtained are essentially numerical expressions of agreement, the correlations reported by Dr. Eley are higher than those of Mr. Pearson.

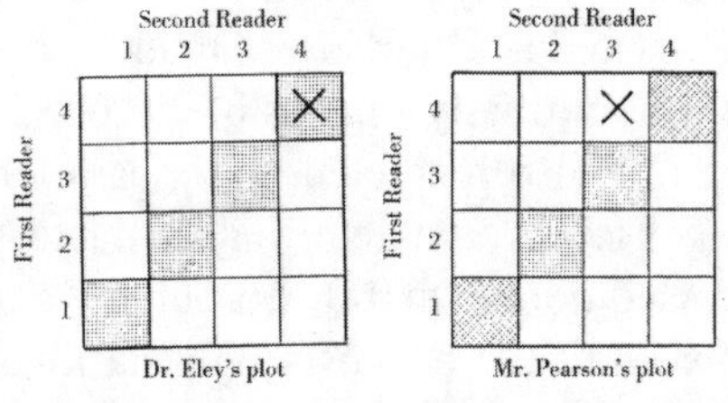

"In simplest and most extreme language, it may be said that those who espouse one or the other of these two viewpoints do not see the same thing when they look at the GCT. They not only see the other side of the same coin; the other side is stamped with a different value in another language." (From the editor's introduction to the Pearson and Eley articles in *College Board Review* [2].) (Source of Photo: *College Board Review* 25 [1955] 21. Copyright © 1955 by College Board. Reproduced with permission. All rights reserved. www.collegeboard.com)

which paper.[50] In addition, the validity was found wanting when the GCT scores were compared with teachers' judgments of their students: SAT Verbal scores "without exception" predicted the teachers' ratings better than did the GCT score.[51]

Eley, in response, argued the appropriateness of considering adjacent scores to be in agreement, evoking metaphor to address lower correlation rates when papers were read a second time by different readers: "It should be noted…that the reading of essays is not precisely analogous to the comparison of samples of iron run through an electric furnace."[52] Further, the instructors' judgments of individual students were not conducted in a test environment in which training was advanced; thus, the lack of correlation between teachers' ratings and GCT scores was no surprise.

To conclude his defense, Eley turned to a discussion of language as a process. "During the twenties, thirties, and early forties, when the prevailing psychology in the United States was mechanistic, that is to say, behavioristic, the professional linguist was busily engaged in the attempt to make an exact science from a humane study, and was happy enough to exclude the investigation of a psychological basis for language behavior from his enterprise. It is not surprising, then, that whatever statement about the psychological basis of human behavior we find among the linguists of the period turns out to be a direct and naive reflection of stimulus-response psychology."[53] (In a footnote, Eley cites Leonard Bloomfield's *Language* as embodiment of this naïveté.) Today, Eley writes, modern psychologists would not accept the label of "mechanistic." "The notion that some kinds of human behavior are complex syndromes of activity which represent wholes that are more than the sum of their parts is today commonly accepted."[54] The "creative or dynamic aspects of human personality resist 'atomization'"—"They must be assessed as wholes or not at all."[55] On the offensive, Eley counters that it is unlikely that objectively scored tests can ever be developed to measure writing, "which is a creative aspect of the human personality."[56] The GCT he had helped to design avoided the impulse toward mechanization and ought to be judged in terms of whether "(1) it satisfies a need in American testing, (2) it satisfies a demand expressed by teachers of English, and (3) it achieves a degree of objectivity appropriate to the kind of instrument that it is."[57] After all, there were consequences here: "The ability to use language creatively is one of the last strongholds of the individual against a growing tendency toward conformity."[58]

In the College Board's *Fifty-Fifth Annual Report of the Director* (1955), Frank H. Bowles answered the question he had posed in 1951. The GCT failed the test of reliability and, thus, was not per se a good test: "The reliability of reading and scoring the papers did not fully meet the standards usually sought for a test used in selection, and the administrative and financial problems of offering the test were severe."[59] Siding with ETS's Richard Pearson, Bowles reported that the GCT was "no better a measure than objective tests already offered by the Board."[60] Moreover, it was not clear that the candidates would be willing to pay the additional fees for the achievement test; nor was it clear that enough readers could have been found to read the tens of thousands of papers that would have poured in if the GCT were made permanent.

The 1956 *College Board Review* announced that the test would be dropped after May 1956. "Certain difficulties" with the GCT had proved persistent since the test was first administered in 1951:

> One was the broad assumption that the test was in English composition alone and that its efficacy should be judged by comparing it with other English tests. The idea of the test from its inception was quite different: it was intended to be an essay in writing English of any kind: literary, scientific, historical. As a matter of fact, the forms of the test were notably short on purely "literary material." The target aimed at was not a bird on a single branch of the academic tree, but a burrowing, insidious creature threatening the whole trunk of learning. That the bird continues to sing unmolested in its lyrical, if incoherent way, is gratifying, but more traceable to nature than to education.[61]

Not only were there problems with the validity of the GCT, but there were also problems with finding "decent reader reliability in a field notoriously lacking it; of finding readers who were competent and who could be counted on to read at a given time; to discover ways and means of keeping the costs of essay testing within reasonable limits."[62] Even the testing population itself was questionable. In May 1954, of the 3,425 independent-school candidates who took the GCT, 2,599 were girls. Girls' independent schools, it seemed, had supported the test more actively than had the boys' schools. "These figures," the article reported, "suggest what is known to be a fact: that proponents of the GCT in the independent schools (and to some extent in the women's colleges) quite legitimately pushed the GCT hard in their anxiety to give the new test a chance to demonstrate its usefulness."[63] But the final argument against the test was the cost. With objective tests, "the cost per user decreases as the number of users increases." This was not at all the case with essay tests. If the costs for the GCT per candidate were not raised and passed on to the candidates, the annual loss to the Board would rise to $80,000, "which would certainly establish any claim of the Board to be a charitable institution incorporated not for profit."[64]

The gap between the concept of the GCT as a reliable and valid test and the concept of the GCT as an aid in encouraging the development of language skills, the article concluded, is "too wide to be bridged at the present time."[65] That gap, readers were told, is part of the landscape of the immeasurable. "And we are afraid," the last sentence of the article states, "that some allowance must always be made for the immeasurable and for differences in judgment, whether they apply to marriage, religion, politics, avocations, or even to the fitness for candidates for college."[66]

Mr. Eley and his associates were thanked for their efforts.

William E. Coffman and the Tests of Developed Ability

If the GCT was a failure, there was hope for two other testing programs that involved essays. As the College Board put it when announcing that the

GCT would be dropped, "We believe that the cause of essay testing and the welfare of education in the United States can be best served at this time by concentrating on and continuing the study of essay material in the Advanced Placement and Developed Abilities Program."[67]

The Tests of Developed Ability were, according to Henry S. Dyer, vice-president of ETS, prompted by Frank H. Bowles, director of the College Board, in his 1949 *Annual Report*. Bowles was writing two years after the Board had contributed "more than two-thirds of its resources, all its staff and facilities concerned with testing, and all its testing activities save those related to college entrance, as its share in the bold experiment which took final form as the Educational Testing Service...."[68] With that experiment now a success, it seemed to Bowles appropriate for the Board to consider its future in terms of likely developments in secondary and higher education. To Bowles, it seemed that the most important force was the concept of general education.

Bowles began his argument by tracing the historical development of "other concepts and other standards" from the past. He made reference to Henry Adams and his recollection of "German thought, method, honesty, and even taste" at Harvard during the mid-nineteenth century, and he quoted Van Wyck Brooks's description of Harvard in *The Flowering of New England* as a place in which the curriculum cultivated "a clear, distinct mentality, a strong distaste for nonsense, steady composure, a calm and gentle demeanor, stability, good principles, intelligence, a habit of understatement, a slow and cautious way of reasoning, contempt for extravagance, vanity, and affectation, kindness of heart, purity, decorum, profound affections, filial and paternal."[69] These former concepts of core education yielded to a new basis for the college curriculum, one in which material that for years had been labeled English, history, economics, foreign languages, philosophy, psychology, science, and mathematics was now being broken down into new groupings with such titles as humanities, communications, social sciences, physical sciences, natural sciences, and life sciences. In this new educational environment, Bowles believed, "aptitude tests will become progressively more important and subject tests progressively less important...." As a result, the former subject tests will become "tests of developed aptitudes."[70] Measurement of "specific details" of subject matter will decrease; measurement of "depth of understanding and the ability to apply knowledge of principles to solutions and problems" will increase.[71] "If these speculations prove to be valid," he proposed, " it may well be that one of the Board's next tasks will be to expend time, effort, and money on further research into aptitude testing with particular attention to a study of the factors that make for success in particular subject fields and the manner in which the development of these factors can be measured and the measurements standardized for use in guidance, selection, and placement."[72]

At ETS, following Bowles's speculations, planning had started in 1952. The "tests of developed aptitudes" became "tests of developed abilities" in that aptitude was seen as a term signifying "something that stays put," while an ability "may grow."[73] In addition to the philosophical shift, three committees were formed to sponsor tests in social studies, humanities, and science. William E. Coffman was put in charge of the program.

As Bowles was forecasting the future of general education in America, Coffman was completing his dissertation from Teachers College under educational psychologist Robert L. Thorndike.[74] Coffman had been at ETS since 1953 and had been a teacher and principal himself; he had also supervised vocational schools and taught in the United States Army Special Training Center in Puerto Rico.[75] Coffman's dissertation, "Teacher Morale and Curriculum Development: A Statistical Analysis of Responses to a Reaction Inventory," had well prepared him for the kind of differential analysis that would later be involved in the design of the Tests of Developed Ability.

Essentially, Coffman's dissertation was centered on three aspects of education: the delineation of the variables of teacher satisfaction; the understanding of teacher morale as it was related to curriculum development—an investigation of shifts in morale that might occur if a curriculum were shifted in the schools in which the teachers worked; and the classification of survey items into scales which would provide a satisfactory group measure of morale in the schools.[76] Delineation and its systematization were activities at the heart of the ETS operation, and the Tests of Developed Ability (TDA) were no exception. Yet Coffman's dissertation also revealed the kind of careful, critical thought that would characterize his approach to all of his research at ETS. When, for instance, one of the scales in his dissertation—General Liking for Teaching—proved internally consistent yet lacked intercorrelations with other scales, he favored a non-mechanistic view of the phenomenon under investigation: "One possible explanation of the independence of the scales may be that the particular influences producing general satisfaction in one individual are not the ones producing it in other individuals. Individuals differ in their needs, interest, and attitudes."[77] Coffman did not follow the logic of a claim for general force of intelligence offered by Charles Spearman and his followers—or for similar concepts such as a generalized construct of teacher morale or developed abilities. While it was true, as E. G. Boring observed, that "what history had given Galton was not a tested nation but a nation being perpetually tested,"[78] the new psychology that had arisen after World War II was more interested in the sub-scores of tests—revelations of complexity—than about single scores. The more one knew about the sub-scores, the more one could understand multi-faceted psychodynamic portraits.[79] Coffman, certainly, was not one for a thermometer approach to testing.

The Tests of Developed Ability did not look like the traditional ETS test. The experimental form of the social studies test, for example, consisted of a 100-item objective section requiring 80 minutes and an essay section requiring 40 minutes. This was a test of achievement, of "knowledge of particular subject matter or achievement in the broad sense of developed ability," and thus it was designed to yield evidence of accomplishment in social studies, humanities, and science.[80] The essay was included in the social science test, Coffman explained, because the test development committee felt that the presence of an essay would encourage more writing in the schools, and evidence of low reader reliability in the past was accepted as a challenge rather than as a potential defeat. (The Humanities Committee experimented with the essay but elected to preserve the two-hour testing period for other material. Regarding the essay, the Science Committee demurred.)

In the field trials in 1956, the tests were administered to over 3,000 secondary school seniors in forty-two different schools. The results "confirm the expectation that the several tests are providing reliable and relatively independent measures—an indication that most of the TDA scores are more independent than the two SAT scores and hence hold more promise than the SAT for distinguishing among students whose likelihood of success in college will vary among prospective major fields of study."[81]

It was, however, the high correlations with the SAT that obviated the need for the tests. While the TDA contributed to an understanding of student development—and thus achieved the best of post-war psychometric analysis, revealing the complexities of academic achievement—it did little to improve the prediction of college success established by the SAT. If the science abilities section of the TDA yielded a .75 correlation with the mathematics section of the SAT, then it could justifiably be argued that the two tests were redundant. By 1957 Bowles himself had come to understand the potential redundancy of the TDA and the SAT. "The optimism concerning these tests as replacements for both the S.A.T. and the Achievement Tests [although the General Composition Test was to have been one of these] has not disappeared," he wrote cautiously, "but it is now tempered by an apparent necessity to devise some combination of the new Tests of Developed Ability with existing examinations if the flexibility and efficiency of the Board's regular battery is to be retained while some of the decided advantages of the new tests are added."[82] Redundant with the other Board tests developed by ETS, the Tests of Developed Ability were dropped from the inventory.[83]

The program failed, but Coffman had not. He had moved ETS beyond the remorseless validation processes of Edith Huddleston, techniques so dependent on item types. His search for defined, subtle assessment procedures led to his work with Frances Swineford and Fred Godshalk and to a system that could be used to evaluate a valid construct of writing through a reliable method. It was a search that proved worthwhile, an effort validated in a classic chapter, "Essay Examinations," that would be published fourteen years later in *Educational Measurement*, a volume edited by his dissertation director.[84]

Frances Swineford and the Advanced Placement Program

If the cause of essay testing and the welfare of education in the United States in 1956 could not best be served by the Developed Abilities Program, then that left the Advanced Placement Program. By all accounts, AP was a dream that came true.

The Advanced Placement Program had grown up alongside of the Developed Abilities Program, but there was a fundamental distinction. The Developed Abilities Program was associated with general education, not linked to any particular course; the Advanced Placement Program was welded to specific high-school courses in American history, biology, chemistry, composition, European history, French, German, Latin, literature, mathematics, physics, and Spanish. In addition, the AP program had grown not so much as a test but as a coherent educational movement associated with Alan B. Blackmer, chairman of the English Department at Phillips Academy in 1952. His report, *General Education in the School and College*, published by Harvard University Press, was the result of a comprehensive effort by three schools (Andover, Exeter, and Lawrenceville) and three universities (Harvard, Princeton, and Yale) to study students in transition from preparatory school to the university. The "three school, three college plan," as it came to be called, advocated an avoidance of waste in the preparatory-school curriculum. The goal was to provide "able students with the opportunity of moving ahead at their own pace in a field of particular strength."[85] Both the College Board and ETS became interested in the "natural outgrowth" of this principle: "a specific proposal for an experimental development of valid advanced placement tests. Constructed, we hope, under the direction of the College Board, these would be offered to all qualified students on a national basis and used, not for admission to college, but for *placement after admission*."[86] Whereas the Tests of Developed Ability were identified with "broad aptitudes rooted in achievement, rather than training in specific subject fields," the Advanced Placement Program was designed to be associated specifically with those defined subject-matter-based courses.[87]

The purpose of the new program was described in the 1954 *College Board Review*: "to encourage superior preparation of college candidates in the secondary schools by providing a method whereby able students with superior training can demonstrate their proficiency and quality for advanced placement. The college will decide whether or not advanced credit will also be granted."[88] Eighteen schools participated, sending 532 candidates. By 1963, 1,681 schools were participating and had sent 21,769 candidates to the examinations.[89] The program was a stunning success for all involved,

Frances Swineford. "Well, I just enjoyed doing the work. It's interesting. I guess I have done a few little things that are stored around and nobody looks at them a second time." (Interview, *ETS Oral History Program* [Princeton: ETS Archives, 1992]: 25.) (Photo Reprinted by Permission of Educational Testing Service. All Rights Reserved.)

its presence concretized by a growing relationship among schools and colleges articulated by College Board.

Behind the AP program was a consistent test validation procedure maintained by Frances Swineford.

Swineford had attended the University of Chicago as an undergraduate, studying and working with Karl Holzinger, a leader in factor analysis techniques, for seventeen years.[90] She had taken a doctorate with fellow statistician Ledyard Tucker, the former head of the Department of Statistical Analysis for the College Board who had moved to ETS.[91] By 1950, Swineford had become head of the Test Analysis Section of the Statistical Analysis Department at ETS.

In her detailed reports for the AP program, Swineford looked closely at reader reliability through a process termed a "double entry" correlation, in which each pair of scores was entered twice to eliminate any bias that might occur if first and second readings are not equally divided among the readers. In a comparison of the essays written on tests of English composition and essays written on tests in literature, for example, Swineford had noted a distinct difference between the correlations: the literature essays had higher inter-reader correlations. "It must be pointed out in this connection," she noted, "that the Chief Reader for Literature reported that a difference of 2 or more points on an essay was discussed by the readers concerned and then adjusted. He added that about 10 per cent of the papers were reread for this purpose. Only the adjusted scores were available for analysis." "Therefore," she concluded, "the reported figures for Literature are somewhat too high to represent the reader reliability for two independent readings. They can not be accepted as reader reliabilities of the reported scores, since we have no data that can be used to estimate how well these scores would agree with scores based on the sums of ratings by different pairs of readers."[92] (Under this view of reliability, one that disallowed adjudication and reliability calculation after the adjudication, it is no wonder that Eley's methods of recording reader reliability in the GCT had been questioned by both Diederich and by Pearson.) On the other hand, the non-adjudicated reliabilities for the composition essays were estimated at .634. It was, however, the American history test that yielded the highest reader reliabilities at .951, "a highly satisfactory value."[93]

Besides establishing the reader reliability coefficients in this particular 1956 test analysis, Swineford also noted the presence of the "halo effect" in the English composition scores. This phenomenon, and the term coined to describe it, had been explained by Edward L. Thorndike in his 1920 article, "A Constant Error in Psychological Ratings." There, Thorndike recalled a 1915 study he had made of employees in two large corporations. He found that different traits, such as intelligence and technical skill, were very highly and very evenly correlated. It appeared that those giving the ratings were "apparently affected by a marked tendency to think of the person in general as rather good or rather inferior and to color the judgments of the qualities by this general feeling."[94] Such correlations, he concluded, are due, in part, to "the constant error of the 'halo,' as we may call it...." Thorndike had become convinced that "even a very capable foreman, employer, teacher, or department head is unable to treat an individual as a compound of separate qualities and to assign a magnitude to each of these in independence of the others." The magnitude of the error, he reflected, seemed "surprisingly large, though we lack objective criteria to determine its exact size."[95] Swineford had, she believed, identified such an error. Each composition test was scored on all three topics by the same reader, but the literature test was scored by different readers, each responsible for one topic. Hence, the intercorrelations—the relationships among the parts of the test—were higher for English composition (.656) than for literature (.286). "Thus," Swineford concluded, "the well known 'halo' entered into the Composition scores but not those on the Literature test."[96]

Swineford had observed two important phenomena associated with the question of reader reliability regarding the AP tests using essay questions. First, she had noted that analytic methods of reading used in the American history test worked very well to produce high inter-reader reliability. Second, she noted that when one reader read the entire test, the presence of the halo effect was observed. Swineford considered the presence of the halo effect problematic. In fact, its presence proved to be of critical benefit.

John French: Factor Analysis and Lack of Independence Among Variables

With Paul Diederich and Sydell T. Carlton, John French, formerly an instructor in psychology at Princeton University, had undertaken a study of the factors in judgments of writing ability with the support of the Carnegie Corporation and had published that study in 1961.[97] The research team hoped that their report would be read by English teachers, many of whom were unfamiliar with factor analysis. With the audience established, a review of the literature was made but with a stated agenda. Since Edith Huddleston's 1954 work, "the College Entrance Examination Board spent six years and a grand total of $97,000 on the development and tryout of its General Composition Test," the authors noted. With the failure of that test, "it was agreed that further progress in grading essays must wait upon a factor analysis of the judgments of a diverse group of competent readers in an unstructured situation." It was hoped that such an analysis would reveal "schools of thought" that would account for systematic differences in grading standards. In addition, it was hoped that some of these "schools" would emphasize qualities "amenable to objective testing" and that the more precise observation of the remaining qualities would lead to greater reader reliability.[98]

John French. "So, if we psychometricians can encourage testing and further clarification of those aspects of writing that objective tests cannot measure, encourage the use of readers who favor grading those particular qualities that are desirable to grade, and see to it that the students are aware of what they are being graded on, we can enlighten rather than merely disparage the polemic art of essay testing" ("Schools of Thought in Judging Excellence of English Themes," ETS Reprint from the 1961 *Proceedings of Invitational Conference on Testing Procedures* [1962] 12). (Source of Drawing: *College Board Review* 27 [Fall 1955] 7. Copyright © 1955 by College Board. Reproduced with permission. All rights reserved. www.collegeboard.com)

In designing the factor analysis study, French and his colleagues recognized that there were four possible sources of error on a composition test: student error (a student can do well one day and do poorly the next day on the very same task); test error (the composition test is, after all, a "one-item test"[99]); scale error (to get all readers for an examination to grade papers on the same scale may, in reality, be a matter of "administrative persuasion"[100]); and reader disagreement (there remains disagreement on what kind of writing is best, even if readers can be persuaded to use the same scale). They had designed a study to investigate reader disagreement, the fourth type of error.

The "stimuli" for the readers in the study were three hundred short essays written as homework by college freshmen, but the essays had been selected to represent a greater percentage of low- and very high-ability students than is normally found in a freshman English course. The low and high clusters of papers would allow easier discrimination among the papers so that the kinds of judgments the readers were making would stand out clearly. Students wrote on two topics: "Who Should Go to College?" and "When Should Teen-agers Be Treated as Adults?" The readers for the experiment were ten English teachers, nine social scientists, eight natural scientists, ten writers or editors, nine lawyers, and seven business executives—"all kinds of persons who have reason to savor or suffer from the quality of writing achieved by graduates of our colleges."[101]

However, the procedure for the readers was radically different than the traditional training used in Board programs in which readers—for three days in advance of reading the actual student papers—came together, discussed the grading criteria, graded sample papers, considered the results, and revised the rules to cover contingencies. In their study, French and his colleagues merely told their readers to "Use your own judgment as to what constitutes 'writing ability.' Do not assume we want you to do this or that."[102] The readers were merely asked to sort the papers into nine piles in order of merit, with at least six of the papers placed into each pile. The readers were also asked to write on the papers their comments on what they disliked or liked about the papers.

The first element the readers examined was the reliability of the readings. The average correlation, despite the fact that the papers had been pre-selected to exhibit low and very high ability, was .31. "You can understand just how low this is, when I tell you that, out of the 300 papers, 101 received all nine different grades, and no paper received less than five different grades."[103] French established that the average inter-reader agreement among English teachers in Board programs was .7, so he wondered if the ratings of the English teachers in the experiment would be higher. They indeed were, with a .41 correlation. English teachers were able to grade with less random error.

In order to discover what "schools of thought" did exist among the readers, the intercorrelations were subjected to factor analysis. In the factor analysis was also included other evaluations of the students: the SAT verbal scores, the SAT mathematical scores, and their English Composition Test scores. These scores were included in the factor analysis, in other words, just as if there had been three additional readers.

The factor analysis—"a mathematical procedure that picks out the basic dimensions or tendencies in a table of correlations"[104]—revealed six sources of variation, but the first factor was so large that it represented a "set of values having importance for all readers," a kind of general factor which could be understood as being supplemented by the other five factors.[105] That factor was the test factor. "The three objective College Board tests appeared close together and quite remote in the dimensional factorial space from any of the readers."[106] The other five factors—ideas, form, flavor, mechanics, and working—were obtained by summarizing and numerically coding the readers' comments, but, significantly, the other five factors were not independent of each other. Readers who had favored one characteristic were favoring other aspects as well. The intercorrelation between ideas and wording, for example, was .55, and between mechanics and wording the intercorrelation was .63. For French, an equally important finding was that the test factor was unrelated to ideas (-.02) or to form (.16) or to flavor (.27). "This tells us," French concluded, "something about the tests, something all of us may not be happy to learn. The test scores are somewhat like the essay grades given by readers of the mechanics and wording schools of thought and they appear to be completely unrelated to the grades assigned by readers who grade on ideas. Isn't this what English teachers have been telling us psychometricians all along—that essay tests of writing ability measure something that objective tests do not measure? They seem to be right."[107]

The results of the factor analysis study were not missed by the team of Godshalk, Swineford, and Coffman. Factor analysis had failed to establish differentiation among the five factors of writing ability. So, if the factors were so inextricably correlated, why not simply ask readers to look at them holistically? In other words, why not make Thorndike's halo effect work to achieve the elusive grail of reliability?

Godshalk, Swineford, and Coffman: Holistic Scoring and the Assessment Solution

Fred I. Godshalk had come to ETS in 1954. He had been a classroom teacher and a high-school principal. He had been both an army colonel and assistant commandant of the Armed Forces Information School and, since 1956, had served as chairman of the Humanities Department of the Test Development Division.

Fred I. Godshalk. "I haven't had any special purpose here, except in so far as the chairman asked me to fill in a gap, but as I have in a way derived a purpose, it is to leave you with the notion that there is 'something in' the English composition test provided that you know it is a *composition* test and not an *English* test" ("Testing the English Composition Test," a talk make extemporaneously at the School and College Conference on English, Barnard College, Feb. 16 and 17, 1962 [Princeton: ETS Archives, Green File, Roll 13] 8–9). (Source of Photo: *College Board Review* 43. Copyright © by College Board. Reproduced with permission. All rights reserved. www.collegeboard.com)

Coffman was an educational measurement specialist, and Swineford was a statistician. But Godshalk was something far different: a subject matter specialist. "I think I should begin by saying that I am not a psychometrician," he said at a conference at Barnard College. "I am a subject matter specialist. I have been an English teacher and have developed the testing specialty on the job. This seems to be the only complete way of learning how to make tests."[108] In 1961 Godshalk undertook a study of the English Composition Test with Frances Swineford; William Coffman was later added to the project. Among them, they invented modern assessment practices and validation techniques.

The English Composition Test had proven to be quite durable and was thus a worthy object of their attention. Begun in 1943, the test had been transformed into an examination of completely objective, limited-response items in 1948. In 1951, an interlinear exercise was added to the test. In this type of item, a poorly written passage required the student to find and correct deficiencies by line-editing the passage. The interlinear exercise, the only free-response section of the test, had proven to have very high scoring reliability but was nevertheless quite complex to evaluate. As Godshalk noted: "It is difficult to handle because it calls for the actual inspection of individual tests by people who must have a considerable degree of expertness. They cannot be simply clerks. They have to have enough familiarity with how to write and what is good and what is not, what is acceptable and what isn't, so that variations from a rubric, a standard book of procedure, an acceptable versus unacceptable determination, can be judged without the necessity of appealing to an authority on every variation found. This is an expensive and, of course, time-consuming, difficult procedure."[109] In that the ECT was quite popular—approximately 100,000 candidates took the March 1960 administration—scoring the interlinear exercise had become a complex job.

Durable at it was, the ECT had also been the object of intense criticism. In meetings on November 5 and 6, 1960, the College Board committee of member colleges responsible for the test had been informed that a number of colleges, including a leading eastern women's college, were considering dropping the test. While no formal action had come from the schools, Godshalk later recollected that "the committee was sufficiently stirred by this hubbub to talk seriously concerning the quality of the work that they were doing." As he recalled:

> The outcome of the discussion was a decision to recommend to the College Entrance Examination Board and to the Educational Testing Service…research into the validity of the English composition test as it was then constituted. The proposal was made in rather general terms. The principal feature was this. Since we are testing a skill and since the skill is called writing competency, should we not for the first time, so far as we know, use as a criterion of writing competency, essays written under standard testing conditions and read by people who normally read such essays and regard themselves, and are regarded, as competent judges of writing skill, of the outcome of good writing? In other words, what was proposed here was a little different from the validity experiments that had been done from

> time to time. Instead of using as a criterion of the success or failure of English composition tests, the outcome in a freshman composition course or in college freshman English in general, we would use simply the single thing that the test was supposed to predict: "How well can the student write? What is the relationship between this one hour, largely objective instrument, and the best judgment of experts concerning the actual writing?"[110]

In their internal ETS research proposal, Godshalk and Swineford delineated the question more formally, stating that they were interested in the efficiency of the item types used on the English Composition Test. On October 2, 1961, they presented a proposal for a study "primarily intended to disclose the differences, if any, between the prediction of a criterion by objective items of various types and by the interlinear exercise, a structured free-response test with controlled scoring of high reliability. Additionally, it is designed to demonstrate differences in prediction of the criterion that might be produced by various combinations of item types into one-hour tests—as a matter of efficient construction, since directions are fairly complex, not more than three kinds of items per test would be considered—so that a best theoretical combination of item types, or several such combinations of almost equal effectiveness, will be known and can be used in test planning."[111] Innovatively, the criterion of the study would be "a series of work samples, free writing under controlled conditions, so devised and graded as to define writing competency in terms of the product produced by writers of a wide range of skill, with the results judged by a panel of qualified critics." They recognized that this criterion was "altogether new and different, and that at this point its justification is merely theoretical."[112]

The essays, Godshalk and Swineford proposed, would be read by means of an experimental procedure, conducted with Osmond E. Palmer at Michigan State University, which had yielded reader reliabilities "in the high .80's."[113] The readings "would be holistic rather than analytical…based upon a group examination and discussion of selected papers, with consensus reached as to the ratings of each paper and the elements that had been considered in arriving at that decision."[114] In other words, the new technique, rather than working to isolate Thorndike's halo effect, would capitalize on it, advancing the general impression that the essay made on the reader. As Coffman would later reflect, "It is possible…that halo is simply another name for the essential unity of any effective essay response. To the extent that a unique communication has been created, the elements are related to the whole in a fashion that makes a high relationship of the parts inevitable. The evaluation of the part cannot be made apart from its relationship to the whole."[115] Indeed, even the evaluative criteria of the essays—their rankings—would be derived inductively and descriptively by the group reading the essays.

The new process embodied the perceptive subtleties characteristic of Coffman and French: hadn't factor analysis confirmed the inextricable nature of the factors of writing ability? The process also suggested the influence of gestalt psychology. Where writing had been understood by Charles Swain Thomas in 1932 as a product of the constants of automatism (mechanics) and creation (active thinking), Godshalk and his team saw essences. The elementalism that drove the scales of Thorndike, Hillegas, and their followers had all but disappeared by 1938 when the University of Michigan's Stuart A. Courtis withdrew his tests from the market because he "had discovered that they did not measure what they were supposed to measure."[116] Influenced by the psychological orientation of Max Wertheimer, Wolfgang Köhler, and Kurt Koffka—the founders of gestalt psychology, all natives of Germany, all immigrants to the United States after the Nazi rise to power—the Godshalk team focused on the emergent wholes of compositions and on the phenomenal, immediate, and impressionistic experience of reading student papers. Following gestalt principles, the team knew that organisms organize consistently in relational patterns that are dynamic; hence, since analysis distorts the whole, the total effect of the composition would be used to train readers to follow relational patterns among levels of papers carefully chosen for their impressionistic value.[117]

Godshalk and Swineford spent considerable time in their proposal on the concept of "English Composition as a skill rather than a body of knowledge."[118] While it is possible, the authors stated, to sample what a student knows of American history or algebra, it is not possible to sample writing skill in the same way. "This is the reason for the considerable number of objective item types that have been developed for tests on English composition, each of which kind is theoretically justified as related to composition skill, but no one of which by itself can possibly do the total testing job."[119] They then formulated their view of composition:

> In the last analysis, therefore, composition skill is like the technique off the diving board or at the piano, with the added complication that mere reproduction is not enough. The judgment of such a skill as writing is an expert judgment in which none of the performance samples is supposed to look like any other, but merely to have certain extremely variable but necessary characteristics; it is further a judgment in which the individual judge is faced with the almost impossible task of "weighting" infinite variations of these characteristics and coming up with a number that other judges will come up with independently.

> The result is a situation in which reliable judgment of free writing is remarkable merely because it exists at all.

Swineford and Godshalk concluded: "Since the English Composition test purports to measure composition skill only, an outside criterion of performance *in the writing of* essays of some sort for which the performance is judged by 'qualified' critics working concertedly, who check each other in setting standards and cross-check the marking of papers as well would seem to be the nearest approach to a 'pure' criterion that can be found."[120] The function of holistic scoring thus followed the form of writing. The allusion to Samuel Johnson's comment—"Sir, a woman's preaching is like a dog's walking on his hind legs. It is not done well; but you are surprised to find it done at all"—was, while not enlightened in its connotation, apt in its conclusion regarding the difficulties involved in the assessment of student compositions. What was needed was a method that used the presence of consciousness (and the reading process inherent in it) to deny analysis and to embrace the *gestalten*.

In the research design, fifty junior- and senior-level students from twenty secondary schools would be given a battery of testing material used in Board programs. Students would be examined using objective items (testing usage, sentence correction, paragraph organization, prose groupings, error recognition, and construction shifts) and the interlinear exercises. The criterion measures would be five free-writing exercises—two essays with a total time allowed of 40 minutes and three extended paragraphs, each to be completed in 20 minutes. Interlinear scoring would be done using the Reader's Manuals.

Essay scoring for the criterion reading would be done using the experimental new holistic procedure. It allowed for speed. As well, "the judgment by total impression, when founded upon rated samples, reasons, and analysis of characteristics, more nearly approximate[d] the method by which any skill is judged in actual practice, whether it be diving, piano playing, or waking out on the runway in a bathing suit."[121] The new method would also, it was hoped, decrease reader bias "towards pet writing aversions"[122] because the papers would be read rapidly. After all, as French and his team had found in their study, if the factors were so inextricably correlated, there was evidence that readers should look at them holistically.[123]

Each paper would receive at least four independent readings to place it on a three-point scale of high, average, or low. All readers would be trained at an orientation session for each of the five kinds of writing. Sample papers would be scored by all readers independently, and their scores would be recorded for discussion. Thus, under guidance, readers would "attempt to arrive at consensus on the characteristics to be considered, their relative weights, and other basic reasons for awarding one score rather than another."[124] Experienced readers would check "maverick writing" in order to answer questions on doubtful papers, and further orientation would "include scoring additional reproduced samples from time to time in the early reading, so that deviations [would be] discovered and corrected."[125]

The experiment would begin on October 5 when letters would be sent to selected schools. The data assembly was to have been completed by January 12. In a draft that was completed very late in 1961, Godshalk, Swineford, and Coffman wrote up their results in a report that would be expanded, but not essentially altered, to form the classic 1966 monograph *The Measurement of Writing Ability*.

In that the writing samples served as the criterion measure for the study, they were of greatest importance: without demonstrated reader reliability, the experiment would have been invalid. The reliabilities were to everyone's satisfaction: "The reliabilities attained in the reading of the twenty-minute essays [were] well above average (.758 for two and .777 for the third), and the total essay test reading reliability of .919 [was] remarkable."[126] The researchers also discovered that essay scores varied according to topics and that topics could not necessarily be used interchangeably, and so options among topics should not be permitted. Stalnaker's 1937 advice had been correct. Each student, it was recommended, should write on each topic presented. Because the total score on all five essays was reliably established, the innovative goal for the study had been met, and it was possible to examine the subtests.

A study of correlations of the various measures used in the study was prepared. Inclusion of the essays increased the multiple correlations among the item types with the essays "from .756 to .767 for seniors and from .733 to .796 among juniors" who had been classified according to performance criteria (their success on usage exercises). Thus, the most reliable direct measure of writing included an essay in combination with objective questions. Among the correlations of other measures, the two highest correlations with the essay were usage (.707) and sentence correction (.705), both tested through objective items. The potential way of improving the English Composition Test suggested in the 1946 *Annual Report*—an essay question read by multiple readers combined with an objective test—had been realized.

And the interlinear, the item type that began the study when Swineford and Godshalk sought its validation? When combined with an objective test, the correlation exceeded .70. But, considering the cost of scoring, “the unique contribution appears to be relatively small when one considers the additional cost of including the interlinear in a test.”[127] Indeed, when the essays were substituted for the interlinear sections, the multiple correlations were “increased *without exception*.”[128] Ironically, the very item type the study had been planned to validate was now found to be too costly to continue.

In 1961, that cost must have loomed especially large. The United Aircraft Company’s Norden Division, famous for developing the World War II bombsight, had just developed a method by which tests could be machine scored and recorded on IBM cards at ETS. A single answer sheet could be used for an entire half-day of testing for the SAT and the Achievement Tests, and the machine could score the tests at a speed of 6,000 sheets per hour.[129] Godshalk and his team were keenly aware of costs, recording that the reading rate per essay “is estimated at from seven to nine 20-minute essays (five readings each) per hour. The reading rate for the 30-minute interlinears has varied from topic to topic but is believed to average about ten per hour.”[130] Thus, if two readers were used on each essay, the reading rate would double that of the interlinear exercises. If money had to be spent on direct assessment, the clear choice now was to allocate that money not to the interlinear (which added little to the ability to measure student ability) but to the essay (which increased the correlations without exception and which could be read rapidly). The objective items would be consigned to the machine (which could “accommodate any foreseeable number of students without undue strain,” as the ETS executives put it[131]).

The stars had aligned, and so the researchers concluded: “Data have been presented constituting strong evidence that a 20-minute essay would not only maintain the current high validity of the English Composition Test as a measure of writing ability but would probably increase such validity by about .025 on the average.”[132]

The final chapter of the 1966 monograph, entitled “The Measurement of Writing Ability—A Significant Breakthrough,” claimed that the essay was now “certified” for regular use to evaluate writing ability.[133] Godshalk, Swineford, and Coffman thus definitively ended the debate begun when S[illegible]aker recanted his 1937 position that essays could be reliably read and [illegible] in 1943 that the “type of test so highly valued by teachers of English, [illegible]equires the candidate to write a theme or essay, is not a worth-while [illegible]evice.”[134] They had also dispelled Edith Huddleston’s 1947 claim [illegible]ssay and the paragraph revision sections have added nothing to the predictive validity" of an examination.[135] Now, just the opposite had been demonstrated to be true: "An essay in the English Composition Test says to the student that skill in actual writing is an important outcome of instruction. It says to the teacher that the ability to answer multiple-choice questions, unless accompanied by the ability to compose answers to essay questions, is not sufficient evidence of effective teaching."[136]

To Edward Noyes, who wrote the introduction to *The Measurement of Writing Ability*, it must have seemed that the end of a very long road had been reached. The measurement of a student's ability to write, he proclaimed, "has at long last been solved, insofar as the current English Composition Tests are concerned."[137] The key to the assessment of writing ability had been found in a combination of objective items and essays. Instinct had proven true: the essays were, after all, worth something.[138]

Borderline People: A Decade of Turbulence

But what? Whose language was it, anyway, that was being assessed? The desegregation mandated by the Supreme Court in the 1954 *Brown* v. *Board of Education* decision had turned aggressive. In 1965 the nation was reading *The Autobiography of Malcolm X*, and in 1966 Stokely Carmichael had proclaimed the following in the *New York Review of Books*:

> For too many years, black Americans marched and had their heads broken and got shot. They were saying to the country, "Look, you guys are supposed to be nice guys and we are only going to do what we are supposed to do—why do you beat us up, why don't you give us what we ask, why don't you straighten yourselves out?" After years of this, we are at almost the same point—because we demonstrated from a position of weakness. We cannot be expected any longer to march and have our heads broken in order to say to whites: come on, you're nice guys. For you are not nice guys. We have found you out.[139]

Watts—Los Angeles' largest black district—had burned for six long August days. While Truman had found popular support in defending South Korea, Lyndon Johnson had found only resentment as hundreds of thousands protested the American commitment to South Vietnam. Even William James could not provide answers, as Reinhold Niebuhr lamented in a 1961 edition of *The Varieties of Religious Experience*. "Our generation is bound to be anxious," he wrote, "not so much about the brevity of our individual life (though that anxiety can never be suppressed) but about the chance of the whole world escaping a nuclear catastrophe. We must worry not only about establishing wholesome relations in the intimate communities of family and friends. We must be concerned about establishing just relations in the increasing intricacies of a technical civilization. Even a genius like James, bound by the limits of his age, cannot help us with these problems of community and the meaning of human history."[140] The 1962 Cuban missile crisis had brought matters of history and faith center-stage as the world waited to see if Khrushchev or Kennedy would blink first. No one, it would appear, was safe.

Even ETS, the agency that had so well served its nation's military-industrial complex, had come under attack with the 1962 publication of Banesh Hoffmann's *The Tyranny of Testing*, as the mathematics professor from Queens College completed the attack he had begun in *Harper's* and the *American Scholar*. Jacques Barzun—dean and provost at Columbia University and recent author of *The Houses of Intellect*, itself a condemnation of the failure of high-riding, well-paid individuals to engage a complex society—set the stage for the attack in the foreword. "Doubts and protests long pent up have at last come forth," he wrote, "because one man was courageous enough to attack an entrenched position. It is therefore clear that the time is ripe for the full, documented, and reasoned account which Mr. Hoffmann gives in this book of the inadequacies and dangers of mechanical testing."[141]

Hoffmann continued the argument that Walter Lippmann had begun in 1923. Citing the conclusions drawn by Brigham in his study of American intelligence based on the army tests, Lippmann had criticized the "Psychological Battalion of Death" and urged his readers to join him "in repudiating the dogmatism of those who preach the predestined incapacity of an overwhelming majority of the nation."[142] Hoffmann's implicit message was at one with Lippmann's, an echo of the journalist's call for rejection of "a doctrine as yet without scientific foundation, which can produce nothing but discredit for psychology, fatalism, and paralysis in the schools, injustice in society, and unnecessary despair or unwarranted conceit among the persons who are tested."[143] In 1962, however, the doctrine was not eugenics but the business of testing itself.

In a chapter entitled "What's in a Name?" Hoffmann paid special attention to the decline and fall of Earle G. Eley's General Composition Test. "Testing is no game," he began the chapter by assuring his readers. "It is in deadly earnest. If tests are misused, the consequences can be far from trifling. Lives can be warped and careers ruined.... The strength and vitality of a nation may be jeopardized."[144] A case in point was the measurement of composition ability. The English Composition Test created by the College Board and the Educational Testing Service had constructed a "synthetic test" in which a set of "fractionalized attributes" of composition—"the ability to punctuate, to choose the appropriate word choice, to place ideas in logical order, to recognize and rectify grammatical error and incorrect usage, to sense whether a particular style is appropriate, and so on." Yet while the College Board and ETS may have felt that "a miracle had been performed," the outcry among educators was immediate. The General Composition Test had been created by Eley in reply to the protest, but it had failed, Hoffmann told his readers, in its ability to reflect the teachers' own grades of their students. It had been outperformed against the multiple-choice items of both the English Composition Test and the verbal section of the SAT. "It all sounds so reasonable, so logical, so scientifically conclusive.... Yet the result feels all wrong. Why? Why is it awry in this pretty picture?" he rhetorically wondered. He charged that the logic lacked self-consistency. If the verbal section of the SAT had performed so well, then why not call it the "New and Improved English Composition Test," he asked? "Was the Board fearful that by going over to the new and improved Scholastic Aptitude model it would make all too plain that neither the new nor the old was in fact a test of English Composition?" And, as for the General Composition Test's failure to reflect the grades of the students' English teachers, Hoffmann wondered, "Were not these ratings based on essays?" To end the story, he reminded his readers that the Board presently sent non-graded essays to colleges under the "official name" of Writing Samples.[145] The College Board, Hoffmann concluded, had forgotten its larger responsibility.

Other criticisms appear in Hoffmann's jeremiad, from a heated exchange conducted with John M. Stalnaker over the National Merit Tests to one with Edward M. Glaser over the Watson-Glaser Critical Thinking Appraisal. The cumulative narrative impact was devastating. Especially telling was the story of a high-school student, told in a chapter entitled "David and Goliath," who had written to ETS with a question regarding two items on the English Composition Test which he had found to be misleading. The student had received no reply and had then written to Hoffmann as well as to the ETS president, Henry Chauncey. That tactic had gotten the attention of ETS. The student was told that he was one who had "just enough knowledge to see possibilities in more than one answer and now enough knowledge to decide which is really correct." "Apparently," the letter told him, "you are one of those borderline people with respect to the two questions about which you have written." A copy of the letter was sent to Hoffmann by ETS with a handwritten note. "I am sure," the note read, "you'll find the attached copies of letters an interesting addition to your file of examples of the relationship—or lack of relationship—between the ability to identify ambiguity in multiple-choice questions and other desirable abilities—such as the ability to write clearly and correctly."[146] The sheer arrogance of it all—the condescending classification of the student as borderline, the attached note to Hoffmann suggesting the incompetence of the student—hit home. His final chapter—"Don't Be Pro-Test—Protest"—was a call to action. Hoffmann had, indeed, found something happening here. And what it was seemed exactly clear.

The attack upon ETS would continue through the 1970s, culminating in a report sponsored by Ralph Nader, Allan Nairn's *The Reign of ETS: The Corporation That Makes Up Minds* in 1980. In New York state, truth-in-testing legislation mandated that ETS publish its old tests, thus forcing a disclosure of the items that were, literally, the capital of testing. Just as Noyes had found footing, the road had turned. Sharply. "Regardless of how it is viewed," Nairn had written, "the underlying fact is inescapable: the ETS test system causes many individuals painful upheavals. Whenever widespread pain is inflicted on people, it is essential to ask why. It is important to keep in the forefront of any such inquiry the experience of victims."[147] The prescience expressed in Specimen 95 fifty-four years before had come true. The rights of man, native or alien, male or female, free or slave, were going to be affirmed—one way or the other.

Endnotes

1 Harry S. Truman, "Statement by the President," June 27, 1950, Truman Presidential Museum and Library, 23 Jan. 2005. <http://www.trumanlibrary.org>.

2 Note, Chauncey Merger File, Miscellaneous Notes (Princeton: ETS Archives). The reference to Richard Nixon is found on a slip of paper initialed by Henry Chauncey dated "4/51." It is significant to note that Truman signed the executive order on March 31, 1951; on March 22, 1951, Chauncey had reported to the ETS Board that he had signed a contract with the Selective Service. Beginning in 1948 under Chauncey's leadership, ETS was involved in testing for student deferment, the program itself demonstrating an active role for ETS in national government. For a history of the SSCQT at ETS, see Thomas J. Frusciano, "Student Deferment and the Selective Service College Qualifying Test, 1951–1967," *Research Memorandum* RM-83-1 (Princeton: ETS, 1980). For another treatment of the SSCQT, see Nicholas Lemann, *The Big Test: The Secret History of the American Meritocracy* (New York: Farrar 1999) 72–80. Lemann's book led me to Frusciano's report.

3 Memorandum for the Board of Trustees, 20 Apr. 1951, Chauncey Merger File (Princeton: ETS Archives) 1. The qualifications of Raymond H. Miller are provided on page 2 of the memo.

4 Public Opinion News Service, 27–28 May 1951, Chauncey Merger File (Princeton: ETS Archives). Gallup, the director of the American Institute of Public Opinion, asked two questions to test public opinion for the deferment. The first question read: "Do you think college students, eligible for the draft, who pass a test of general ability should or should not be allowed to complete their college work before being called into the Armed Forces?" The answers revealed the following: 55 percent said they should; 36 percent said they should not; 9 percent were undecided. (Gallup also posed this question to a cross-section of those listed in *Who's Who in America*, and 66 percent reported that the exemption should stand; 31 percent reported that it should not; and 3 percent had no opinion.) The second question was designed to elicit opinions on whether students majoring in all academic subjects should be exempted. The question read: "If some college students are permitted to finish their college courses before they are drafted into the Armed Forces, do you think this should apply to all college students—or to those students taking special courses, such as medicine, science, engineering, etc.?" Forty-six percent reported that the exemption should stand for all students; 44 percent reported that the exemption should stand for special students only; and 10 percent were undecided. The relationship between the two questions was reported as follows: "Persons who favored the idea of allowing college students to finish their training were more inclined to think that all students should be included in this plan."

5 Selective Service College Qualifying Test, *Bulletin of Information*, Mar.–June 1951 (Princeton: ETS Archives).

6 The northern states, Yerkes and his colleagues had found in *Psychological Examining in the United States Army* (Washington: GPO, 1921), were "highest in intelligence," the more northern and western southern states were "intermediate in intelligence," and the more southern and eastern southern states were "lowest in intelligence" (731). Civil engineers, lawyers and teachers, and students had scored the highest, while teamsters, barbers, and laborers had done the worst on examination alpha (Table 375, 821).

7 Lyndon B. Johnson, Memorandum to Major General Lewis B. Hershey, 13 June 1951, Chauncey Merger File (Princeton: ETS Archives).

8 Paul B. Diederich, Memorandum to Henry Chauncey, 16 May 1951, Chauncey Merger File (Princeton: ETS Archives). Lemann's book led me to Diederich's letter.

9 Henry Chauncey, Interview, Part Six, 8 Nov. 1977, *ETS Archives Oral History Program* 11. In *The Big Test* Lemann also notes the Chauncey interview and writes that he carried on a "substantial correspondence with Chauncey, much of it consisting of his clarifying or elaborating on details in the history of testing" (351).

10 John E. Burchard, "Science Education and the Liberal Arts," *College Board Review* 33 (1957): 16. The article (13–18) is a classic of Cold-War rationality in its adoration of science and its relegation of the humanities (and the social sciences) to supporting roles.

11 This poll is reported in George Q. Flynn, *The Draft, 1940–1973* (Lawrence: UP of Kansas, 1993) 148.

12 Major Lenox R. Lohr, *Chemical and Engineering News*, 7 Apr. 1955, 700. Noted in Flynn, *The Draft, 1940–1973* 148.

13 Dwight D. Eisenhower, "Military-Industrial Complex Speech," *Public Papers of the Presidents of the United States* (Washington: Federal Register Division, National Archives and Records Service, General Services Administration, 1961) 1035–1040. 23 Jan. 2005 <http://www.yale.edu/lawweb/avalon/>.

14 Edith M. Huddleston, "Recent Studies of the English Composition Test," *College Board Review* 1.4 (1948): 45.

15 Huddleston, "Recent Studies of the English Composition Test" 50.

16 *Forty-Sixth Annual Report of the Executive Secretary* (New York: College Entrance Examination Board, 1946) 7.

17 *Forty-Sixth Annual Report of the Executive Secretary* 7.

18 *Forty-Sixth Annual Report of the Executive Secretary* 8.

19 Huddleston, "Recent Studies" 50.

20 Huddleston, "Recent Studies" 51.

21 Huddleston, "Recent Studies" 52.

22 Huddleston, "Recent Studies" 52.

23 The Commission on English, *Examining the Examination in English: A Report to the College Entrance Examination Board* (Cambridge: Harvard UP, 1931) 213. In Appendix D the commission found that "The Scholastic Aptitude Test, although not specifically designed to test pure English ability, seems to do so in a much more effective manner than does the College Entrance Examination Board English Examination"; Appendix C provided a formula for combining the three factors.

24 Huddleston, "Recent Studies" 53.

25 The dissertation was printed by the Educational Testing Service in August 1952. The article was published in the *Journal of Experimental Education* 22.3 (1954): 165–213. References are made to the article because it is more widely available and because the dissertation was printed in its entirety in the *Journal*.

26 John M. Stalnaker, "Question VI—The Essay," *English Journal* 26.2 (1937): 133–140.

27 Edith M. Huddleston, "Measurement of Writing Ability at the College-Entrance Level: Objective vs. Subjective Testing Techniques," *Journal of Experimental Education* 22.3 (1954): 171.

28 G. F. Kuder and M. W. Richardson, "The Theory of the Estimation of Test Reliability," *Psychometrika* 2 (1937): 151–160. Huddleston provided this citation on the formula, as well as one by her ETS colleague Ledyard R. Tucker: "A Note on the Estimation of Test Reliability by the Kuder-Richardson Formula (20)," *Psychometrika* 15 (1949): 117–119.

29 Huddleston, "Measurement of Writing Ability at the College-Entrance Level" 189.

30 Huddleston, "Measurement of Writing Ability at the College-Entrance Level" 189.

31 Huddleston, "Measurement of Writing Ability at the College-Entrance Level" 204.

32 *Fiftieth Annual Report of the Director* (New York: College Entrance Examination Board, 1950) 3.

33 *Fiftieth Annual Report of the Director* 2.

34 *Fiftieth Annual Report of the Director* 3.

35 *Fiftieth Annual Report of the Director* 4.

36 Frank D. Ashburn, "Progress Report—Committee on English Testing," *College Board Review* 11 (1950) 141.

37 Earle G. Eley, "An Analysis of Writing Competence," diss., U of Chicago, 1953. Braddock, Lloyd-Jones, and Schoer cite Eley's dissertation in the bibliography of *Research in Written Composition*. The 504-item bibliography was more than just a list of works cited; rather, it was a list of studies examined by the Committee on the State of Knowledge about Composition (a ten-member committee chaired by Braddock), cooperating colleagues, and the directors of the project. Hence, Eley's dissertation was considered significant.

38 Earle G. Eley, "The Experiment in General Composition," *College Board Review* 15 (1951) 217.

39 Eley, "The Experiment in General Composition" 218.

40 Eley, "The Experiment in General Composition" 220.

41 *Fifty-First Annual Report of the Director* (New York: College Entrance Examination Board, 1951) 9. The General Composition Test had been off to a promising start. Sketches were drawn by Educational Testing Service artist Rosamond Rollins to accompany a Christmas reading conference at New Jersey's Lawrenceville School. The cover of this book shows one of the sketches. See "Reading Conference," *College Board Review* 19 [1953]: 324–326.

42 *Fifty-First Annual Report of the Director* 9.

43 Stalnaker, "Question VI—The Essay" 134.

44 Paul B. Diederich, Memo for Mr. Dobbin: The CEEB General Composition Test, 3 Oct. 1951, Diederich Papers (Princeton: ETS Archives) 2.

45 Diederich, Memo for Mr. Dobbin 2.

46 Diederich, Memo for Mr. Dobbin 3.

47 Diederich, Memo for Mr. Dobbin 4.

48 Diederich, Memo for Mr. Dobbin 4.

49 "Should the General Composition Test Be Continued?" *College Board Review* 25 (1955): 2. Eley's article was noted eight years later in *Research in Written Composition* by Braddock, Lloyd-Jones, and Schoer as emblematic of critics of "multiple-choice tests of composition" (40–41).

50 Richard Pearson, "The Test Fails as an Entrance Examination," *College Board Review* 25 (1955): 6.

51 Pearson, "The Test Fails as an Entrance Examination" 7.

52 Earle G. Eley, "The Test Satisfies an Educational Need," *College Board Review* 25 (1955) 11.

53 Eley, "The Test Satisfies an Educational Need" 13.

54 Eley, "The Test Satisfies an Educational Need" 13.

55 Eley, "The Test Satisfies an Educational Need" 13.

56 Eley, "The Test Satisfies an Educational Need" 13.

57 Eley, "The Test Satisfies an Educational Need" 13.

58 Eley, "The Test Satisfies an Educational Need" 13.

59 *Fifty-Fifth Annual Report of the Director* (New York: College Entrance Examination Board, 1955) 40.

60 *Fifty-Fifth Annual Report of the Director* 40.

61 "The GCT Experiment: Final Report," *College Board Review* 29 (1956) 31.

62 "The GCT Experiment: Final Report" 31.

63 "The GCT Experiment: Final Report" 32.

64 "The GCT Experiment: Final Report" 32.

65 "The GCT Experiment: Final Report" 32.

66 "The GCT Experiment: Final Report" 32.

67 "The GCT Experiment: Final Report" 32.

68 *Forty-Ninth Annual Report of the Director* (New York: College Entrance Examination Board, 1949) 49.

69 *Forty-Ninth Annual Report of the Director* 49.

70 *Forty-Ninth Annual Report of the Director* 51.

71 *Forty-Ninth Annual Report of the Director* 51.

72 *Forty-Ninth Annual Report of the Director* 51.

73 Henry S. Dyer, "The Test of Developed Abilities," *College Board Review* 31 (1957): 5.

74 Robert L. Thorndike had been at Teachers College since 1936. A renowned measurement specialist, he would restandardize the Stanford-Binet Intelligence Test in 1972.

75 William E. Coffman, Annual Service Recognition Dinner, 27 Apr. 1968 (Princeton: ETS Archives). By 1968, Coffman had been assistant, associate, and director of test development within an eight-year period. In 1968, he was serving as acting director of developmental research.

76 William E. Coffman, "Teacher Morale and Curriculum Development: A Statistical Analysis of Responses to a Reaction Survey," diss., Teachers College, Columbia U, 1949, 10.

77 Coffman, "Teacher Morale and Curriculum Development" 85.

78 Edwin G. Boring, *A History of Experimental Psychology*, 2nd ed. (New York: Appleton, 1950) 577.

79 R. W. Kamphaus, Martha D. Petoskey, and Anna Walters Morgan, "A History of Intelligence Interpretation," *Contemporary Intellectual Assessment: Theories, Tests, and Issues*, eds. Dawn P. Flanagan, Judy L. Genshaft, and Patti L. Harrison (New York: Guilford P, 1997) 36–38.

80 William E. Coffman, "Development of the Tests," *College Board Review* 31 (1957): 7.

81 Coffman, "Development of the Tests" 9.

82 *Fifty-Sixth Annual Report of the Director* (New York: College Entrance Examination Board, 1957) 39.

83 In *The Big Test*, Lemann writes that Chauncey had proposed the test and that it was designed by ETS insiders. "The Tests of Developed Ability," he claims, "would have represented a decisive symbolic break for ETS with its origins in IQ testing" (94). He writes that the TDA might have appeased test developer E. F. Lindquist, "the most influential testing figure who wasn't concerned with ETS in some way" (94). Lemann also finds that the abandonment of the TDA resulted in Lindquist beginning American College Testing, the organization that today remains the most active competitor of ETS. As well, Lemann claims that the loss of the TDA had "spiritual consequences" for Henry Chauncey, who then "stopped thinking of ETS as being in the process of moving beyond aptitude testing" (95). I can find no textual evidence for any of these claims, but it is possible that the interviews Lemann conducted with Chauncey substantiate these findings. It is, nevertheless, clear that the TDA was based on a shift in American education toward general education, a change that was perceptively sensed by Frank Bowles of the College Board. The test was designed by ETS test development specialists (insiders) working with representatives from College Board member schools at Exeter Academy, Kenyon College, Harvard University, and Simmons College (outsiders). (For more on the two cultures involved in writing assessment—the college community and the corporate educational measurement community—see Chapter 5, note 2. The college composition *research* community, however, had not yet emerged when Coffman was working on the TDA.) Since the TDA was designed as an achievement test in social science, humanities, and science, it is not clear—though it is possible—that those involved with the TDA could have believed that it was being developed in order to signal a break with an IQ testing tradition. If Lemann's claims are true, then an early instance can be identified of the dichotomy identified by Richard C. Atkinson in his 2001 decision to abandon the SAT (the aptitude test) for University of California applicants in favor of the SAT Subject Tests (the achievement tests). For more on Atkinson's decision, see Chapter 5.

84 William E. Coffman, "Essay Examinations," *Educational Measurement*, 2nd ed., ed. Robert L. Thorndike (Washington: American Council on Education, 1971) 271–302.

85 Alan R. Blackmer, "The Three School, Three College Plan," *College Board Review* 18 (1952): 303.

86 Blackmer, "The Three School, Three College Plan" 303.

87 Frank D. Ashburn, "Recommendations for Achievement Testing," *College Board Review* 18 (1952): 314. This issue of the *Review* clearly revealed "new patterns of transition from school to college," as the editors put it, emerging during the early 1950s (298). Included were articles not only by Ashburn and Blackmer but also by Alvin C. Eurich, the first president of the State University of New York, and Gordon K. Chalmers, president of Kenyon College. Chalmers had just published *The Republic*

and the Person: A Discussion of Necessities in Modern American Education (Chicago: Regnery, 1952).

88 *College Board Review* 24 (1954): 2.

89 David A. Dudley, "The Beginnings of the Advanced Placement Program," Dec. 1963 (Princeton: ETS Archives).

90 For an example of Swineford's work on factor analysis with Holzinger, see her "Factor Analysis in Educational and Vocational Guidance," *The School Review* 46.10 (1938): 760–762. For her work with Holzinger and Charles Spearman on the Unitary Trait Study, see "The Effect of Motivation on Scores on a Grammar Test," *The School Review* 44.6 (1936): 434–444. For her review of twenty-five years of advances in educational measurement, see James B. Stroud, et al., "Educational Measurements," *Review of Educational Research* 26.3 (1956): 268–291. With Warren G. Findley of ETS, Swineford had compiled the section of the review on "Statistical Methods Related to Test Construction" (281–283).

91 Frances Swineford, Interview with Barbara Pitcher, 1992, *ETS Oral History Program* (Princeton: ETS Archives). In interviewing Swineford, Gary Saretzky of ETS noted that she was "by far the most prolific author of reports." An unusual glimpse of Swineford's powers of explanation—rather than her powers of analysis as found in the reports—may be found in "Questioning the Questions" (*College Board Review* 11 [1950] 142–147). There, with John Landis, Swineford explained the item-analysis procedure that became the foundation of ETS test construction. The explanation of the biserial correlation (an expression of the discriminating power of a test item) aimed at teachers was especially lucid.

92 Frances Swineford, "Test Analysis of College Entrance Examination Board Advanced Placement Tests," Sept. 1956, SR-56-28 (Princeton: ETS Archives).

93 Swineford, "Test Analysis of College Entrance Examination Board Advanced Placement Tests" 14.

94 Edward L. Thorndike, "A Constant Error in Psychological Ratings," *Journal of Applied Psychology* 4.1 (1920): 25.

95 Thorndike, "A Constant Error in Psychological Ratings" 28–29.

96 Swineford, "Test Analysis of College Entrance Examination Board Advanced Placement Tests" 5.

97 Paul B. Diederich, John W. French, and Sydell T. Carlton, "Factors in Judgments of Writing Ability," *Research Bulletin* RB-61-15 (Princeton: ETS, 1961). The study was popularized by John W. French in "Schools of Thought in Judging Excellence of English Themes," an ETS Reprint from the 1961 *Proceedings of Invitational Conference on Testing Procedures* (1962). The study remained a popular handout at ETS when I was there in 1982; my copy was given to me by Gertrude Conlan so that I could better understand writing assessment techniques.

98 Diederich, French, and Carlton, "Factors in Judgments of Writing Ability" 3.

99 French, "Schools of Thought" 9. This is the first mention I have found of this familiar writing assessment aphorism.

100 French, "Schools of Thought" 9.

101 French, "Schools of Thought" 4.

102 French, "Schools of Thought" 5.

103 French, "Schools of Thought" 5.

104 Diederich, French, and Carlton, "Factors in Judgments of Writing Ability" J2, the Glossary for English Teachers. Again, the teacher-centeredness of this document is clear. Contemporary interpretations that denounce factor analysis as merely a reflection of positivistic (and therefore elementistic) methodology are historically incorrect, as are the implications of French and his ETS colleagues as number-crunching reductionists. (Raw denouncements of the positivism of Auguste Comte, the logical positivism of Rudolf Carnap, or the writing assessment methods informed by such theories are also misleading.) Indeed, as I maintain in note 97 above, factor analysis established the conditions under which holistic scoring emerged, an assessment system that asked readers not to interrupt their total impression of an essay in order to condemn errors in grammar. Were it not for factor analysis, systems of counting errors—such as those recollected by Richard Lloyd-Jones in his memoir of his collaboration with Richard Braddock on *Research in Written Composition*—would have endured and been tested with the same force that had been present in the early 1950s. It may not be too imaginative to claim that the review of *The Measurement of Writing Ability*—again, research that may not have been undertaken in the absence of the factor analysis study—that appeared in the first issue of *Research in the Teaching of English* in 1967 (especially noted by Lloyd-Jones in his memoir) signaled the end of the belief that school grammar was a precondition for the achievement of successful academic writing ability within the corporate educational measurement community. That signal was noted among informed members of the newly emerging college composition research community. For the eventual outcome of communication between these two cultures, see Chapter 6, note 2. For the Lloyd-Jones memoir, see "Richard Braddock," *Traditions of Inquiry*, ed. John C. Brereton (New York: Oxford UP, 1985) 153–170.

105 French, "Schools of Thought" 6.

106 French, "Schools of Thought" 6.

107 French, "Schools of Thought" 11. In "Factors in Judgments of Writing Ability," this information is found on 41. It is significant to note that the conference paper by French took a much stronger stand regarding the potential of essay tests than did the research report. French clearly advocated explaining complex studies to audiences of varied statistical background. See, for example, his "What Is Factor Analysis?"

College Board Review 10 (1950) 129–131. For a brief history of the method of factor analysis, see Boring, *A History of Experimental Psychology* 481.

In 1959, C. Remondino of the Industrial Psychology Laboratory of the Fiat School in Turin published "A Factorial Analysis of the Evaluation of Scholastic Compositions in the Mother Tongue" in *The British Journal of Educational Psychology* 29 (1959). Wesdorp, Bauer, and Purves—who reference this work in "Toward a Conceptualization of the Scoring of Written Composition," *Evaluation in Education* 5.3 (1982): 301—state that it is unknown if Diederich, Carlton, and French knew of this work when completing their own factor analysis. The question of influence is difficult to answer. Certainly, Diederich, French, Carlton were quite familiar with Remondino's work when *analyzing* their data. The ETS researchers cited Remondino's 1959 article and referenced it to distinguish their own methods, in which the factors were based entirely on correlations among grades on general merit, from those used by Remondino, in which the readers had been asked to evaluate essays on seventeen particular categories (Diederich, French, Carlton 11). Did the ETS team know of Remondino's work when *designing* their study? The ETS study began in November, 1958, when 600 papers (from which 300 would later be used to generate the factors) were collected from students at Cornell, Middlebury, and the University of Pennsylvania. Remondino first presented the paper that led to 1959 article in Rome during April, 1958. Thus, to be influenced by Remondino's design, the ETS team would have to have known of that presentation, given eight months earlier at the International Conference of Applied Psychology.

Remondino interviewed twenty teachers of literary subjects in different secondary, technical, vocational, and lyceum schools in Italy and asked: "What are the qualities of a school composition that you generally succeed in discriminating?" (243). About a dozen replies were obtained from each teacher and were grouped into categories. Seventeen categories were then developed: readability; aesthetic arrangement; appearance; spelling; morphographic exactness; syntax; organization of ideas; wealth of ideas; adequacy of thoughts; factualness; comprehensiveness; conciseness; language use; style; originality; maturity; and imagination (244). Using these categories, a team of ten markers (four teachers with experience in assessing essays and six non-teachers with experience in technical and administrative fields) were then asked to define the "intensity" of each category on 230 essays written by 15- and 16-year-old-boys to the topic "Write about Yourself." The readers were asked to use a "+" sign to indicate a degree of intensity above the average, a "-" sign to indicate the contrary case, and a "O" sign to indicate cases in which a distinction from the average was not possible (243–244). Regarding reliability, Remondino noted "an absence of systematic differences between teachers and non-teacher ratings" (246) and discarded from the analysis one teacher whose markings were not "in close agreement" with the other readers' marks (246). The factorial analysis, therefore, was undertaken using only the ratings of the three teachers found to be in agreement. Using Holzinger's factor analysis techniques, Remondino extracted four factors: graphic representation (including readability, arrangement—the "harmonious and pleasing fluency of the letters," including "good taste in the arrangements"—and appearance); language use (including spelling, word formation and inflexions, grammatical use, correct use, and style); content and arrangement (including organization of ideas, richness or wealth of ideas, adequacy of thought to subject, objective accuracy of facts, and completeness); and "subtle traits that were difficult to define and recognize in essays" identified as originality, maturity, and imagination (246–247). In his conclusions, Remondino noted that, while the seventeen correlational structures had been solved factorially to give a simple pattern, some of the categories had very similar factorial content. This was no surprise, he stated, because the pattern is "related to the halo effect whose existence is revealed by the large number of high correlations present in the matrix analyzed," yet it was nevertheless interesting, he found, "to note how even certain parameters which apparently seem to be independent of each other and very distinguishable . . . are instead factorially identical, as shown by the factual evidence" (247).

It is, thus, significant that in 1958 Remondino had come to the conclusion that Diederich, Carlton, and French would also reach in their 1961 publication: the factors of writing ability were not independent of each other. Further, in establishing the presence of Thorndike's halo effect, Remondino perceptively noted the key that would lead American researchers Godshalk, Swineford, and Coffman to their moment of epiphany: if the factors of writing ability were so inextricably correlated, then readers could be asked to look at essays holistically in order to make the presence of the halo effect serve in the quest for reliable direct assessment techniques.

108 Fred I. Godshalk, "Testing the English Composition Test," School and College Conf. on English. Barnard College, New York. 16 and 17 Feb. 1962. Green File, Roll 13. Princeton: ETS Archives.

109 Godshalk, "Testing the English Composition Test" 4.

110 Godshalk, "Testing the English Composition Test" 3–4.

111 Frances Swineford and Fred I. Godshalk. "Memorandum for All Concerned; Subject: CEEB Research Proposal—Validity of the Interlinear," 2 Oct. 1961 (Princeton: ETS Archives) 1.

112 Swineford and Godshalk, "Memorandum for All Concerned" 2.

113 Swineford and Godshalk, "Memorandum for All Concerned" 3.

114 Swineford and Godshalk, "Memorandum for All Concerned" 2–3. This memo contains the first reference to holistic scoring that I can identify.

115 William F. Coffman, "Essay Examinations," *Research Memorandum* RM-69-18 (Princeton: ETS Archives). The chapter would appear as Chapter 10 in *Educational Measurement*, 2nd ed., ed. Robert L. Thorndike (Washington: American Council on Education, 1971) 293.

116 Stuart A. Courtis, "Forty Years of Educational Measurement: An Appraisal and a Prophecy," *The National Elementary Principal* 25 (1946): 19. The history of the scales has been analyzed by William A. Younglove, "A Look at Behavioristic Measurement of English Composition in United States Public Schools 1901–1941," California Educational Research Association, 17–18 Nov. 1983 (ERIC ED 246

109). In 1929 Rollo L. Lyman addressed the development, strengths, and weaknesses of the scales in Chapter IV of his *Summary of Investigations Relating to Grammar, Language, and Composition* (Chicago: U of Chicago P, 1929) 134–197. While the use of scales had been quite popular—Courtis had used them in his study of the Gary, Indiana, public schools—they had also endured criticism from the beginning. Lyman identified the weakness in the scales: "Composition scales attempt to measure very complex products" (195). In this attempt, they were often shown to have been inadequate in their failure to account for the context of the student writer in the classroom and the "inventive elements of expression" (196). "In general," Lyman concluded, "measurements in the field of composition, quite in line with the customary practices in teaching, have exalted mechanical and rhetorical elements and have neglected originality, freshness, and inventiveness" (197). For the use of scales in achievement surveys by another maker of scales, see M. J. Van Wagenen, *Educational Diagnosis and the Measurement of School Achievement* (New York: Macmillan, 1926). For the most succinct criticism of the scales, see Edward William Dolch, Jr., "More Accurate Use of Composition Scales," *English Journal* 11 (1922): 536–544. For the most devastating criticism of the Hillegas scale, see Isidore Kayfetz (of Public School No. 84 in Brooklyn, New York), "A Critical Study of the Hillegas Composition Scale," *Pedagogical Seminary* 21 (1914): 559–577. Kayfetz found that the methods used to derive the scale were faulty, that the scale was not truly objective, that the scale was flawed in its use of literary and not pedagogical samples, that the procedure which produced the scale was flawed, that the selections did not represent the real expression of children, and that the scale ignored process and context issues of composition.

117 I am here indebted to Boring's analysis of the history and principles of gestalt psychology in *A History of Experimental Psychology* 589–619.

118 Swineford and Godshalk, "Memorandum for All Concerned" 3.

119 Swineford and Godshalk, "Memorandum for All Concerned" 3.

120 Swineford and Godshalk, "Memorandum for All Concerned" 4–5.

121 Swineford and Godshalk, "Memorandum for All Concerned" 9.

122 Swineford and Godshalk, "Memorandum for All Concerned" 9.

123 Fred I. Godshalk, Frances Swineford, and William E. Coffman, *The Measurement of Writing Ability* (New York: College Entrance Examination Board, 1966) 4. It is important to note that the researchers specifically reference the factor analysis study as justification for use of holistic scoring in their own study. What is unexpected, however, is that they saw the low inter-reader correlation on the French study (.31) as encouraging. "A little calculation," they believed, "indicated that a sum of 20 of these readings would produce a reading reliability of .90. With a modest period of training readers might be able to read more reliably" (5).

124 Swineford and Godshalk, "Memorandum for All Concerned" 8.

125 Swineford and Godshalk, "Memorandum for All Concerned" 8.

126 Fred I. Godshalk, Frances Swineford, and William E. Coffman, "A Study of the English Composition Tests of the College Entrance Examination Board as Predictors of an Essay Criterion," Green File, Roll 13 (Princeton: ETS Archives, 1961) 21. An analysis of variance method was used to estimate the reliability because there were five readers, rather than the usual correlation coefficient that was traditionally used when a paper was read by two readers. The analysis of variance method also allowed a detailed study of variation of topic types.

127 Godshalk, Swineford, and Coffman, "A Study of the English Composition Tests" 24.

128 Godshalk, Swineford, and Coffman, "A Study of the English Composition Tests" 34.

129 Robert B. Bartnik and William W. Turnbull, "A Revolutionary Change in Test Scoring," *College Board Review* 40 (1960): 21–23.

130 Godshalk, Swineford, and Coffman, "A Study of the English Composition Tests" 36.

131 Bartnik and Turnbull, "A Revolutionary Change in Test Scoring" 23.

132 Godshalk, Swineford, and Coffman, "A Study of the English Composition Tests" 36.

133 Godshalk, Swineford, and Coffman, *The Measurement of Writing Ability* 39.

134 *Forty-Third Annual Report of the Executive Secretary* (New York: College Entrance Examination Board, 1943) 24.

135 Huddleston, "Recent Studies of the English Composition Test" 52.

136 Godshalk, Swineford, and Coffman, *The Measurement of Writing Ability* 39. The study, as Gertrude Conlan would later note, nevertheless did not disprove the validity of multiple-choice questions. "It is perhaps one of the great ironies of educational research," she wrote, "that the Godshalk, Swineford, and Coffman study, published as 'The Measurement of Writing Ability,' should have as its fundamental objective proving that the interlinear, a free-response editing exercise, and various types of multiple-choice questions used in the College Board English Composition Test are valid measures of writing ability. For the study not only offered that proof but also demonstrated that essays—direct measures of writing ability—can be scored quickly, efficiently, and reliably and can therefore be used in measuring the writing ability of large groups of students" ("Comparison of Analytic and Holistic Scoring Techniques" [Princeton: ETS, 1978]).

137 Edward S. Noyes, introduction, *The Measurement of Writing Ability*, by Godshalk, Swineford, and Coffman, iv.

138 *The Measurement of Writing Ability* was reviewed in the first issue of *Research in the Teaching of English* in the spring of 1967. In a section of the journal entitled "Roundtable Review," Richard Braddock, the editor, invited "stalwart authors who wish to obtain the benefits of full and frank review" to submit copies of their work (76). Godshalk had sent along the ETS monograph. Samuel L. Becker of the University of Iowa provided a positive methodological review: "This is the best designed and most carefully conducted study of its kind I have seen" (76). In a conceptual review, however, Martin Steinman, Jr., of the University of Minnesota was negative. He began by offering his view that effective writers make choices based on grammatical rules, rhetorical rules, and "other rules" that may be logical or psychological in nature (80–81). Steinman found that these concepts were not supported in the ETS study from knowledge gained from the profession of English and other relevant disciplines. "It is not that the test lacks statistical validity," he found. "My objection is that, all pretenses to the contrary, it lacks conceptual validity: far from contributing to knowledge of writing ability, it is not even supported by such knowledge. And I say this, not because it fails to reflect my explication of the concept of writing ability and my typology of choices (which may well be mistaken), but because it fails to reflect any serious theoretical concern with this concept (compared to concern with such concepts as statistical validity and reliability) and any research in the relevant disciplines" (83). In "A Reply to the Critics," Godshalk reported conversations with his co-authors. Coffman agreed that there was much to be done: "We need to be cautious about feeling that we've solved the problem [of assessing writing ability]" (85). Swineford, on the other hand, felt that conceptual validity was not the point of the research. *The Measurement of Writing Ability* was a standard validation study, she held: "We are not concerned with writing as an art, which is what I think he [Mr. Steinman] has in mind…but with writing ability as a tool. Before the art can be produced, skill in handling the tools must be developed. We cannot expect all college students to become 'writing artists'; we can expect them to have mastered the tools" (86). Or, as Godshalk put it, "One can hardly be called to account for failure to design and blueprint an interplanetary vehicle if he has decided, or has been asked, to judge the blueprint for a tricycle" (86).

139 Stokley Carmichael, "What We Want," *New York Review of Books* 22 Sept. 1966: 5.

140 Reinhold Niebuhr, introduction, *The Varieties of Religious Experience*, by William James (1902; New York: Collier, 1961) 8.

141 Jacques Barzun, Foreword to *The Tyranny of Testing* (New York: Collier, 1952) 7.

142 Walter Lippmann, "A Defense of Education," *Century Magazine* May 1923: 95–103. *Disability History Museum*, 23 Jan. 2005. <http://www.disabilitymuseum.org>

143 Lippmann, "A Defense of Education" paragraph 61.

144 Banesh Hoffmann, *The Tyranny of Testing* (New York: Collier, 1962) 103.

145 Hoffmann, *Tyranny* 122.

146 Hoffmann, *Tyranny* 204.

147 Allan Nairn, *The Reign of ETS: The Corporation That Makes Up Minds* (New Jersey: Nairn and Associates, 1980): 27. The State of New York Assembly Act S. 5200-A on Standardized Testing (called "Truth-in Testing Legislation") is appended in Nairn 530–532.

Chapter 5
Lone Wolves, 1966–2005

Between 1955 and 1965, college enrollment in the United States rose from 2.5 million to 5.7 million students.[1] In 1953, approximately 35 percent of all high school students were going to college; by 1960, that number had risen to 43 percent.[2] The post-war boom of babies had arrived. As was the case with returning soldiers after World War II, this shift was not merely an increase in numbers. In 1968, it was clear that the change was going to be, once more, in the backgrounds of students now appearing to make good the promises of education in a democracy. This time, however, the change would be radical.

William Turnbull, executive vice-president of ETS and soon to be its new president, saw this clearly. From the early years of the Truman administration to the election of John F. Kennedy, American education had succeeded in expanding the top quarter of high school students who would go on to college, perhaps to the extent, Turnbull believed, that little or no further gains would be made in this group. "Automatically," he concluded, "this means that all of the further increase in the proportion of students going beyond high school must come from the second, third, and fourth ability groups. This is not a new thought, but I think the cold statistics of the SAT scale may serve to drive it home: these students are largely from the score range in the 200s and 300s."[3] For these new types of students, new kinds of skills and aptitudes had to be identified. In metaphor, Turnbull declared the Procrustean model of education a thing of the past. What was needed was not a uniform, razor laden bed of fit; rather, the flexibility of Proteus was needed.

In the profession of English, the tensions involved in the metaphoric shift from Procrustes to Proteus were evident in *Freedom and Discipline in*

English. This report, a detailed proposal issued by the Commission on English, had been begun in 1959 by the Board. Edward Simpson Noyes, representing the College Board, was among the commission members, as was Louise M. Rosenblatt, author of the acclaimed *Literature as Exploration*, from New York University.[4] Through James Squire, executive secretary of the National Council of Teachers of English, and George Stone, executive secretary of the Modern Language Association, the commission was thus in direct contact with that profession's best scholars and largest professional associations.[5] Implicit in the report was the effect of America's growing uneasiness as a global force, emblematic in the fear surrounding the launch of *Sputnik* in 1957. With the publication of Vice-Admiral H. G. Rickover's *Education and Freedom* in 1959 and the increase of funds to mathematics and science education from the National Defense Education Act that same year, the teaching of English was no longer on the agenda as an academic subject of national significance. As the report stated, "The English curriculum in the average secondary school today is an unhappy combination of old matter unrenewed and new matter that rarely rises above the level of passing concerns. *Macbeth* vies with the writing of thank-you notes for time in the curriculum, and lessons on telephoning with instruction in the process of argument."[6] In addition, the failed General Composition Test—and the notion that a writing sample would be taken at College Board test centers and sent, unscored, directly to the colleges—led to the conclusion by the Board that a serious study of the goals of English needed to be undertaken.

The commission, finally constituted in 1959, took its title from an essay in Alfred North Whitehead's *The Aims of Education* and explained the relevance of the title in the chapter on composition. In "The Rhythmic Claims of Freedom and Discipline," Whitehead recorded what he saw as a cyclic, orderly progression of the intellect. The commission adapted his ideas for its purposes. The first stage of the intellect should be, the commission authors told their readers, one of romance in which the teacher is "a friendly enemy, a confessor, a deeply attentive listener, a dramatist of the student's imagination."[7] In the second stage, the emphasis should be on form—"on those matters of arrangement, logic, and conventional correctness that make up the body of most books on composition."[8] In the third stage, the instructor should witness the development of style which was "the most austere of all mental qualities…an aesthetic sense, based on admiration for the direct attainment of a foreseen end, simply and without waste, effective enough to warrant recommendation as the vital principle for organizing instruction in writing."[9]

Scott Elledge saw the report as emblematic of a period of experimentation. Elledge, who had been an associate professor of English at Carleton College in 1952 when he had helped Edith Huddleston with her dissertation, was now professor of English at Cornell University. At the College Board in 1969, he reported, only three English evaluation programs had survived: the verbal section of the SAT, the English Composition Test (now proudly sporting a 20-minute essay scored holistically) and an achievement test in English Literature (newly developed by Alan C. Purves, formerly of ETS and a new associate professor of English at the University of Illinois). "Movements," Elledge felt, "that seek to modify conventional assumptions about the aims and methods of teaching English are already afoot."[10] And when these movements succeed, he believed it likely that some of the College Board's English tests would become obsolete.

Among those movements was, simply, the growing resistance to tests. Because they foster competition, one school of thought concluded, tests corrupt. To carry competition—a concept associated with war and other forms of destructive aggression—into the classroom, many now felt, was "a crime against students." Elledge doubted whether testing and grading would ever play the same part in American education that it had played in the past.[11]

Perhaps it was the images of Newark burning that were in Elledge's mind, or perhaps it was the memory of the thousand students barricading themselves at Columbia University to protest the university's expansion into Harlem. Whatever the images, the message was radical. The day of the old spiritual, nuanced by James Baldwin, was at hand. The warning sign had been sent: no more water, the fire next time.

Elledge was wrong in one sense. Richard Nixon would end the draft in 1973 and announce a settlement to end the war in Vietnam. Life would return, in many ways, to the normal predictability of the world Elledge and Edith Huddleston inhabited in 1952. But he was right in another. The era of protest had ushered in a new sense of the individual and shown the door to static conceptions of society. Organized protests would end, but the sensitivity toward the language of protest—the observation that testing encouraged destructive competition, for example, and that crimes against students could occur in that environment—remained. For writing assessment, the emphasis was no longer on institutional models sponsored by the College Board and executed by the Educational Testing Service. Now, classroom instructors sought to influence the destiny of students, increasingly diverse, that they saw each day in the rows of desks before them.

Promoting Assessment: Paul B. Diederich

Diederich first saw the need for local influence, for information gathered by teachers themselves about those sitting before them.

Paul B. Diederich. "As a test of writing ability, no test is as convincing to teachers of English, to teachers in other departments, to prospective employers, and to the public as actual samples of each student's writing, especially if the writing is done under test conditions in which one can be sure that each sample is the student's own unaided work." (From *Measuring Growth in English* [Urbana: NCTE, 1974] 1.) (Photo Reprinted by Permission of Educational Testing Service. All Rights Reserved.)

Diederich both was, and was not, an Educational Testing Service insider. He had been close to a great many projects—among them the Selective Service College Qualifying Test, the General Composition Test, and the factor analysis study of reader judgment—but his true audience did not seem to be within the ETS organization. The publication of Diederich's *Measuring Growth in English* in 1974 was emblematic of a new approach in writing assessment, one which provided strategies for classroom instructors to evaluate writing on their own without the help of assessment professionals in organizations such as ETS. The impulse to help teachers design their own assessment programs—an old impulse driven again by an enrollment surge similar to that which drove Thorndike to create scales extended and modified by Hillegas and Trabue early in the century—emerged again. That earlier instructor-centered impulse had been overshadowed by the power of machine-scored objective tests and their remorseless reliability—organizationally solidified by the College Entrance Examination Board and its contractor, ETS. But the tests themselves had been so massively questioned by Banesh Hoffmann and others since his 1962 publication *The Tyranny of Testing* that the face validity of the tests was no longer evident. The publication of Diederich's *Measuring Growth in English* by the National Council of Teachers of English was, simply, good news.

An observation made by Stanford University professor Lewis M. Terman in 1948 was to be proven true at the century's end: the individuals working alone would be the ones to break new ground. On September 24, 1948, Terman—a eminent measurement specialist who had helped to revise the Stanford-Binet Scale in 1937—had written to Don Marquis of the Department of Psychology at the University of Michigan. Marquis had observed the need for cooperation in testing-related research and was supportive of a plan for a national testing organization, a plan that would launch ETS. Terman disagreed with Marquis:

> I'm not sure how far I agree with you on the necessity of cooperative research at the level of program design. I know it is possible for such cooperation to be very fruitful at times, especially if it has to do with applied problems,—whether atomic research, pilot selection, a psychologist, or what-not. I'm not sure that cooperative research is equally successful in breaking new ground. I've always felt that the individual working alone was the one who was most likely to do that. Besides, most scientists even in psychology are individuals and don't work together in teams very satisfactorily. On the army mental test of the first world war I think that our committee did a fairly good job, but I also think that at least two or three members of it could have done just as good a job without the help or hindrance of the others. I was one of the committee that made the National Intelligence Test on a grant of $25,000. I'm pretty sure I could have done a better job all alone on $5,000! You may recall that some years ago there was a movement to get Spearman, Thurstone, Kelley, and all the other factor-analysis people working together to iron out their difficulties. Apparently nothing ever came of it. I don't believe Spearman could ever work with anyone cooperatively, and I'm sure that Thurstone and Thorndike are the sort that had to be lone wolves.[12]

In *Measuring Growth in English*, Diederich was introduced as such a lone wolf by Robert F. Hogan, the executive secretary of the National Council of Teachers of English. Imagine, Hogan wrote in his foreword to the slim volume, an agent of the Internal Revenue Service who arrives to audit a return. While the tax auditor may be a helpful person—"gregarious and affable, who writes poetry in his free time and who will help us by showing how we failed to claim all our allowable deductions"—it is doubtful. So, too, is the profile of the specialist of measurement, one who thinks only of children as "they distribute themselves across deciles."[13] But as a measurement specialist, Diederich is as pleasant a surprise as would be the helpful IRS agent. This is a role that Diederich warmed to in his introduction. "First let me surprise these critics [those who believe that there is too much measurement] by saying that I agree with practically everything they say. This is not a rhetorical trick; I really mean it. During my twenty-five years at the Educational Testing Service, one of my principal duties had been consulting with secondary schools on problems of measurement, grading, record-keeping, and reporting. I have had to visit more classes than I care to remember, and my predominant impression has been that these classes are fantastically over evaluated."[14] What to do? Diederich called for common sense.

His common sense, however, was of a particular kind. It was functionalist, an orientation evident in his analysis of his own diagnosis of cancer. In a letter, "To All My Friends and Well-Wishers," dated March 6, 1966, a sixty-year-old Diederich analyzed his surgery for a malignant tumor. His surgeon had told him that the cancer had been detected and removed "early enough," a statement that Diederich denounced as a medical rationalization. "If it had remained localized and they get all of it, it is 'early enough'; but if it has broken up and started growing in other places, which some tumors do at quite an early stage, it is 'too late.' Somehow this seems to put the patient in the wrong if the operation does not come off, but there is very little he can do about it, since the tumor often gives no sign of its presence until anyone could call it 'too late.'" His father had died from the disease—"Too late in his case."

Reflecting on God and eternity, Diederich wrote that he had come to realize how "little basis" he had for imagining attributes ("mind, purpose, or meaning") of the creator. He was left with only one conviction: "God invented the body; man invented the soul." God "is something matter is or does, just as the mind is something that the body is or does." Diederich thus proclaimed himself a devout materialist, "believing that matter is the most wonderful thing known to us, and what most unmistakably bears the stamp of the designer of the cosmos." His conviction about the nature of the divinity of the body stood up, he concluded, in the face of death: "I have been just a mortal—no more, no less—as I would have been had I believed in heaven, hell, and judgment." (He ended the letter with a P.S.: "Nothing in this statement is confidential.")[15]

Diederich's analysis of the constructed nature of causation suggested a deeply felt functionalist approach to his life and his work. It was an approach to thought that did not allow Diederich to align himself completely with ETS. The work at ETS was basically conducted in the psychological experimental tradition of Wilhelm Wundt, the founder of modern psychology. Projects at ETS centered on a Wundt-based view of testing, a laboratory exercise carried on in the field, a genre with findings documented and reported formally, and with new categories constructed that would yield new tests. The mental measurement movement in America that had begun early in the century—with Alfred Binet's constructed scales of age norms and with Spearman's 1904 argument for general ability, *g*—had been incorporated into the kind of cooperative research undertaken at the Educational Testing Service, measurement systems that had fueled testing during two world wars and one conflict in Korea. By the early 1970s, the epistemological orientation toward discovery that had begun with Wundt had become fully incorporated into American culture.

It was not so much that Diederich did not participate in the work derived from such an orientation but, rather, that he held such work at a distance, aligning himself with the traditions of William James, Edward Thorndike, and John Dewey. For Diederich, the construction of relationships was just that: clever, interpretative designs that did not necessarily reflect reality. Diederich's kind of functionalism was at one with the interpretation of experience that Dewey had argued for in his famous 1896 paper "The Reflex Arc Concept in Psychology." In that paper, Dewey had brought into play the realization that descriptions are only constructs, analyses that may not be, finally, valid. Traditional wisdom holds, Dewey began, that a child sees a candle flame, imagines it may be pleasurable to play with the flame, and thus is burned and withdraws his hand. Yet this account assumes that the parts are prior to the whole; in fact, it is only the whole environment that matters. There is no stimulus and response, no desire to play with the flame and the burn. The reflex arc concept of stimulus and response is, he argued, "defective in that it assumes that every sensory stimulus and motor response as distinct psychical existences, while in reality they are always inside a co-ordination and have their significance purely from the part played in maintaining or reconstructing the co-ordination."[16] As Dewey put it, "The burn is the original seeing, the original optical-ocular experience enlarged and transformed in its value. It is no longer mere seeing; it is seeing-of-a-light-that-means-pain-when-contact-occurs."[17] Thus there is no arc; there is, instead, a circle: "The circle is a co-ordination, some of whose members have come into conflict with each other."[18] There is no cause and effect, no stimulus and response; there are, instead, acts which are "strictly correlative and contemporaneous."[19] Or, as Diederich found in the case of his own health, no early or late diagnosis—only the cancer and the operation. The orientation—radically questioning that which is interpreted as too little or too late—was pure functionalism.

So Diederich, while working at ETS, had adopted the position of lone wolf, of a functionalist working in a testing organization. The 1974 publication of *Measuring Growth in English* was, in fact, the culmination of years of work undertaken in the service of enabling teachers to assess the writing abilities of students within their own classrooms and schools—not work undertaken solely in the service of testing. As early as 1961, he had published "Readers, Aides, and Technicians" in the *Harvard Graduate School of Education Association Bulletin*. There, he summarized his plan, begun in 1956, for using college-educated housewives as readers—"good wenches," a colleague from the Deep South had termed them—to handle rising enrollment patterns. "There are," he claimed, "hundreds of thousands of these bright, well-educated women sitting at home in the morning watching television and growing increasingly restless and neurotic." A part-time job working as readers of essays would "bring them out like bargain-day at Macy's."[20] His plan, coined "The Rutgers Plan for Reducing the Teaching Load in English," was sponsored by the Ford Foundation in 1959, and it had become very successful: applicants poured in to work as technicians with the teachers by monitoring their reading and helping to design and score exercises on fundamentals in vocabulary, spelling, grammar, and punctuation.

The lay readers were selected by means of four tests: a verbal ability test, a paper-grading test, a paper-correcting test, and an essay test of their own writing ability. When hired, the readers would meet with the school department head to review the curriculum. The teacher then worked with the readers during the term. For each assignment, the teacher asked the reader to study the text upon which the assignment was based and the rationale for the assignment. The teacher then reviewed the papers written in response to the assignment, revealing what she would have awarded the paper and what points she would have emphasized. By 1962, Diederich reported that there were at least two hundred school systems employing readers.[21]

To examine the impact of the program, an experiment in 1959–1960 was conducted on sixteen school systems, half of which were using lay readers and half of which were not. There was, as would have been expected, no significant difference in growth between the experimental and control groups: no one expected the teachers to have written comments that could have improved writing ability in one year. More important, however, was that the lack of difference indicated that there was no handicap evident in those schools that had employed the lay readers. "All we had hoped to prove," Diederich wrote, "was that teachers could be relieved of half or more of their impossible load of paperwork without handicapping their students. We found no such handicap in any of our 16 cities."[22] The gains to the school were clear. The English teacher had fewer class preparations and marked fewer papers because the lay readers worked with students in both marking papers and in monitoring their reading. In addition, the teacher never met with more than twenty students "except on the rare occasions when he delivers a lecture, which may be to as many as 2,000 students in an auditorium or to any number of students on TV."[23] Diederich had created an economic model for a self-sustaining school system, one which monitored its curriculum and assignments meticulously and which used readers to manage increased class size. He had designed a contextually based system to meet the need for local control, a system that allowed information to be gathered by the teachers themselves about those sitting in the desks in front of them. Diederich's functional approach, in fact, had eradicated the need for systems created by the College Board and its agent, the Educational Testing Service. The system was entirely and strictly correlative and contemporaneous.

All the system needed was a kind of handbook for evaluation. Diederich had produced a set of guidelines for the Association for Supervision and Curriculum in 1967.[24] But it was in *Measuring Growth in English* that he provided the full program. Here were discussions of inter-reader reliability. (He had come to expect .80 as a standard correlation when practical decisions were to be made but backed down to .70 as a more achievable correlation.) There were directions on ways to compute reliability in essay tests. (Diederich advocated a method he termed "top quarter tetrachorics" in which the evaluation coordinator would ask two readers to place essays into four quartiles representing four levels of judgment, calculate the percentage of papers placed by both readers into two categories, and then step up the correlation by the Spearman-Brown Prophecy Formula. The method, he believed, was easier to use than the standard product-moment correlation and, though it had twice the standard error, was "better than nothing.") And there were directions on ways to compute reliability in objective tests. (He provided a simplified version of the Kuder-Richardson formula.) There was a review of the 1961 factor analysis study that he had conducted with John French in order to identify the elements of judgment involved in measuring writing. (Diederich emphasized the five factors—rather than the lack of differentiation among the factors as French had—so that teachers understood that readers measured writing according to the ability of a student to articulate rich ideas, avoid error, establish organization, arrange skillful phrases, and develop style. The unaccounted variance from the study—the 57 percent of the variance that was unexplained by the factor analysis—was described by Diederich as an indication of unique ideas that readers have about essays and of the presence, simply, of error.) There is even a model design for an examination in English language arts. (Diederich's model suggested objective and essay tests in the morning, as well in the afternoon, so that multiple writing samples could be taken from each student to increase the weight given to the writing samples.) There were also appendices (including descriptions that teachers could use to operationalize assessment criteria based on the five factors from the factor analysis study, topics for essay tests, sample objective items, and a guide to effective writing based on rhetorical goals).

Ultimately, Diederich's advice to his reader was deeply contextual. Those procedures that "you adopt must be suited to your course of study, your student population, and the conviction and preferences of your staff. But one requirement is almost universal. At some point someone with authority—usually the principal or dean—must tell that staff to stop arguing and try something—no matter what. Without that push, nothing will happen."[25] For his part, he had indeed tried something. He had advocated a system that allowed classroom instructors to take control of their own professional lives. He had empowered teachers to take charge.

Differentiating Assessment: Charles Cooper and Lee Odell

The year after the publication of *Measuring Growth in English*, the National Council of Teachers of English held a conference in San Diego on describing and measuring growth in writing. That 1975 conference produced what would become an enormously influential volume on writing assessment, Charles R. Cooper and Lee Odell's *Evaluating Writing: Describing, Measuring, Judging*.[26] While Diederich's volume was centered on empowering teachers to judge writing collectively within their schools, Cooper and Odell's collection of essays was more nuanced, directed toward the more varied assessment aims of describing and measuring writing ability. For Cooper and Odell, diagnosis and prescription were the aims of assessment.

The editors introduced the volume with a rhetorical technique that exemplified their research orientation: they began not with statements but with questions: What should we look at when we describe and measure writing? The product or the process? How can we identify the abilities of the individual writer so that efficient, focused instruction can be planned to bridge gaps and strengthen abilities? How can longitudinal studies be planned? How can students themselves be involved in evaluation?

As for answers provided by means of standardized tests of the sort available through the Educational Testing Service—this was the era of the Test of Standard Written English with its multiple choice items—such information was dismissed. "We all knew at the outset that we were unwilling to settle for the kinds of information provided by published standardized tests of writing because we did not believe they assessed students' ability to compose for different purposes and audiences," the editors wrote.[27] After providing a summary list of the articles in the volume—articles on holistic scoring, primary trait scoring, computer-assisted assessment, syntactic fluency, writing strategies, and student involvement—attention was, again, turned to the absence in the volume of standardized tests of writing. These tests measure only editorial skills, readers were told, and were not valid measures of writing performance. Their only justifiable use is for "prediction or placement" or for "the criterion measure in a research study with a narrow 'correctness' hypothesis."[28]

With standardized tests and all they connoted dismissed, the aims of writing evaluation—administrative, instruction, and evaluation and research—may be achieved, it was inferred, by the methods described in the volume, strategies that were based on findings taken not from test items but, rather, on "actual pieces of writing, on some writer's real performance."[29] Emblematic of the editors' orientation in the volume was the description of reliability. There was no mention of reader agreement, a radical omission since it had been the single obsession among researchers for most of the century. For Cooper and Odell, reliability was discussed in terms of multiple samples taken from the same student. They wrote:

> If a measure or measurement scheme is reliable, it is fair to writers, permitting them to demonstrate what they can really do. For purposes of a quick, tentative screening or placement decision, we need only ask a writer for one piece produced under the best conditions we can arrange. However, from previous research we know that either a comprehensive description of writing performance or a reliable rank ordering of a group of writers can be achieved only by asking for more than one piece of writing on more than one occasion and then involving two or more people in describing or rating each piece. Even then, we have reliable measurement of writing ability in only one mode. To test ability to write in different modes (personal narrative, explanation, dramatic dialogue, reportage, prose fiction) or to write for different purposes (explanation, persuasion, expression), we need multiple pieces on multiple occasions. As an example, we know from previous research that syntactic patterns vary from mode to mode, and further, that the best writers display most variation.[30]

In a single paragraph, Cooper and Odell set the stage for a new type of assessment by ignoring what had been the single most pressing issue in collaborative assessment to date, inter-reader agreement. For them, the new focus was to be on a reliability tied to increased validity, a reliability not achieved between readers but among tasks. Odell and Cooper had quietly closed the curtain on debates that had engaged the writing assessment community for most of the century—the Hillegas scale of 1917; Stalnaker's 1937 assurance of reliability in College Board direct assessment methods and his 1943 recantation; the 1955 argument of Richard Pearson and Earle G. Eley in the pages of *College Board Review*, the 1966 breakthrough findings of Godshalk, Swineford, and Coffman. The new writing assessment stage, as far as Cooper and Odell were concerned, would be filled with discussions of modes and purposes of writing, with ample dialogue devoted to the marriage of validity with reliability.

In terms of collaborative assessment of writing, two essays were to become of seminal importance: Charles Cooper's "Holistic Evaluation of Writing" and Richard Lloyd-Jones's "Primary Trait Scoring." Together, they were to establish for the profession of English the two methods of direct writing assessment that would be most used during the later twentieth century.

Cooper's focus was on the usefulness of holistic scoring to rank order students. He presented an overview of what he described as seven types of holistic evaluation: an essay scale (the use of a series of complete essays arranged according to quality and accompanied by comment of the evaluators regarding the scale criteria); an analytic scale (such as the kind discussed by Diederich in 1974 listing a series of prominent features such as general merit and mechanics ordered according to low, middle, and high scores); a dichotomous scale (a series of statements which can be affirmed or denied by readers); feature analysis (focusing on a particular aspect such as structure); primary trait scoring (used to focus the reader's attention on discourse features); general impression marking (such as that used by Godshalk, Swineford, and Coffman in their 1966 *The Measurement of Writing Ability*); and center-of-gravity response (coined by Peter Elbow as a formative response used for feedback to students in his 1973 *Writing Without Teachers*). Regarding anxieties about inter-reader reliability, Cooper set the reader's fears aside in italics ("reliability can be improved to an acceptable level *when raters from similar backgrounds are carefully trained*"), assuring his readers that raters trained with guides can achieve reliabilities in the high eighties and low nineties. Cooper also cited William E. Coffman's 1971 *Research in the Teaching of English* article to establish that teachers, when made aware of discrepancies in scoring, move their ratings in the direction of the group and, thus, tend to become more reliable. In sum, Cooper wrote, when we need scores, the use of holistic scoring ensures that "we are obtaining them in a valid way, from human responses to actual pieces of writing."[31]

For Richard Lloyd-Jones, primary trait scoring was understood as a type of holistic scoring, potentially more valid than atomistic tests, such as vocabulary or usage or syntax tests. Lloyd-Jones tied primary trait scoring not only to the universe of discourse but also to the products of specific types of writing tasks. While the methods perfected by ETS assume that excellence in one sample predicts excellence in other modes, he wrote, primary trait scoring methods do not assume that a writer of a good technical report may be able to produce an excellent letter to a city council. "A precise description on census of writing skills is far richer in information if the observations are categorized according to the purpose of the prose. The goal of primary trait scoring is to define precisely what segment of discourse will be evaluated (e.g., presenting rational persuasion between social equals in a formal situation), and to train readers to render holistic judgments accordingly."[32] Thus, to design a primary trait scoring system, one had to define the discourse model (James Kinneavy's model given in his 1971 *A Theory of Discourse* was considered, but its complexity was rejected in favor of a simpler model of explanatory, expressive, and persuasive discourse), to design writing exercises which sampled that mode (a delicate job in which a stimulus for writing is designed which, at once, allows each writer to respond to the topic but which, nevertheless, limits the topic to a particular situation), to ensure that the writers could and would give writing samples (through preliminary trials), to devise workable scoring guides (consisting of the exercise itself, a statement of the elicited primary writing trait, an hypothesized interpretation of the exercise, an interpretation of how the situation of the exercise is related to the primary trait, the guide itself, samples of papers which have actually been scored, and rationale of the scores), and to use these guides when assessing the essays. Lloyd-Jones even provided a scoring guide for an expressive prompt that had been given in order to evaluate the primary trait of a writer's ability to demonstrate imaginative expression of feeling through inventive elaboration of a point of view. Clearly, for Lloyd-Jones, specificity was everything.

By 1977, holistic scoring had been in use with large and influential national assessment programs such as the English Composition Test and the Advanced Placement Test, but Cooper's was the first description of the process that had been written for teachers. The primary trait assessment system, on the other hand, was an innovation that had been developed to serve a system that would become that nation's report card on its schools in the second half of the century: the National Assessment of Educational Progress.

Accountability: The National Assessment of Educational Progress

Following the call for accountability that led to the Elementary and Secondary Education Act of 1965, a mainstay piece of legislation of Lyndon Johnson's war on poverty, the United States Congress had mandated a national assessment project—the 1969 National Assessment of Educational Progress (NAEP)—to evaluate the skills of students enrolled in the nation's schools in the areas of reading, mathematics, science, history, geography, and writing. Richard Lloyd-Jones and his colleagues from the National Council of Teachers of English had participated in a scoring conference, along with William Coffman, to elaborate on the system Lloyd-Jones explained in his chapter in Odell and Cooper's volume. By 1984, that system was being effectively used to provide detailed information on the writing performance of students aged nine, thirteen, and seventeen.

Using the methods developed by Lloyd-Jones and his colleagues, Arthur N. Applebee, Judith A. Langer, and Ina V. S. Mullins reported the results of ten years of writing assessment data in *Writing Trends across the Decade, 1974–84*. Ninety-five thousand students—participating in assessments that had taken place in the school years ending in 1974, 1979, and 1984—had written papers on the three types of writing models that Lloyd-Jones had identified: explanatory writing (now called informative writing), persuasive writing (the name was retained), and expressive writing (now called imaginative writing).[33] Papers had been evaluated using both primary trait scoring and holistic scoring; the former was used to "isolate particular features of the writing essential to accomplishing the task and developing criteria for various levels of performance based on those features," and the latter was used "to provide an estimate of the relative fluency of the writing."[34] For the primary trait system, a 20 percent random subsample of all the papers scored in 1983–1984 was scored by a second reader, and the exact agreement and reliability coefficients were reported. "By either measure," Applebee and his colleagues reported, "the rater reliabilities were very high."[35] The lowest reliability coefficient was reported at .73 and the highest at .95. To establish the reliability of the holistic scores, a 20 percent subsample was also rescored. They too were high—from .94 to .71—though lower than the corresponding primary trait scores. Applebee and his coauthors supposed that the lower holistic score correlation was "probably because the general impression procedure does not require readers to evaluate papers against specific criteria as with primary trait scoring, but rather to familiarize themselves with sets of essays that illustrate different levels of performance of a specific task ('range finders')."[36] Indeed, the low correlational relationship between the primary trait scores and the holistic scores—as low as .29 for the persuasive writing task—suggested that the two types of scoring were measuring different aspects of student writing.[37] So effective were the scoring guides for the primary trait method that they had surpassed the reliability of the holistic scoring method.

The scoring system was sound, a culmination of refinements in techniques that had been advanced by the Godshalk research group in 1966 in their holistic methods and that had been refined by Lloyd-Jones and his colleagues in 1977 as primary trait measurement. Yet the findings of the assessment were similar in their orientation to so many reports of the distressingly poor nature of writing, reports that seemed little different than the findings of Charles Francis Adams and his colleagues in their 1892 *Report of the Committee on Composition and Rhetoric*. But instead of freshmen at Harvard, the problem was now, it seemed, a national one. "American students are writing no better in 1984 than they were ten years earlier," Applebee and his colleagues report, and "performance of these 9-, 13- and 17-year-old-students is distressingly poor."[38] In addition, at all three ages, "Black and Hispanic students generally showed lower writing achievement levels than White students."[39]

The system developed by Lloyd-Jones and his colleagues continued to endure in the twenty-first century. In 2002, approximately 276,000 students from 11,000 schools wrote on topics that were informative (Lloyd-Jones's explanatory discourse) or persuasive (Lloyd-Jones's original term); the expressive, imaginative discourse of Lloyd-Jones had been replaced by a narrative task. A six-level scoring guide had been used, and exact reader agreement ranged from 83 percent (for the fourth grade essays) to 78 percent (on the twelfth grade papers).[40] The results? Students' average scores increased between 1998 and 2002 at grades four and eight, though no significant difference was noted between the two assessment years in the performance of twelfth-graders. Only 24 to 31 percent of the students in each of the three grades had performed at or above the proficient level.[41]

And what of the writing ability of those who attended Title I schools—schools that received federal funds because their students lived in areas with high concentrations of low-income families? Title I schools, the NAEP reported, had lower average writing scores than students who attended schools that did not participate in Title I funding.[42] Class now, it appeared, had taken its place with race as a factor associated with poor writing skill. On January 8, 2002, President George W. Bush would attempt to rectify the disparity by renewing Lyndon Johnson's 1965 initiative, the Elementary and Secondary Education Act. The new No Child Left Behind Act included both a goal of increased literacy and a reliance on accountability through measurement. The act was designed to meet "the educational needs of low-achieving children in our Nation's highest-poverty schools, limited English proficient children, migratory children, children with disabilities, Indian children, neglected or delinquent children, and young children in need of reading assistance" the Statement of Purpose noted. And the nation would know that these needs were being met when all children would be able to "reach, at a minimum, proficiency on challenging State academic achievement standards and state academic assessments."[43] The racial disparities that William Turnbull and Scott Elledge witnessed in the late 1960s had not been fully addressed. Now, the matter of income, assessment revealed, could be added to the ever-growing list of disparities. And assessment would demonstrate if these achievement gaps were being bridged. In the new century, perhaps more so than in the old, so much depended on a scale.

Cultural Context: The Map of Alan C. Purves

In 1975 Alan C. Purves was concerned about disparity. He relished the fact that one size does not fit all; he was incensed at those who sought to incorporate a single rule on others. In *Common Sense and Testing in English*, a National Council of Teachers of English Report on the Task Force on Measurement and Evaluation in the Study of English, Purves and his colleagues had prepared a list of questions parents should ask about the published tests that their children were taking in school. "Do the tests ask your children to know or to do the same kinds of things they are being taught?" "Do the tests discriminate against children because they do not speak a particular type of English or because they come from a particular part of the United States?" At the end of a list of ten such questions, the following warning appeared in italics: "*You should bring these questions to the attention of teachers, school administrators, and citizens' groups. If they cannot answer these questions satisfactorily your children are in danger of having their lives ruined by bad tests badly used.*"[44]

If anyone could make such a statement with impunity, it was Purves. From 1965 to 1968 he had served as an examiner in humanities at the Educational Testing Service. In 1968, as a newly appointed associate professor of English at the University of Illinois, he reflected on the design of the College Board's first one-hour, multiple-choice Achievement Test in English in *College Board Review*. The committee Purves had been charged with coordinating decided to measure a student's ability to paraphrase, to comprehend structure, to comprehend language and style, to comprehend rhetorical and literary devices, to comprehend the ways that meaning is created, to classify a text according to genre, tradition, or period, to understand allusion, and to deal with general aspects of literary study such as theme. To demonstrate the ways that such questions could be operationalized into a multiple-choice test, he provided the text of "Medusa" by Louise Bogan, and ten questions. It is clear in the article that only the final two questions really interested him. Designed to prompt interpretation, the questions show Purves to be especially engaged with asking students to reflect on tense changes in the poem. The correct choice would reveal that a student understood the difference between historical reality and the interior life of the mind. Inferences based on language nuance were important, he explained. "All of these experiments seek to make the test of literary acumen one which finds out how deeply students examine a poem, by following a pattern of questions," he wrote. "This pattern attempts to move from a test of sharpness of observation to a test of depth of understanding, the two qualities which seem to mark the mature reader of literature."[45] His analytic technique, constant throughout his career, was to problematize what seemed most obvious so that the wonderful complexity of an idea could be realized.

Purves engaged writing assessment in all its complexity in his role as Chair of the International Project Council for the International Association for the Evaluation of Educational Achievement (IEA). Since 1981 the IEA had conducted a study designed to examine the teaching and learning of written composition in the schools of fourteen countries: Chile, England, Finland, the Federal Republic of Germany (Hamburg), Hungary, Indonesia, Italy, The Netherlands, New Zealand, Nigeria, Sweden, Thailand, the United States, and Wales. In 1984, Purves, Söter, and their colleagues, Sauli Takala and Anneli Vähäpassi of Finland's University of Jyväskylä, had published their design for a domain-referenced system for classifying composition assignments along fifteen dimensions: instruction, stimulus, cognitive

Alan C. Purves. "Just after I finished a draft of this paper, the secondary school with which I work was visited by W. S. Merwin, who gave a reading. After he finished each selection, some of the students would ask him what the selection meant or what something symbolized. He tried various evasive answers, but the students kept pressing him. At the back of the room, one of the English teachers turned to me and said, 'My god! They're asking him all the questions we English teachers ask…and they're the wrong questions!'" (From "Implications of the IEA Studies in Reading and Literature for College English Departments," *ADE Bulletin* 72 [1982]: 1.)

demand, purpose, role, audience, content, rhetorical specifications, tone, advanced preparation, length, format, time, draft, and criteria.[46]

In 1988 the first volume of the study appeared, complete with a comprehensive examination of the scoring scheme and its distinctions between holistic scoring (general impression marking that, in its dependence on a cultural sharing of norms among the group, was not practical for an international study), primary trait scoring (used to connect the scoring scheme to a specific task, thus forcing the test constructor to consider the score when devising the topic, a method again not practical for an international study which would involve analysis of performance across tasks), and analytic scoring (designed to take into account specific features of writing in relation to a general framework, thus allowing performance across tasks).[47] In 1992 the second volume of the study appeared in which Purves found that the ability to write a composition had more to do with cultural contexts than with a universal capacity for cognition, that there was variation among nations regarding what was valued in compositions, and that girls uniformly had higher scores in the assessment, a finding that "cuts across languages, cultures, and stages of economic development."[48] Across a seven-year period, Purves had managed the largest, most comprehensive writing assessment venture in history. In his explanation of the methods he designed with his colleagues and his analysis of the findings, Purves brought into application the very best practices of writing assessment, educating the profession—as he had always done—in the process.

At the end of his career, Purves once more nudged his readers toward a more comprehensive understanding of the complex life of the mind. He died late in December of 1996, and his last book, *The Web of Text and the Web of God: An Essay on the Third Information Transformation*, was posthumously published in 1998. In that contemplative study, he asked his readers to consider the possibilities of hypertext as a way to achieve fulfillment in a new community. Granted, a singular sense of modern consensus had eroded, yet Purvis, rather than documenting a sense of unwitting despair, advocated looking deeply into the condition of the erosion itself, following what Martin Heidegger had concluded in "The Question Concerning Technology." As Heidegger had written, "The closer we come to the danger, the more brightly do the ways into the saving power begin to shine and the more questioning we become. For questioning is the piety of thought."[49] For Purves, truth was aligned with complexity, and he asked that we find hope in the new (and potentially dangerous) technologies of hypertext and hypermedia by looking into (the saving power) of five themes: anarchy ("Ah, but look at me—I don't fit your neat scheme"), authority

("There is a simple abuse of the authority of things"), community ("A community respects the individual and yet finds a common ground"), idolatry ("We see the world as if it were what we had made it on paper, in our models, statistics, and programs. We do not see these as images or icons, to pierce through to a deeper understanding of that world"), and networks ("It may be through networks that we are finally able to cope with the vastness and complexity of our society"). Even the greatest danger, idolatry, could have positive aspects if it yielded deeper vision. For vision could lead to Whitman's noiseless, patient spider itself, immanent in the links as well as in the webs of the transcendent spinner.[50]

It was our job to understand, and that understanding must begin with a simple realization: "There is no 'best map' of the world. There is no single rule. What is sauce for the goose is not sauce for the gander. One size does *not* fit all." Culturally informed conclusions were, in the end, the brightest.

A Place to Come to: The National Testing Network in Writing

NAEP had concentrated on writing in the school, and the IEA Study had concentrated on international writing assessment. By 1982—the year that Purves had first offered his thoughts on the implications of his work to an audience of U.S. teachers—it was evident to Karen Greenberg and her colleagues that writing assessment programs had mushroomed. With Harvey S. Wiener and Richard A. Donovan, Greenberg wanted to establish a broad national forum on writing that advanced new methods, a community of specialists that would allow teachers, administrators, and researchers "to exchange ideas, to investigate existing tests and testing programs, and to pool resources and data."[51]

Supported by the Fund for the Improvement of Secondary Education (FIPSE), Greenberg and her colleagues began simply with a paperback booklet, *Notes from the National Testing Network in Writing*, published in October 1982. Greenberg and her colleagues had developed a series of questions and sent them off to nationally known theorists, designers, administrators, and evaluators of writing tests, asking them to respond openly for the pages of the *Notes*. Deceptively humble in its concept and idea, the National Testing Network in Writing (NTNW) gathered together in that first, eighteen-page issue the nation's leaders in writing assessment to answer a series of questions:

> What can tests tell, or what can they not tell, teachers or administrators about students' writing problems?
>
> What should a teacher—or parent, school administrator, school board

member, or legislator—know about testing—especially about the implications and limitations of test results?

What have been the effects of local and centralized minimum competency programs on a) test designs, b) procedures, c) curriculum, and d) writing program development? What are the most effective ways to respond to a mandated test of minimum competency in writing?

On the basis of your experience, what mistakes or pitfalls can those interested in testing writing avoid in the future?

What are the major concerns that the classroom teacher should have about a college-wide testing effort, and how should the classroom teacher participate in test development and use?

Based on your conversations and/or research, how do students perceive writing tests—their purpose and use?

What are the unresolved issues in testing writing? In what direction should the field be heading? What research should be conducted?

What should a teacher—or parent, school administrator, school member, or legislator—read to be the most informed on current issues in testing writing?[52]

These were questions directed not only to researchers, administrators, and policymakers, but also to the community of shareholders impacted by writing assessment, to parents and teachers. Turnbull's 1968 Protean model of inclusion had come to life, and the nation's leaders in writing assessment responded. Lynn Quitman Troyka, then the immediate past chair of the Conference on College Composition and Communication, wrote on a decade of that organization's resolutions and what they revealed about "the uses and abuses of writing tests."[53] Richard Lloyd-Jones, another past chair of CCCC and a designer of primary-trait scoring, provided the balanced advice that "not all tests be abandoned but that interpretations of results all be expressed within limits."[54] Lester Faigley, Stephen P. Witte, James Kinneavy, and John Daily reported on their own FIPSE-funded project regarding the evaluation of college writing programs, advocating a pluralistic approach to program evaluation that included the components of cultural and societal context, institutional context, program structure and administration, curriculum, and instruction—five components that would rest at the center of Witte and Faigley's *Evaluating College Writing Programs* published a year later.[55] Lee Odell noted that attention in essay assessment needed to be paid to selection of topics, the areas of audience and purpose, and—perhaps most important—the relationship between the ways that writing is taught and how it is assessed.[56] Also addressing the issue of topic design, Gertrude Conlan of ETS, representing the role of corporate testing, reported on the "humility" needed to design effective writing topics.[57] Edward M. White, professor of English at the California State College, San Bernardino, also listed needed research, focusing on product/process issues, mode of discourse issues, cognitive development and curriculum issues, program evaluation issues, needed definition of writing sub-skills, and remaining problems with equity. Three years later, he would answer his own call "to resist the routine oversimplification" of writing assessment by publishing *Teaching and Assessing Writing: Recent Advances in Understanding, Evaluating, and Improving Student Performance*, a book that, in two editions, would guide a generation of administrators, teachers, and researchers to "reduce bad practice in the testing of writing" through informed practice.[58]

In March 1983 Greenberg and her colleagues launched the first NTNW conference in New York, beginning a series of conferences held across the United States and Canada that would continue until November 1990, the final New York conference. NTNW continued to attract the nation's leaders to present and publish their abstracts yearly in the *Notes*. Greenberg and her colleagues had fostered the first national community for writing assessment. As Richard Hendrix observed in his foreword to *Writing Assessment: Issues and Strategies*—a tangible result of NTNW that had been edited by Greenberg, Weiner and Donovan, the CUNY faculty who had served as co-directors on the project—"NTNW's most important achievement may in fact be in giving voice to writing teachers in a forum that usually had been dominated by researchers and policymakers." Gone was the observation made twenty years earlier by Richard Braddock, Richard Lloyd-Jones, and Lowell Schoer in *Research in Written Composition* that composition research "taken as whole, may be compared to chemical research as it emerged from a period of alchemy: some terms are being defined usefully, a number of procedures are being refined, but the field as a whole is laced with dreams, prejudices, and makeshift operations."[59] To those who were watching, the new city on the hill was to be seen as populated by a cohesive group of researchers focused on writing assessment. Its members would rejoice in each other's accomplishments. While the question of English remained as tied to the question of competence as it had for Barrett Wendell, the answers about its assessment would now be offered by a community of researchers, policymakers, and teachers. Such, at least, was the hope of NTNW.[60]

The Vision of Edward M. White

For Edward M. White, answers about writing assessment may have come from a community, but some of the individuals within that community—

educational researchers, statisticians, and policy makers—were suspicious; and process was laced with intrigue. "The modern era of writing assessment began during the fall of 1971," he would reflect in 2001, "when the English departments of the California State University (CSU) system, then consisting of 19 separate campuses, were able to defeat an administrative move to institute an external multiple-choice test for first-year English equivalency for the entire system."[61] The policymakers ("a determined system-wide administration") and the researchers (the Educational Testing Service) stood in opposition against the English department faculty (coordinated on nineteen separate campuses by the CSU English Council). At the end of the day, the faculty captured the right to determine which examinations would be used. Yet the responsibility of designing, conducting, and reporting the assessment process would fall to the faculty as well.

White's narrative of the events during 1970–1971 at California State University was reminiscent of the antics of the Nixon administration itself. The CSU system chancellor, a dark prince named Glenn Dumke, had secretly developed an assessment plan by which college freshmen would be able to skip required first-year composition class. The College Level Examination Program (CLEP) of ETS would provide the examinations, utilizing multiple-choice questions only, free of change to all entering students in exchange for widespread publicity of the test. The tests would function efficiently and would allow high-scoring students to skip six semester units of freshman composition. The chancellor's agents, plumbers in the spirit of G. Gordon Liddy and E. Howard Hunt, were everywhere. But the private arrangement with ETS was thwarted by the Daniel Ellsberg character, Gerhard Friedrich, a former officer of the National Council of Teachers of English who was then serving as vice chancellor for academic affairs. Friedrich leaked information from the system chancellor's office to White in a series of undercover meetings. White and his colleagues, stringers for the *Los Angeles Times* and the *San Francisco Chronicle*, called in their debts to those newspapers. The chancellor, now reading front-page stories about instant sophomores with the same expression that Nixon must have held when reading the Pentagon Papers in the *New York Times*, capitulated. The arrangement with ETS and the CLEP program would be dropped until the tests could be evaluated by the faculty, and the faculty themselves would be given university funding to implement an assessment program.

In the falling action—a wave before entering the helicopter—we see the emergence of the new order. The CSU resolution that Friedrich placed before the shaken Dumke in those final hours found its way, through White, into the widely read little volume *Equivalency Testing: A Major Issue for*

College English in 1974. The resolutions called for autonomous faculty governance (departments were responsible for determining what equivalency examinations should be used and what "cutting scores" should be used to grant exemption and credit), enhanced construct validity for the examination (equivalency examinations in English "must include student writing"), and increased student participation ("significant numbers of minority groups" should be present in such planning).[62]

Triumphant as Carl Bernstein and Bob Woodward would be in their *Washington Post* offices, White and his colleagues had won the day in the fall of 1971. Realizing, however, that in dreams begin responsibilities, the faculty now had to invent a system to assess the writing ability of students. When White and his CSU English Council colleagues met some weeks later as a committee to relish their victory, as White recalled, "we had to make good on our statement that we were the ones to assess whether or not students had achieved on their own whatever it was we were teaching in first-year composition. We looked at one another in dismay. Remember, these were the days before composition studies, before holistic scoring was well known, before anyone in an English department had more than the vaguest notions about assessment theory. The Chancellor had offered to fund the test we had suggested we should give. Now what?"[63]

White had been trained as a literature specialist under Harry Levin and Reuben Brower at Harvard University, and his dissertation, "Jane Austen and the Art of Parody," must have seemed especially apt to his present situation. Parody, he had written in 1960, "remains as a technique of humor through which the obscure fact of truth may be glimpsed."[64] In that the pointer had stopped at White, he began to research what little existed, glimpsed what was there, and built consensus among the CSU English departments. On May 12, 1973, the Freshman Equivalence Examination was administered to 4,071 students. As White claimed in his 1973 report, *Comparison and Contrast*, the results demonstrated that the program was a "major success" for all involved, including the 1,362 students who earned six semester units of college credit by means of the examination, the English faculties, and the CSU system itself. The project, White concluded, "embodied a constructive resolution to what had seemed to be an irreversible and bitter conflict."[65]

The authenticity of the first examination was compelling. The State of California had given the university $64,003 for the project. Following the recommendation of the 1966 Godshalk, Swineford, and Coffman research for combined assessment methods, the California examination employed both a 90-minute essay test of two 45-minute questions (designed by the

CSU faculty and graded by 75 English professors drawn from 19 campuses) and a 90-minute objective test (the CLEP Subject Examination, Analysis and Interpretation of Literature). (The CLEP General Examination in English Composition had been declared inappropriate, as had the CLEP Subject Examination in English Composition.) The reliability of the essay test—scored on a 6-point scale—was .7183. The cost to the state of California per credit hour earned was approximately $9.00, much less, White noted, than the usual expense for instruction. White had helped to build the nation's first college writing assessment community.[66]

In 1982, White summarized the number of applicants and their success rates on the English Equivalency Examination. In nine years' time, 31,092 students had taken the examination, and 33% of those students had passed the examination, earning some 61,470 semester units of college credit for freshman composition. White recalled that a "decade of solid achievement has been accomplished."[67] White also noted in the 1982 report the relationship between the English Placement Test (EPT), implemented in 1977 to identify students with poor preparation in English, and the English Equivalency Examination. In 1980, for example, 2,290 students (47.6%) had been exempted from the former because of satisfactory scores on the later. If this number of students was added to the 1,417 students (29.5%) who received credit for freshman English through the English Equivalency Examination, approximately 77% of the 1980 students received "some form of pass."[68] Thus, White concluded, the two tests in combination provided substantial benefit to the students in affording them course exemption.

In 1981, White, with Leon L. Thomas (the associate dean of institutional research for the California State University and College system), used scores from the EPT to analyze the impact of such tests on racial minorities. In the fall of 1977, 10,719 admitted CSU freshmen had taken both the EPT and the Test of Standard Written English (TSWE) offered by the College Entrance Examination Board as part of the Scholastic Aptitude Test for college admission.[69] The TSWE, a fifty-question, multiple-choice test, was designed to evaluate the ability to recognize standard written English; the EPT, longer and more diagnostic in nature, included an essay section calling for a forty-five-minute writing sample, a thirty-five-minute multiple-choice reading test, and two additional thirty-five-minute multiple-choice sections on sentence construction and on logic and organization. While the TSWE focused on correctness, White and Thomas noted, the EPT avoided isolated questions of usage unless such questions related to sentence structure or to logic and organization. In addition, the essay portion of the EPT was scored holistically, a focus on the overall quality (not the correctness) of the writing.

Of the 10,719 students who had taken both the EPT and the TSWE, 7,300 identified themselves ethnically: 5,246 as white, 585 as black, 449 as Mexican American, and 617 as Asian American. While the scores of the white students on both tests were similar in their distribution, the TSWE scores of black students were dramatically different. Of the black students, the TSWE had grouped eleven percent at the lowest possible score and distributed those students in a different pattern of performance than that demonstrated for the majority of students. "It might be argued," White and Thomas wrote, "that such a distribution reflects the writing ability of this [minority] group, if those same students had not performed otherwise on the EPT. While these students have a lower EPT total mean score than the majority, they are distributed along the whole range of scores, and their pattern reflects the left-skewedness [stretched out and tailed off in the lower ranges] that is desirable for placement testing."[70] In an analysis of the Mexican American and Asian American student scores, the multiple-choice items of TSWE again "rendered a much more negative judgment of these students' use of English than did the evaluators of their writing." The conclusions were clear, as were the cautions: "The TSWE does not distribute minority students the same way trained and accurate evaluators of writing samples do. (It may be that multiple-choice usage tests in general share this disparity.) Those who use the TSWE, or other such tests, should be aware of possible differences in measurement for minority students." The contrast-gainer was clearly direct writing assessment, a method "likely to produce more accurate distributions of scores, at least in relation to faculty judgments of writing ability."[71] If impact on diverse groups of students was emerging as a central issue in large-scale writing assessment programs, an iron wedge was again driven between indirect and direct assessment methods. Changes in student populations, White had claimed, had rendered multiple-choice usage tests—to borrow the language John Stalnaker had used against essay tests in 1943—not worthwhile testing devices.[72] The year was 1981, and the publication of *Hunger of Memory* would have everyone—whether they felt affirmed or betrayed by the educational experiences of Richard Rodriguez—attending to the fact that diversity was rapidly becoming part of American higher education. If tests of writing ability must fit the times, this was the age of direct assessment.

Key to the direct assessment method had been the technique of holistic scoring, and in 1984 White produced the first comprehensive statement of the development of holisticism in English testing. In 1980 Miles Myers—then Administrative Director of the Bay Area Writing Project who would, from 1990–1997 serve as the Executive Director of the National Council of Teachers of English—had published *A Procedure for Writing Assessment and Holistic Scoring*. That sixty-nine-page monograph, written primarily for K–12 teachers, had been widely used as a practical handbook for those wishing to learn more about selecting topics, designing directions for administering the topic, scoring the papers, and writing the report of the process. Using a more philosophical approach, White chronicled holistic scoring as a process standing in opposition to "the dominant tendency of our time, the analytic spirit, which breaks things down into constituent parts in order to see how they work."[73] As a philosophy that stands against reductionism, holisticism "is the form that humanism takes when confronted with analytic reductionism. Holisticism says that the human spirit and its most significant form of expression (writing) must be seen and understood not in parts, but as a whole, face to face as it were, almost sacramentally."[74] There were acknowledged shortcomings of the method. It was, after all, only a means of rank-ordering papers and thus gave no meaningful diagnostic information beyond the comparative ranking; it could not represent an absolute value and thus yielded no steadfast cut score to divide strong from weak papers; and its proponents often overestimated inter-reader reliabilities. Yet that advent of holisticism was a manifestation of the spirit of process research in composition and poststructural criticism in literature.

In 1954 Edith Huddleston had proclaimed the triumph of scientific formalism and product analysis regarding the efficacy of multiple-choice tests of writing and their apparent objectivity. Now, thirty years later, White rejected such cold logic and embraced "the rediscovery of the functioning human being behind texts."[75] Early in the century, Thorndike had made use of a specimen of high quality in which the writer claimed the need for a Christian element to fulfill the dream of the city-state of Plato and Aristotle to include the humblest man, the lowliest woman, and the most defenseless little child. For White, holisticism provided just that form of anointed vision at the century's end. "Even the meanest bit of halting prose, even the most down-trodden of our fellow creatures," he wrote, "deserves to be taken as a living and vital unit of meaning, an artistic and human whole, not merely as a collection of scraps and parts."[76] His 1984 *College English* article would become Chapter 2 of *Teaching and Assessing Writing: Recent Advances in Understanding, Evaluating, and Improving Student Performance* the next year. That book would become a touchstone for a generation of teachers in schools and universities who needed detailed guidance in evaluating student writing. Stressing the importance of identifying connections between assessment and instruction, White ended his book on a note of optimism: "The more we know, and the more we help our students know about assessing writing, the more effective our teaching will become."[77]

State-Based Assessment: At Lunch Tables

In 1989 Robert E. Lynch, a professor of English at New Jersey Institute of Technology, was serving as a member of the state's community of writing assessment. He was, by all accounts, an effective teacher, deeply involved in writing assessment. With his colleagues Anthony D. Lutkus of the New Jersey Department of Higher Education and Paul A. Ramsey of the Educational Testing Service, he had presented a paper at the National Testing Network in Writing, focusing on one of the nation's premier assessment programs, the New Jersey Basic Skills Placement Test (NJBSPT). They had posed questions in their presentation about large-scale assessment and provided answers: What are the outcomes of a statewide placement test that uses a writing sample? What are the implications of a state-mandated writing assessment program for college remedial programs?[78] The answers to the questions reflected the complexity of the issues themselves. That year, 35 percent of the state's freshmen entering public institutions of higher education—16,966—were found to lack proficiency. Forty-one percent (19,593) lacked proficiency in some areas, and only 24 percent (11,480) appeared to be proficient.[79] That was the bad news. The good? The assessment was working to place students into appropriate college courses. Eighty-six percent of students who passed the basic writing courses into which they were placed by the NJBSPT passed a re-test of the placement test (a procedure brought forward when Lynch served as chair of the New Jersey Basic Skills Council, the group that monitored the test); 48 percent of students who took and passed basic writing courses were still in college after four semesters; 84 percent of those who passed basic writing courses also passed subsequent traditional writing courses; and the cumulative grade-point average of students who took and passed the basic writing courses was 2.27 after four semesters of college.[80] As Lynch reported to the NTNW, a program designed in 1977 to provide colleges with guidance in placing students in appropriate freshman math and English courses—and to report to the New Jersey Board of Higher Education on the status of basic skills preparedness in reading, writing, computation, and elementary algebra—was universally seen as successful. Two years later, Robert Lynch, a member of the Basic Skills Council since 1984 and the chair of the council from 1987 to 1991, presented the work of the NJBSPT in a conference in The

Netherlands. "I think the positive public reception of our report was due to its honest attempt to tackle complex assessment issues without oversimplifying them but also without hiding behind educational jargon and bland, neutral language," Lynch reported of the conference presentation.[81]

In May 1994 he made a very different presentation, this time to give public testimony before the New Jersey Board of Higher Education in response to a proposal by the recently elected governor, Christine Todd Whitman, to restructure higher education in the state by eliminating the state's Board of Higher Education and, with it, the NJBSPT. Without the testing system, Lynch argued, the embarrassing data would disappear, but the problem of basic skills would not. The faculty, he maintained, would continue to confront the problem in their classes. "It was the Basic Skills Program," he said, "that allowed wide access to public education while assuring that the quality of academic programs was maintained."[82] Harold Shapiro, then in his eighth year as Princeton's president, agreed. The governor, he believed, should re-think her plan to eliminate the state's Board of Higher Education and its attendant programs.[83] Testimonies and warnings yielded nothing; the fix, as the saying goes in New Jersey, was in. In her March budget message, the governor, exercising her power, announced that the Board of Higher Education would no longer exist as of July 1. New Jersey's program of basic skills placement testing had, in a political heartbeat, ended.

Ten years later, Bob Lynch had been named the Jim Wise Professor of Dramatic Literature at New Jersey Institute of Technology. The NJBSPT was a memory, fading more with each undergraduate section he taught of "Shakespeare and Film," with each graduate seminar on "Technical Editing." As a street-wise kid running around Brooklyn, he had done well on the New York Regents Examinations and enjoyed taking tests. Educated at New York University in Middle English and Renaissance drama, he had written his dissertation on popular insurrection in Elizabethan and Jacobean drama. The dominant literary theory at the time was the New Criticism, and its implicit attention to formal textual elements—not necessarily to the culture that produced the text—was the point of view that drove interpretation. Lynch knew from the first that he wanted to teach both writing and literature. The subtleties involved in the analysis of language on the page—the sort of explication Cleanth Brooks had executed in *The Well Wrought Urn*—had captured his imagination. "Formalism wasn't quantitative, but it was focused," he recalled.[84]

At first, his assessment of student writing was private, made public only over the university lunch table. His first experience in the formal system of writing assessment was with the New Jersey Basic Skills Council at its origin in 1977. It became clear from the first that faculty would need to be involved if the program were to be successful, and so he became a reader of student essays. Training papers were selected by ETS staff and given to table leaders to score and to use as scoring guides. Once the table leaders scored the training papers and found their own scores reflecting the given scores (usually a process that took place a day before the group scoring of papers), the sample papers were used to train the group to reach agreement. A four-point scale was initially used (later changed to six), and there were, in 1977, no scoring criteria. Discussions of reliability were centered, he recalled, not so much on reader reliability but, rather, on how individual parts of an exam—including the one-item test of writing and the abundant multiple-choice items—worked with other parts of the examination so that one administration would produce the same scores as another administration, a process known as equating the forms. Even though the study of Godshalk, Swineford, and Coffman was by then sixteen years in the past, the use of holistic scoring in large-scale programs such as the NJBSPT was still an emerging technique.

Early meetings were held at ETS, the contractor for the test, and centered on the design of multiple-choice test items and their pre-testing. (Lynch recalled being upset that the results of the pre-testing were released to the newspapers by representatives from the state. Participating faculty had thought that it was the items that were being assessed at this early stage, not the abilities of students.) At ETS he was impressed by the magnitude of that operation and the professionalism of the staff there. The notion that opinion could be substantiated by data was new to most English teachers. Opinion at the ETS lunch table was thus restrained unless it could be supported by data.

In 1984 Lynch became a member of the council, and complexities of the reporting structure became clear. These were public findings, communicated from committees to the state legislature and, often, as he had found, to the newspapers in the process. The political implications of testing were clear. In 1987 he became the chair of the council for two terms. The council met monthly, crafted memos (in that time before e-mail when each word mattered), and wrote bi-annual reports. The controversial post-testing program had just begun (now it was the colleges, not the high schools, who were to be judged) when the governor decided to undertake higher education's restructuring (the fix). College administrators breathed a sigh of relief: they were no longer responsible for reporting to the Board of Higher Education, and they no longer needed to acknowledge the extent of remediation at the post-secondary level. The entire venture, as the education editor of the state's leading newspaper put it, was a waste of money, hope, and effort. No one was blaming the Department of Higher Education or the colleges. "The fault might be found elsewhere," he wrote, "in the schools, perhaps, that year after year produce a bumper crop of academic losers who believe they should go to college, enroll, and then fail or drop out for some other reason."[85]

Lynch had spent seven years in the service of the NJBSPT. The benefit of table talk among members of the state's county colleges, colleges, and research universities—along with on-going discussion among these teachers with researchers from the Educational Testing Service and administrators from the state—was gone. That was the bad news. The good? The weekly drive from Newark to Trenton was over. Would he bring all of it back if he could? Yes, if only for the conversation.

A Room of Their Own: The Founding of a Journal

Since the end of the National Testing Network in Writing in the fall of 1991, there had been no national forum for the field of writing assessment, no way to continue the conversation enjoyed by Robert Lynch and his colleagues. The journal *Research in the Teaching of English* had been founded in 1967 and had remained an avenue for rigorous research. Yet a forum for assessment practice, such as that undertaken by Lynch and his colleagues, had disappeared.

The idea for a journal devoted to writing assessment arose at the Miami University of Ohio New Directions in Portfolio Assessment Conference in October 1992. As Professor Brian Huot of the University of Louisville wrote in his introduction to the first issue of the new journal in 1994:

> We had no real, focused or concentrated space to initiate, continue, or contribute to an ongoing dialogue about writing assessment. This lack of space was made all the more poignant by our experience at Miami University because we were pleasantly aware of the wealth and depth of scholarship going on just about portfolios. At one of the social activities during the evening, the talk turned to the obvious lack of space for talking about writing assessment on a regular basis. There were many voices in that conversation. I remember Pat Belanoff's, Peter Elbow's, and Liz Hamp-Lyons' (all members of the editorial board) as prominent in the discussion that eventually prompted Kathy Yancey and me to exchange e-mail addresses for the purpose of establishing a journal in writing assessment.[86]

The new journal, *Assessing Writing*, would become a forum for experimentation and discussion. The 2004 issue alone substantiated the initial promise of the journal: traditional experimental research was offered by Sara Cushing Weigle, associate professor in the Department of Applied Linguistics and ESL at Georgia State University and author of *Assessing Writing* (2002), regarding her development of an integrated reading and writing competency test for non-native speakers of English[87]; and a discussion was begun by Liz Hamp-Lyons, professor at the Hong Kong Polytechnic Institute and co-author, with William Condon, of *Assessing the Portfolio: Principles for Practice, Theory, and Research* (2000), regarding advances in establishing a common basis for proficiency in language use in the European Common Union—work that has occurred abroad subsequent to the IEA study by Allan C. Purves and his colleagues.[88]

In addition, the journal—available on-line through subscription—took full advantage of the Internet, including an articles-in-press service that allowed readers to study articles that had been accepted for publication yet remained in the process of proof correction. Combined with GIF images that allowed readers to review lengthy rubrics and surf through hyperlinked bibliographic notes, the journal's use of technology allowed innovative research conducted by the field's best practitioners to be presented in timely and detailed ways.

Involving Students: Portfolio Assessment

Mary H. Beaven's chapter "Individualized Goal Setting, Self-Evaluation, and Peer Evaluation" ended Cooper and Odell's 1977 *Evaluating Writing*. On one level, it was out of place, a discussion of one woman's methods of helping individual students; but on a deeper level, it set the stage, by its recollection of individual student talent, for the strategy that was to become the most-discussed method of assessment in the 1980s and 1990s, a method so popular that by 1994 its power had helped to crystallize plans for the field's first journal. As Huot wrote in the first issue of *Assessing Writing*, the silence from the classroom "ended in a resounding noise" with the advent of that most authentic of strategies, portfolio assessment.[89]

Beaven began her chapter simply: "When one looks for research that might help classroom teachers evaluate student writing more effectively, nothing is available that seems immediately applicable."[90] Indeed, her interest was not in summative, end-of-process assessment but, rather, in formative assessment within the classroom. She examined three approaches for responding to student writing: individualized goal setting, self-evaluation, and peer evaluation. Her assumption was that growth in writing was a highly individualistic process, and so she told stories of her students: the high-school student who worked full time and locked herself in the bathroom from 3:00 to 5:00 a.m. each morning to compose; the college student who could write nothing but expository essays because crafting poetry or short stories opened up memories of three cancer-related deaths in her family. There were, after all, Beaven reminded her readers, writers behind the essays, and teachers might best discover strategies for formative growth rather than employ edicts for summative judgment.

It was such knowledge of the writing process—sometimes approached experientially (as in Janet Emig's 1971 *The Composing Process of Twelfth Graders*, sometimes approached cognitively (as in Sondra Perl's 1979 account of the composing process of unskilled college writers and in Linda Flower's series of articles in *College Composition and Communication* and *Research in the Teaching of English* between 1980 and 1981)—that drove Educational Testing researcher Roberta Camp to propose a writing portfolio project in her January 19, 1982, report.[91] Among the objectives of the proposed portfolio project were those formative, process-oriented elements of writing that Beaven, Emig, Perl, and Flower and Hayes had identified. Camp identified four objectives in what may be the earliest comprehensive statement of portfolio assessment:

> A. To provide a comprehensive measure of writing ability that would allow secondary school students to demonstrate a wide range of writing experiences.
>
> B. To provide a focus for the improvement of secondary school writing curricula by demonstrating the value of writing in assessment, by formulating a set of writing tasks commonly recognized among teachers of writing, and by enhancing the professional development of teachers of writing; to provide the instructional and descriptive materials necessary to the integration of the portfolio into existing writing programs and a forum for discussion of writing and writing instruction in which can be developed 1) common standards for the evaluation of writing, 2) awareness of strengths and weaknesses exhibited by student writers and 3) a context for curriculum improvement
>
> C. To facilitate, eventually, the transition from secondary to post-secondary institutions by providing information less subject to distortion than that provided by the current application process and by improving communication between secondary and post-secondary institutions.[92]

ETS had begun a process of securing advice from secondary and post-secondary teachers of writing which included interviews with major figures in the field of composition: Toby Fulwiler, Maxine Hairston, William D. Lutz, Frank O'Hare, and Janet Emig. As well, ETS had sponsored a Writing Portfolio Conference held on November 13–14 in Philadelphia. The participants felt, Camp recorded, that "the portfolio held great promise, both as a method of assessment appropriate to writing as currently taught and as a means of enhancing writing instruction."[93] The formative nature of writing demonstrated in a wide range of writing experiences, as well as the creation of a forum for writing and writing instruction, were the goals of Beaven and of her fellow writing-as-process researchers. These aims were also apparent—and fully articulated in a programmatic orientation—within the ETS organization in 1982.

But the movement from theory into practice took place not within ETS but within the university. When Peter Elbow and Pat Belanoff started their portfolio experiment in 1983 at the State University of New York at Stony Brook, they incorporated the same aims and values into their program that Camp had articulated in her 1982 proposal. Reflecting in 1997 on what they termed the "portfolio explosion," Elbow and Belanoff recalled a great "hunger for a different way to evaluate writing," a hunger that was "echoed in so many colleges in the widest variety of institutional settings."[94] They saw the events at Stony Brook as paradigmatic of the times: at Stony Brook, the faculty had decided "not to trust the grades given by first-year writing teachers (especially graduate-assistant teachers) and therefore mandated a proficiency exam that overrode course grades: no one could satisfy the writing requirement without passing the exam—even if they got an A in the course itself."[95] Elbow and Belanoff resisted the system because it made a "mockery" of the writing-as-process, collaborative strategies advocated in the classroom. It was, no doubt, the manifestation of the accountability movement in their own university that drove Elbow and Belanoff to launch that which had remained on the ETS drawing board.

Key to the assessment process, Elbow and Belanoff believed, is an emphasis on collaboration and negotiation. Collaboration, they found, prompts teachers "to have to articulate for others (and thus for themselves) the basis for their judgments." And negotiation was the method by which the portfolios would be evaluated. Together, these processes had a way of "permeating" the assessment program.[96] Indeed, portfolios have "kicked back" at testing itself, they reported.[97] Inter-reader reliability was difficult to achieve, Elbow and Belanoff admitted, a complexity demonstrating the kick-back principle that presents itself when single numbers were assigned to portfolios. "Thus," they concluded,

> portfolios have put the assessment process in a pickle. They finally give more trustworthy pictures of ability (making us realize how little we could trust those old conventional single-sample pictures), but in the same stroke they undermine any trust we might want to put in the scoring of these pictures. Of course people

> have been calling into question holistic scoring, grading, and single-dimension-ranking for a long time. But portfolios have finally made this critique stick better.[98]

Portfolios were, Elbow and Belanoff claimed in 1997, simply the best current system to assess writing.

Colleagues at Washington State University agreed and launched the most widely used and most-documented system of portfolio assessment in the nation.[99] At Washington State, the portfolio assessment in 2004 was some thirteen years old, embedded within a university-wide writing program, including a placement examination for entering students, a writing-across-the-curriculum strategy for general education courses, a writing center, and a junior-level qualifying assessment in which the portfolio is used. An administrator of the program, Richard Law, described the development of the writing assessment program as emerging within this "package of policies" that began in 1986 and continued in response to the Washington State Higher Education Coordinating Board's mandate to collect data about students at several points, including entry-level information and mid-career progress.[100]

In the junior year, at the completion of sixty credits of coursework, the assessment system described in 2005 required that the student submit three pieces of writing from coursework in the portfolio; students also sat for a timed writing sample taken under controlled conditions. The portfolio, including the timed sample, was then scored on three levels: pass with distinction, pass, or needs work. At the top level, the achievement was noted on the transcript; at the bottom level, additional coursework in writing was recommended, including advisement for planned coursework.[101] Regarding reliability, the system yielded overall ratings that are consistent more than 85 percent of the time and simple passes that are consistent 95 percent of the time.[102]

The program's viability remained fueled, its developers claimed, by its responsiveness to its stakeholders—from students to faculty to administrators to legislators and their constituents. Indirect examinations such as the Scholastic Aptitude Test, however, regrettably also endured, their viability akin to Dracula's own: "no one has quite been able to find a sufficient wooden stake to put this invalid use of the exam to rest." Yet perhaps the stakeholders, the sponsors pray, will "have the power to finally lay the indirect exam to rest never again to see night or day."[103]

From Floor to Ceiling: Lee Odell and Outcomes of Assessment

In 1977 Lee Odell had been similarly disposed in discussing the objective items associated with standardized tests said to measure writing ability. He had been reticent about their use for any but the most elementary administrative decisions of placement. In 2004, he had added another point of reticence: the value of large-scale assessment. He had granted its value, a tail that had given a much-needed wag to a complacent dog. Yet the ultimate worth of it all was questionable.

In 1988 Lee Odell collaborated with Charles Cooper on a sequel to their 1977 text. The new volume, *Evaluating Writing: The Role of Teachers' Knowledge about Text, Learning, and Culture*, revealed the changes in writing assessment that had occurred in twenty-one years: the shift away from the sole use of multiple-choice testing, the acknowledgment that writing was a complex process, and the realization that writing tasks controlled both the writer's process and assessed product. In that volume, Fran Claggert had presented a model for an integrated reading and writing task based on her experience with the California performance assessment program in 1985, as well as her work with the New Standards project, a system of performance standards at the elementary, middle, and high school levels sponsored by the National Center on Education and the Economy in Washington, D.C., and the Learning Research and Development Center at the University of Pittsburgh. Gaining critical momentum in the 1990s, New Standards specialists such as literacy researcher Lauren Resnick of the University of Pittsburgh, as well as thousands of classroom teachers, worked to establish an international system to benchmark and indicate performance levels that students should demonstrate in English and the language arts (as well as in mathematics, science, and applied learning). Claggert's chapter documents enormous teacher involvement, with the essays of nearly one million students in California assessed annually. "While teachers, state department assessment personnel, politicians, and statisticians are still coping with the logistics of administering and scoring such a complex instrument," she concluded, "the work to date has shown that large-scale authentic assessment—from design to construction to scoring—can be accomplished by teachers working together with administrative support."[104]

For Lee Odell, a professor of composition theory and research at Rensselaer Polytechnic Institute, the outcome was perhaps not worth the effort if valuable writing instruction was not, in the first place, offered to the students—a theme he had advanced in 1982 for the National Testing Network in Writing. After all, he felt, the basic concern of assessment was diagnosis and prescription. Unless assessment told students what they had done and how they might do better, the subject failed to energize him. With Charles Cooper, he held steadily to the belief that assessment and teaching are closely related and mutually influential. The complex logistics, the formulaic essays of large-scale assessment—he had elected to stay as far away from it as he possibly could.[105]

Odell was educated at the University of Michigan in the doctoral program in English and education. The curriculum afforded a great deal of freedom but little training in rhetoric. His dissertation, directed by Richard E. Young, was a turning point.[106] The theory of tagmemics developed by Young and his colleagues Alton L. Becker and Kenneth L. Pike was a heuristic that was a sure match for Odell, particularly in its explicit taxonomic complexity and in its implicit call for good citizenship. The ideas of contrast, variation, and distribution, key to the taxonomy, were of seminal importance to Odell's thinking.[107] These ideas, as Young's co-author Kenneth Pike had said, were the characteristics of rationality itself. As Odell's advisor, Young also paid careful attention to language, especially to Odell's own writing. He was, Odell recalled, "incredibly generous with his time and his intellect."

Jean Piaget also was an influence, although a lesser one, particularly through his ideas of the ways that we try to restructure our internal and external notions of the world.[108] There was a Cartesian dichotomy there, Odell realized, but there was nevertheless something in the external world that we must reckon with daily, something that—as Samuel Johnson demonstrated in his refutation of Bishop Berkeley's assertion that matter did not exist—may thus be found by kicking a stone. We do stub our toe on something, and we try to have an influence on that something. We act on a world around us; we move back and forth between what we perceive and what we encounter at a given moment. This movement between worlds, Odell realized, was a powerful concept, one that encourages us to try to decenter, to try to understand that which is not us. The shift involved in decentering takes place over a range of shared features, Young had realized. And over the years, perhaps because of his research on writing in non-academic settings, Odell had also come to realize that the reference points of these features must be identified if we are to move an audience from where its members are to some other point. For him, the happiest teaching moments were those that involved transactional writing, that involved enabling students to do something in the world. Odell had learned to think of writing as a cognitively complex, transactional act occurring within myriad social contexts. Writing assessment, it followed, should engage such complexity.

Odell's particular interest in assessment stemmed from his own college experience in observing grades given by professors on papers he and his fellow students had written: "How the hell did he figure that out? How did he get that?" Thoughts about grading animated the way he spent his time at Michigan, especially regarding his dissertation. His interest in assessment, thus, came out of a long-standing frustration with grading. In his later work with discourse-based interviews, research evident in *Writing in Non-Academic Settings*, he had wanted to get at the choices that writers make. Do writers elaborate or not, define or not? Such questions led to the context in which a text arose. And so it was that Odell combined an interest in the formal features of the text with an interest in the choices writers made—especially tacit choices—in particular contexts.

As a high-school teacher in Knoxville, Tennessee, Odell had learned to make his assessment goals clear to students. Individualized, classroom-based evaluation went well. At Michigan, however, his recollection of a collaborative writing assessment was quite the opposite. The head of the freshman writing program would reproduce student essays and encourage discussion of those essays. "A proverbial room full of monkeys could have gotten the same level of agreement that we had gotten." The discussion was even worse. Eventually, the unproductive process ended. Common paper readings among the teaching assistants were equally disastrous. He realized, of course, that essays could be read reliably, and there were times when that was useful. Nevertheless, people bring agendas, even when they look at the same thing. "It is almost impossible to talk."

In his later work with the New Standards project on collaborative assessment, Odell had similar problems. In that case, it was difficult to render a valid assessment because the work that he and his fellow readers were reviewing was mediocre, falling always toward the middle of the scale. Because the writers—children—had by and large not had the benefit of good composition instruction, it was thus very difficult to render a valid assessment that was significant. "If there is a failure of instruction, there is little that assessment can reveal," he had come to believe. "It is hard to have meaningful assessment unless there has been good teaching. Otherwise, the papers used as range finders will be mediocre and will not allow useful distinctions among different levels of performance." His position was strikingly similar to that expressed by George Hillocks, Jr., in *The Testing Trap: How State Writing Assessments Control Learning*. "If states really want student writing to improve," Hillocks had concluded in his study of state-mandated writing assessment programs, "they need to insure that teachers have adequate time to teach writing well."[109] In essence, Odell believed, there can be no informed talk about context, variation, and distribution, about how writers render the world, about how shared features are identified in order to move audiences—the desired outcomes, really—that will be of value in the absence of perceptive teaching. Even advanced students are often taught to write to a formula, he had concluded, and assessment often rewarded solely those rote formulas. Such formulaic instruction has little epistemic or rhetorical value and remains uninformed and superficial. "What might be the floor becomes the ceiling." The really profound assessment criteria he had once hoped for had not been forthcoming.

For Odell, as had been the case for Dewey and Diederich, there was no reflex arc. There was only a desired circle of teaching and assessing writing in which informed assessment criteria shape and are shaped by instruction. Within that circle students and their teachers would examine heuristics, study adaptation achieved through the cognitive processes of assimilation and accommodation, identify reference points used to move audiences, and use—for the common good—rhetorical structures designed to allow us to do a worthwhile something in the world. For assessment to be valid there would be no cause or effect, no stimulus of writing, and no response evaluated by means of restrictive criteria. Teaching and assessing writing would be strictly correlative and contemporaneous.

Was the curriculum better in 2004 than it was in 1977? Has such a circle emerged for students? Was there evidence of valid assessment, of the burn that was the original seeing? From his vantage point—"a highly personal, idiosyncratic view"—the teaching of writing had not become as thoughtful and as well informed as he had hoped. In 2002, he recalled, he had visited the school district where he had gone to high school in order to give a writing workshop. It soon became clear that the teachers wanted his help to develop one semester of literature and one semester of grammar—literally, the same curriculum that had been in place fifty years earlier when he had been a student, the same kind of dualistic instruction in grammar that Rollo Lyman had concluded should be abandoned in 1929. Even the California assessment program described by Fran Claggert—so wonderful in its potential—had become undermined by funding and administrative failure, he felt. Why the lack of progress? The teaching of writing itself was "just so dammed hard." The sheer burden of instruction, combined with a load of one hundred and fifty students a day and the conflicting pressures of the community and the testing organizations, made progress just another myth.

Lee Odell was not against assessment. It was not wrong. It was not bad. He was simply wary of the presence of the assessment machine in the mind's garden, its tendency to reduce mechanistically that which was most valuable: the writer's power to understand and to create and to do something of value in the world.

Technology in the Garden: E-rater

The computers of the 1950s were slow behemoths that used batch processing, but innovations such as time sharing, pioneered at institutions such as Dartmouth College, made the computers of the 1960s more accessible and led, eventually, to the first generation of personal computers. As the cost dropped—from $85,000 in 1961 to $18,000 in 1965—the usefulness of the machines was soon apparent.[110] The promise of something good to come was there.

Even Hollywood knew it, as the 1957 film *Desk Set* demonstrated. Richard Sumner, holder of a Ph.D. from MIT and the creator of the Electromagnetic Memory and Research Arithmetical Calculator, did not in the end replace the head of the research department, the college-educated Bunny Watson (who was going to take a Ph.D. herself but ran out of money). The pink slips issued to everyone in the building were a simple mistake of EMRAC. As Spencer Tracy and Katharine Hepburn showed in the triumph of their sexy-smart characters, the machine was only making everything more efficient. All along, EMRAC was there just to help.

In 1966, Ellis Page also recognized the usefulness of such efficiency. There was, he argued, an imminent day at hand when essays would be graded by computers. Since language had its own observable—and thus countable—features, the problem's solution rested in the sentences themselves. These intrinsic elements of writing he called "trins," features such as syntactic complexity. In that a computer can count features such as the number of prepositions and conjunctions—which he termed "proxes"—then a tabulation of the "proxes" would reflect the true value of the "trins." By 1968, Page designed an experiment in which the grades established by computer tabulation of approximately thirty proxes correlated quite well with grades assigned by four human judges. Indeed, the correlations were stronger between machine and human than they were among four human judges. "We will soon be grading essays by computer," Page prophesied, "and this development will have astonishing impact on the educational world."[111] Thus, in 1977, it seemed that it might be possible, Patrick J. Finn explained in Cooper and Odell's *Evaluating Writing*, to use computer tabulations to check on evaluation "as one would use a second reader."[112]

Finn himself reported on an experiment in which he demonstrated that classes of words, such as undistinguished word choices and mature word choices, could be identified and placed into a computer. Once the words were placed into the computer, teachers could classify the words used on an individual theme within seconds. Evaluation would be achieved in a fraction of the time it would take a human reader to judge an essay. Yet Finn was hesitant, realizing that word choice was merely one component of writing. Nineteen years later, Hunter Breland of ETS was, in fact, not willing to go much further, and certainly he was not going as far as Page had gone in envisioning a new city on the hill. Although Breland had found that the computer analysis program WordMap produced an evaluation of an expository essay that was as reliable as a single human reader in a correlation of prediction, he backed away from claiming that essays could be graded by a computer. "Grading is a high-stakes event," he warned, "that can affect other important events, such as college admission; accordingly, grading seems an unlikely task for the computer."[113] By 1998, his warning would prove without foundation in light of the ETS prototype for the electronic essay rater, E-rater.

E-rater was designed by ETS researchers, chief among them Jill Burstein.[114] Burstein was trained in linguistics at the City University of New York and had worked at the Borough of Manhattan Community College, teaching students who were learning English as a second language. At Empire State College, she had taught electricians. To be union certified, electricians had to earn an associate degree. Part of that degree included a strong writing curriculum in essay and researched writing. Since holistic scoring had been used at the conclusion of courses to certify proficiency, Burstein had early contact with scoring methods. In teaching writing to non-traditional students, she had become a specialist in non-standard dialect.

Her work at ETS in developing automated essay scoring was initially based on the evaluative criteria made explicit in scoring rubrics. What was there in the rubrics, she and her colleagues had asked, that could be captured computationally and would enable essays to be scored by machine? To answer that question, Burstein and her colleagues used natural language processing, a battery of computer science techniques used to address written (or spoken) language, in the e-rater's development. Discourse analyzers were also used to identify the presence and absence of relevant essay-based discourse elements, including introductory material, thesis statements, main ideas, supporting ideas, and conclusions. Rhetorical parsers were used to assign, for example, comparison and contrast techniques. At the end of the day, e-rater had been designed to extract features from essays that had been written by students and scored by human readers.

The first application—a high-stakes venture begun in 1995–1996 and launched in February 1999—would be the Graduate Management Admissions Test (GMAT). The scoring was to take place between human reader and machine. E-rater was, of course, 100 percent reliable within itself, unlike its human counterpart, who would give different scores across time and circumstance. The GMAT test development statisticians had specified a measure of agreement: E-rater had to achieve an 87 percent agreement with human readers, a percentage based on the lowest recorded human reader agreement (measured by exact plus adjacent scores) for the test. Burstein's creation easily achieved its goal. By 2004 it had regularly achieved exact plus adjacent agreement upwards of 97 percent.

Because the computer's scoring system was based on defined topics, the issue of validity had been concurrently linked to reliability. Solving one solved the other. On the GMAT, there were two tasks, one that asked students to present an argument and one that asked students to take a stand on an issue. Students were to use different rhetorical strategies in responding to the different tasks, and e-rater was designed to capture essays written in response to both. That is, the software of e-rater was specifically structured to identify five predictor variables in writing samples submitted to address argumentative and issue topics—surface features, structural features, rhetorical structures, content vector analysis, and argument-content vector analysis.[115]

The five variables were well designed, a reflection of the rubric—itself a series of predictor variables—used by human readers. Surface features of an essay were captured and measured based on variations in word count. In 1996, Hunter Breland of ETS had found a .74 correlation between the number of words written for the College Board's English Composition Test essay and the essay score based on a six-point rubric; hence, surface features promised a correlative ability in the software design.[116] Structural features were defined as those elements of a writing sample embodying syntactic variety—subordinate clauses, infinitive clauses, relative clauses, and subjunctive modal auxiliary verbs such as "would" for each sentence in an essay. A linear regression model was then used to select predictor variables of structural features based on essay type: the total number of modal auxiliary verbs for argumentative essays; the total number of infinitive clauses for issue essays. The third variable, an analysis of rhetorical structure, was operationalized by an automated argument partitioning an annotation program designed to segment the essay into units based on "clue words" signaling where an argument begins and ends, phrases such as "in summary" or "in conclusion." Content vector analysis in the study was undertaken using content vector analysis, a statistical weighing technique used to identify relationships between words and documents. The word "pterodactyl" would, for example, have a high salience because few documents contain that word. The final variable, argument-content vector analysis, was used to identify the associations between the words in each argument of an essay and the essay score assigned by the human rater.

The researchers had thus, in effect, matched the software to the six-point holistic rubric—guides that were, in effect, predictor variables of the value of an essay as measured on a scale of six (the highest score) to one (the lowest score). The word counts—the surface features used by Page and Finn—were incorporated as a single variable into a rich array of variables that now reflected the ETS-developed scoring guide. Because the computer program had been designed to be topic specific, its designers had used the most current academic research to align task and scoring criteria—Leo Ruth and Sandra Murphy's *Designing Writing Tasks for the Assessment of Writing*, and Gordon Brossell's summary of the research to date regarding topic variables of wording, subject matter, mode of discourse, and rhetorical specification. In addition, one year later, Hunter Breland and his ETS colleagues had replicated the Godshalk study and paid special attention to the writing tasks, developing scoring guides independently for each of the three topics (narrative, expository, and persuasive) and scoring the papers according to the topic.[117] Thus, e-rater had been designed to embody the most current research on writing assessment in its design. Its software fastened the scoring criteria to topic design with a technical efficiency unimaginable to Lloyd-Jones and Purves.

And with a performance efficiency as well. On the argumentative topic, the inter-reader correlation between two human readers was .853. The inter-reader correlation between the first human reader and the machine on the argumentative topic was .848 and .857 between the second human reader and the machine. On the issue topic, the inter-reader correlation between two human readers was .864. The inter-reader correlation between the first human reader and the machine on the issue topic was .879, and .880 between the second human reader and the machine. As Burstein and her team modestly declared, "These statistics suggest that agreement, reliabilities and correlations between two human raters, or between a human rater and the machine are comparable."[118] The trial test had worked. In 2005, the

GMAT writing assessment essays were scored twice—once by a human reader, and once by a machine.

Of the many questions that would be asked and answered regarding the ability of e-rater, one stood out. Was it possible to trick the machine? Donald E. Powers and his team of researchers asked carefully selected readers—assessment specialists, researchers in computational linguistics and cognitive science, members of the academic writing community critical of automated scoring methods, and specialists in English as a second language—to write essays in response to Graduate Record Examination (GRE) writing-assessment prompts. The specialists were given information about the design of e-rater as well as the scoring guides used by the human readers. Winners were awarded $250 if they submitted an essay that was either greatly undervalued or greatly overvalued by the computer.

There was one clear winner, a professor of computational linguistics who simply wrote several paragraphs and repeated them thirty-seven times. E-rater assigned the paper the highest possible score, while the human raters awarded the paper the lowest score. Powers and his colleagues felt, however, that such an essay would be "downgraded by trained readers in the 'real world' of high stakes testing."[119]

The human reader, in the end, would make all the difference in the world.

Paul Ramsey and ETS in the Twenty-First Century

The new technology was most promising, Paul Ramsey believed.[120] The future of writing assessment would be determined, in part, by the development of programs such as e-rater. By 2004, some 500,000 students—five times more users than in 2001—were using an on-line essay evaluation system, Criterion, developed by ETS. The system included two companion tools, e-rater and Critique. A school would subscribe to the ETS service, and its students would write and submit essays on-line. The teacher would select topics from an ETS pool, and the student would write to that topic. The student would then receive a score from 6, the highest, to 1, the lowest (from e-rater) and a diagnostic analysis of the essay's elements (from Critique). The teacher would also receive the score and the analysis. As Miles Myers himself had to admit, Criterion had brought a dialogue into the classroom that had not previously existed.

The Criterion system, with its two tools, was both reliable and affordable; indeed, the feedback that ETS researchers received from Critique, as well as from experienced teachers annotating dimensions of writing on student essays, was being used in August 2004 to improve the scoring capability of e-rater—evidence that Daniel Coit Gilman's 1885 assurance that intricate systems and ingenious methods would eliminate error had come to pass, at least in the venue of computer-assisted writing assessment. Yet in its implicit claim that a machine was as good as a person when it came to essay evaluation, the process of computer-based scoring flew in the face of humanism. Computer-based scoring, Ramsey acknowledged, was still seen as an affront to an academic tradition. Such scoring did a good job, but that was not, he knew, the point with many teachers. Nevertheless, in time he felt that the stakeholders of writing assessment would certainly come to a compromise in order to gain a better process.

About paths leading to better results (often gained amid controversy), Ramsey knew a good deal. In 2004 he was senior vice-president for School & College Services and International Development—one of the most senior corporate officers at ETS. He was, he recalled, part of a generation of African American intellectuals who had been influenced by their parents under an obligation to do well. That he had clearly accomplished. His mother had been head of testing in an historically black college in Ohio, Central State College, during the 1970s. ETS had established a relationship with Central State College in order to help black students perform better on ETS tests. Through a connection at ETS established by his mother, Ramsey's résumé was forwarded to Princeton—his dissertation had been a critical edition of James Shirley's *Pastorale*, and his early scholarly work dealt with city and myth in Rome and the Renaissance—and he became a visiting scholar at ETS, taking a year off from his tenure-track position as an assistant professor of English and co-director of the writing center at the State University of New York at Binghamton.

Shortly before coming to ETS, Ramsey had written an article in *College English* in which he recalled his experiences teaching a graduate seminar entitled "The Teaching of Writing to Speakers of Dialect." Since the graduate students were "no fools," and since Ramsey was black, everyone knew that the seminar would be about teaching black students enrolled in remedial courses to write. Fearing to be "unmasked as being as unenlightened and unexotic" as his white colleagues—he knew little of the subject—he told the students not to pre-register. The course did not fold, and he began teaching a useful course: he learned a lot, he recalled, by teaching it. Essentially, the message Ramsey carried was that these courses were not needed; rather, what was needed was general writing instruction. "What I saw," he wrote, "for the first time was that this obsession with black dialect was really a new form of racism at work in the field of writing." He feared that teachers, in their obsession with black dialect, were seeing "the student's pigmentation," not the paper. "If enough college teachers assume this humble I-don't-know-how posture," he warned, "the effect will not be unlike that of the slave laws which forbade 'them' to learn to read and write."[121]

Ramsey decided to stay at ETS. There he found that writing assessment was a refuge from multiple-choice testing. His self-described compulsive personality had fit well with his dissertation and would serve well his interest in writing assessment. When he became involved in language assessment at ETS in the literature and writing division, no essays were used for assessment. In 1979 he became the first person in that division at ETS to use essays as an assessment device in the Pre-Professional Skills Test (PPST), partly at the encouragement of Edward P. J. Corbett, who was on that test development committee and had argued for an essay. Writing assessment quickly became an area of his own as he worked with ETS researcher Trudy Conlan.

A graduate of Montclair State College, Conlan taught grades seven and eight before joining ETS. With her mentor, Fred Godshalk, she initiated and refined the holistic scoring process and would become the doyenne of writing assessment. Under her guidance at ETS, the apparatus for writing assessment—the method of holistic assessment, the resolution of reliability issues—was in place by the late 1970s.

While the College Board had used a four-point scale, the PPST was to employ a six-point scale in 1979, a device not much in use at that time. (The New Jersey Skills Placement Test had used, in its early administration, a four-point scale.) As much as anyone, Paul Ramsey was responsible for

Gertrude Conlan. "Each paper is read by at least two readers. The essays are read quickly for an over-all impression. You and the other readers are asked to react immediately to a paper and to score it on the basis of that first impression. You are asked *not* to reread papers or to analyze specific points of view. The basic assumptions of the holistic reading are that each of the factors [note the influence of French's factor analysis here] involved in writing skill is related to all the others and that no one factor can be separated from the others." (Gertrude Conlan, "How the Essay in the College Board English Composition Test Is Scored: An Introduction to the Reading for Readers" [Princeton: ETS, 1978] 2.) (Photo Reprinted by Permission of Educational Testing Service. All Rights Reserved.)

the new scale through his attempt to delineate more finely the skills of professionals. The PPST committee, for example, was also unhappy with the discrepancy range for the four-point scale: one reader could give a score of 3 and a second rater a score of 1, but that score was not considered discrepant. As part of an advisory committee apart from the PPST test development committee, Miles Myers of NCTE had taken issue with that discrepancy range and had argued for any score that was not adjacent to be considered discrepant and to be resolved by a third reader. In the end, Myers—who the next year would publish *A Procedure for Writing Assessment and Holistic Scoring* for NCTE, with the advice to teachers to "have papers read twice by different readers and a third time if the two scores differ by more than one point"—had prevailed.[122] Ramsey thus put into place what was to become the most popular contemporary writing assessment system: a six-point scale, holistic in orientation, with discrepancy considered as any score that was neither identical nor adjacent.

In those early days, Ramsey recalled, there were no scoring guides. Conlan, who had been instrumental in designing the NJBSPT scoring system for the writing sample, had argued that the guides undercut the holistic nature of the reading. Table leaders read holistically and inductively defined levels of the papers. That the levels thus emerged from the group without a scoring guide was considered "a very sacred part of the process." Due to a need for an expressed comparability across forms and administrations of a test, the scoring guides that were to be so common in writing assessment arose from the PPST. Ramsey and his colleagues began calling the new process modified holistic scoring because a scoring guide was used. With the scoring guide in hand, sample papers were then selected by table leaders to present to the readers for training. Conlan, Ramsey recalled, was "very upset about the scoring guide," feeling that it "undercut" the essence of holistic scoring. As her paper "Comparison of Analytic and Holistic Scoring Techniques" reveals, she believed that analytic scoring "has its roots in the traditional system of teaching writing," and that holistic scoring "grew out of the needs of a researcher [presumably her mentor Godshalk] and developed through its use in evaluating the essay components of writing tests administered to large groups of candidates."[123] The guide, she must have felt, had the potential to interrupt the efficiency of holistic scoring and blur the division between research methods and classroom instruction to the detriment of both.

Objections aside, the process of consensus building based on student writing samples triumphed. The scoring process Ramsey and others had built during the late 1970s would become the one most commonly used in schools and colleges across the nation, the emergence of calls for tighter discrepancy standards and for fully articulated rubrics a reflection of the growing certainty of the profession's ability to assess writing.

In 1986, Ramsey returned to the subject of minorities and standardized tests in a volume published by the National Council of Teachers of English. His essay, "Minorities and Standardized Tests," was a return to the themes of the *College English* article, but this time the application was both to teaching and to testing. His premise was clear: "Sure evidence of racism is neither in our tests nor in our classrooms but in our ignorance." We would know more about bias in tests "if white students over the last generation had done as poorly as minority students have on standardized tests." Either we would know more, he wrote, or we would have different tests. His advice to teachers was practical. If a school system adopts a standardized test, then it is important to gain information on differential racial and gender performance. In addition, because much was to be learned from the test-taking experience, teachers should take the tests themselves. The more the teachers knew, the better students, who should never go into a test cold, could do. Retired practice tests could be procured at a minimal fee, so that the students could become familiar with the test items. Indeed, teachers could assign students to compose a letter to a testing company requesting study materials—an assignment that "would almost surely do more for most students than would a five-page essay on a topic of their or anyone else's choice."

Ultimately, teachers should be encouraging success on these tests, not programming failure. As Hoffmann had nearly a quarter of a century before, Ramsey called for protest, for a belief "that it is the collective power of educators that will change the world of testing for the better." He ended his chapter with an allusion to *The Defence of Poesie*. "When you, the people who use the tests, unite and speak, your voice is heard and, to paraphrase Sir Philip Sidney, it moves—though it may not delight—the makers of standardized tests."[124] In 2001, as the keynote speaker at the Council for Basic Education, he reflected on the Praxis test for teachers that he and his colleagues had created. To criticisms of the test, he responded simply: "Work with me to create a test you're willing to stand behind."[125] It was there again: Ramsey's knowledge about emerging processes leading to better results that were so often gained amid controversy.

In 2004 new areas of development, he felt, would be in the technology, the way we score on-line, the way that we use the technology to ensure that readers are achieving agreement, are "on point." Essay scoring, he felt, would become more affordable because of its ability to be scored on-line.

And the assessment of writing ability through multiple-choice testing, the device most associated with ETS? In the twenty-first century, it was counterintuitive, an idea that no longer had traction in the English community. As James Grey of the National Writing Project once said to Ramsey, "You know, Paul, to talk about assessing writing in a multiple choice format is like assessing swimming in a multiple choice format." It was a great statement, he recalled, of the dilemma of writing assessment. At the end of the day, multiple-choice testing would endure, but direct assessment would prevail. Educators liked to see student achievement demonstrated on realistic tasks evaluated by other educators. As Ramsey simply stated, "People like the validity of human essay scoring."

A Way We'll Live Now: The SAT I Essay in the Twenty-First Century

So, it appeared, did Richard C. Atkinson.[126] As deputy director of the National Science Foundation, and then its director, he had worked hard to execute educational policy grounded in scientific research. From 1980 to 1995 he served as chancellor of the University of California at San Diego. In 1995 he was named president of the University of California system. Admissions tests should measure achievement rather than aptitude, he argued, so he did the unthinkable for a university administrator: he challenged the SAT I: Reasoning Test, the Board's key college admissions test, and argued that the University of California system should no longer use it. It was an archetypal lone-wolf act of inspired defiance, a challenge that would lead the College Board to revamp the SAT I to lend greater emphasis on achievement. When the controversy was over, the SAT I would include a test of writing ability. Beginning in March 2005, all students taking the SAT Reasoning Test would write an essay to be scored holistically. In the new millennium, admission to college would be dependent on a student's ability to compose.

Atkinson was a skeptic about intelligence tests. He admired Stephen Jay Gould's *The Mismeasure of Man*, a study that had, with guns blazing, analyzed the history of measurement, including a thorough condemnation of Princeton's Carl Campbell Brigham. Atkinson's direct involvement with the SAT began in the 1980s when he chaired the Board on Testing and Assessment, an agent of the National Research Council charged with advising the federal government on issues of testing and assessment. At a meeting of the Board on Testing and Assessment—what Atkinson referred to as "the defining moment"—representatives of the College Board and the Educational Testing Service presented their views on admissions testing. As he recalled, he "left the meeting less than satisfied." The technical, statistical, administrative aspects of the SAT were clearly controlled by the Board and ETS, he recalled, but "the notion that the SAT was a true measure of intelligence still seemed to dominate their perspective." On the way home from the meeting, he stopped in Florida to visit his granddaughter, then in seventh grade, and found her diligently preparing for the SAT. She was studying lists of verbal analogies. Was this, he wondered, how he wanted his granddaughter to spend her study time?

On February 18, 2001, Atkinson was asked to give the keynote address at the American Council on Education. On the suggestion of a colleague in the president's office, Pat Hioshi, then a member of the board of directors of the College Board, Atkinson decided to focus on the admissions process of the University of California. In the address, he announced that he intended to recommend to the faculty that the university stop using the SAT I (a measure of aptitude) and rely on the SAT II (subject-matter tests that were measures of ability) until appropriate achievement tests could be developed to replace the SAT. "If the Academic Senate responds favorably to these recommendations," he concluded, "then UC would reaffirm its commitment to assessing achievement in ways appropriate to the 21st century—a commitment to assess students in their full complexity. Such decisions are difficult because they involve making sense of grades earned in different courses taught at very different schools. They require that judgments be made about the opportunities available to individual students. They call on admissions officers to look into the future and make judgments about what individual applicants might contribute to campus life and, later, to society. These are extraordinarily tough decisions that require both wisdom and humility. But the stakes are too high not to ensure that the job is done right."

Because a draft copy of his address had been leaked to the *Washington Post*, the *Los Angeles Times*, the *Chicago Tribune*, and the *New York Times*, the auditorium was packed when he arrived for his presentation, as were the overflow rooms. The place was alive with reporters and television cameras and satellite feeds. "Clearly," he recalled, "the topic hit a deep chord in the American psyche." Over the course of the next several months, he received hundreds of letters, appeared on *The Jim Lehrer NewsHour* on March 30 with Gaston Caperton,[127] and saw *Time* magazine feature a picture of him and President George W. Bush with the caption underneath asking, "What do these two men have in common?"

Both supported the idea of standardized testing, Nicholas Lemann, author of *The Big Test*, had reported. Bush had made his first major address as president, proposing a new federally mandated system of standardized tests for public schoolchildren in which every student from grades three through eight would be tested in math and reading; it would be, Lemann emphasized, "the first Washington-ordered standardized educational test" and would thus increase the scope of testing. On the other hand, Atkinson had proposed dropping the SAT. Lemann then gave the history behind Atkinson's decision, emphasizing that Atkinson had not proposed abolishing all standardized admissions tests but, rather, had proposed using achievement tests that measured success in specific high-school subjects. "It's all the same idea," Lemann told his readers. "Half a century ago, Conant and Chauncey created, in the SAT, national education standards for the most gifted and best educated few. Now Bush and Atkinson are proposing to create national education standards for the many."[128]

It was not standardized testing that Atkinson had come to question but, rather, the SAT and its effectiveness and fairness as an admissions test that had been required since 1968 at the University of California and had become a formal part of the admissions process in 1979. In 1995, under Atkinson, the university had given greater weight to the SAT II tests in the admissions process. The use of these tests had allowed nearly 78,000 student-admission protocols to be studied: SAT scores, the SAT II scores (three tests were required, among them the SAT II writing test), family income, family educational background, high-school grades, the quality of the high school attended, as well as the race and ethnicity of the student. As well, the grades the student had received in the first year at the University of California were included in the protocol. The predictive validity study by two members of the Office of the President—Saul Geiser, director of Research and Evaluation, and Rodger Studley, senior research analyst in Admissions and Outreach—was released on October 29, 2001.

In *UC and the SAT: Predictive Validity and Differential Impact of the SAT I and the SAT II at the University of California*, Geiser and Studley had looked at the University of California admissions data and drawn three striking conclusions. First, there was strong evidence that students' scores on the SAT II achievement tests were "superior predictors" of freshman grades. If the prediction of college success as measured by freshman GPA were the standard by which admissions tests should be judged, as the College Board and others had emphasized in the vast majority of validity studies, then the SAT II achievement tests were the clear choice as an instrument upon which to base admissions decisions, the researchers argued. Second, the researchers found that the predictive validity of the SAT II was "much less affected" by differences in students' socioeconomic background than the SAT I. That is, after statistically controlling for socioeconomic factors, the predictive power of the SAT II was "undiminished," while the relationship between the SAT I and UC freshman grades "virtually disappear[ed]." "These findings" they concluded, "suggest that the SAT II is not only a better predictor, but also a fairer test in college admissions insofar as it is demonstrably less sensitive than the SAT I to differences in family income and parents' education." Significantly, the researchers also found that the SAT II writing test had "the greatest predictive weight among General/Undeclared majors and students in the Social Sciences and Humanities but not, as might be expected, among students in the Biological and Physical Sciences, Mathematics and Engineering, for whom the SAT II Mathematics test is the best predictor of freshman grades." Third, the researchers found that, with respect to racial and ethnic impact, there were only minor differences between the SAT I and the SAT II. Thus, eliminating the SAT I would have little effect on rates of UC eligibility and admission among students from different racial/ethnic groups."[129]

It was, thus, the efficacy of predictive validity—not solely the remembered scene of his granddaughter's time wasted on analogies—that had moved Atkinson to recommend a shift in admissions policy. As Geiser and Studley assured their readers in the first line of their report, Atkinson's "proposal to discontinue use of the SAT I in college admissions in favor of achievement tests, such as the SAT II, did not come out of the blue."

The College Board's reception was "less than enthusiastic," Atkinson recalled. His decision had moved, though not delighted, the owners of the SAT. In time, however, Gaston Caperton, a former governor of West Virginia and president of the College Board, encouraged the SAT revision. In March 2002 Caperton announced that the SAT would be eliminated and replaced, on a national basis, with a new test that would abandon analogies but would include an essay. A revolutionary change had been made, he recalled, and a clear message had been sent: learning to write was of critical importance.

At the College Board, it fell to Wayne Camara to make the new test work.[130] With a Ph.D. from the University of Illinois at Urbana-Champaign, Camara had been trained in school psychology as well as in industrial and organizational psychology. He had been associated with the Illinois state civil service and with military and employment testing. He had worked to assist federal agencies in developing regulations that addressed the Americans with Disabilities Act and had testified before Congress and state legislatures on his work. He had worked with the American Psychological

Association in Washington, first as director of testing and, later, as assistant executive director of science. He gathered national panels of experts in order to advise the discipline of psychology on various policy issues. There he also served as project director for the 1999 revision of the *Standards for Educational and Psychological Testing*, the essential guidelines for the profession of testing.

In the 1999 *Standards*, perhaps the most striking revision since the first edition of the standards was published in 1954, he had included some 30 percent new material; about 10 percent of the material had been dropped from the 1985 edition. The chapter on fairness was new, and the chapter on validity had been revised to include material on portfolios used as tests. ("Whether it is a multiple choice test or whether it is a designed constructed response or a portfolio…you need validity and you need reliability, you need to meet the same technical requirements, and you may do it in a different way—but in no way is your burden to demonstrate that technical relevance and rigor for your instrument are somehow minimized if you call it an assessment versus a test," he believed.) Camara was an advocate both of scientifically based testing as well as the appropriate use of tests. His work in analyzing employment settings for the private sector and in explicating judgmental situations for the military had led him to understand deeply the attributes necessary for success. In colleges, he felt, writing should be understood as a criterion for admissions. The fact that something was hard to measure did not mean that "we should give up and ignore it." By education, experience, and disposition, he was thus the ideal candidate when he came to the College Board in late 1994 to fill the position of executive director for Research and Development. Now, as the vice-president for Research and Development, he would oversee the most significant revision in the history of the SAT.

In looking at the Graduate Management Admissions Test, the new Graduate Record Examination, the National Assessment of Educational Progress, and at many state tests, Camara had come to the conclusion that testing in general had been "getting writing assessment right" for some time and, thus, could again get it right in the new version of the SAT. Although he was surprised that a minority remained who still questioned issues of rater reliability, the emphasis on the importance of writing and its ability to be scored reliably had been accepted. The Board's own experiences with writing assessment were substantial: the SAT II (taken by approximately one-sixth of SAT I test-takers), the Advanced Placement Program (where well over 1.1 million students took AP examinations each year, all of which, except those in studio art, involved extensive constructed response items, some essays, and some explication of problems), and the former Test of Standard Written English (that had employed an essay once a year as well as multiple choice items until 1994 when the test had been deleted from the Board's inventory). Such experiences had convinced Camara that the Board could, indeed, use a scored writing sample to inform admissions decisions.

Camara was further convinced by the recommendations included in *Beyond Prediction*, a 1990 report of the College Board. The authors of the report, the Commission on New Possibilities for the Admissions Testing Program, included co-chairs Derek C. Bok, president of Harvard, and the former president of the University of California, David B. Gardner, as well as Diane Ravitch, who would become assistant secretary of education the next year. The authors of *Beyond Prediction* had expressed directly their concerns about testing in the transition to college:

> Consider the oft-repeated claim that the SAT trivializes learning by using multiple-choice questions rather than higher intellectual skills. One can respond by pointing out that the multiple-choice format actually tests much more than memory, that it predicts college performance as accurately as more elaborate tests, and that it costs less to score, thus lowering the price for students. For these reasons, multiple-choice questions can be defined as the cheapest, most reliable way of carrying out the Board's primary mission of helping admissions officers to select students. But this response takes too narrow a view of the issue. Because of the challenges facing American education, the Board must pursue broader aims than simply helping admissions officers choose a class. For better or for worse, the format of a test as important as the SAT sends a strong signal to high school students about the types of thinking and learning that are valued in our society. A multiple-choice format carries a subtle message that recognizing the right answer is more important than working out one's own solutions, and that passive learning is sufficient to get ahead. In this way, the SAT can unintentionally weaken the very forms of active problem solving and critical thinking that most need to be emphasized in high school reforms.[131]

The statement was the most direct criticism of the validity of item types that had ever been issued by a group representing American education, a reflection of Banesh Hoffmann's long-forgotten conclusion that there was "a place for multiple-choice tests, but it is a strictly limited one, and its bounds have long since been overstepped."[132] The commission also questioned the "limited predictive power" of the SAT. The fact remains, the authors noted, that the added predictive power of the SAT is limited and measures only one of the attributes that admissions officers seek in selecting a freshman class: "creativity, practical judgment, perseverance in completing academic work, love of learning and ideas, to name only a few." Testing for college admissions was still, the authors cautioned, "an imperfect act that requires continued effort to help colleges find a fully effective, enlightened means of choosing students."[133] Again, the conclusions of Hoffmann—that "all methods of evaluating people have their defects—and grave defects they are. But let us not therefore allow one particular method to play the usurper. Let us not seek to replace informed judgment, with all its frailty, by some inexpensive statistical substitutes"—were echoed by the commission.[134] One generation's howl had become another generation's informed commission.

In short, the committee recommended that writing and problem-solving, rather than the singular use of multiple-choice format, be used in the SAT. The commission also recommended that the aptitude and the achievement measures should be brought together. The Board would indeed have implemented these changes, Camara believed, but Atkinson's position hastened their implementation.

Camara and his staff began to make visits to the University of California and met with the Board of Admissions and Relations with School (BOARS) committee, the faculty group now advocating the change with Atkinson. It was at that point, Camara recalled, that the importance of writing came forward and that the analogies were seen as problematic. The Board had been studying analogies and had considered their questionable instructional and consequential validity, although they had high predictive validity and did not impact English-as-a-second-language learners unfairly. Using an item response theory model, a computer-based method of analysis that allowed analysis of SAT items that had been in use over a fourteen-year period, ETS researchers concluded that it was possible to "maintain measurement precision for the new SAT critical reading section without analogy items," although some modification of other item difficulty would be necessary to obtain precision at the ends of the score scale.[135]

During 2003 the Board continued to work with the University of California. As well, the College Board talked widely with other institutions and constituencies across the nation—academicians and guidance counselors and admissions officers—to get information on the kinds of work that would be needed to revise the SAT. By August 2003 the University of California announced that students applying for admission to the 2006 entering class would submit SAT scores that would include a writing sample.

The new SAT would include a 25-minute essay and 35 minutes of multiple-choice items. The topics for the essay were to be academic and rigorous in nature, accessible to students regardless of content. Longer stimulus passages—lengthy passages, for example, of material to read before writing—were rejected, because it was important to maintain the distinction between reading and writing, as well as to retain the scoring scale. (Changing the scoring scale—the result of such a shift—would, in addition, have rendered comparisons before and after March 2005 complex.) Camara recalled being disappointed at how little existed in the literature of topic design, especially regarding performance differences according to discourse mode (e.g., persuasive compared to narrative) and how the topic impacted various sub-groups. So, the Board did its own study in 2003 under ETS researcher Hunter M. Breland, a comparison of SAT II prompts and persuasive prompts.

Breland and his staff prepared two types of prompts. The first was based on the SAT II writing test and encouraged students to discuss a topic in 25 minutes:

> Consider carefully the following statement and the assignment below it. Then plan and write your essay as directed.
>
> > Failure often contains the seeds of success.
>
> Assignment: The statement above suggests that failure may be the source of success. In an essay, discuss the statement above, using an example (or examples) from literature, the arts, history, current events, politics, science and technology, or your experiences or observations.

The second prompt was also on the topic of failure but provided more information—what had been called "information load" in Gordon Brossell's 1986 study reported for the National Testing Network in Writing. In addition, the modification encouraged persuasive writing:

> Consider carefully the following excerpt and the assignment below it. Then plan and write an essay that explains your ideas as persuasively as possible. Keep in mind that the support you provide—both reasons and examples—will help make your view convincing to the reader.
>
> > The principle is this: each failure leads us closer to deeper knowledge, to greater creativity in understanding old data, to new lines of inquiry. Thomas Edison experienced 10,000 failures before he succeeded in perfecting the light bulb. When a friend of his remarked that 10,000 failures were a lot, Edison replied, "I didn't fail 10,000 times, I successfully eliminated 10,000 materials and combinations that didn't work."
> >
> > —Miles Brand, "Taking the Measure of Your Success"
> >
> > Assignment: What is your view on the idea that it takes failure to achieve success? In an essay, support your position using an example (or examples) from literature, the arts, history, current events, politics, science and technology, or your experience or observation.[136]

Similar prompts were prepared on the topic of happiness. Four ethnic groups—African American, Asian American, Hispanic, and white—were sampled, with approximately six hundred students in each group writing on the two types of prompts. The essays were evaluated on a six-point scale, and those with a discrepancy of two or more score points were read by a third rater. The researchers found that there was no pattern in the types of prompts they studied—opinion or argumentative, briefer or longer, and task specification. "The results of this study," they found, "indicate that there should be no significant impact on any ethnic group of changing from an SAT II type writing prompt to a persuasive prompt for the type examined in this study."[137] A note of caution, however, was expressed about the performance of African American students. Perhaps, for this group of students, there was an advantage in using that SAT II prompt, at least for the subject of failure.

In 2004, lengthy discussions of inter-reader reliability were no longer needed. Attention was now turned to the reliability of student performance over time. Most poorly scoring students who repeated a test of writing skill after a four-month period received similar or slightly higher scores; over half of students whose scores were average or above average received scores within one point of their original score.

With the prompt design established, all that remained was the management of the reading. The essays were to be scored by two readers using a six-point scale. In case of a discrepancy of more than one point (e.g., a score of 6 and a score of 4), a third reading would be given by a master reader. Previous Board experience led to an expectation that approximately 97 percent of the essays would fall within a two-point range (e.g., a score of 6 and a score of 4), and approximately 94 percent of the papers would fall within a one-point range (e.g., a score of 6 and a score of 5). Approximately 60 to 65 percent of papers would receive identical scores (e.g., two scores of 6).

Technology, however, would play a role as never before. Although ETS would develop the prompts, the essays were to be scanned and scored online by NCS Pearson. In 2002 the world's largest integrated education company had won an $83-million, five-year contract for scoring the National Assessment of Educational Progress and had gained both experience and reputation in essay evaluation. In addition, students would be able to practice for the new writing sample using ScoreWrite, a system developed by Vantage Laboratories. Even the scored essays written for the SAT would be sent to the colleges for local review.

While Wayne Camara, a researcher, believed that the new SAT would have a great impact on the teaching of writing in secondary schools, it was Brian Bremen, a classroom teacher, who would be able to give a detailed account of the extent and nature of that impact. Bremen had been a high-school teacher at New Jersey's prestigious Peddie School in Hightstown and had spent his summers in Vermont studying in the graduate program at Middlebury College's Bread Loaf School of English. He had taught at The Peddie School for eight years before returning to Princeton University for his Ph.D.[138] His dissertation on William Carlos Williams had been directed by two of the nation's most eminent literary scholars, A. Walton Litz and Sandra Gilbert. He had been associated with the College Board since 1978 when he had taught advanced placement English and started grading the AP examination at ETS. While studying at Princeton he had worked part-time at ETS in test development on the Graduate Record Examination in 1988–1989. He had also been involved with the English Composition Test, the predecessor of the SAT II test of writing, and he had learned about the subtleties of assessment under Gertrude Conlan. In 1990 he had been recruited by the University of Texas at Austin, where he trained the admissions staff to read essays holistically. (Two admissions essays, evaluated by the admissions staff, had been required at the university since 1995.) In September 2002, the College Board had approached Bremen, now an associate professor and author of *William Carlos Williams and the Diagnostics of Culture*, to work on the writing sample for the new SAT. As the chair of the Test Development Committee for the SAT II writing test, he was the logical choice to work on the SAT revision.

The writing sample for the new SAT was to be a first-draft piece of writing. As a member of the committee that designed the writing task, Bremen had advocated the open task allowed by the SAT II. That is, he pressed for language that asked students to "develop a point of view" rather than "argue a position"—two different rhetorical constraints of the task. Word choices such as "persuade," he had argued, should not be used for the new essay. (While everything may be an argument, as his colleague, the rhetorician John Ruszkiewicz had claimed in a recent textbook, the use of such language overly constrained the task, Bremen felt.) Hence, a further refinement had been made in the prompt evaluated by the Breland study. The final form of the prompt appeared in *A Guide to the New SAT Essay*, a book that in 2004 had been sent to every high-school principal in the nation:

> Think carefully about the issue presented in the following quotations and the assignment below:
>
> 1. While secrecy can be destructive, some of it is indispensable in human lives. Some control over secrecy and openness is needed in order to protect identity. Such control may be needed to guard privacy, intimacy, and friendship.
>
> Adapted from Sissela Bok, "The Need for Secrecy"

> 2. Secrecy and a free, democratic government, President Harry Truman once said, don't mix. An open exchange of information is vital to the kind of informed citizenry essential to healthy democracy.
>
> Editorial, "Overzealous Secrecy Threatens Democracy"
>
> Assignment: Do people need to keep secrets or is secrecy harmful? Plan and write an essay in which you develop your point of view on this issue. Support your position with reasoning and examples taken from your reading, studies, experience, or observation.[139]

The content was as suited to its times as had been the April 1943 question used for the English Composition Test, a period when Churchill, Stalin, and Roosevelt had met in Tehran to set the invasion of France. Then, under the direction of Noyes and Stalnaker, students had been asked to illustrate by description their position on the impact of the radio after reading a passage critical of its impact on American life. For Breland and Camara, opinions potentially informed by the 2001 Patriot Act, passed a month after the tragedy of September 11, 2001, would provide the topic for essays that could, in a global framework, debate the benefits of enhanced domestic security and surveillance versus the costs of a federal search of library and medical records without probable cause.[140]

The new SAT scoring guide, Bremen noted, established that success could be gained whether the student decided to use "a narrative, expository, or argumentative approach; or whether the essay is structured through cause and effect or comparison or contrast or any other rhetorical strategy; or whether the student uses one example that is substantially developed or several examples that build an argument."[141] Without trying to be prescriptive, Bremen and his colleagues had allowed a wide range of possibilities in rhetorical mode and strategy for students to address in their SAT essays. "Students could do what they feel they could do best," he said. Procedurally, ETS would design and pre-test the tasks according to specifications designed by Bremen and the members of the test development committee at the College Board.

The new test would not claim, Bremen believed, to measure a student's writing ability; rather, the writing sample was valid because it was predicted, based on similar studies performed on the SAT II, that there would be a high correlation between scores on the writing sample and success in freshman composition courses. The issue of face validity had been important in the decision to use a direct writing sample. Indeed, in the future, the essay could be used as part of the admissions package in place of, for example, the two essays required at the University of Texas at Austin. In addition, there was the hope that the revision would promote writing instruction in high schools, that it would make writing instruction an important part of secondary-school education.

Within Bremen's own university setting, *The Neglected "R": The Need for a Writing Revolution*, a College Board report published in April 2003, had an impact. In the College of Liberal Arts at the University of Texas, a college-wide committee had been established to reassess writing instruction across the curriculum, and a new person was hired to head up the innovations. The findings of the National Commission on Writing in America's Schools and Colleges, a group that included among its members David M. Bloome, the president of the National Council of Teachers of English, had looked at the 1998 NAEP data and found that students could not systematically produce writing at the skill level required in a complex, modern society. In calling for a "cultural sea change," the committee had made recommendations for a new national writing agenda, recommendations that had been taken to heart at Bremen's university.[142] The *Chronicle of Higher Education* article the year before, "Why Johnny Can't Write, Even Though He Went to Princeton," had also had an impact. A real recognition was emerging, Bremen believed, that students were best served in institutions having an active and successful writing program.[143]

Bremen had fears, of course. The design of the tasks—perhaps a student would freeze when the question was encountered—worried him, as did the ever-present concern of reader reliability. But there were quality controls in place. While a score of 6 and a score of 3 would generate a third reading on the SAT II writing test, the new SAT would have tighter controls (a score of 6 and a score of 4 would generate a third reading). And, of course, every paper would be rated twice by human readers. Bremen would personally be involved in selecting the training papers for the readers and annotating them for the on-line readers at each administration. The on-line system developed by NCS Pearson, he believed, would allow close monitoring, thus allowing greater quality control. An accuracy score, for example, would have to be met by the readers before live SAT papers could be scored. (At live readings, everyone would be trained [an assumption], then readings of the live papers would occur; the new on-line system designed by NCS Pearson would afford proof that the readers could achieve agreement on the sample papers—proof demonstrated by an accuracy score achieved before the business of rating began.)

It was Bremen's hope that the inclusion of a writing sample on the new SAT would influence the way essay writing was taught and assessed. Hopefully, the formulaic five-paragraph essay would become a relic of the past, a detriment to good writing. With the faculty at Washington State, he hoped to drive in a few stakes himself, to begin again in the light of a new day. In his own *Introduction to American Literature*, a course required for all students at his university, a series of two-page essays was required that would enable students to crystallize their thinking, to make apparent to others the nature of their thinking. In the graduate seminar in pedagogy he taught, Bremen used these undergraduate student papers to train the new graduate students in holistic scoring, a process they would then use in their own teaching and assessment practices. With its return to the classroom, the assessment of writing had come full circle, had become part of an informed educational process. Bremen had found a world to put all together: his research on the vastly human world of the physician William Carlos Williams, his detailed work with the College Board, his well-designed undergraduate American literature class, and his responsibility to train informed graduate students who would, in time, create the future of English with their own research and teaching. His was the ultimate act of meaning in a postmodern world: in a culture of flux, students would negotiate their ideas in essays, and their instructors would assess the essay's value on its own terms by means of holistic scoring. The gap between pragmatism and postmodernism had been bridged. There was, after all, reason to be hopeful.

To Richard C. Atkinson's granddaughter, none of this mattered. She would be among the first to take the new SAT. She was not hesitant to accuse her grandfather of complicating her future. She had liked the old SAT.

Endnotes

1 "Why a Commission on Tests?" *College Board Review* 65 (1967): 14.

2 William W. Turnbull, "How Can We Make Testing More Relevant?" *College Board Review* 67 (1968): 7.

3 William W. Turnbull, "How Can We Make Testing More Relevant?" 8.

4 Louise M. Rosenblatt, *Literature as Exploration* (New York: Appleton, 1938). For the history of this important book written for the Commission on Human Relations, see Arthur N. Applebee, *Tradition and Reform in the Teaching of English: A History* (Urbana: NCTE, 1974) 123–125.

5 John A. Valentine, *The College Board and the School Curriculum: A History of the College Board's Influence on the Substance and Standards of American Education, 1900–1980* (New York: College Board, 1987) 119–120. The list of association members is provided on 119.

6 Commission on English, *Freedom and Discipline in English* (New York: College Entrance Examination Board, 1965) 3.

7 Commission on English, *Freedom and Discipline in English* 9.

8 Commission on English, *Freedom and Discipline in English* 90.

9 Commission on English, *Freedom and Discipline in English* 91.

10 Scott Elledge, "For the Board's English Tests: An Old Era Ends, What Lies Ahead?" *College Board Review* 71 (1969): 22.

11 Elledge, "For the Board's English Tests" 22.

12 Lewis Terman, "Letter to Don Marquis," 24 Sept. 1948, *Lewis Terman Papers*, Stanford University (SC038/Box 15/Folder 5). Permission to quote from the letter given by Margaret J. Kimball, University Archivist, Stanford University Libraries.

13 Robert F. Hogan, Foreword to Paul B. Diederich, *Measuring Growth in English* (Urbana, IL: NCTE, 1974) iii.

14 Diederich, *Measuring Growth in English* 2.

15 Paul B. Diederich, "To All My Friends and Well-Wishers," 6 Mar. 1966, Diederich Papers (Princeton: ETS Archives).

16 John Dewey, "The Reflex Arc Concept in Psychology," *The Early Works, 1882–1898*, ed. Jo Ann Boydston, vol. 5 (Carbondale and Edwardsville: Southern Illinois UP, 1972) 99. The importance of this essay has also been noted by Edwin G. Boring, *A History of Experimental Psychology*, 2nd ed. (New York: Appleton-Century-Crofts, 1950) 554; and Louis Menand, *The Metaphysical Club: A Story of Ideas in America* (New York: Farrar, Straus and Giroux, 2001) 328–329.

17 Dewey, "The Reflex Arc" 98.

18 Dewey, "The Reflex Arc" 109.

19 Dewey, "The Reflex Arc" 109.

20 Paul B. Diederich, "Readers, Aides, and Technicians," *Harvard Graduate School of Education Association Bulletin* 6.1 (1961): 2–3.

21 Paul B. Diederich, "Innovations in English Teaching," *Needed Research in the Teaching of English: Proceedings, English Research Conference, 5–7 May 1962* (Princeton: ETS Archives): 72–78. In the copy of the paper in the ETS Archives, Diederich noted in the margin that this was the "best available account of lay readers." He also noted in the margin that in 1964, "about 16% of the members of the National Association of Secondary Schools and Principals reported that they were then employing lay readers."

22 Diederich, "Innovations in English Teaching" 75.

23 Diederich, "Innovations in English Teaching" 78.

24 Diederich and Frances R. Link provided two extensive, detailed chapters on assessment in *Evaluation as Feedback and Guide*, prepared by the ASCD Yearbook Committee and edited by Fred T. Wilhelms (Washington: Association for Supervision and Curriculum Development, NEA, 1967). See Chapter 6, "A Cooperative Evaluation Program," and Chapter 7, "Cooperative Evaluation in English."

25 Diederich, *Measuring Growth in English* 50.

26 Charles R. Cooper and Lee Odell, eds., *Evaluating Writing: Describing, Measuring, Judging* (Urbana, IL: NCTE, 1977).

27 Cooper and Odell, *Evaluating Writing* (1977) viii.

28 Cooper and Odell, *Evaluating Writing* (1977) viii.

29 Cooper and Odell, *Evaluating Writing* (1977) ix.

30 Cooper and Odell, *Evaluating Writing* (1977) xi.

31 Charles R. Cooper, "Holistic Evaluation of Writing," *Evaluating Writing* (1977), eds. Cooper and Odell 20.

32 Richard Lloyd-Jones, "Primary Trait Scoring," *Evaluating Writing* (1977), eds. Cooper and Odell 37.

33 Arthur N. Applebee, Judith A. Langer, and Ina V. S. Mullins, *Writing Trends Across the Decade, 1974–84*, ETS Report No. 15-W-01 (Princeton: ETS, 1985) 3. The 1985 report did not include data from the first writing assessment of 1969–1970 in that the samples were minimal (about 2,500 papers), written in response to one imaginative task, thus rendering comparison useless (63). It is also worthwhile to note that by 1985 NAEP had assessed approximately 1,300,000 students across subject areas.

34 Applebee, Langer, and Mullins, *Writing Trends* 67–68.

35 Applebee, Langer, and Mullins, *Writing Trends* 68.

36 Applebee, Langer, and Mullins, *Writing Trends* 68–69.

37 Applebee, Langer, and Mullins, *Writing Trends* 69–70.

38 Applebee, Langer, and Mullins, *Writing Trends* 3.

39 Applebee, Langer, and Mullins, *Writing Trends* 6.

40 Persky, Hilary R., Mary C. Daane, Ying Jin, *The Nation's Report Card: Writing 2002* (Washington: U.S. Department of Education, Institute of Education Sciences, and

National Center for Education Statistics, 2003) 189. 22 Jan. 2005 <http://nces.ed.gov/nationsreportcard/pdf/main2002/2003529.pdf>

41 Persky, Daane, and Jin 17–20.

42 Persky, Daane, and Jin 54.

43 No Child Left Behind Act of 2001, Pub. L. 107–110, 8 Jan. 2002, Stat. 115.1425, Sec.1001. Statement of Purpose.

44 Alan C. Purves et al., *Common Sense and Testing in English: Report of the Task Force on Measurement and Evaluation in the Study of English* (Urbana: NCTE, 1975) 33.

45 Alan C. Purves, "Designing the Board's New Literature Achievement Test," *College Board Review* 67 (1968): 20.

46 Alan C. Purves, A. Söter , Sauli Takala, and Anneli Vähäpassi, "Towards a Domain-Referenced System for Classifying Composition Assignments," *Research in the Teaching of English* 18.4 (1984): 385–406.

47 Alan C. Purves, Thomas P. Gorman, and Sauli Takala, "The Development of the Scoring Scheme and Scales," in *The IEA Study of Written Composition I: The International Writing Tasks and Scoring Scales*, ed. T. P. Gorman, A. C. Purves, and R. E. Degenhart (Oxford: Pergamon P, 1988) 45–46. With Hildo Wesdorp of the University of Amsterdam's Center for Educational Research, Purves and Barbara A. Bauer had argued that an analytic scheme provided the greatest amount of information for any given community in "Toward a Conceptualization of the Scoring of Written Composition," *Evaluation in Education* 5.3 (1982): 299–315. Also included here is an excellent international historical survey of essay marking.

48 Alan C. Purves, "A Comparative Perspective on the Performance of Students," in *The IEA Study of Written Composition II: Education and Performance in Fourteen Countries*, ed. A. C. Purves (Oxford: Pergamon P, 1992) 146. In "Implications of the IEA Studies in Reading and Literature for College English Departments," *ADE Bulletin* 72 (1982), Purves emphasized the differences among cultures and pedagogies, stressing his reticence "to propound how reading and literature should be taught in cultures far different" from those found in America (1). He did, however, offer some perspectives to his audience based on five findings of the IEA Study regarding the reading and interpretation of literature: girls outperform boys in tests of comprehension of literature; students have difficulty reading nonnarrative prose; students who do not comprehend a text are concerned with "peripheral" matters such as the biography of the author; students have difficulty answering questions about formal and technical aspects of prose; and able students—those most likely to take college English courses—were found to have developed patterns in responding to fiction that consider meaning, content, and moral implications of that fiction.

49 Martin Heidegger, "The Question Concerning Technology," *Basic Writings*, ed. David Farrell Krell (New York: Harper, 1977) 317.

50 Alan C. Purves, *The Web of Text and the Web of God* (New York: Guilford P, 1998) 201–219. "God," Purves wrote, "is Whitman's 'noiseless patient spider' forever spinning the web, the immense hypertext of which we become readers and participants" (218).

51 Karen L Greenberg, Harvey S. Weiner, and Richard A. Donovan, eds., *Notes from the National Testing Network in Writing* (New York: The City University of New York, 1982) 1–2. CompPile 23 Jan. 2005 <http://comppile.tamucc.edu/>. The history of the CUNY Instructional Resource Center and its relationship to the NTNW are both documented by Marie Jean Lederman in "Evolution of an Instructional Resource Center: The CUNY Experience," *ADE Bulletin* 82 (1985): 43–47. 23 Jan 2005 <http://www.mla.org/ade/bulletin/N082/082043.htm> "The national trend to assess the writing skills of college students," Lederman noted, "prompted the Fund for the Improvement of Postsecondary Education (FIPSE) to award a three-year grant jointly to the Chancellor's Task Force on Writing of the Freshman Skills Assessment Program and to the Office of Academic Affairs to establish CUNY as the site of a National Testing Network in Writing (NTNW)."

52 Greenberg, Weiner, and Donovan, eds., *Notes from the National Testing Network in Writing* (New York: The City University of New York, 1982) 1–2. CompPile 23 Jan. 2005 <http://comppile.tamucc.edu/>. It is of interest to place these assessment questions alongside the series of twenty-four questions raised as "unexplored territory" in the teaching and learning of written composition nineteen years earlier by Braddock, Lloyd-Jones, and Schoer: "1. What kinds of situations and assignments at various levels of schooling stimulate a desire to write well? 2. What do different kinds of students prefer to write about when relieved of the expectations and requirements of teachers and others? 3. What are the sources of fear and resentment of writing? 4. How do the kinds of writing which adults compose vary with their occupation and other factors? 5. What is the effect on writing of having the student compose his paper for different kinds of readers? 6. At which levels of maturation does it seem appropriate to introduce the various modes of discourse—narration, poetry, drama, exposition, argument, and criticism? 7. What is the relative effectiveness of writing shorter and longer papers at various levels of maturity and proficiency? 8. At which levels of maturation does it seem appropriate to introduce the various rhetorical elements of writing? 9. What are the effects of various kinds and amounts of reading on the quality and kinds of writing a person does? 10. What are the direct and indirect effects of particular sensory experiences and guided observations upon writing? 11. At what stages of maturity do students spontaneously seek specific help in improving particular aspects of writing, such as specificity of details, transitions, parallel structure, and metaphor? 12. At which levels of maturation can particular aspects of writing most efficiently be learned? 13. Does the oral reading of rough drafts help the elementary child strengthen "sentence sense"? How does it? 14. What techniques of composition most effectively help build self-discipline and pride in clarity, originality, and good form? 15. What procedures of teaching and learning composition are most

effective for pupils of low socioeconomic patterns? 16. What procedures of teaching and learning composition are most effective for pupils learning to write English as a second language? 17. Can the study of newer types of linguistics help writers? 18. Can formal study of rhetorical theory or of logic help writers? 19. How is writing affected by extensive study and imitation or parody of models? 20. What forms of discourse have the greatest effect on other types of writing? For example, does writing poetry help a writer of reports? 21. What is involved in the act of writing? 22. How does a person go about starting a paper? What questions must he answer for himself? 23. How does a writer generate sentences? 24. Of what does skill in writing really consist?" (*Research in Written Composition* 52–53). When George Hillocks, Jr., began work in 1978 on what would become his meta-analysis of experimental treatment studies in written composition—research published in 1986 as *Research on Written Composition: New Directions for Teaching*—he observed that many investigators had followed the suggestions made by Braddock, Lloyd-Jones, and Schoer for further research. The first chapter of his study was devoted to answering question 21. Indeed, it seems reasonable to conclude that by 1982 enough empirical information was known about certain practices in the teaching of writing so that Greenberg and her colleagues could pose valid questions designed to investigate (1) if those teaching practices were being followed, (2) the extent to which known assessment practices could capture evidence of the success or failure of those practices, and (3) what happened when the two practices (teaching and assessing writing) failed to align.

53 Lynn Quitman Troyka, "Looking Back and Moving Forward," Greenberg et al., eds., *Notes from the National Testing Network in Writing*. CompPile 23 Jan. 2005 <http://comppile.tamucc.edu/>.

54 Richard Lloyd-Jones, "Skepticism About Test Scores," Greenberg et al., eds., *Notes from the National Testing Network in Writing*. CompPile 23 Jan. 2005 <http://comppile.tamucc.edu/>.

55 Lester Faigley, Stephen P. Witte, James Kinneavy, and John Daily, "The Writing Project Assessment Project," Greenberg et al., eds., *Notes from the National Testing Network in Writing*. CompPile 23 Jan. 2005 <http://comppile.tamucc.edu/>.

56 Lee Odell, "New Questions for Evaluators of Writing," Greenberg et al., eds., *Notes from the National Testing Network in Writing*. CompPile 23 Jan. 2005 <http://comppile.tamucc.edu/>.

57 Gertrude Conlan, "Panning for Gold: Finding the Best Essay Topics," Greenberg et al., eds., *Notes from the National Testing Network in Writing*. CompPile 23 Jan 2005 <http://comppile.tamucc.edu/>.

58 Edward M. White, "Some Issues in the Testing of Writing," Greenberg et al., eds., *Notes from the National Testing Network in Writing*. CompPile 23 Jan. 2005 <http://comppile.tamucc.edu/>.

59 Richard Braddock, Richard Lloyd-Jones, and Lowell Schoer, *Research in Written Composition* (Urbana: NCTE, 1963) 5. The emergence of NTNW validates the existence of the second wave of writing assessment noted by Yancey in "Looking Back and We Look Forward: Historicizing Writing Assessment," *College Composition and Communication* 50.3 (1999): 483–503. As well, the presence of NTNW validates Yancey's similar observations that, by the early 1980s, the evaluation of student products had become as important as the design of multiple-choice items and that ethical concerns continue to emerge regarding the appropriate use of tests. See "A Brief History of Writing Assessment in the Late Twentieth Century: The Writer Comes Center Stage," *History, Reflection, and Narrative: The Professionalization of Composition, 1963–1983*, Eds. Mary Rosner, Beth Boehm, and Debra Journet (Greenwich, CT: Ablex, 1999) 115–128.

60 The last issue of *Notes from the National Testing Network in Writing* was published in March 1990. A list of researchers who had presented papers in the previous year's conference demonstrates the power of Greenberg and her City University of New York colleagues to bring together national leaders in writing assessment: Pat Belanoff, Gordon Brossell, Roberta Camp, Sybil B. Carlson, Fran Claggett, R. Elaine Degenhart, Michael Flanigan, Thomas Flynn, Liz Hamp-Lyons, Brian Huot, Richard L. Larson, Anthony D. Lutkus, Ina V. S. Mullins, Robert E. Lynch, Sandra Murphy, Lee Odell, Alan C. Purves, Paul A. Ramsey, Leo Ruth, Harvey S. Wiener, Edward M. White. As the FIPSE funding ended, the last conference was held in New York in November, 1990. Issues of *Notes* from 1982–1990 are located at <http://comppile.tamucc.edu/NTW/index.htm>

61 Edward M. White, "The Opening of the Modern Era of Writing Assessment: A Narrative," *College English* 63.3 (2001): 308.

62 Forrest D. Burt and Sylvia King, eds., *Equivalency Testing: A Major Issue for College English* (Urbana: NCTE, 1974) 48–50.

63 White, "The Opening of the Modern Era of Writing Assessment: A Narrative," 315.

64 White, "Jane Austen and the Art of Parody," diss., Harvard U, 1960, 15.

65 White, ed., *Comparison and Contrast: The 1973 California State University and Colleges Freshman English Equivalency Examination* (ERIC ED 114825) 1.

66 In "College-Level Equivalency Exams in English Draw Fire," published in the *Chronicle of Higher Education* on March 12, 1973, Edward R. Weidlein reported that White put the following statement forth: "The combination of objective items (which measure accurately some skills involved in writing) with an essay (which measures directly, if somewhat less accurately, the writing itself) proved to be more valid than either type of item alone" (6). Weidlein noted that the statement came from *The Measurement of Writing Ability*. The *Chronicle* article was appended to the 1973 report. White's report includes a fact sheet (11–12), and the individual essay reliability scores on both essays are reported as .6951 and .6824 in an appendix (89). White was careful to note the .7813 reliability within a band of plus or minus .1802.

67 White, ed. *Comparison and Contrast: The 1980 and 1981 California State University and Colleges Freshman English Equivalency Examination* (ERIC ED 227511) 4.

68 White, ed. *Comparison and Contrast: The 1980 and 1981 Examination* 3.

69 The Test of Standard Written English (TSWE) was a separate, multiple-choice instrument that assessed basic writing skills. After three years of experimental testing, the 30-minute TSWE became part of the SAT test book during the 1976–1977 test year. In the fall of 1986 a task force of College Board and Educational Testing Service specialists began the New Possibilities Project (NPP). Driven by a belief that new developments in educational theory and test design would allow a thorough review of the SAT, task force members of the NPP began a process that led to specific recommendations to improve the SAT testing program. The name of the program changed from the Admission Testing Program to the SAT program. The test names changed as well. The Scholastic Aptitude Test became the SAT I: Reasoning Test; the Achievement Tests became the SAT II: Subject Tests. In March of 1994 the SAT I: Reasoning Test was offered for the first time and the TSWE was dropped from the testing program. The SAT II: Subject Tests were also introduced in the 1993–1994 period; one of these tests, the Writing Test, included both multiple-choice questions and a writing sample. These changes in the SAT program are summarized in Sue Frisch-Kowalski's invaluable *The SAT®: A Timeline of Changes* (New York: College Board, 2003).

70 White, and Leon L. Thomas, "Racial Minorities and Writing Skills Assessment in the California State University and Colleges," *College English* 43.3 (1981): 280.

71 White and Thomas 281–282.

72 *Forty-Third Annual Report of the Executive Secretary* (New York: College Entrance Examination Board, 1943) 24.

73 White, "Holisticism," *College Composition and Communication* 35.4 (1984): 400.

74 White, "Holisticism" 409.

75 White, "Holisticism" 400.

76 White, "Holisticism" 409.

77 White, *Teaching and Assessing Writing: Recent Advances in Understanding, Evaluating, and Improving Student Performance* (San Francisco: Jossey-Bass, 1985) 289. For White's account of the ideas represented in this book as they are situated within the larger assessment movement (in this case, within The Assessment Forum of the American Association of Higher Education), see "Language and Reality in Writing Assessment," *College Composition and Communication* 41.2 (1990): 187–200.

78 Anthony D. Lutkus, Robert E. Lynch, and Paul A. Ramsey, "Three Major Issues in Large Scale Essay Assessment," in *Notes from the National Testing Network in Writing*

14 (New York: The City University of New York, 1990). CompPile 23 Jan. 2005 <http://comppile.tamucc.edu/>.

79 *New Jersey College Basic Skills Placement Testing, Fall 1991* (Trenton: Department of Higher Education, 1991) Table 1, 31.

80 *Effectiveness of Remedial Programs in New Jersey Public Colleges and Universities, Fall 1987–Spring 1989* (Trenton: Department of Higher Education, 1992). The results were widely reported in New Jersey by Bill McCleary in *Composition Chronicle* 5.6 (1992) 1–3, 11.

81 Robert E. Lynch, Interview, *Composition Chronicle* 5.6 (1992) 3.

82 Robert E. Lynch, "Testimony Before New Jersey Board of Higher Education," 12 May 1994, 7.

83 Robert J. Braun, "Educator Faults Whitman College Plan," *Star-Ledger* 23 Mar. 1994: 1.

84 Structured interview conducted with Robert Lynch, Nov. 19, 2003. The interview was taped. Lynch provided corrections and annotations to the interview on January 22, 2005. Interviews with Brian Bremen, Jill, Burstein, Wayne Camara, Lee Odell, and Paul Ramsey all followed the same protocol. Each individual was identified because of both a demonstrated and unique role in contemporary writing assessment. After an initial contact, each individual received a list of questions based on four variables of interest: education and formal training in writing assessment; first encounters with writing assessment; unique contributions of the individual; and the future of writing assessment. A final question was open ended. After the interview, each individual was sent a copy of this chapter with an invitation to review the entire manuscript. When corrections and annotations were provided, they were included in the text and notes of the chapter.

85 Robert J. Braun, "Remediation Helps Boost Return on Investment," *Star-Ledger* 26 Jan. 1992: 52.

86 Brian Huot, "Editorial: An Introduction to *Assessing Writing*," *Assessing Writing* 1.1 (1994): 1.

87 Sara Cushing Weigle, "Integrating Reading and Writing in a Competency Test for Non-Native Speakers of English," *Assessing Writing* 9.1 (2004): 27–55.

88 Liz Hamp-Lyons, "Writing Assessment in the World," *Assessing Writing* 9.1 (2004): 1–3. In 2003, citing tensions with Elsevier (the publisher of *Assessing Writing*), Brian Huot and Kathleen Blake Yancey began a new publication, *Journal of Writing Assessment* (published by Hampton Press).

89 Huot, "Editorial: An Introduction to *Assessing Writing*" 3.

90 Mary H. Beaven, "Individualized Goal Setting, Self-Evaluation, and Peer Evaluation," *Evaluating Writing: Describing, Measuring, Judging* (1977) 135.

91 Janet Emig, *The Composing Process of Twelfth Graders* (Urbana: NCTE Research Report 13, 1971). In focusing on the way students approached reflexive and extensive writing assignments, Emig concluded that perhaps the chief value of her study was "its steady assumption that persons, rather than mechanisms, compose" (5). See Sondra Perl, "The Composing Process of Unskilled College Writers," *Research in the Teaching of English* 13 (1979): 317–336; Linda S. Flower and John R. Hayes, "The Cognition of Discovery: Defining a Rhetorical Problem," *College Composition and Communication* 31 (1980): 21–32; Flower and Hayes, "A Cognitive Process Theory of Writing," *CCC* 32 (1981): 365–387; Flower and Hayes, "The Pregnant Pause: An Inquiry into the Nature of Planning," *RTE* 15 (1981): 229–244. A lengthy internal report written by Sybil B. Carlson and submitted to Winton H. Manning on March 25, 1982, establishes the profound extent that such research had within the Educational Testing Service. In her *Survey of ETS Writing Activities* (Princeton: ETS, 1982), Carlson organized her summary around the following core concept about writing: "Clearly, as more questions are being formulated about writing, particularly about improving the quality of writing, more focus is being placed on writing as a process and on instructional interventions that make a difference. Evaluation becomes increasingly important because we need to be able to identify and encapsulate the many facets of writing that are of importance" (I–3). In summarizing the then-emerging ETS Writing Portfolio Project, Carlson stated: "The major objectives of the project are to bring methods of *assessment closer to instruction*, and to raise the level of writing in secondary schools" (her emphasis, IV–44). Carlson's report documented the extent to which the lone-wolf researchers had influenced writing assessment within ETS. In a section entitled "Bibliography: Background and Significant Issues" of her report, she noted the following researchers: Carl Bereiter, Charles Cooper, Dixie Goswami, Elaine P. Maimon, James Moffett, Lee Odell, Janice Redish, Marlene Scardamalia, and Mina P. Shaughnessy (VI–1,2). See also Chapter 6, note 2.

92 Roberta Camp, "Proposal for Writing Portfolio Project, Phases I and II and Progress Report for Writing Portfolio Project, Phase I," 15 Jan. 1982 (Princeton: ETS). The ideas in this proposal are also found in Roberta Camp, "The ETS Writing Portfolio: A New Kind of Assessment," 17 Mar. 1983, draft for a paper to be presented at the Conference on College Composition and Communication (Princeton: ETS).

93 Camp, "Proposal for Writing Portfolio Project, Phases I and II and Progress Report for Writing Portfolio Project, Phase I" 11. The list of consultants for the writing portfolio project is found in Appendix A.

94 Peter Elbow and Pat Belanoff, "Reflections on an Explosion: Portfolios in the '90s and Beyond," in *Situating Portfolios: Four Perspectives*, ed. Kathleen Blake Yancey and Irwin Weiser (Logan: Utah State UP, 1997) 23. Elbow and Belanoff cite the following as among the earliest published essays on portfolio assessment: Roberta Camp, "The Writing Folder in Post-Secondary Assessment," *Directions and Misdirections in English Education*, ed. Peter J. A. Evans (Ottawa: Canadian Council of Teachers of English, 1985); Chris Burnham, "Portfolio Evaluation: Room to Breathe

and Grow," *Training the New Teacher of College Composition*, ed. Charles W. Bridges (Urbana: NCTE, 1986); and their own "State U of New York: Portfolio-Based Evaluation Program," *New Methods in College Writing Programs: Theory into Practice*, eds. Paul Connolly and Teresa Vilardi (New York: MLA, 1986).

95 Elbow and Belanoff, "Reflections" 23.

96 Elbow and Belanoff, "Reflections" 24.

97 Elbow and Belanoff, "Reflections" 25.

98 Elbow and Belanoff, "Reflections" 26.

99 The program's documentation is found in Richard H. Haswell, ed., *Beyond Outcomes: Assessment and Instruction Within a University Writing Program* (Westport, CT: Ablex, 2001).

100 Richard Law, "The Continuing Program: A Retrospective View," *Beyond Outcomes,* ed. Haswell 5.

101 Washington State University, "WSU Writing Programs: Junior Writing Portfolio Final Rating Categories." 23 Jan. 2005 <http://www.wsu.edu>.

102 Galen Leonhardy and William Condon, "Exploring the Difficult Cases: In the Cracks of Writing Assessment," ed. Haswell, *Beyond Outcomes* 77. The researchers did, however, identify cases in which reliability scores were low: "gray area portfolios" (writing that the evaluation system revealed was not easily placed) and "disciplinary dissonance between raters and students" in which evaluations and students did not share the same academic background (74–78).

103 Diane Kelly-Riley, "Whither? Some Questions, Some Answers," *Beyond Outcomes*, ed. Haswell 192.

104 Fran Claggert, "Integrating Reading and Writing in Large Scale Assessment," *Evaluating Writing,* eds. Cooper and Odell 363.

105 Structured interview conducted with Lee Odell, Apr. 12, 2004. The interview was taped. Odell provided corrections and annotations to the interview on December 28, 2004.

106 For a widely referenced article based on Odell's dissertation, see "Measuring the Effect of Instruction in Pre-Writing," *Research in the Teaching of English* 8.2 (1974): 228–241.

107 Young, Richard E., Alton L. Becker, and Kenneth L. Pike, *Rhetoric: Discovery and Change* (New York: Harcourt, 1970). See especially the heuristic procedure described in Chapter 6, 119–136.

108 See "Piaget, Problem-Solving, and Freshman Composition," *College Composition and Communication* 24.1 (1973): 36–42.

109 George Hillocks, Jr., *The Testing Trap: How State Writing Assessments Control Learning* (New York: Teachers College P, 2002) 205.

110 Roy A. Allan, *A History of the Personal Computer: The People and the Technology* (London: Allan Publishing, 2001). See Chapter 2, "Personal Computing in the 1960s."

111 Ellis B. Page, "The Imminence of Grading Essays by Computer," *Phi Delta Kappan* 47 (1966) 238.

112 Patrick J. Finn, "Computer-Aided Descriptions of Mature Word Choices in Writing," in Cooper and Odell, eds., *Evaluating Writing* 71.

113 Hunter M. Breland, "Computer-Assisted Writing Assessment: The Politics of Science versus the Humanities," in *Assessment of Writing: Politics, Policies, Practices*, ed. Edward M. White, William D. Lutz, and Sandra Kamusikiri (New York: Modern Language Association, 1996) 255.

114 Structured interview conducted with Jill Burstein, May 17, 2004. The interview was taped. Bunstein provided corrections and annotations to the interview on August 9, 2004.

115 Jill Burstein et al., "Computer Analysis of Essay Content for Automated Score Prediction: A Prototype Automated Scoring System for GMAT Analytical Writing Assessment Essays," ETS Research Report 98–15 (Princeton: ETS, 1998) 5. For Burstein's more contemporary work, see *Automated Essay Scoring: A Cross-Disciplinary Perspective*, ed. Mark D. Shermis and Jill Burstein (Hillsdale, NJ: Erlbaum, 2003). In her annotation of this section of the manuscript in August, 2004, Burnstein noted that "surface" features and "rhetorical structure" were no longer accurate terms. In 1998, however, both terms were used in the report.

116 Hunter M. Breland et al., *Factors in Performance on Brief, Impromptu Essay Examinations*, College Board Report No. 95-4 and ETS Research Report 95-41 (New York: College Board, 1996).

117 Karen Greenberg, *The Effects of Essay Questions on the Writing of CUNY Freshmen* (New York: City University of New York Instructional Research Center, 1981); James Grey and Leo Ruth, *Properties of Writing Tasks: A Study of Alternative Procedures for Holistic Writing Assessment*, NIE Final Report G-80-0034 (Berkeley: U of California Graduate School of Education, Bay Area Writing Project, 1982); Leo Ruth and Sara Murphy, *Designing Writing Tasks for the Assessment of Writing* (Norwood: Ablex, 1986); Gordon Brossell, "Current Research and Unanswered Questions in Writing Assessment," in *Writing Assessment: Issues and Strategies*, ed. Karen L. Greenberg, Harvey S. Wiener, and Richard Donovan (New York: Longman, 1986); Hunter M. Breland et al., *Assessing Writing Skill*, Research Monograph No. 11 (New York: College Board, 1987).

118 Jill Burstein et al., "Computer Analysis of Essay Content for Automated Score Prediction" 16.

119 Donald E. Powers et al., *Stumping E-Rater: Challenging the Validity of Automated Essay Scoring*, GRE Board Professional Report No. 98-08bP and ETS Research Report 01-3 (Princeton: ETS, 2001). The study, Burstein noted, was undertaken using an older version of e-rater than existed in 2004.

120 Structured interview with Paul Ramsey conducted Nov. 25, 2004. The interview was taped. The material in the interview, as well as the manuscript for the book, was reviewed by ETS.

121 Paul A. Ramsey, "Teaching the Teachers to Teach Black-Dialect Writers," *College English* 41.2 (1979): 199.

122 Miles Myers, *A Procedure for Writing Assessment and Holistic Scoring* (Urbana, IL: NCTE, 1980) 46. It is interesting to note that Myers makes no mention of the Godshalk study in the volume but does claim that Diederich "has done more than anyone else to develop holistic scoring procedures for use in the schools" (2).

123 Gertrude Conlan, "Comparison of Analytic and Holistic Scoring Techniques" (Princeton: ETS, 1978) 2.

124 Paul A. Ramsey, "Minorities and Standardized Tests," in *Consensus and Dissent: Teaching English Past, Present, and Future*, ed. Marjorie N. Farmer (Urbana: NCTE, 1986) 93.

125 Paul A. Ramsey, "Are There Equity Implications in High-Stakes Teacher Testing?," Keynote Address, Standards-Based Teacher Education Project Conference, 11 June 2001, Washington. 23 Jan. 2005 <http://www.c-b-e.org >.

126 Richard C. Atkinson, "AERA Public Service Award Address," 14 Apr. 2004, American Education Research Association, San Diego, CA. A transcript of his address appeared at "Standardized Tests and Access to American Universities," 18 Feb. 2001, the 2001 Robert H. Atwell Distinguished Lecture, 83rd Annual Meeting of the American Council on Education, Washington, DC. 23 Jan. 2005 <http://www.ucop.edu/welcome1.html>.

127 The March 30, 2001, segment on the SAT and the discussion following it were posted at the website for the *NewsHour* with Jim Lehrer. 23 Jan. 2005 <http://www.pbs.org>.

128 Nicholas Lemann, "What Do These Two Men Have in Common?" *Time* 4 Mar. 2001, 23 Jan 2004 <http://www.time.com/time/nation/article/0,8599,101322,00.html>.

129 Saul Geiser and Roger Studley, *UC and the SAT: Predictive Validity and Differential Impact of the SAT I and the SAT II at the University of California* (Berkeley: Office of the President, Oct. 29, 2001) 22. 23 Jan. 2005 <http://www.ucop.edu/welcome1.html>.

130 Structured interview conducted with Wayne Camara, May 4, 2004. The interview was taped. The material in the interview was reviewed by Dr. Camara.

131 Commission on New Possibilities for the Admission Testing Program, *Beyond Prediction* (New York: College Board, 1990) 3.

132 Banesh Hoffmann, *The Tyranny of Testing* (New York: Collier, 1962) 216.

133 Commission on New Possibilities for the Admission Testing Program, *Beyond Prediction* 3.

134 Hoffmann, *The Tyranny of Testing* 216.

135 Jinghua Liu, Miriam Feigenbaum, and Linda Cook, *A Simulation Study to Explore Configuring the New SAT Critical Reading Section Without Analogy Items*, College Board Research Report No. 2004-2, ETS RR-04-01 (New York: College Entrance Examination Board, 2004) 1.

136 Hunter M. Breland et al., *New SAT Writing Prompt Study: Analysis of Group Impact and Reliability*, College Board Research Report No. 2004-1, ETS RR-04-03 (New York: Board, 2004) 10–11. An earlier study on the placement of the essay in the new SAT had been performed a year earlier by Hyeon-Joo Oh and Michael Walker. That study had found that students who had taken the essay first as part of the new SAT had done better on the essay section of the test. The study had also found that a one-line prompt and a contextual prompt had a similar impact on test-takers' performance. See *The Effects of Essay Placement and Prompt Type of Performance of the New SAT*, ETS Statistical Report ST-2003-72 (Princeton: ETS, 2003).

137 Breland et al., *New SAT Writing Prompt Study* 8.

138 Structured interview conducted with Brian Bremen, Apr. 6, 2004. The interview was taped. Bremen provided corrections and annotations to the interview on September 13, 2004.

139 *A Guide to the New SAT Essay* (New York: The College Board, 2004) 4.

140 In his September 13, 2004, annotation to the interview, Bremen noted that "as important, if not more important, was that secrecy could be as effectively discussed at a personal or a local level." Such was also the case with the 1943 essay question. Bremen's annotation demonstrated the great complexities involved in topic design. Indeed, in annotating his interview, Robert Lynch recalled a case in which an identical topic given in two different test administrations of the NJBSPT produced quite different responses. In the 1981–1982 administration, the following topic had been given: "Some people believe that media—movies, news, radio, and especially television—have too great an influence on what we think about the world around us and what we think of life. Do you agree? Why or why not? Be sure to be specific." In the 1986–1987 administration, the same topic had been given again because the test developers wanted to investigate the degree to which scores varied and, thus, suggest reasons for the potential decline, stability, or rise of student scores (e.g., improved secondary

school instruction). Two cultural events had occurred, however. The New Jersey high schools had, during the five-year period between the two test administrations, developed courses in media. In addition, just after the replicated topic had been approved—but before the NJPSPT had been administered—a news story broke alleging that a young child had fallen to his death after watching *Superman IV: The Quest for Peace*. When the 40,000 or so papers were read, Lynch recalled, the same example—a child falling to his death after watching a Christopher Reeve film—was repeated over and over. As well, the students appeared very able to handle the topic, and so displayed a sense of rhetorical and organizational sophistication that was not evident in the 1981–1982 administration. The topic may have been the same, Lynch observed, but the social context in which the students lived had changed.

141 *A Guide to the New SAT Essay* 9.

142 National Commission on Writing in America's Schools and Colleges, *The Neglected "R": The Need for a Writing Revolution* (New York: College Board, 2004) 17.

143 Thomas Bartlett, "Why Johnny Can't Write, Even Though He Went to Princeton," *Chronicle of Higher Education*, 3 Jan. 2003: A39. On November 7, 2004, the Education Life supplement of the *New York Times* also played off the famous 1975 *Newsweek* article by Merrill Sheils. The cover featured a cereal box with the message: "The New SAT: Bigger Scores! More Math! Less Reasoning! Essay Included!" And an article by Charles McGrath, "Writing to the Test," was featured for the supplement cover as "Why Johnny Can't Write, and What the SAT Is Doing About It" (24+).

Chapter 6
Now and Then: An Analysis

By 1984 the college composition research community had achieved professional standing within the educational measurement community. The standing had not been achieved by protest. Since Isadore Kayfetz of P.S. 84 in Brooklyn lodged his grievance against the Hillegas scales in the 1914 issue of the *Pedagogical Seminary*, informed complaints had been within earshot. Indeed, the Kayfetz analysis—supported by Rollo Lyman in his 1929 *Summary of Investigations Relating to Grammar, Language, and Composition*—was archetypal. When teachers voiced their opposition to writing assessment, the lines of argument echoed those established by Kayfetz: the methods and procedures were wrong, true objectivity had not been achieved, classroom applications had been ignored, and the statistical results were all that seemed to matter.[1] By 1984, however, when the educational measurement community at ETS heard voices, they were no longer those of complaint. The accomplishments of the lone wolves scattered across the nation's universities had made such an impact that the Educational Testing Service was now to begin adjusting its assessment practices.

Peter L. Cooper's 1984 research summary for the Graduate Record Examination Board demonstrated this impact. In his report, *The Assessment of Writing Ability: A Review of Research*, the ETS examiner informed his view of assessment practices by reference to Richard Braddock, Richard Lloyd-Jones, and Lowell Schoer's review of research in written composition; to Francis Christensen's rhetoric program; to Allen Purves' ideas for common sense and testing in English; to Miles Myers' procedures for holistic scoring; to James Moffett's writing across the curriculum program; to Charles Cooper and Lee Odell's strategies for defining and assessing competency in writing; and to Edward M. White's research presented at the National Testing Network in Writing.[2] What James Berlin found in his study of writing instruction in American colleges is clearly validated in the history of writing assessment: the Renaissance that rhetoric had undergone following World War II had reached full flower. The signs were everywhere.[3]

As is evident in Peter Cooper's discussion of discourse mode as a source of variance in essay tests, the signs signified a radical shift. "Just as any given writer is not equally equipped to write on all topics, so he or she is not equally equipped to write for all purposes or in all modes of discourse, the most traditional being description, narration, exposition, and argumentation," Cooper wrote. His statement exemplified a shift of position for ETS, an agency that had previously viewed writing ability as uniform regardless of topic design.[4] In his analysis of research on topic design, Cooper evoked, though did not cite, the enduring modes of discourse classified by Robert J. Connors in his popular *College Composition and Communication* article of 1981, the absence of citation perhaps documenting the prevalence of Connors' scholarship among all assessment researchers, including those at ETS.

But there was more than the influence of Connors' historical scholarship here.[5] There was also the experimental influence of researchers Edys S. Quellmalz, Frank J. Cappell, and Chih-Ping Chou, a collaborative California team whose work had been funded by the National Institute of Education. The Quellmalz group had called into question the 1966 research of Godshalk, Swineford, and Coffman in which performance variability of topic was not differentiated from writing performance. Quellmalz's random assignment of homogeneous students to discourse-based writing conditions and the analysis undertaken by a multitrait multimethod factor analysis—standard methods for differentiating variables across groups—had been published in the influential *Journal of Educational Measurement*.[6] ETS had taken notice, and Cooper quotes the Quellmalz study itself in his report to emphasize that the researchers themselves had

> cast doubt on the assumption that "a good writer is a good writer" regardless of the assignment. The implication is that writing for different aims draws on different skill constructs which must therefore be measured and reported separately to avoid erroneous, invalid interpretations of performance, as well as inaccurate decisions based on such performance.[7]

Cooper concluded: "Obviously, any given writing exercise will provide an incomplete and partially distorted representation of an examinee's writing ability."[8] Obviously, a shift had occurred within ETS.

Three years later, when Hunter M. Breland and his ETS research team sought to replicate the Godshalk study, the effort was undertaken because of the major changes that had occurred "over 20 years in the way English composition is taught and in the way that skills in it are assessed."[9] Breland's references included Linda Flower and John Hayes's well-known 1981 article calling for a cognitive-based theory of writing.[10] In the discussion of writing tasks Breland cited not only the Quellmalz study but also Leo Ruth and Sandra Murphy's *Designing Writing Tasks for the Assessment of Writing* published the year before.[11] When Breland reported his results in 1987, it was clear that topic variance was important: "Factor models that took into consideration topic variance provided the best fit to the data. This is unfortunate in that a student could appear to be a good writer given one topic and a mediocre writer given an alternative topic within the same mode."[12] If even the way the topic was phrased mattered, then identifying a single construct of writing ability that endured across time and context was going to be difficult, if not impossible, to determine. The matter was, Breland and his colleagues found, even more complex than Quellmalz thought. Variance in writing ability was to be found not only across different modes of writing: variance was also to be found within the individual modes.

Every word mattered. Obviously, things had changed.

In the Desks: Enrollment Trends

When Barrett Wendell was offered a job reading sophomore themes at Harvard by his old teacher, Adams Sherman Hill, the American educational system was just beginning to emerge into an era of systematization. Charles Eliot, the great promoter of change, had come to Harvard in 1865, had hired Hill in 1880, and had approved Hill's recommendation of Wendell because the president was, as Wendell recalled, "fond of experiments with inexperienced teachers."[13] Wendell became part of the attempt to systematize, a teacher, as Wallace Douglass put it in his 1985 essay, who could be accused of seeking to "remove writing from any concerns of living and turn it into the construction of beginnings and endings, the filling out of plans, the narrowing and the simplification of material and analysis...."[14]

One hundred and twenty-five years later, the College Board announced plans to shift its traditional methods of verbal assessment, abandoning item types such as analogies (a measure of ability assessed through limited response items) and substituting a writing sample (a measure of ability assessed through a scored writing sample). The new SAT to be offered in March 2005 was to be, on one hand, the result of the systematization of American education fostered by Eliot, Hill, and Wendell; on the other hand, the new testing program could also be viewed as the result of pressure to develop more valid ways of measuring the performance of a very diverse group of American students.

Emerging across this 125-year period has been a tremendous growth in American education in terms of enrollment trends. As the table below demonstrates, the population shifts have been dramatic.

Educational Enrollment, 1879–1989[15]

Available Data	**Benchmark Event in Writing Assessment**	**United States Population**	**Enrollment in Elementary and Secondary Education**	**Enrollment in Higher Education**
1879–1880	1880s: Barrett Wendell teaches composition at Harvard	50,156,000	9,868,000	115,850
1919–1920	1917: Milo Hillegas, "A Scale for the Measurement of Quality in English Composition by Young People," published by Teachers College Press; M. R. Trabue, "Supplementing the Hillegas Scale," *Teachers College Record*	104,541,000	21,578,000	597,880
1949-1950	1945: Edward S. Noyes, William M. Sale, and John M. Stalnaker publish *Report on the First Six Tests in English Composition*	149,199,000	25,111,000	2,444,900
1969–1970	1966: Fred Godshalk, Frances Swineford, and William Coffman publish *The Measurement of Writing Ability*	201,385,000	45,550,000	8,004,660
1988–1989	1987: Portfolios based on Pat Belanoff and Peter Elbow's system initiated at Washington State University	245,807,000	40,189,000	13,538,560

The history of writing assessment in America must be understood in terms of these patterns of growth. Public education at the elementary and secondary levels rose from 9.86 million in 1879–1880 to 40.1 million in 1988–1989, and the percentage of school-aged children (5- to-17-year-olds) attending classes grew from 65.5 percent to 88.5 percent. Seen in light of the increases in elementary and secondary school enrollment, the decision by Teachers College to publish (for eight cents) "The Thorndike Scale" (ready to pin on a wall) takes on new meaning: Thorndike, as his biographer Geraldine M. Joncich points out, was training a new kind of educator.[16] The new school administrator, able to manage the number of students pouring into the nation's elementary- and secondary-school classrooms—between 1909–1910 and 1919–1920, the percentage of high-school enrollment for all persons aged fourteen to seventeen rose from 14 to 31 percent[17]—would be informed not by untested tradition but, rather, by state-of-the-art theory and evaluation practices defined in Thorndike's own *Educational Psychology* (1903) and *Education: A First Book* (1912) and by the work of his disciples, Milo Hillegas and Marion Trabue. Seen in terms of a growing population of students, the 1945 report of Noyes and his colleagues prepared the college admissions system for the flood of students who would enter college under the Serviceman's Readjustment Act (the G.I. Bill) under which, by 1949, about 2.4 million students enrolled in higher education—about 15 per 100 18- to-24-year-old students.[18] The 1966 experiment by the Godshalk research team responded to a similar growth in which enrollment would rise by 120 percent in the nation's colleges.[19] (The enrollment decline after 1971 was caused by the end of the baby boom.) The 1987 portfolio strategy of Belanoff and Elbow, in part a response to a 17 percent enrollment growth between 1979 and 1989,[20] should also be understood as a reaction to an expanding student population and the resulting need to assess the writing ability of that population. The popularity of the NTNW from 1982 to 1990 should also be seen in this light.

The phenomenon under investigation in this book—the evolution of writing assessment in America—must be seen as an artifact associated with population growth. In October of 1999, more than one-fourth of the population of the United States—72 million people—were enrolled in school. Eight million were enrolled in nursery school and kindergarten, 33 million were enrolled in elementary school, 16 million were enrolled in high school, and 15 million more were enrolled in college.[21] In 2005 writing assessment is a permanent part of the American educational culture that will undeniably be part of the foreseeable future of education in America.

The table below demonstrates the continued nature of that growth, a pattern that will necessitate the need for increased assessment:

Education Projections, 2001–2005[22]

Projected Data	Benchmark Event in Writing Assessment	Enrollment in Grades K-8 and 9-12 of Elementary and Secondary Institutions	Total Enrollment in Degree-Granting Institutions
2001	2001: Donald E. Powers et al., *Stumping E-Rater*	53,890,000	15,484,000
2005	College Entrance Examination Board implements writing sample on the SAT	54,615,000	16,679,000

In elementary and secondary education, enrollment reached a record in 2001, representing a 19 percent increase since the fall of 1988. Between 2001 and 2013 (the most remote date for which projections were available in 2005), an additional 5 percent growth is expected.

Enrollment in degree-granting institutions witnessed similar patterns. From 1988 to 2001, enrollment increased 17 percent. Between 2001 and 2013, middle-range projections estimate a 19 percent growth. At the high end of the projections, it is estimated that by 2013 there could be 18.8 million students enrolled in American higher education—a growth of 22 percent. Seen in light of the increases in college enrollment, the decision by the Educational Testing Service to pursue e-rater takes on new meaning: ETS had developed a new method of writing assessment in anticipation of increased cost. As ETS's Hunter M. Breland predicted in 1983: "Recent technological developments in text processing may afford an opportunity to improve direct assessments of writing skill. There is hope that the present impasse between the unreliability of the usual assessments and the labor intensiveness of more reliable and valid assessments can be broken by appropriate applications of technology."[23] How much more cost efficient this technology will seem if enrollment indeed rises from 12.46 million—the college enrollment total in 1983 when Breland wrote this statement—to 18.8 million in 2013, a time in which each and every student will stand ready to be assessed.

The Ontology of Accountability

In "Historical Reflections on Accountability," Richard Ohmann identified 1965 as a key date in the origin of the movement toward outcomes assessment in American education.[24] Part of Lyndon Johnson's Great Society program, the Elementary and Secondary School Act of 1965 was seen as a key to the nation's war on poverty. Programs such as Head Start and the national emphasis on bilingual education were part of that legislation.[25] In January 2002, George W. Bush reauthorized the 1965 legislation as the No Child Left Behind Act, a program resplendent with accountability measures. In 2004 it is clear that the accountability movement in American education has developed into an enduring part of a fully developed culture of assessment. The modest prediction of Frank J. Sciara and Richard K. Jantz in their *Accountability in American Education*, a 1972 volume of articles edited in the thick of the then-emerging accountability movement, has proven truer than imagined: "The age of accountability is dawning in American education and could well become one of the most important educational movements in the decade of the 1970s. Beginning as a flickering spark in the twilight of the 60s, and fanned into a flame by the federal government, politicians, taxpayers, unhappy parents, as well as private learning corporations, accountability has been transformed from a theoretical notion to a formidable force in American education."[26]

For Ohmann, accountability as it existed in 2003 was distinct from obligation and responsibility, a plague of managerial logic that can be countered only by organized militant actions leading to unionization.[27] For George Hillocks, Jr., writing in *The Testing Trap: How State Writing Assessments Control Learning,* the kind of accountability offered by the Bush administration was no more than a reformer's dream. "If there are real, substantive academic gains, then we could say that this reform truly worked. In fact, we know that testing programs tend to restrict the curriculum to the kinds of knowledge and skills tested. They are likely to generate drill and memorization in classrooms. Teachers are likely to feel considerable stress because they are held accountable for the level reached by their students even though there is no measure of the same students at the beginning of the school year."[28] In Hillocks' study of the ways that mandated assessment impacted writing instruction in Illinois, Kentucky, New York, Oregon, and Texas, the conclusions are as bleak as those drawn by Ohmann. Tests cannot assure that good teaching is in play. Perhaps, Hillocks wonders, the master plan behind testing is an Orwellian scheme to keep students from thinking at all.[29]

Yet the permanence of accountability—the reckoning gained from educational effort—may also have its advantages. It is possible, as well, to talk about the advantages of assessment as Charles R. Cooper and Lee Odell did in their 1999 *Evaluating Writing: The Role of Teachers' Knowledge about Text, Learning, and Culture*, a sequel to their 1977 classic. In 1977, Cooper and Odell were "unwilling to settle for the kinds of information provided by published standardized tests of writing" because they did not believe in the validity of those tests as measures of the ability to compose for different audiences and purposes.[30] Twenty-two years later, their position was, on one hand, the same when they discussed the connections between classroom teaching and large-scale assessments at the local, state, and national level. "First," they candidly reminded us, "bad, large-scale assessments can be truly bad, especially those that consist principally of short-answer, 'objective' questions. These can only trivialize writing instruction and subvert the efforts of good writing teachers."[31] In acknowledging that valid assessment had emerged during those twenty-two years, however, they noted in 1999 that there are good instructional programs that are informed by good instructional practice. (In fact, Cooper's chapter, "What We Know about Genres," was structured around essays from the California Department of Education, and his modes for genre assignments are taken from a California writing assessment handbook.[32]) Second, Cooper and Odell noted that in perhaps the majority of American classrooms, students rarely write anything longer than a paragraph. "If large-scale assessment accomplishes nothing else, it will do everyone an enormous favor by helping to change instructional practices in these classrooms."[33] For Cooper and Odell, assessment can have transformative value. Sometimes, they admit, the dog needs wagging.

Epistemology: Knowing About Writing Ability

Analysis of the phenomenon of accountability does not, however, provide sufficient detail for us to understand the unique historical strategies used to assess writing ability. After all, in 1999 Cooper and Odell acknowledged the power of informed assessment to transform banal instruction, an admission that they would not have made twenty-two years before when the Test of Standard Written English (TSWE)—"consisting of indirect measures that indicate whether a student is ready for the expository writing typically required of college freshmen," as Sybil Carlson described it in her 1982 report—was in its heyday.[34] Methods of assessing the writing ability of students varied across the twentieth century, and two competing views of the impact of those methods—dialectic and materialist in nature—endure into the twenty-first century.

The first view is found in Diane Ravitch's view of outcomes assessment as a dialectic activity. Ravitch presents the dialectic by identifying competing traditions. One, evident in the tradition of Thorndike to Odell, is what Ravitch has called the professional education paradigm. This is work characterized by Ravitch as research conducted to strengthen the profession, not to increase public oversight of schools. The other tradition, that of public accountability described above—the efforts of locally based assessments (such as the portfolio system developed at Stony Brook by Elbow and Belanoff in the "catalytic situation" of 1986), state-based assessments (such as those described by Hillocks), the Educational Testing Service, the College Entrance Examination Board, and the National Assessment of Educational Progress—is placed by Ravitch with its origin in 1966 with the publication of *Equality of Educational Opportunity*. In that report, sociologist James S. Coleman wrote about performance outcomes of students.[35] This shift from input to results, as Ravitch proposes, set the stage for the current accountability movement. She writes: "In the near term, American education will continue to be driven by the two paradigms: the professional Education paradigm, which deeply believes that the profession should be insulated from public pressure for accountability and which is deeply suspicious of the interventions of policymakers; and the policymaker paradigm, which insists that the public school system must be subject to the same incentives and sanctions based on its performance as are other large scale organizations."[36] The future of American education, Ravitch believes, will be based on how this conflict is resolved.

Ravitch holds a Hegelian view, one in which a dialectic—armies clashing by night—will determine a new world. Ohmann's view in "Historical Reflections on Accountability" is materialist—market forces will determine an Orwellian future (envisioned also by Hillocks) of mass systematization and individual resistance. Yet Ravitch and Ohmann's interpretative views neglect the lure of systematization itself. Thorndike and Odell both may be viewed as lone wolves, but both want a kind of methodological analysis that is, itself, a system; and ETS may be viewed as the very incorporation of systematization, but it too is influenced by the world of the individual lone-wolf researchers, some of whom (as was the case with Diederich and Ramsey) are among its ranks. It is best not to allow determinist views, either Hegelian dialectic or Marxist materialism, to pre-construct perspectives on the history of writing assessment.

A more accurate method of analysis by which to understand the historical context of writing assessment is to look closely at the techniques of determining information—the epistemology of assessment—and how these techniques have developed in the twentieth century. In the assessment of writing, two investigative areas have undergone significant development: the proof of validity and the establishment of reliability. To understand how our ideas about reliability and validity have changed, we first have to look at how the definitions of these terms have themselves shifted over time.

Validity: 1929–1999

In order to form an analytic framework for contextual analysis, we need to understand just how recent the concept of validity itself is to researchers. In her classic 1929 *Studies in the History of Statistical Method*, Helen M. Walker does not list the term "validity" in her chapter on the origin of technical terms, and the word does not appear in the index.[37] In their 1997 analysis of the history of test development, Richard F. Ittenback, Irvin G. Estes, and Howard Wainer established 1937 as the date in which H. E. Garrett, in his *Statistics in Psychology and Education*, provided the original definition as the "degree to which a test measures what it was intended to measure." As Ittenback, Estes, and Wainer found, it was not until the 1930s and 1940s that it became apparent that all tests were not appropriate for all persons.[38] Before that period, the authors of the tests were themselves the best judges of the validity of a test, and thus the test developers were the corporeal evidence of validity.

If the very concept of validity existing independently of the test developer was not presented until 1937, it is also striking to note that a differentiation of the concept was not offered until 1946 when J. P. Guilford presented new standards for test evaluation. In the journal *Educational and Psychological Measurement*, Guilford established what still stands in the early twenty-first century as the most enduring and significant process used to produce evidence of validity: correlation-based validity. Validity, Guilford claimed, could be established if a test correlated to a measure similar to one of interest but external to the test itself. As Ittenback, Estes, and Wainer put it, "the proof was in the correlations."[39]

In 1954 the first set of standards appeared for those involved in assessment. That date may be established by the publication of *Technical Recommendations for Psychological Tests and Diagnostic Techniques*, a monograph prepared by a joint committee of the American Psychological

Association, the American Educational Research Association, and the National Council on Measurement Used in Education, and published by the American Psychological Association.[40] Aimed at providing a set of uniform standards that all tests should meet so that consumers could be assured that they were using tests of high quality, the recommendations defined validity as follows: "Validity information indicated to the test user the degree to which the test is capable of achieving certain aims."[41] That definition differed from one offered by Garrett seventeen years earlier in its recognition of the role of test users, but even more significant was the codification in 1954 of four "aspects"—a carefully chosen word to suggest the gathering of validity information and not types—of validity.[42] Important in the case of achievement and proficiency measures, the joint committee told its readers, was the first aspect: content validity. This type of validity was to be "evaluated by showing how well the content of the test samples the class of situations or subject matter about which conclusions are to be drawn."[43] The joint committee identified the second aspect of validity as predictive validity, "evaluated by showing how well predictions made from the test are confirmed by evidence gathered at some subsequent time."[44] As was the case in 1946, correlation was the key: "The most common means of checking predictive validity is correlating test scores with a subsequent criterion measure."[45] The third type of validity, concurrent validity, was to be evaluated "by showing how well test scores correspond to measures of concurrent criterion performance of status." Concurrent validity and predictive validity were quite similar, "save for the time at which the criterion is obtained."[46] The fourth kind of validity, construct validity, was to be "evaluated by investigating what psychological qualities a test measures, i.e., by demonstrating that certain explanatory constructs account to some degree for performance on the test." In studying construct validity, the authors of the recommendations reminded their readers, researchers were in fact validating the theory underlying the test, and such investigation was to be established in two steps in which two questions were to be asked: "First, the investigator inquires: From this theory, what predictions would we make regarding the variation of scores from person to person or occasion to occasion? Second, he gathers data to confirm these predictions."[47] Which is the most important among these types of validity? Construct validity, the joint committee found, "greatly overshadows" the others.[48] Thus, by 1954, the concept of validity had been fully articulated for the first time in one document.

The articulation of different methods used to establish validity evolved through American Psychological Association-sponsored editions of 1955,

1966, 1974, and 1985. However, a major shift occurred in 1999 under the leadership of Wayne Camara in his role as project director for the revision of the standards at the American Psychological Association. The 1999 edition of the *Standards for Educational and Psychological Testing* represented a shift emblematic of the growing presence of innovative types of assessment, such as the assessment of writing ability, in the culture of American education. In 1954 the *Technical Recommendations* were aimed at two groups: producers and users of tests.[49] By 1999 the *Standards* identified six uses: to evaluate a student's achievement and growth in a content domain; to diagnose strengths and weaknesses in those domains; to plan intervention; to place students in appropriate educational programs; to select applicants into programs with limited enrollment; and to certify individual achievement. In addition, tests could be used of accountability: to judge and monitor program quality and to infer the success of policy.[50] Gone was the world of test manuals, of isolated test developers and a unified group of test users. Present was an American ontology of shared accountability, a complex culture of evaluation and planning and policy conducted by shareholders.

It is no wonder, then, that in 1999 validity was defined in terms of the uses of tests. In an elegant and subtle sentence worthy of any reader-response theorist, the committee wrote: "It is the interpretations of test scores required by proposed test uses that are evaluated, not the test itself."[51] At the end of the millennium, the test itself was not, after all, the matter under investigation in a consideration of validity. It is the interpretation that matters, as we find in the very next sentence: "When test scores are used or interpreted in more than one way, each intended interpretation must be validated."[52] At modernist mid-century, when the conditions for establishing knowledge were understood to be scientifically constructed into patterns not bound to tradition, test construction was about design. At century's postmodern end, as the conditions for knowledge establishment themselves came under question and the grand meta-narratives collapsed, testing was about context. Hence, validity had become defined as follows: "Validity refers to the degree to which evidence and theory support the interpretations of test scores entailed by proposed uses of tests."[53] Theory itself had a new role, and the aims of test development were now to be aligned with issues of impact. Gone were universal applications; present were contexts.

In 1954 an instance of the relationship between validity and test uses was found in the example of vocabulary tests. "Thus," that committee wrote, "a vocabulary test might be used simply as a measure of present vocabulary, as a predictor of college success, as a measure of discriminating schizophrenics from organics, or as a means of making inferences about 'intellectual capacity.'"[54] In 1999 the example was a new kind of assessment that had not been noted in the 1985 *Standards*. "Tests used in educational settings," we are told, "range from tests consisting of traditional items to performance assessments including scorable portfolios."[55] Where once were vocabulary tests (and before that, scales) were now portfolios.

Portfolios were worthy, in fact, of extended discussion and definition in the 1999 *Standards*: "An individual portfolio may be used as another type of performance assessment. Scorable portfolios are systematic collections of educational products typically collected over time and possibly amended over time. The particular purpose of the portfolio determines whether it will include representative products, the best work of the student, or indicators of progress."[56] There is process here and purpose and audience—all lessons popularized by the composition movement begun in 1960 (as documented by James Berlin) and by the growth of the writing portfolio movement in the early 1980s (as documented by Peter Elbow and Pat Balanoff).[57] And there are achievable standards for this new type of performance assessment that should be "judged by the same standards of technical quality as traditional tests of achievement."[58] Portfolios had moved beyond show-and-tell classroom projects.[59] As Edward White claimed in his 1994 discussion of the criteria for scoring reliability, the work of establishing such technical standards "pays off for the staff and the curriculum as well as for the assessment."[60]

Evidence of validity, a key epistemological technique of determining information, had changed radically since Edward L. Thorndike had taken Barrett Wendell's course but found that he preferred "Philosophy 2A: Advanced Psychology" with William James. Between the world of Wendell and his student and the world of the new SAT writing sample in 2005, ideas about measurement emerged, were given definition, were challenged, and were recast—sometimes sequentially, often concurrently, ever in flux.

In 1954 there was a remorseless modernist, archetypal certainty about validity. In 1999 there was a postmodern contextualism. Plausible rival hypotheses should be considered when gathering evidence of validity, readers were reminded at the close of the twentieth century, and consideration should be given to construct underrepresentation and construct-irrelevant variance. If, readers were told, a test of reading comprehension is designed, that test might fail because it underrepresented the intended construct by failing to contain a sufficient variety of reading material. An emotional reaction to a test? Construct-irrelevant variance—the degree to which scores are affected by processes that are extraneous to the intended construct—may be present.[61] While validity may be a unitary concept, there are multiple methods to integrate validity evidence. After all, it is the proposed uses that are being validated, not the test itself.

The 1999 *Standards* thus served as a dramatic statement of the profound impact that researchers—significant among them those who studied the assessment of writing—have had on the very concept of validity. At the same time, those *Standards* demonstrate that it was not enrollment alone that explained the shifts in writing assessment that occurred since Wendell came to Harvard (any more than it was the presence of the traveling conestoga that shaped something Frederick Jackson Turner thought was the American character). The shifting concept of validity is itself testament that an analytic reliance informed solely by theories of embattled Hegelian factions or materialist Marxist critiques cannot explain adequately a history in which the very definitions themselves have evolved.

Validity in Writing Assessment: From Scales to Portfolios

In 1911, Edward Thorndike's announcement in the *Journal of Educational Psychology* of his "ideal scale for merit in English writing" was emblematic of a period of scale building in which writing, like handwriting or reading, was a behavior validated by judges.[62] There was no attempt to explicate the variables of writing, no consideration of modes of discourse or topic, of critically thinking writers and culturally bound receivers. The warning of the Committee of Ten—that "there are serious theoretical and practical objections to estimating a student's power to write a language on the basis of the theme composed not for the sake of expounding something that he knows or things, but merely for the sake of *showing his ability to write*"—had not been heeded.[63] Rather, Thorndike was building scales, a scientific process that focused on distributing scores across a continuum. In 1929 Helen M. Walker provided an excellent contemporary overview of that process as it originated with Galton in his 1869 *Hereditary Genius*. "In assigning marks of excellence of any sort, whether prizes or test scores," Walker began, "the first requisite is the ability to arrange all the members of the group in an order of merit."[64] Among the earliest scales developed by Galton was one designed to arrange the ranking of men who obtained mathematical honors at Cambridge University along a continuum that ranged from below 500 to 8,000 by intervals of 500, "the senior wrangler obtaining nearly twice as many marks as the second wrangler, and more than thirty-two times as much as the last man," as Walker explained.[65] In his 1889 *Natural Inheritance*, Galton termed these "schemes for distribution," and Walker quotes Galton at length to establish the uses of these schemes:

> A knowledge of the distribution of any quality enables us to ascertain the rank that each man holds among his fellows, in respect to that quality. That is a valuable piece of knowledge in this struggling and competitive world, where success is to the foremost and failure to the hindmost, irrespective of absolute efficiency. A blurred vision would be above all price to an individual in a nation of blind men, though it would hardly enable him to earn his bread elsewhere. When the distribution of any faculty has been ascertained, we can tell from the measurement, say, of our child, how he ranks among other children in respect to that faculty, whether it be a physical gift, or one of health, or of intellect, or of morals.[66]

Here is Galton summarizing his method of scaling variation, of establishing the value of a group above and below the mean:

> It will, I trust, be clearly understood that the numbers of men in the several classes in my table depend on no uncertain hypothesis. They are determined by the assured law of deviations from an average. It is an absolute fact that if we pick out of each million the one man who is naturally the ablest, and also the one man who is the most stupid, and divide the remaining 999,998 men into fourteen classes, the average ability in each being separated from that of its neighbors by equal grades, then the numbers in each of these classes will, on the average of many millions, be stated in the table.... Thus the rarity of commanding ability, and the vast abundance of mediocrity, is no accident, but follows of necessity, from the very nature of things.[67]

And here is Thorndike on his scale in 1911, asking readers to rank eighteen samples given in the article:

> Examine the following specimens and rank them in order for what you regard as merit in English writing by young people. Number the worst specimen 1, the next worse 2, the next worse 3, and so on. Then let the four-inch line below represent the total difference in merit between the specimen which you rank 1, or worst, and the specimen which you rank 18, or best, and place the letters designating your numbers 4, 7, 10, 13, and 16 at appropriate points, so that the distances between these points represent the respective differences in merit between 1, 4, 7, 10, 13, 16 and 18 in your judgment. Then decide what sort of English writing would possess zero, or "just not any," merit as writing by young people and locate this zero point where it belongs on the line or an extension of it.[68]

Following Galton, Thorndike saw the possibilities of distribution. As historian Theodore M. Porter observed, Galton saw in the error curve—known more popularly as the normal distribution—"both the possibility of increasing the impressiveness of his study and a technique for quantifying a range of attributes that previously had resisted exact investigation."[69] If two hundred competent judges, Thorndike reasoned, established the value points on the distribution—a technique that increased validity of the ranking—then the scale would achieve its promised value. Scale-building was a method of ranking, as Porter points out in his analysis of the method used by Galton, not of measurement. Individual differences did not matter, and information about those differences did not have to be recorded differently. Everything that needed to be known, as Porter writes, "could be learned simply by arranging the group in order, beginning with those possessing the lowest degree of the attribute in question and proceeding to the highest."[70] And so Thorndike and his students Hillegas and Trabue worked on the scales from 1911 to 1917. Scale-building was a valued contribution to American education for the first quarter of the century.[71]

The concept of writing ability as a unitary skill is evident not only in the scales but also in the literacy tests used by Robert M. Yerkes and his colleagues in the army intelligence tests. During World War I, literacy became the arbiter that was either absent or present—so that the second, more meaningful test, that of intelligence—again, a unitary concept—could be given. As Yerkes had written, "The task of separating the illiterate and semi-literate from the literate was recognized previous to the fall [1917] examining in the Army."[72] And so the Thorndike Reading Scale, the Kelley Literacy Test, and the Devens Literacy Test were used from the beginning to segregate men into examination alpha and examination beta. Yet while the literacy tests were varied both in their administration and usefulness, Yerkes and his colleagues nevertheless claimed that the results indicated conditions of public concern in that nearly 30 percent of the examinees were sent to the beta test due to the presence of non-Nordic native and immigrant groups. Yerkes had discovered evidence of a literacy crisis without establishing evidence of such decline. This pattern—a rhetorical move in which the limits of the data were fully explored and conclusions were drawn that were not supported by the data—would remain part of American culture to occur again, as Richard Ohmann has pointed out, at the end of the Cold War when the popular press claimed that Johnny could not read.[73] In the twenty-first century, the pattern had emerged again—in, for example, the 2003 impressionistic account offered in "Why Johnny Can't Write, Even Though He Went to Princeton"[74]; and in the 2004 interpretation of the 1998 NAEP writing assessment data by the National Commission on Writing in America's Schools and Colleges whose authors found that the achievement of four out of five students in grades four, eight, and twelve at or above the basic level of writing was evidence that students "cannot systematically produce writing at the high levels of skill, maturity, and sophistication required in a complex, modern economy."[75] If professors could cite "a host of writing-related shortcomings among students, most often their inability to construct the sort of lengthy, sophisticated research papers required in upper-division courses" for the *Chronicle of Higher Education*—and if a blue-ribbon committee elected to ignore the fact that 84 percent of students in grades four and eight and 78 percent of students in grade twelve in America's diverse educational system were at or above basic levels of writing—then it could be concluded that colleges were failing to build the edifice on which the rest of education rests and that grade-school children were not being equipped to meet the demands of writing in the workplace. The more badly nuanced the information, the greater the crisis. As was the case in 1921, here were failures of the very aims of democratic capitalism itself.

Just as *A Nation at Risk* would capitalize in 1983 on the widely promoted literacy crisis of 1975, so too the absence of literacy among the army recruits had set the stage for Carl Campbell Brigham's 1924 *A Study of American Intelligence*. There, literacy was a pre-condition for intelligence and, as such, its absence was evidence of mental inferiority. Using the army data gathered by Yerkes, Brigham established what he claimed was a scientific basis for "the study of race differences in mental traits."[76] Groups who had failed to demonstrate evidence of literacy in the army were markedly inferior in intelligence, Brigham found, and many should be in custodial institutions.[77] Brigham's interest in verbal ability as a valid determinant of intelligence was carried forward into his admission tests used locally at Princeton University and, by 1926, nationally in the Scholastic Aptitude Test. A follower of the literary critic I. A. Richards and his principles of close textual analysis, Brigham had seen the potential in a scientific study of language and its errors, "an experimental epistemology," as he had termed this new type of study in his 1932 *A Study of Error*.[78] Brigham would recant because his own constructs had shifted. Within an individual's language use, he had come to believe, could be found evidence of "what is happening to an individual in his culture."[79] That legacy of language use—that language is a window to the culture and the individual within—remained with Brigham as he investigated the increased validity gained by the College Board's shift to the Comprehensive Examinations. The Restrictive Examinations that had been in use since 1900 were being phased out, and Brigham's 1934 study, *The Reading of the Comprehensive Examination in English*, was evidence of his commitment to bring method to "the new spirit" that had entered the classroom.[80]

The tradition of careful attention to language that Brigham established was continued by Edward Noyes and John Stalnaker in their *Report of the English Examination of 1937*. For Noyes and Stalnaker, however, there was a new articulation of validity that Brigham had not had in his 1934 report covering the Comprehensive Examinations from 1929 to 1933. Noyes and Stalnaker had taken in hand the authority of the 1931 report *Examining the Examinations in English*. The requirements in English delineated by that important committee—to "develop in the student (1) the ability to read with understanding, (2) knowledge and judgment of literature, and (3) accurate thinking and power in oral and written expression"—were quoted by Noyes and Stalnaker in the opening pages of their report.[81] Demonstrated ability in these areas, moreover, related to work in other subjects and could serve as a significant "index either of past attainment or of future promise."[82] In the 1937 report of Noyes and Stalnaker there was thus evidence of a definition of writing, provided by the Commission on English, that served to provide construct validity for the study; and there was a desire to investigate this strength of the construct by reference to other measures of performance, to other criteria such as the SAT. Noyes and Stalnaker's report established those elements that endure in the assessment of writing: the need for a defined construct and the desire to correlate that construct with other forms of assessment in order to establish the construct's relationship with past, present, and future performance.

Thus, when Edith Huddleston studied the nature of writing ability between 1948 and 1954, a known method of establishing evidence of validity was in place as she sought to correlate—as did Galton, Thorndike, Brigham, Noyes, and Stalnaker before her—writing performance to other measures. Huddleston claimed relationships between her objective tests and other measures, such as course grades, instructors' evaluations of students, and the SAT antonym section. March 1954 saw the publication of both the American Psychological Association's *Technical Recommendations for Psychological Tests and Diagnostic Techniques* and of Huddleston's "Measurement of Writing Ability at the College-Entrance Level," and both documents are informed by the growing sense of remorseless certainty in establishing validity evidence through "criterion measures," the very term used by Huddleston.[83] When she claimed that she had found evidence of correlation, she drove home her finding: that ability to write was no more than verbal ability.[84] And since verbal ability could be tested through multiple-choice questions that were economically efficient because they were machine scored, there was every reason to proceed with efficient tests that measured the only factor evident: verbal ability.

By 1950 most tests of writing ability were symptomatic tests, as the College Board termed them, which asked the candidate to "perform exercises which are related to competence in composition and which, therefore, could be judged on technical standards alone."[85] Earle G. Eley's 1951 objection was based on the validity of this kind of test. The construct of objective tests—"the ability to recognize grammatically incorrect constructions, the ability to select from several alternatives a correct construction to fit a context, the ability to rearrange previously concocted sentences into a well organized paragraph"—was not, he claimed, congruent with the ability to write.[86] In substitution of symptomatic tests, he proposed to measure writing on use of mechanics, style, organization, reasoning, and content. These elements, he claimed, combined with a set of topics in which background readings were provided to the students, would constitute a valid assessment of writing ability. When the College Board elected not to use the General Composition Test developed by Eley in 1956, the failure was due to the stronger criterion validity demonstrated by the SAT and by teachers' appraisals of their own students involved in the study. It was, in fact, the power of the SAT that stopped William E. Coffman's Tests of Developed Ability in 1957. The proof of irrelevancy was in the correlations: if direct measures correlated with the SAT, then those measures were duplicative. Huddleston's legacy remained, her multiple choice tests an enduring form of writing assessment.

The Advanced Placement Program was, however, successful in its use of essay tests because, unlike the General Composition Test and the Tests of Developed Ability, the construct validity of the program was established through the content of the courses articulated within the program. While Eley and Coffman's programs were associated with general education, the Advanced Placement Program was integrated into subject matter courses, with credit-bearing sections of American history and of literature. As well, the program focused on placing students in college-level courses after they had been admitted, and this low-stakes testing—rewarding achievement rather than testing skills—became the occasion for the nation's first widespread use of direct assessment. The assessment process was overwhelmingly viewed as successful, and by 1963 the Advanced Placement Program had evaluated the content knowledge of over 21,000 students by means of direct assessment.

The English Composition Test, which had been in use since 1943, had a much more troubled history than the Advanced Placement Program's essays when Fred Godshalk and his colleagues William Coffman and Frances Swineford examined it in 1961. A high-stakes test used in admissions decisions, the English Composition Test had become a field-test site for objective and interlinear items. While the test remained popular—some 100,000 candidates had taken a 1960 administration—member colleges questioned the validity of the item types and their ability to capture writing competency. In the most ironic moment in the history of writing assessment, the development of the criterion measure—a writing sample scored holistically—became the most enduring legacy of the study.

It was an essay's total impression, Thorndike's halo effect, which would be harnessed from the essays themselves. The validity was not to be found in discrete generalized traits but within the samples themselves. As Coffman would later explain it in 1971, the halo was "simply another name for the essential unity of any effective essay response. To the extent that a unique communication has been created, the elements are related to the whole in a fashion that makes a high interrelationship of the parts inevitable. The evaluation of the part cannot be made apart from its relationship to the whole."[87] Instead of a stimulus-response, behavioral model of validity—criteria are provided that readers then identify in essays—Coffman offered a validity model taken from the gestalt psychology of Max Wertheimer, Wolfgang Köhler, and Kurt Koffka. Dealing with wholes or phenomena, these gestalt psychologists were radically opposed to behaviorism and believed that consciousness reacted to wholes. As E. G. Boring described gestalt psychology, "In perceiving a melody you get the melodic form, not a string of notes, a unitary whole that is something more than the total list of its parts or even the serial pattern of them. That is the way experience comes to man, put up in significant structured forms, Gestalten."[88] For Coffman, the global rating scale had proven capable of capturing in a valid fashion the complex phenomenon of writing. Even the primary trait-scoring system developed by Richard Lloyd-Jones and his colleagues in support of the National Assessment of Educational Progress during the early 1970s—a scoring system informed by a behavioral model of stimulus-response relationships established in a reflex arc—established the entire gestalt circuit of the assessment in the scoring guides by including the exercise, the rhetorical trait under investigation, an interpretation of the exercise, an interpretation of the context of the exercise, a system of reporting descriptions of the writing, samples of scored papers, and rationale of the scored samples.[89]

If, indeed, the context established the gestalt, the situation in which the writing assessment episode emerged, then the more that could be known about the context, the more valid the assessment episode would become. By 1982 Edys Quellmalz and her colleagues had established the significance of the writing topic.[90] And by 1988 Leo Ruth and Sandra Murphy had published *Designing Writing Tasks for the Assessment of Writing*. For the first time, the writing assessment community had a model of a writing assessment episode (of iterative stages involving the test-maker, the text, the test-taker, and the test-rater) and of a procedurally oriented method of task design (of planning and development, and evaluation).[91]

Yet a single sample taken on a single day remained a questionable strategy by which to establish validity, as Charles Cooper and Lee Odell argued as early as 1977. "To test the ability to write in different modes (personal narrative, explanation, dramatic dialogue, reportage, prose fiction)," they stated, "or to write for different purposes (explanation, persuasion, expression), we need multiple pieces of multiple occasions."[92] The development of portfolio assessment in the early 1980s at the Educational Testing Service and at the State University of New York at Stony Brook throughout the 1990s allowed avoidance of what the 1999 *Standards* would soon term construct underrepresentation. As Sara Cushing Weigle stated in her 2002 *Assessing Writing*, "Portfolio assessment clearly has the potential for greater construct validity for school-based writing assessment at all levels of education where learning to write is a central curricular goal."[93] And, as demonstrated at Washington State University, in 2004 it was possible to capture, validly, an individual's ability to write in an academic context through portfolio assessment.[94]

But was it possible to capture that ability in a reliable fashion?

Reliability: 1929–1999

As Roberta Camp correctly observed in 1996, the concept of validity changed during the last quarter of the twentieth century, and writing was viewed in the last decade of the twentieth century as "a rich, multifaceted, meaning-making activity that occurs over time and in a social context, an activity that varies with purpose, situation, and audience and is improved by reflection on the written product and on the strategies used in creating it."[95] While reliability had undergone a similar transformation, its achievement remained a major concern. In fact, in the inaugural issue of *Assessing Writing* in 1994, Grant Wiggins warned his readers: "In performance tests of writing we are too often sacrificing validity for reliability; we sacrifice insight for efficiency; we sacrifice authenticity for ease of scoring."[96] During the twentieth century, reliability remained the obsession of writing assessment, an enduring constant reified in correlation coefficients, the rock against which studies were broken. To understand the significance of reliability in writing assessment, we must first understand its development in the broader field of measurement.

There was no definition of validity evident in Helen M. Walker's 1929 compilation of the origin of technical terms used in statistical method, but there is no such absence regarding reliability. Reliability is ever present in Walker's volume, and she devoted Chapter 5 to the topic. Charles Spearman, as she documented, "used the term to describe the correlation between two comparable measures of the same trait" and had employed the concept first in 1904 in "The Proof and Measurement of Association Between Two Things," published in the *American Journal of Psychology*—the same issue which carried his "'General Intelligence,' Objectively Determined and Measured."[97] And, as Spearman observed in his article, the concept was first introduced in 1896 in the *Philosophical Transactions of the Royal Society of London* under the title "Mathematical Contributions to the Theory of Evolution. III. Regression, Heredity, and Panmixia."[98]

A cousin of Charles Darwin, Francis Galton had been forever changed by the 1859 publication of *The Origin of Species*. "Its effect was to demolish a multitude of dogmatic barriers by a single stroke," he wrote in his *Memories*, "and to arouse a spirit of rebellion against all ancient authorities whose positive and unauthenticated statements were contradicted by modern science."[99] The birthplace of the idea of correlation took place when, seeking shelter from a rainstorm on the grounds of the medieval Naworth Castle, it came to him that the laws of heredity could be captured with deviations expressed in statistical units. The concept of correlation became widely known after the 1889 publication of *Natural Inheritance*, and by 1899 Pearson had fully explicated the usefulness of the method in service to the theory of heredity in the *Philosophical Transactions of the Royal Society of London*. For Pearson, the complexities of inheritance, regression, assortative mating and panmixia could be approached by direct quantitative treatment. The causes of heredity had achieved "a certain prevalence of almost metaphysical speculation"[100] to such a degree that studies of individual cases of inheritance had to be abandoned. Instead, researchers had to "proceed from inheritance in the mass to inheritance in narrower and narrower classes" by statistical methods.[101]

With Pearson, Spearman used correlation to demonstrate the power of unity. He began "The Proof and Measurement of Association Between Two Things" with a simple statement: "All knowledge—beyond that of bare isolated occurrence—deals with uniformities."[102] And he proceeded to define the nature of these uniformities mathematically with an imagined case taken from education. Suppose, he asked, we wanted to determine the merits of instruction given in writing or given orally. Using his rank correlation, he finds that of 2,000 visual impressions, 900 were correctly remembered, while 700 auditory impressions were retained. He then calculated the probable error to be .02. Thus, he had demonstrated that the superiority of giving instruction in written form had occurred and, in fact, could only have occurred by chance once in 100,000 times.[103]

But it is in the other 1904 article—"'General Intelligence,' Objectively Determined and Measured"—that Spearman showcased the true power of correlation. After reviewing previous studies of intelligence—such as that conducted in 1902 of Papuan children who were shown to be of lower intelligence than Europeans of any age and who, as Pearson put it, "on returning to the more congenial occupations of pearl-diving and cannibalism" sunk to lower levels of intelligence—Spearman described his own study.[104] Using a school in Berkshire located within one hundred yards of his house, Spearman had tested children on their perceptions of light (to discriminate among shades of light and dark), weight (among a graduated series of weights), and sound (among tones), each believed to be preeminently intellective operations. The students were also ranked according to "Native Capacity" by a procedure determined by taking the difference between each boy's rank in school in subjects (such as classics, French, English, and mathematics) and his rank in age.[105] Teachers were asked, as well, to identify the brightest students, and the older children were also interviewed and asked to give judgments about the other children based on "sharpness and common sense out of school."[106]

In the findings, sex and age were removed as irrelevant factors for their failure to correlate with the ability to discriminate along physical lines—the perceptions of light and weight and sound. But factors such as talent in classics, French, English, and mathematics correlated with physical discrimination by an average of .51 with a probable error of .03.[107] Spearman thus drew his conclusion, complete with italics: "*Whatever branches of intellectual activity are at all dissimilar, then their correlations with one another appear wholly due to their being all variously saturated with some common fundamental Function (or group of Functions).*"[108] In the correlation coefficients he had, he believed, discovered *g*—a general intelligence, a "universal Unity of the Intellectual Function."[109]

Spearman had used correlations to identify what he believed "must inevitably become one of the foundation pillars of any psychological system claiming to accord with actual fact—and the majority of prevalent theories may have a difficulty in reckoning with it."[110] By 1929, Walker could provide a definition of correlation that stood in 2005, a measurement of association invented to identify general intelligence:

> When *r* [the coefficient of correlation] is neither zero nor 1, the contour lines are ellipses whose axes are oblique to the axes of *x* and *y*. As the numerical value of *r* increases these ellipses become more and more elongated, until when correlation

> is perfect—no matter whether positive or negative—the ellipses have collapsed into a straight line, all the points being now located on a single regression line of perfect correlation.[111]

By 1954, the definition of reliability and presence of correlation had become unified. *The Technical Recommendations for Psychological Tests and Diagnostic Techniques* divided the quality of reliability—"a generic term referring to many types of evidence"—into three types of correlation coefficients: those of internal consistency (correlations obtained on a single trial of a test), those of coefficients of equivalence (correlations obtained between two forms of a test given at the same time), and those of coefficients of stability (correlations between tests and retests).[112] Internal consistency, equivalence, and stability remain the major forms of classical test theory in the twenty-first century.

The use of high-speed computing in the second half of the twentieth century led to an alternative to classical theories of reliability. In that computers could rapidly provide scores for individuals that could be compared to scores for groups, studies could be undertaken to determine what happens when a candidate of a certain ability encounters a certain item of a determined level of difficulty. Through this new type of test design, termed in the 1980s Item Response Theory (IRT), a test could be built that, as Richard Ittenback, Irvin Estes, and Howard Wainer put it, is "optimized for the circumstance."[113] Such automated test construction selects items that are neither too hard nor too easy for the candidate. As the candidate completes the test, the automation updates its idea of the level of proficiency and offers questions more suited to the ability of the individual. In addition, the automation allows the test to stop when a level of proficiency has been reached. "This allows fairer testing," Ittenback, Estes, and Wainer found, "because each individualized test will be as accurate as necessary for that individual rather than only on average over the entire examinee population." The use of Item Response Theory was evident in the late 1980s when the National Assessment of Educational Progress used it to build a series of items across school ages that would be appropriate for each school age and thus stand as common measure across grades and schools.[114] IRT was also used in 2004 by ETS researchers to configure the new SAT without analogy items.[115]

In the 1985 *Standards for Educational and Psychological Testing*, Item Response Theory was barely mentioned, but by 1999 it was a driving force behind an expanded view of reliability in the *Standards*. While reliability was still defined as consistency of measurement "when the testing procedure is repeated on a population of individuals or groups," the definition of measurement procedure itself had, the *Standards* admit, "broadened significantly in recent years."[116] The expanded definition was due, in part, to broadened views of reliability drawn from IRT, a procedure designed to vary with the examinee's ability. At one time, the *Standards* admit, the chief features of standardized tests—consistency of materials from examinee to examinee, strict adherence to administration procedures, the use of prescribed scoring rules—were, in fact, what made a test "standardized." But more flexibility in assessment procedures—and here the *Standards* cite portfolios of student work that had been substituted for traditional end-of-year achievement tests—had led to new ways of thinking about reliability. The cost-benefit analysis used to open the door to new ways of thinking about reliability was striking: "Each step toward greater flexibility almost inevitably enlarges the scope and magnitude of measurement error. However, it is possible that some of the resultant sacrifices in reliability may reduce construct irrelevance and construct underrepresentation in an assessment program."[117]

By 1999 reliability and validity were no longer the Scylla and Charybdis of evaluation. Writing assessment researchers would now sail to a single island on which constructs waited to be conjured into existence by means of expanded definitions of validity and reliability. The lure remains great.

Reliability in Writing Assessment: From Specimens to Portfolios

In some writing assessment studies during the twentieth century, when *r* was, say, .9, the line of correlation looked as if sand had been poured along a ruler laid at a forty-five-degree angle; in other cases, when *r* was, say, .4, it looked as if a stiff wind had scattered the sand. In many writing assessment studies, it was easy to determine the value of *r* and even to discover the origin of the absence and presence of the wind. But the interpretation of *r* in the history of writing assessment was as tremulous and elusive as wind blown through glass.

For Teachers College researchers Thorndike and Hillegas, reliability was not a major concern: they were looking for agreement. They were building scales, assembling rankings in a system in which the validity of the specimens was self-evident: the placement on the scale was the only evidence of validity needed. The higher the placement, the procedure assumed, the better the writing. There was a problem, as Hillegas recognized: "Variation among the judges was very great," he admitted, "and to make a perfect scale would require the services of many more judges that it was possible to secure for the study." Nevertheless, this was the beginning of the age of measurement certainty: "The scale is accurate enough to be of very great practical value in measuring the merit of English compositions written in the upper grades of the elementary school and in the high school."[118]

By 1917, however, Marion R. Trabue had designed the Nassau County Supplement and controlled for inter-reader agreement. He rid the supplement of artificial samples, controlled for topic by asking students to write compositions "of the same general narrative type, which in fact gives one a simple basis for the recognition of improvement in quality as one passes upward from quality 0 to quality 9," used "at least two trained judges, and in case the first two independent ratings differed, a third judgment had been made by still another judge" and employed a homogeneous group of readers, "all college graduates who had had experience in teaching and administrative or supervisory school work, and were at the time of making these judgments members of classes in educational administration at Teachers College."[119] Trabue identified a greater sense of inter-reader agreement in his study than had been obtained by Hillegas, noting that his 139 Columbia University judges agreed with each other because they were all "school people" and because the compositions were all of the same type.[120]

Trabue also cautioned, as Cooper and Odell would in their 1977 discussion of reliability, that a comprehensive description of writing performance could be achieved only by seeking more than one piece of writing on more than one occasion and by having two or more readers rate each piece. "One composition is not a complete measure of an individual child's ability in English composition," Trabue wrote, "but one set of compositions is a fairly reliable measure of the ability of a class. Whether the compositions are rated on the Hillegas Scale or on the Supplement matters little, unless it be in the ease the judges find in using one or the other. An added validity is given to any measurement of a class if each composition is rated independently by at least three judges before its final rating is determined."[121]

Inter-reader reliability in essay scoring during the first quarter of the century was not established through the use of correlation coefficients, and it is more accurate to think of the measurement of association between readers as an account of inter-reader agreement. If a given study was, in fact, designed to reveal difference, as was the 1912 *School Review* study by Daniel Starch and Edward C. Elliott, and agreement was found to be "shocking"—their findings revealing that "the range of marks given by different teachers to the same paper may be as large as 35 or 40 points"—

then the difference was demonstrated by distribution curves.[122] The techniques developed by Pearson (1896) and Spearman (1904) were first used widely by Yerkes and his team of army psychologists during World War I, their results published in 1921 in *Psychological Examining in the U.S. Army* and popularized in 1923 by Brigham in his *A Study of American Intelligence*. It is only after World War I that the correlation coefficient begins to be used to establish inter-reader reliability in the assessment of writing ability.

However, it is instructive to note that among its earliest uses, *r* was not used as a measure of inter-reader reliability. When Earle Huddleston of the University of Minnesota reported the results of his study of the effect of objective standards on the judgment of composition teachers in the December 1925 issue of the *Journal of Educational Research*, he found that the use of agreed-upon standards increased inter-reader agreement. He reported that agreement with lines drawn across the three raters to show, in a visual fashion, pre- and post-standardization among three readers—lines crossing vertically at pre-training, lines assuming horizontal patterns after post-training. His use of the correlation coefficient was to demonstrate a relationship among the individual raters and their intelligence quotients. After the teachers had practiced using a scale to standardize scoring for four hours, their scores on the essays correlated with their intelligence quotients at .69, and after sixteen hours of practice their correlation was .735. Huddleston concluded: "There is evidence that ability to use general merit composition scales reliably is a fair measure of the same factors of intelligence that our mental tests now measure."[123] The more training given in the use of scales, the more the judgments aligned with the very intelligence of the teachers. Referencing the work of Huddleston, British researchers Godfrey H. Thomson and Stella Bailes, among the first to use *r* to establish inter-reader reliability, used a specified scoring scale in 1926 and reported correlation coefficients among readers that ranged from .64 to .89. They found that the correlations were "on the whole, high, and point to a considerable measure of agreement—in excess of what is commonly held to be true." But caution was to be exercised, and the correlations were not to be compared with two applications of an intelligence test. On those tests, correlations were very high, and the correlations found in their own study "by their *comparative* lowness emphasize the fluctuating and subjective nature of a judgment on an essay."[124]

The pattern was set: correlations were in use, but the high correlations obtained by other tests—such as the ever-present intelligence quotient that appeared to be, as Spearman proposed, independent of circumstance and, thus, consistent across multiple administrations—dwarfed the correlations established by essay readers. By 1925, a pattern of reference emerged by which the strength of the correlation—from 0.00 (a hurricane of variance) to 1.00 (absolute, unified calm)—could be judged. The intelligence tests of Stanford University's Lewis M. Terman and his colleagues, based on the *g* identified by Spearman, were widely used. The period from 1910 to 1920 was, as Boring termed it, "the decade of intelligence testing."[125] The high test-retest correlations on intelligence tests that Thomson and Bailes alluded to in their closing paragraph—"practically unity," they had written[126]—had been established and were known to researchers. In that high correlations were found in studies from biology to psychology—Stephen Jay Gould noted the correlations identified by American biologist Raymond Pearl as well as those of Spearman[127]—the inter-reader correlations in writing assessment would have to compare with those nearly perfect relationships being identified on both sides of the Atlantic.

Thus, when Brigham reported on the College Board's Comprehensive Examination in English in 1934, he found that the readings from 1929 to 1932 failed to establish acceptable measures of agreement. The reading of 1929 was significant as the first time, according to Brigham, that quantitative analysis techniques were used to study the Comprehensive Examination in English. For two independent readings, the correlation, established using Spearman's techniques, was .70.[128] But the correlations across the readers varied: six readers achieved correlations between .99 and .95; twenty-one achieved .94 to .90; forty-nine received .89 to .85; thirty-five achieved .84 to .80; fifteen achieved .79 to .75; nine achieved .74 to .70; and four achieved .69 to .65. As Brigham concluded, the correlation coefficients were not comparable from reader to reader; there was even suspicion that second readers would erase their marks and substitute other marks after conference with their colleagues.[129] A similar range of correlations was reported for the reading of 1930 and 1931.

Even the new scoring methods of 1932 and 1933 produced somewhat questionable correlations. In 1932 the correlations on the essay questions—one allowing 50 minutes of writing, the other allowing 60 minutes—ranged from .10 to .85. Brigham's observation is worth recalling:

> It should be noted that 42 to 58 coefficients are .60 or higher, indicating a substantial degree of correlation between the candidates' scores on question three and question six. These coefficients include, of course, the halo effect of reader's mood, candidate's handwriting, and all miscellaneous factors which tend to produce excess correlation over and above the intrinsic similarity between the two

> performances. The coefficients may be accepted as spuriously high, but they probably bracket fairly well the range of correlations to be expected.[130]

For the first time, the *r* of .60 appears—a measure of inter-reader relationship that, Brigham felt, reflected what could realistically be expected.

The 1933 reading was designed to achieve that standard, and Brigham did his best to eliminate sources of reader variance during the evaluation of 6,970 answer books. When it was over, the correlations of .52, .56, .56, .48, and .49 between readers on the six questions in the examination were "far too unreliable to be reported."[131] Only the grading committee of experts who examined the books for discrepancies saved the day and allowed a reported .988 for 6,657 cases of agreement between readers and a conversion key that had been established on the basis of 2,034 candidates who had previously taken the Board examinations.[132] The readers never did agree, but they did align their scores to match the conversion key that contained the approximate grade which would be assigned if the weighted sum of the numerical grades were translated directly into Board marks. Brigham's solution was to identify readers who had agreed with each other in the past. His goal was not to correlate reader with reader but to correlate reader with group judgment at .60 for some questions and .50 with others.[133]

The strategy of using the constructed scale had succeeded, but Brigham was disappointed at the true inter-reader reliability and reported failure: "The factors making for unreliability are now so great that the examination should be discontinued unless progress can be made in getting a single stable score which is descriptive of the candidate."[134] Indeed, he suggested that the achieved correlation must exceed .75 in order to give the individual candidate a mark with "'respectable error.'"[135]

In 1937, Brigham's recruited understudy, John Stalnaker, reported success in *School and Society*.[136] Earlier problems in inter-reader reliability had been resolved, Stalnaker reported, and the 1937 College Board report demonstrated that papers had been read with reliabilities of over .98. The new methods developed by Stalnaker and Edward Noyes—inductively prepared scoring guides that varied according to topic, a more limited scale range, intensive training with mimeographed typical answers, a process of scoring by question—had yielded an inter-reader correlation of .84 for the entire test—a correlation in excess of Brigham's standard—and .68 for the essay.[137] The method allowed Stalnaker and Noyes to claim victory over the problem of reliability.

World War II offered an opportunity to use solely objective items that could be scored very reliably, often perfectly, by clerks. Since its first offering in 1926, the SAT had grown in popularity, and college admissions directors were losing their skepticism about the measurement capability of the test, which now included both a mathematical and a verbal test. There was a war on, and resources were scarce—even the gasoline to drive to the testing centers was rationed. And so in 1942 only objective-type questions were used. When English teachers demanded a return to the essay test in 1943, it was reinstated as a one-hour test. When Noyes, Sale, and Stalnaker published their report in 1945 on the six administrations of the test that had been given since its reinstatement, over 10,000 students had written essays for the achievement test in English composition during each of the April sessions. "If the number of candidates taking it is the only criterion," the investigators wrote, "the English composition test has been successful from the start. Few tests of the essay type have been written by so many individuals."[138]

While the reliability for the reading of the essay question was about the same as it had been before the war—.67 for the April 1943 examination and .66 for the June 1943 examination—the correlations, especially when compared to the .99 of the objective tests, were now seen as "too low to be satisfactory."[139] It is not that the investigators had shifted standards but, rather, that the earlier Comprehensive Examinations had six questions; so, when Noyes and Stalnaker reported .84 as the correlation obtained in 1937, they were reporting on the average of all six questions on 1,149 re-readings of the examination booklets.[140] In 1943, with only a single item, the essay, under evaluation and no other items to offset it—such as the pre-war Question 5, requiring only a 20-minute revision exercise that had been read in 1937 with a .87 recorded reliability coefficient—the inter-reader correlations on the essay seemed appallingly low. The essay had become a one-item test.

Through April 1944 the same scoring plan remained in place that had been used in 1937. When a reliability coefficient of .58 was identified, an adjustment in the scoring process was implemented in June 1944 in which ranges of high, middle, or low were used with eleven points of value (0–10) to be given within each range. The impulse to obtain increased precision—a change from a twelve-point set scale to the thirty-three-point scale—yielded only a .59 correlation. No doubt recalling their 1937 study of the .84 inter-reader correlations demonstrated for the entire comprehensive test—and, no doubt, feeling the comparative pressure of the .99 correlations yielded by objective tests scored expeditiously by clerks—the investigators drew the only responsible conclusion: "Reliabilities of reading should be of the order of .85 or higher before the reading can be deemed satisfactory."[141] Stalnaker declared that the essay test should be outlawed forever in the College Board's 1943 *Annual Report* and called, instead, for a series of well-defined tasks.[142] When those were implemented in the September 1944 examination, the reliability rose to .89. "The 'write-a-theme-on' type of exercise was completely abandoned in the September examination; as was predicted, the results showed a distinct improvement," the 1944 *Annual Report* recorded.[143]

In the same 1944 report, the College Board noted that it had received government contacts for the army-navy screening tests, the development of the achievement tests for the navy B-12 program, and other restricted projects from the Office of Scientific Research and Development. While the test fees had remained relatively stable from 1943 ($163,261) to 1944 ($179,033), these special government projects gave rise to a new category and a new source of revenue. An additional $337,422 was added to the College Board's revenue in 1944.[144] The new government tests would all be objective in nature, the content domains of the tests more precisely established than those "write-a-theme-on" tasks. In essence, the door was now effectively opened for some sixteen years of objective tests developed by Henry Chauncey's newly established Educational Testing Service for the College Board.

Edith Huddleston, and the era of limited-response testing she helped to usher in between 1948 and 1954, was historically the first through that door.[145] Concurrently advancing the reliability of multiple-choice methods—so easy to score—and their correlation with criterion measures, such as the verbal portion of the SAT, she was able to reify her claim that writing ability was no more than verbal ability through her use of correlation coefficients. The essays, after all, could not even be read reliably. The correlation between readers of .55 was about the same as between height and weight.[146] But the verbal portion of the SAT yielded a .76 correlation with instructors' ratings (the first criterion variable) and a .77 correlation with the average English grade (the second criterion variable). Huddleston's objective items also correlated well with the two criterion variables, yielding .58 and .60, respectively. The essay placed a distant third, with correlations of .40 and .41.[147] The items that Huddleston designed and the verbal portion of the SAT achieved excellent criterion correlation. She had designed her study to capture concurrent validity in exactly the form established by the 1954 *Technical Recommendations*, and she had demonstrated a high degree of correlation between objective tests and concurrent criterion of writing performance. By 1954 the burden of proof that writing ability was anything other than verbal ability rested with the investigator.

In 1956 Earle Eley's General Composition Test fell before standards set by Huddleston and the *Technical Recommendations*, faltering both in observed inter-reader reliability correlations and in criterion measures needed to establish concurrent validity. Inter-reader correlations on his five standards of judgment, calculated by Frances Swineford, were all low: .57 for style, .43 for organization, .53 for mechanics, .42 for reasoning, and .44 for content. As Richard Pearson of ETS concluded: "It appears evident that reader disagreement was a major source of error in GCT scores reported to schools and colleges and that those of individual students should be used with that in mind."[148] His test also failed to correlate as well with teachers' ratings of students in the study—the criterion measure—as well as the ever-present SAT, now the gold standard for the criterion measure of any new test. The SAT, Pearson found, would result in more students properly placed and fewer students improperly placed; even if the GCT scores were added to the placement decision, there would be an increase in the number of misplaced students.[149]

In 1957 William Coffman's Tests of Developed Ability would also yield only redundancy with the SAT, the need for his test obviated by the very criterion measure identified to establish its validity: If the science section of Coffman's test had a .75 correlation with the mathematics section of the SAT, then why have two tests evaluating the same ability? Only the structure of the Advanced Placement (AP) Program, a low-stakes evaluation system in which students were placed into existing courses after college admission was already secured, allowed Frances Swineford's calculated correlation in 1956 of .656 for the English composition AP test to remain unchallenged. Taken as an entire program, the low inter-reader reliabilities on the English test were overshadowed by estimated reader reliability on the essay sections of other tests such as the American history test, recorded at .951, "a highly satisfactory value."[150]

After the failure of the General Composition Test, researchers at ETS took a hard look at essay scoring. In their 1961 *Factors in Judgments of Writing Ability*, Paul B. Diederich, John W. French, and Sydell T. Carlton introduced their study by reminding readers that since Edith Huddleston's 1954 article in the *Journal of Experimental Education*, the College Board had spent six years and $97,000 on the development and tryout of the failed GCT. They reviewed all the efforts that had been made to increase reliability in that two-hour test of writing ability: presenting extensive stimulus material for background and content; training the readers to score on the five defined qualities; using a four-point scale (from 4: might be excused from the freshman composition course to 1: unprepared for college work); allowing for borderline scores; and resolving resolution by a third or even fourth reader. When the last administration of the test was given in 1956, Swineford had calculated the inter-reader correlation coefficients one last time, and they had not improved from the previous year: they had ranged from .46 for reasoning to .66 for mechanics, the sum of the composite score resting at .69.[151]

After reviewing the GCT's other failures in their criterion measures, Diederich and his colleagues revealed that an internal ETS decision had been made: Further work on grading essays had to wait for a factor analysis of the judgments of readers. The Carnegie Corporation had provided a grant for the study of an analysis that would reveal "schools of thought" in grading essays, and a classification of these kinds of responses would account for differences in grading standards. It was also hoped that these "schools of thought"—really, the ways that readers respond to texts—would emphasize "qualities amenable to objective testing, and that more precise observations of the remaining qualities could then lead toward closer agreement."[152] When their elegant analysis was complete, Diederich and his colleagues had identified five factors: mechanics (which could be measured by objective tests); wording (which could also be measured in similar fashion); and ideas, form, and flavor (which could serve as a new focus for readers to turn to when preparing evaluation criteria and rubrics for reading).

In reviewing the literature for their own study of 1961, Fred Godshalk, Frances Swineford, and William Coffman saw something in the Diederich factor analysis study that the authors had not fully emphasized: the five factors were "far from independent."[153] Diederich and his colleagues had observed in only one part of their study that it was unexpected to find "just these five groups and no others, and that they would hang together in the particular ways that were here discovered."[154] Yet the observation that the factors of writing ability were somehow hanging together was the beginning of the end of inter-reader reliability as an insurmountable problem in writing assessment.

When Godshalk, Swineford, and Coffman changed the research design to advance writing itself as the criterion variable, they had a great deal at stake: if the papers could not be read reliably through their new method of holistic scoring, then the existence of the criterion measure itself could not be established. Their design was clever: five topics would be read by five readers; as a result, every reader contributed to the total score for each student so that any difference in standards from reader to reader was eliminated.[155] The correlations among the five readings ranged from .435 to .592, but the design allowed the researchers to report the total score of five readers on all five essays. The design paid off, and the inter-reader reliabilities were identified at .739 to .777, with the total essay score at .921.[156] The soundness of the criterion measure had been established, and it was then possible to evaluate the various types of multiple-choice questions in the English Composition Test (ECT). When those correlations were established, five of the six types of questions used in the ECT were shown to be "remarkably efficient for predicting scores on a reliable criterion of writing ability."[157] Indeed, when the essay was combined with the multiple-choice tests, the multiple correlations increased. Of the four studies that combined multiple choice tests with essays, the lowest reported was .715 and the highest was .736.[158] The conclusions were indeed the breakthrough that Edward S. Noyes had described in the introduction: a promising way had been identified to evaluate writing ability, and the most efficient predictor of writing ability appeared to be a test which included both essay questions and objective questions.

The primary trait system developed by Richard Lloyd-Jones and his colleagues for the National Assessment of Educational Progress (NAEP) also demonstrated reliability by 1974, no doubt because it utilized, on one hand, an intrinsically holistic approach by providing actual models of student writing for each of the traits and, on the other hand, because the articulation of the traits had great precision due to the specific domains of discourse identified by the researchers. Even the earliest NAEP papers had been read using primary trait scoring with no inter-reader correlation lower than .82 in 1974.[159] Significantly, the holistic scores (an estimate of overall fluency), although "acceptably high for comparing group performance"—the lowest was .70 in 1979—were not as high as the primary trait scores. By 1985, Arthur N. Applebee and his colleagues were able to report that primary trait scoring produced even higher inter-reader correlations because the global judgment required by the range finders in holistic scoring did not require readers to evaluate essays around the specific criteria used in primary trait scoring.[160] The combination of harnessing gestalt impression and specifying trait-based discourse analysis had worked. As is clear in Applebee's 1985 report on the NAEP, both holistic and primary trait scoring had been found to be reliable methods of assessing writing.

By 1986, with inter-reader reliability an achieved feature of writing assessment, attention now turned to the question of inter-topic reliability as Leo Ruth and Sandra Murphy published the summary of their National Institute of Education work in *Designing Writing Tasks for the Assessment of Writing*. A year later, when Hunter Breland and his ETS research team replicated the Godshalk study, they attended carefully to narrative, expository, and persuasive writing by providing topics on each. An advanced, computer-based system of factor analysis was used and revealed that while there was one dominant factor of writing ability that explained about 78 percent of the common variance among topics, there were definable subfactors based on the topics.[161] In addition, the topics seemed to be capturing different levels of ability. One of the narrative topics, for example, correlated higher with the multiple-choice questions (.584 with the SAT Verbal, .663 with the Test of Standard Written English, .649 with the English Composition Test), an observation leading the investigators to write that "a familiar topic, administered under controlled conditions, is most similar to standardized measures of writing ability."[162] That is, if narrative topics correlated with multiple-choice measures—themselves designed to measure basic writing skills—then narrative topics best captured the skills of basic writing.

In their conclusion to the study, the Breland research team wrote that they wished to extend the complexity of types of writing even beyond that identified by Edys Quellmalz in her 1982 study. Not only are different types of writing important, but the different topics assigned might elicit different skills or knowledge even within the same type of writing. Thus, by 1987, the Breland research group designed a study that revealed that narrative topics were best used to assess basic skills of writing. The study was able to validate empirically what Ruth and Murphy had written as a cautionary message after reviewing the literature on the impact of modes of writing on assessment design: "A single writing task measures only one of many kinds of functional writing skills. Different skills are likely to be associated with different tasks."[163] The topic now had become a source of reliability variance.

Yet what better way to solve the problem of inter-topic reliability than to have students present their writing according to different topics? A longitudinal sample of writing, taken under authentic, non-timed writing conditions, would decrease the complexities of topic variance, because the students themselves would select their best writing across modes of discourse and types of writing tasks. The validity implications were clear.

But was it possible to capture that ability in a reliable fashion? In their 2000 volume, Liz Hamp-Lyons and William Condon reported success in inter-reader reliability of their portfolio program. From 1994 to 1999, approximately 5,000 entering freshmen and transfer students submitted writing portfolios that included an information sheet, a reflective statement that described the writing in the portfolio, one piece of writing from a class other than English, one piece of writing that responded critically or analytically to something the student has read, and one best piece that the student identified as a best, favorite, or most representative sample. The researchers reported better placement decisions into a basic writing course, an introductory composition course, or exemption from the latter. And as for the reliability, they reported readers' agreement on scores exceeding .8. "After 4 years of reading—two pilot studies and 2 years of running a full-scale entry-level portfolio assessment on more than 5,000 students a year, ECB [English Composition Board] methods have resulted in an overall interrater reliability of .85." These results, they wrote, "place the reliability of portfolio readings at or above the .8 benchmark for holistic ratings of timed ratings."[164] Hamp-Lyons and Condon believed that portfolio-based writing assessment remained an experimental process, and they set forward a research agenda based on dimensions of consequences, meaningfulness, transfer and generalizability, cognitive complexity, content quality, content coverage, and cost and efficiency.[165] The research agenda for portfolios, as they claimed, was generative.

(Re)Articulating Writing Assessment

In 1937 Noyes and Stalnaker's report established those elements that were to endure in the assessment of writing: the need for a defined construct and the desire to correlate that construct with other forms of assessment in order to establish the construct's relationship with past, present, and future performance. This method remained in place in 2004 as the College Board prepared for the March 2005 written essay by forecasting its prediction power based on correlation coefficients of previous studies. A combined multiple-choice and essay assessment did a fairly good job of predicting first-year college grade-point average and did nearly as well as the SAT verbal section.[166] Even that granite criterion measure, the SAT, endured.

However, a unified research method designed to establish construct validity and verify its correlative power through predictive validity was questioned in 1990 by the Commission on New Possibilities for the Admissions Testing Program. Derek C. Bok and his colleagues gave credence to instructional validity in their critique of multiple-choice questions and raised serious questions regarding the limited predictive power of tests such as the SAT. In a period in which educators, researchers, and administrators were asked to attend to instructional validity and move beyond prediction—a period that also witnessed the radical reformation of concepts of validity and reliability in the pages of the 1999 *Standards for Educational and Psychological Testing*—Brian Huot launched a new writing assessment agenda. With Hamp-Lyons and Condon, Huot believed that the future of writing assessment was generative. And he had assured readers of *College English* that portfolios were a positive force in the teaching of writing, a method that had "the potential to disrupt the prevailing negative discourse of assessment and its adverse effects on teaching and learning."[167]

Huot was the ideal messenger to bring a new gospel. As an assistant professor of English at the University of Louisville, he had published a magnificent review of the literature of direct assessment in *Review of Educational Research*.[168] In 1993, with Michael M. Williamson, he had co-edited *Validating Holistic Scoring for Writing Assessment: Theoretical and Empirical Foundations*.[169] In 1994 he had become a founding editor of *Assessing Writing*. Then, in 2002, he launched his full agenda in *(Re)Articulating Writing Assessment for Teaching and Learning*. As Richard Rorty said of Orwell's success, exactly the right book had been written at exactly the right time.[170] Its title was reflective: the book could not be thought of as an act of reclaiming because no teacher ever owned the act of writing assessment, and its ideas could not be thought of as an act of re-imagining because such a project was simply too abstract. Even its conclusion was imaginative: the reader realized that, unlike what Dorothy found at the end of the yellow brick road, the answers had not been here all along. Huot's analysis of a particular historical contingency was just what was required to make a difference to the future of writing assessment.

To establish the context for his study, Huot identified the isolation that had historically taken place between college English and educational measurement and called for work centered on a new definition of validity. In advancing Lee Cronbach's sense of validity as an argument that linked concepts, evidence, social and personal consequences and values, Huot recognized the potential for a new writing assessment community of teachers and measurement specialists to look not merely at technical and statistical explanations but also at the decisions that are made as a result of an assessment practice and the theories and pedagogical implications of that practice. In the classroom, instructive evaluation would extend the traditional boundaries of formative and summative evaluation and provide ways for writers to become participants in the evaluation process, to become aware of how drafts match desired linguistic and rhetorical targets and how those targets may be attained.

In place of the theoretical assumptions of traditional test theory—a reliance on the ability of the test to perform in uniform fashion across populations, an adherence to concepts of validity and reliability established by statistical rigor—Huot called for a new theory of writing assessment that emphasized procedures that were linked to local instruction. Among the principles he offered for his work in progress were concepts linked to context. Assessment, he believed, should be site based, locally controlled, context sensitive, rhetorically centered, and accessible.[171] In addition, Huot advanced recent research on reading and writing to demonstrate the complexities involved in responding to student writing. A new transformative notion of response, he believed, was needed to correct mechanistic notions of writing and to instill wonder and struggle in students. Reading through the use of rubrics, a kind of technology designed to resolve problems of reader reliability, was unlike any situation in which most readers review student essays. A new notion of response would, therefore, allow new research into the ways that students write and the programs in which they are taught. While assessment may be a permanent part of the educational process, it need not be undertaken as an act of discipline and punishment worthy of Foucauldian analysis. Understood, rather, as a social action, writing assessment has the power, Huot proposed, to promote the fundamental right of literacy for all students. "This volume," he concluded, "is just a beginning, a challenge for all of us who are dissatisfied with past and current writing assessment to create a new future."[172] It was a postmodern call for solidarity of action within a new community.

Somewhat similar hopes for a more informed vision of assessment had been advanced before, by Walter Lippmann in 1923, by Banesh Hoffmann in 1962, by Paul Diederich in 1974. But now things were different. This time, tradition was beginning to be called into question by the individual talents of educational leaders such as Derek Bok, Wayne Camara, and Richard C. Atkinson. In the early twenty-first century there was, once again, something happening here.

Endnotes

1 For more on Kayfetz, see Chapter 4, note 116. Lyman's summary of the criticism of the scales echoed those of Kayfetz: the statistical methods are not suited for opinions and judgment; the scales neglected the conditions under which the students wrote; the nature of the judgments made by the readers was not known; standardization of the scales was not justified; comparisons were impossible; and the types of writing were not correlated (Rollo L. Lyman, *Summary of Investigations Relating to Grammar, Language, and Composition* [Chicago: U of Chicago P, 1929] 152–156). Although the specific topic at hand was the criticism of the scales, the lines of argument apply to writing assessment in general.

2 Peter L. Cooper, *The Assessment of Writing Ability: A Review of Research*, GRE Board Research Report, GREB No. 82-15R, and ETS Research Report 84-12 (Princeton: ETS, May 1984). The lengthy note that follows documents an early recognition of college composition research within the corporate educational measurement community. In 1984, ETS examiner Cooper was clearly knowledgeable about work being done in college composition. The following citations of research appear in "References and Bibliography" 42–46: Richard Braddock, Richard Lloyd-Jones, and Lowell Schoer, *Research in Written Composition*; Francis Christensen, *The Christensen Rhetoric Program*; Allen Purves, *Common Sense and Testing in English*; Miles Myers, *A Procedure for Writing Assessment and Holistic Scoring*; James Moffett, *Active Voice: A Writing Program Across the Curriculum*; Lee Odell, "Defining and Assessing Competence in Writing," *The Nature and Measurement of Competency in English*, ed. Charles Cooper; and Edward M. White, "Some Issues in the Testing of Writing," *Notes from the National Testing Network in Writing*. (Recall that ETS researcher Gertrude Conlan had provided material for the first issue of the *Notes* in 1982.)

It is worth noting an earlier internal report from Sybil E. Carlson, *Survey of ETS Writing Activities* (Report to Winton H. Manning, Mar. 26, 1982), in order to push the date of recognition back a bit. Carlson had surveyed significant writing areas at ETS. (See also Chapter 5, note 90.) In the process she had interviewed those within ETS who were experts in writing assessment (among them Hunter Breland, Roberta Camp, Mary Fowles, and Paul Ramsey). These were experts, she carefully noted, who also had "knowledge of current trends and research findings outside of ETS," individuals who "interact with the 'real world' of educators and writers" (I-2). Carlson's analysis of findings from the field of composition, given in the section "Viewpoints About Writing," is worth quoting in its entirety as evidence of an emerging view of writing as a complex cognitive activity, a procedural act undertaken in diverse communities to effect a subtle range of purposes: "Clearly, as more questions are being formulated about writing, particularly about improving the quality of writing, more focus is being placed on writing as a process and on instructional interventions that make a difference. Evaluation becomes increasingly important because we need to be able to identify and encapsulate the many facets of writing that are of importance. Whatever forms these evaluations take, they must serve as valid measures of the 'real' process, and must be reliable from instance to instance. In fact, the field of writing today, from our limited observations, appears to be in the process of developing an operational definition of writing. Writing can no longer be viewed as simplistically as it was in the past. Now writing is being explored in its complexity, as a form of human communication that cuts across disciplines and that involves the integration of numerous human skills and abilities. Investigators are asking questions concerned with how we learn to write—to what extent is writing skill influenced by human development? Greater emphasis is placed on discourse rather than on mechanical skills. In addition, we need to know more about the contributions of mechanical skills to writing, and about the diagnosis of writing skills at different stages and levels in the writing process. These problems are discussed in the following portions of this section of the paper" (I-2). This statement is significant, a record that demonstrates the impact of the college composition research community on the corporate educational measurement community.

The sections that follow in Carlson's report are devoted to an elaboration of that impact: the composing process, learning to write, diagnostic indicators, discourse level development, mechanics and writing, writing across the curriculum, and writing and other skills and abilities. In her bibliography (VI-1 to VI-2), Carlson cites the better-known texts, such as Cooper and Odell's *Evaluating Writing*, James Moffett's *Active Voice*, and Mina P. Shaughnessy's *Errors and Expectations*. Yet Carlson also reveals in-depth knowledge of the work of the university community. She cites Dixie Goswami and Janice C. Redish's *Writing in the Professions*, a writing manual (reproduced in photocopy) from the Document Design Center at the American Institutes for Research in Washington. That thirteen-year project directed by Redish would reveal a great deal about the nature of non-academic, transactional writing, and the fact that Carlson had an advanced copy (the citation for the volume reads "in preparation") suggests the depth of her knowledge about the college composition research community. Carlson also cites a paper by Elaine P. Maimon regarding writing across the curriculum, a movement begun by Maimon at Beaver College that received National Endowment for the Humanities funding in 1977. (For an account of the origin of this important movement in composition studies, see David R. Russell, *Writing in the Academic Disciplines: A Curricular History* 2nd ed. [Carbondale: Southern Illinois UP, 2002] 284–286). Carlson also notes a chapter by Canadian researcher Marlene Scardamalia on how children cope with cognitive demands of writing. Along with Linda Flower, Scardamalia was becoming known as a leader in the study of cognition and composition through the 1981 publication of *Writing for Results: A Sourcebook of Consequential Composing Activities* (Toronto: Ontario Institute for Studies in Education, 1981). In 1987 Scardamalia would co-author *The Psychology of Written Composition* (Hillsdale, NJ: Erlbaum, 1987).

On a personal note, I can add that, by the summer of 1984 when I worked part-time at ETS, a great deal of attention was paid to the newly emerging college composition research community. Sybil Carlson, Mary Fowles, and I worked that summer on a glossary of terms used in holistic scoring in an environment that was stimulated by the interaction of the two cultures. (We had in our hands a copy of the fourth draft of what would become the 1985 *Standards for Educational and Psychological Testing*, as well James Grey and Leo Ruth's final 1982 National Institute of Education report, the study that would become *Designing Writing Tasks for the Assessment of Writing*. We had paid special attention to Chapter 1, Parts I and II, by Leo Ruth and Catharine Keech, "Designing Prompts for Holistic Writing Assessments: Knowledge from Theory, Research, and Practice" 32–259. Looking back, I believe that it was clear that the work of researchers such as Scardamalia had led ETS researchers to conclude that the college composition research community had demonstrated satisfactorily that writing was a complex cognitive activity. As well, work by Goswami, Redish, and Maimon confirmed that the college composition research community had evidence demonstrating the significance of purpose and context on writers. Concepts such as inter-topic reliability offered by Ruth and his colleagues, however, were still hotly debated within ETS in 1984, at least within the Literature and Writing Group; the ETS work on inter-topic reliability of Hunter Breland in 1987 and in 2004 remained in the future.

Three observations may be made when Carlson and Cooper's documents are considered. First, two writing assessment cultures existed in 1982, a fact that is evident in Carlson's emphasis that those she interviewed had experience in both the research world (us) and the "real world" of educators and writers (them). Thus, Pamela Moss's 1998 identification of these cultures (a college assessment community that may be "seriously isolated from the larger educational assessment community" [113]) may be documented by reference to the Carlson report. (For what may be the first interaction between the two communities, see Chapter 4, note 104.) Second, Huot's observation in *(Re)Articulating Writing Assessment for Teaching and Learning* that isolation exists on both sides was and is equally true (30); however, in light of the information referenced and the positions taken by Carlson and Cooper, the communities had begun to commingle twenty years ago. With two decades of interaction in place, the stage was set for Huot's call in 2002 for "a unified field of scholars who recognize and respect each other's work" (189). Thus, the third observation: Huot had written the right book at the right time.

The bad news, however, is that the second part of Huot's call—"to ensure that the main thrust of decisions based on assessment must be for the promotion of teaching and learning" [190]—may be much harder to implement. The culture of corporate-based testing, as Carl Campbell Brigham had presciently warned in 1937, is quite a different culture than that of university-based research. "We-build-'em, we-don't-fly-'em" is the appropriate mantra, testing corporations maintain, if the tests the organization produces are to maintain their marketability across time and circumstance. While certain groups may work together—the college composition research community and the corporate educational measurement community interested in writing—these are, in reality, small tribes that exist within much larger cultures of national, state, and regional policy. If we in the college community are to unify our efforts and focus them on the promotion of teaching and learning, then history tells us that we should use three strategies. First, we should attend to our specific institutional tribes as best we can. Second, we should undertake rigorous research in the tradition of those whose works appear in the citations of the corporate educational measurement community. (Since so much remains to be known about prompt design at the present writing, for example, a series of research studies replicating the sampling plan and analytic methods of Breland's *New SAT Writing Prompt Study*—while varying the prompt [according to, say, Purves' 1984 domain-references for classifying composition assignments] across African American, Asian American, Hispanic, and white writers—would surely catch the attention of ETS researchers the same way that Quellmalz had caught fire there in 1982.) Third, as we tend our fires and light new ones, we should follow Wilson Farrand's call for continued agitation and legislation in order to catch the attention of those who are watching us.

3 James A. Berlin, *Rhetoric and Reality: Writing Instruction in American Colleges, 1900–1985* (Carbondale: Southern Illinois UP, 1987) 183.

4 Cooper, *The Assessment of Writing Ability* 5.

5 Robert J. Connors, "The Rise and Fall of the Modes of Discourse," *College Composition and Communication* 32 (1981): 444–463. Peter L. Cooper's use of the

word "mode" in his ETS report suggests the prevalence of Connors' treatment of these enduring discourse forms, a widespread way of thinking about discourse that by 1984 had become so prevalent that they no longer required citation. (After all, Connors did not invent the forms, but he did bring their endurance forward with such compelling force that the academic community had begun referring to the modes of discourse in ways that had not been referenced since the nineteenth century. It is the absence of citation by Cooper that provides the most compelling evidence that the research in composition had had a great impact on ETS researchers.)

6 Edys S. Quellmalz, Frank J. Cappel, and Chih-Ping Chou, "Effects of Discourse and Response Mode on the Measurement of Writing Competence," *Journal of Educational Measurement* 19.4 (1982): 241–258. The use of the LISERL program for data analysis, just then becoming popular, would surely have caught the notice of ETS researchers.

7 Quellmalz, Cappel, and Chou, "Effects of Discourse and Response Mode on the Measurement of Writing Competence" 255–256.

8 Cooper, *The Assessment of Writing Ability* 5.

9 Hunter M. Breland et al., *Assessing Writing Skill* (New York: College Board, 1987).

10 Linda S. Flower and John R. Hayes, "A Cognitive Process Theory of Writing," *College Composition and Communication* 32 (1981): 365–387.

11 Leo Ruth and Sandra Murphy, *Designing Writing Tasks for the Assessment of Writing* (Norwood, NJ: Ablex, 1988).

12 Breland et al., *Assessing Writing Skill* 47.

13 Howe, M. A. DeWolfe, *Barrett Wendell and His Letters* (Boston: Atlantic Monthly Press, 1924). See also Wallace Douglass, "Barrett Wendell," in *Traditions of Inquiry*, ed. John C. Brereton (New York: Oxford UP, 1985) 3–25.

14 Douglass, "Barrett Wendell" 18.

15 Thomas D. Snyder, ed., *120 Years of American Education: A Statistical Portrait* (Washington: National Center for Education Statistics, 1993). The columns listing the available data periods and the enrollment in elementary and secondary education are taken from Table 8, Historical summary of public elementary and secondary school statistics: 1869–1870 to 1989–1990 (34–35). The U.S. population information is taken from Table 1. Population, by age and race, live births, and birth rate: 1790–1991 (11–13). The columns listing the data on higher education enrollment are taken from Table 24. Enrollment in institutions of higher education, by sex, attendance status, and types of control of institutions: 1869–1870 to fall 1991 (76–77). When Snyder edited the portrait in 1993, the higher education data for 1991 were noted as a preliminary estimate.

16 Geraldine M. Joncich, *The Sane Positivist: A Biography of Edward L. Thorndike* (Middletown, CT: Wesleyan University P, 1968). See Chapter 1, note 133.

17 Snyder, ed., *120 Years of American Education* 26.

18 Snyder, ed., *120 Years of American Education* 65.

19 Snyder, ed., *120 Years of American Education* 66.

20 Snyder, ed., *120 Years of American Education* 66.

21 Amie Jamieson, Andrea Curry, and Gladys Martinez, *Current Population Reports: School Enrollment in the United States—Social and Economic Characteristics of Students, October 1999* (Washington: US Census Bureau, 2001) 1. 23 Jan. 2005 < http://www.census.gov/prod/2001pubs/p20-533.pdf>

22 National Center for Education Statistics, *Projections of Education Statistics to 2013* (Washington: National Center for Education Statistics, 2003). 23 Jan. 2005 <http://nces.ed.gov/pubsearch/>. Since 1964 the National Center for Education Statistics had annually prepared ten-year projections. The columns listing the projected data in enrollments in elementary and secondary education are taken from Table 1: Enrollments in grades K–8 and 9–12 of elementary and secondary schools, by control of institution, with projections: fall 1988 to fall 2013. The columns listing the projected data on higher education enrollment are taken from Table 10: Total enrollment in all degree-granting institutions by sex, attendance status, and control of institution, with alternative projections: fall 1988 to fall 2013. The middle alternative projections have been noted, but the National Center also provides low and high alternative projections. In 2004, this report provides the best source of information compiled since Snyder's *120 Years of American Education: A Statistical Portrait.*

23 Hunter M. Breland, *The Direct Assessment of Writing Skill: A Measurement Review*, College Board Report No. 83-6, ETS Research Report No. 83-32 (New York: College Board, 1983) 18.

24 Richard Ohmann, "Historical Reflections on Accountability," *Politics of Knowledge: The Commercialization of the University, the Profession, and Print Culture* (Middletown: Wesleyan UP, 2003) 143. Ohmann cites Frank J. Sciara and Richard K. Jantz's *Accountability in American Education* (Boston: Allyn and Bacon, 1972) as an important document in establishing the history of accountability.

25 For more on the Elementary and Secondary School Act of 1965, see Joel Spring, *Conflicts of Interest: The Politics of American Education* (New York: McGraw-Hill, 1997).

26 Sciara and Jantz, *Accountability in American Education* 3. Of special interest in this volume is William A. Mehrens' account of the then newly established National Assessment of Educational Progress (290–295).

27 Ohmann, "Historical Reflections on Accountability" 148.

28 George Hillocks, Jr., *The Testing Trap: How State Writing Assessments Control Learning* (New York: Teachers College P, 2002) 12.

29 Hillocks writes in *The Testing Trap*, "Is there a plan to keep students from thinking, a kind of subtle 1984?" (204).

30 Charles R. Cooper and Lee Odell, introduction, *Evaluating Writing: The Role of Teachers' Knowledge about Text, Learning, and Culture* (Urbana: NCTE, 1999) viii.

31 Cooper and Odell, introduction xi.

32 Charles R. Cooper, "What We Know about Genres, and How It Can Help Us Assign and Evaluate Writing," *Evaluating Writing: The Role of Teachers' Knowledge about Text, Learning, and Culture* 23–52.

33 Cooper and Odell, introduction xi.

34 Sybil E. Carlson, *Survey of ETS Writing Activities* (Princeton: ETS, Mar. 26, 1982) II-11. Carlson noted that the TSWE was a "companion test" of the SAT.

35 James S. Coleman et al, *Equality of Educational Opportunity* (Washington: GPO, 1996). The *Oxford English Dictionary* identifies the date of the first use of the concept of assessment—"the process or means of evaluating academic work; an examination or test"—as 1956 ("Assessment," Def. 5b, 2nd ed., 1989).

36 Diane Ravitch, "Testing and Accountability, Historically Considered," *School Accountability: An Assessment by the Koret Task Force on K–12 Education*," eds. Williamson M. Evers and Herbert J. Walberg (Stanford: Hoover Institution P, 2002) 21.

37 Helen M. Walker, *Studies in the History of Statistical Method, with Special Reference to Certain Educational Problems* (Baltimore: Williams and Wilkins, 1929) 228. The *Oxford English Dictionary* establishes 1957 as the first use of the concept of validation—"to examine for incorrectness of bias; to confirm or check the correctness of" ("Validate," Def. 2b, 2nd ed., 1989).

38 Richard F. Ittenback, Irvin G. Estes, and Howard Wainer, "The History of Test Development," *Contemporary Intellectual Assessment: Theories, Tests, and Issues*, eds. Dawn P. Flanagan, Judy L. Genshaft, and Patti L. Harrison (New York: Guilford P, 1997) 22.

39 Ittenback, Estes, and Wainer, "The History of Test Development" 22. See J. P. Guilford, "New Standards for Test Evaluation," *Educational and Psychological Measurement* 6 (1946): 427–438.

40 American Psychological Association, American Educational Research Association, National Council on Measurement Used in Education, *Technical Recommendations for Psychological Tests and Diagnostic Techniques* (Washington: American Psychological Association, 1954). This volume was published as a supplement to the *Psychological Bulletin* 51.2 (Mar. 1954).

41 American Psychological Association et al., *Technical Recommendations* (1954) 13.

42 American Psychological Association et al., *Technical Recommendations* (1954) 13.

43 American Psychological Association et al., *Technical Recommendations* (1954) 13. Ittenback, Estes, and Wainer acknowledge that the idea that a test must measure a construct in its content was established as early as 1915 but that a name was not given to the idea until the publication of the *Technical Recommendations*, a time in which the concept was reified (23). An important early discussion on content validity, although it was not called by that name, is E. G. Boring's "Intelligence as the Tests Test It," *New Republic*, 6 June 1923: 35–37. Boring's essay is an implicit critique of the study of intelligence in works such as Robert M. Yerkes' *Psychological Examination in the U.S. Army* (1921) and Carl Campbell Brigham's *A Study of American Intelligence* (Princeton: Princeton UP, 1923), although Boring states in a note that his essay is "not a reply to Mr. Lippmann's latest series, having been written before it appeared" (35). Walter Lippmann was an avid opponent of intelligence testing, but Boring is not writing to debate. Rather, his essay may best be understood as an explication of content validity: What do scores on intelligence tests mean? "They mean in the first place that intelligence as a measurable capacity must at the start be defined as the capacity to do well in an intelligence test. Intelligence is what the tests test" (35). Boring here presents, to a popular audience, the first discussion of validity evidence: the items on a test operationalize the construct under investigation. If there is a true relationship between defined construct and test content, then validity is present; if not, then there is evidence of construct underrepresentation, as the 1999 *Standards* would define it seventy-six years later. Boring's 1923 essay is an excellent validation of Ittenback, Estes, and Wainer's finding that the idea of content validity existed before the 1954 *Technical Recommendations* but was not given identification until 1954—and, we may add, not given its fullest treatment until 1999.

44 American Psychological Association et al., *Technical Recommendations* (1954) 13.

45 American Psychological Association et al., *Technical Recommendations* (1954) 13.

46 American Psychological Association et al., *Technical Recommendations* (1954) 14.

47 American Psychological Association et al., *Technical Recommendations* (1954) 14.

48 American Psychological Association et al., *Technical Recommendations* (1954) 18.

49 American Psychological Association et al., *Technical Recommendations* (1954) 2. The heading for the section is entitled "Information Standards as a Guide to Producers and Users of Tests." The emphasis in 1954 was on the information that should be contained in test manuals.

50 American Educational Research Association, American Psychological Association, and National Council on Measurement in Education, *Standards for Educational and Psychological Testing* (Washington: American Psychological Association, 1999) 137.

51 American Educational Research Association et al., *Standards* (1999) 9.

52 American Educational Research Association et al., *Standards* (1999) 9.

53 American Educational Research Association et al., *Standards* (1999) 9.

54 American Psychological Association et al., *Technical Recommendations* (1954) 13.

55 American Educational Research Association et al., *Standards* (1999) 137.

56 American Educational Research Association et al., *Standards* (1999) 138.

57 Note the title of Berlin's chapter, "The Renaissance of Rhetoric," *Rhetoric and Reality: Writing Instruction in American Colleges, 1900–1985* (Carbondale: Southern Illinois UP, 1987) 120–138; Peter Elbow and Pat Belanoff, "Reflections on an Explosion: Portfolios in the '90s and Beyond," *Situating Portfolios: Four Perspectives*, eds. Kathleen Blake Yancey and Irwin Weiser (Logan: Utah State UP, 1997) 21–42.

58 American Educational Research Association et al., *Standards* (1999) 138.

59 William Condon and Liz Hamp-Lyons report this characterization by Brian Huot in "Maintaining a Portfolio-Based Writing Assessment: Research That Informs Program Development," *New Directions in Portfolio Assessment*, ed. Laurel Black et al. (Portsmouth, NH: Boynton/Cook, 1994) 277.

60 Edward M. White, *Teaching and Assessing Writing: Recent Advances in Understanding, Evaluating, and Improving Student Performance*, 2nd ed. (San Francisco: Jossey-Bass, 1994) 129. The growth of portfolio assessment may be seen as well by noting the term's absence in the index of White's 1985 first edition of his book.

61 American Educational Research Association et al., *Standards* (1999) 10.

62 Edward L. Thorndike, "A Scale for Merit in English Writing by Young People," *Journal of Educational Psychology* 2 (1911): 367.

63 National Education Association of the United States, *Report of the Committee of Ten on Secondary School Studies, with the Reports of the Conferences Arranged by the Committee* (New York: American Book Company, 1894) 94.

64 Walker, *Studies* 88. The *Oxford English Dictionary* documents that 1898 was the first use of the psychological definition of a scale—"a graded series in terms of which the measurements of such phenomena as sensations, attitudes, or mental attributes are expressed; sometimes preceded by the name of the person to whom a particular scale is attributed (as Binet scale; cf. Guttman Scale, or some other qualifying word)" ("Scale," Def. 5c, 2nd ed., 1989).

65 Walker, *Studies* 89.

66 Qtd. in Walker, *Studies* 89. From Francis Galton, *Natural Inheritance* (London: Macmillan, 1889) 37.

67 Qtd. in Theodore M. Porter, *The Rise of Statistical Thinking, 1820–1900* (Princeton: Princeton UP, 1986) 142. From Francis Galton, *Hereditary Genius: An Inquiry into Its Laws and Consequences* (London: Macmillan, 1869) 34–35.

68 Thorndike, "A Scale for Merit in English Writing by Young People" 361–362.

69 Porter, *The Rise of Statistical Thinking* 141.

70 Porter, *The Rise of Statistical Thinking* 144.

71 William A. Younglove, "A Look at Behavioristic Measurement of English Composition in United States Public Schools, 1901–1941," California Educational Research Association, 17–18 Nov. 1983, ERIC ED 246 109.

72 Robert M. Yerkes, ed., *Psychological Examining in the United States Army* (Washington: GPO, 1921) 472.

73 Richard Ohmann, "English and the Cold War," *Politics of Knowledge: The Commercialization of the University, the Profession, and Print Culture* (Middletown, CT: Wesleyan UP, 2003) 20. Rudolph Flesch attracted national attention with the publication of *Why Johnny Can't Read—And What You Can Do About It* (New York: Harper, 1955).

74 Thomas Bartlett, "Why Johnny Can't Write, Even Though He Went to Princeton," *Chronicle of Higher Education*, 3 Jan. 2003: A39.

75 National Commission on Writing in America's Schools and Colleges, *The Neglected "R": The Need for a Writing Revolution* (New York: College Board, Apr. 2004) 16–17. 23 Jan. 2005 <http://www.writingcommission.org/>.

76 Brigham, *American Intelligence* xx.

77 Brigham, *American Intelligence* 153.

78 Carl Campbell Brigham, *A Study of Error* (New York: College Entrance Examination Board, 1932) 45.

79 Brigham, *Error* 46.

80 Carl Campbell Brigham, *The Reading of the Comprehensive Examination in English: An Analysis of the Procedures Followed During the Five Reading Periods from 1929–1933* (Princeton: Princeton UP, 1934) i.

81 Edward S. Noyes and John M. Stalnaker, *Report on the English Examination of June 1937: A Description of the Procedures Used in Preparing and Reading the Examination in English and an Analysis of the Results of the Reading* (New York: College Entrance Examination Board, 1938) 7.

82 Noyes and Stalnaker, *Report* 7.

83 Edith M. Huddleston, "Measurement of Writing Ability at the College-Entrance Level: Objective vs. Subjective Testing Techniques," *Journal of Experimental Education* 22.3 (1954): 171.

84 Huddleston, "Measurement of Writing Ability at the College-Entrance Level" 204.

85 *Fiftieth Annual Report of the Director* (New York: College Entrance Examination Board, 1950) 3.

86 Earle G. Eley, "The Experiment in General Composition," *College Board Review* 15 (1951) 217.

87 William E. Coffman, "Essay Examinations," *Educational Measurement*, ed. Robert L. Thorndike (Washington: American Council on Education, 1971) 293.

88 Edwin G. Boring, *A History of Experimental Psychology*, 2nd ed. (New York: Appleton-Century-Crofts, 1950) 588.

89 Richard Lloyd-Jones, "Primary Trait Scoring," *Evaluating Writing: Describing, Measuring, Judging*, eds. Charles R. Cooper and Lee Odell (Urbana: NCTE, 1977) 45.

90 Edys S. Quellmalz, Frank J. Cappel, and Chih-Ping Chou, "Effects of Discourse and Response Mode on the Measurement of Writing Competence," *Journal of Educational Measurement* 19.4 (1982): 241–258.

91 Leo Ruth and Sandra Murphy, *Designing Writing Tasks for the Assessment of Writing* (Norwood, NJ: Ablex, 1988), Figure 7.1 (128) and Figure 12.1 (239).

92 Cooper and Odell, introduction, *Evaluating Writing: The Role of Teachers' Knowledge about Text, Learning, and Culture* xi.

93 Sara Cushing Weigle, *Assessing Writing* (New York: Cambridge UP, 2002) 202.

94 Richard H. Haswell, ed., *Beyond Outcomes: Assessment and Instruction Within a University Writing Program* (Westport, CT: Ablex, 2001). In 2004 the program remained in place.

95 Roberta Camp, "New Views of Measurement and New Models for Writing Assessment," *Assessment of Writing: Politics, Policies, and Practices*, eds. Edward M. White, William D. Lutz, and Sandra Kamusikiri (New York: MLA, 1996) 135.

96 Grant Wiggins, "The Constant Danger of Sacrificing Validity to Reliability: Making Writing Assessment Serve Writers," *Assessing Writing* 1.1 (1994): 129.

97 Walker, *Studies* 187. See Charles Spearman, "The Proof and Measurement of Association Between Two Things," *American Journal of Psychology* 15 (1904): 72–101. Spearman cites Pearson's 1896 article (cited below) in note 2 (77). The *Oxford English Dictionary* agrees with Walker and establishes 1904 as the first use of the

statistical concept of reliability—"the extent to which a measurement made repeatedly in identical circumstances will yield concordant results" ("Reliability," Def. 2, 2nd ed, 1989).

98 Karl Pearson, "Mathematical Contributions to the Theory of Evolution. III. Regression, Heredity, and Panmixia," *Philosophical Transactions of the Royal Society of London* 187 (1896): 253–318.

99 Qtd. in Walker, *Studies* 103.

100 Pearson, "Mathematical Contributions" 255.

101 Pearson, "Mathematical Contributions" 255.

102 Spearman, "The Proof and Measurement" 72.

103 Spearman, "The Proof and Measurement" 82–83.

104 Charles Spearman, "'General Intelligence,' Objectively Determined and Measured," *American Journal of Psychology* 15 (1904): 230–231.

105 Spearman, "'General Intelligence'" 250.

106 Spearman, "'General Intelligence'" 251.

107 Spearman, "'General Intelligence'" 265.

108 Spearman, "'General Intelligence'" 273.

109 Spearman, "'General Intelligence'" 284.

110 Spearman, "'General Intelligence'" 273.

111 Walker, *Studies* 93.

112 American Psychological Association et al., *Technical Recommendations* 28.

113 Ittenback, Estes, and Wainer, "The History of Test Development" 25. The standard text on Item Response Theory is by ETS Distinguished Research Scientist Frederick. M. Lord, *Applications of Item Response Theory to Practical Testing Problems* (Hillsdale, NJ: Erlbaum, 1980).

114 Eugene G. Johnson and Rebecca Zwick, *Focusing the New Design: The 1988 NAEP Technical Report*, ED 325 496 (Princeton: ETS Technical Report, 1988). In 1983 ETS became the grantee of the NAEP, and IRT models were introduced (4). In 1988 the writing assessment design benefited by a method of sampling termed Average Response Method (ARM), used to estimate the student's composite value of writing ability, because each student in the NAEP wrote on only a subset of the questions (275). This technique of sampling is known as Focused BIB spiraling (5).

115 Jinghua Liu, Miriam Feigenbaum, and Linda Cook, *A Simulation Study to Explore Configuring the New SAT Critical Reading Section Without Analogy Items*, College Board Research Report No. 2004-2, ETS RR-04-01 (New York: College Board, 2004).

116 American Educational Research Association et al., *Standards* (1999) 25.

117 American Educational Research Association et al., *Standards* (1999) 26.

118 Milo B. Hillegas, "A Scale for the Measurement of Quality in English Composition by Young People," *Teachers College Record* 13.4 (1912): 50.

119 M. R. Trabue, "Supplementing the Hillegas Scale," *Teachers College Record* 18 (1917): 56–57.

120 Trabue, "Supplementing the Hillegas Scale" 73–74.

121 Trabue, "Supplementing the Hillegas Scale" 84.

122 Daniel Starch and Edward C. Elliot, "Reliability of the Grading of High-School Work in English," *School Review* 20 (1912) 442–457. "The range of possible marks is indicated along the base line of each chart and the number of times each grade was given is indicated by the number of dots above that grade" (449).

123 Earle Huddleston, "The Effect of Objective Standards upon Composition Teachers' Judgments," *Journal of Educational Research* 12.5 (1925): 339.

124 Godfrey H. Thomson and Stella Bailes, "The Reliability of Essay Marks," *Forum of Education* 4.2 (1926): 91.

125 Boring, *A History of Experimental Psychology* 547.

126 Thomson and Bailes, "The Reliability of Essay Marks" 91.

127 Stephen Jay Gould, *The Mismeasure of Man* (New York: Norton, 1981) 256.

128 Brigham, *Comprehensive Examination,* Appendix A, written by Cecil R. Brolyer, explains the method.

129 Brigham, *Comprehensive Examination* 2–4.

130 Brigham, *Comprehensive Examination* 18.

131 Brigham, *Comprehensive Examination* 26.

132 Brigham, *Comprehensive Examination* 21–22.

133 Brigham, *Comprehensive Examination* 30.

134 Brigham, *Comprehensive Examination* 41.

135 Brigham, *Comprehensive Examination* 41.

136 John M. Stalnaker, "Essay Examinations Reliably Read," *School and Society* 46 (1937) 671–672.

137 Noyes and Stalnaker, *Report* 50.

138 Edward Simpson Noyes, William Merritt Sale, Jr., and John Marshall Stalnaker, *Report on the First Six Tests in English Composition, with Sample Answers from the Tests of April and June, 1944* (New York: College Entrance Examination Board, 1945) 7.

139 Noyes, Sale, and Stalnaker, *Report on the First Six Tests* 11.

140 Noyes, Sale, and Stalnaker, *Report on the First Six Tests* 50–51. The chart for the correlations on all six questions is found on 51. The correlation for the 60-minute essay, Question 6, was .68.

141 Noyes, Sale, and Stalnaker, *Report on the First Six Tests* 67.

142 *Forty-Third Annual Report of the Executive Secretary* (New York: College Entrance Examination Board, 1943) 24.

143 *Forty-Fourth Annual Report of the Executive Secretary* (New York: College Entrance Examination Board, 1944) 24.

144 The government contacts are announced in the *Forty-Fourth Annual Report of the Executive Secretary* 4. The comparative revenue charts are found, for 1943, in the *Forty-Third Annual Report* (21) and the *Forty-Fourth Annual Report* (20).

145 Huddleston, "Measurement of Writing Ability at the College-Entrance Level" 165–213.

146 Huddleston, "Measurement of Writing Ability at the College-Entrance Level" 166.

147 Huddleston, "Measurement of Writing Ability at the College-Entrance Level," Table 15 (197).

148 Richard Pearson, "The Test Fails as an Entrance Examination," *College Board Review* 25 (1955): 6.

149 Pearson, "The Test Fails as an Entrance Examination" 9.

150 Frances Swineford, "Test Analysis of College Entrance Examination Board Advanced Placement Tests," Sept. 1956, SR-56-28 (Princeton: ETS Archives). The English composition correlation is given in Table 4 (6) and the American history correlation is given in Table 7 (14). It is worth noting that Swineford identified a .851 inter-reader correlation on the literature test but dismissed it. "It must be pointed out," she wrote, "in this connection that the Chief Reader of Literature reported that a difference of 2 or more points on an essay was discussed by the readers concerned and then

adjusted. He added that about 10 percent of the papers were reread for this purpose. Only the adjusted scores were available for analysis. Therefore, the reported figures for Literature are somewhat too high to represent the reader reliability of the sum of two independent readings. They cannot be accepted as reader reliabilities of the reported scores, since we have no date that can be used to estimate how well these scores would agree with scores based on the sums of readings by different pairs of readers" (6). The passage demonstrates not only Swineford's meticulous sense of integrity but also yields an inside look into just what Earle Ely was up against within ETS in attempting to present an alternate way of resolving discrepant scores.

151 Paul B. Diederich, John W. French, and Sydell T. Carlton, *Factors in Judgments of Writing Ability* RB-61-15 2 (Princeton: ETS, 1961).

152 Diederich, French, and Carlton, *Factors in Judgments of Writing Ability* 3.

153 Fred I. Godshalk, Frances Swineford, and William E. Coffman, *The Measurement of Writing Ability: A Significant Breakthrough* (New York: College Entrance Examination Board, 1966) 4.

154 Diederich, French, and Carlton, "Factors in Judgments of Writing Ability" 55.

155 Godshalk, Swineford, and Coffman, *The Measurement of Writing Ability* 14.

156 Godshalk, Swineford, and Coffman, *The Measurement of Writing Ability* 15.

157 Godshalk, Swineford, and Coffman, *The Measurement of Writing Ability* 29.

158 Godshalk, Swineford, and Coffman, *The Measurement of Writing Ability* 37.

159 Arthur N. Applebee, Judith A. Langer, and Ina V. S. Mullins, *Writing Trends Across the Decade, 1974–84*, ETS Report No. 15-W-01 (Princeton: ETS, 1985). Table A.3 (68) presents the primary trait correlation coefficients. Table A.4 (69) presents the holistic scoring correlation coefficients.

160 Applebee, Langer, and Mullins, *Writing Trends Across the Decade, 1974–84* 69.

161 Hunter M. Breland, Roberta Camp, Robert J. Jones, Margaret M. Morris, and Donald A. Rock, *Assessing Writing Skill*, Research Monograph No. 11 (New York: College Entrance Examination Board, 1987) 45. Table 7.1 (41) presents the estimates of factor loadings assuming a single factor model. It is also important to note the analysis of variance model that Breland and his colleagues employed to estimate reliability (25–26). That structural equation model appears to be the first of its kind to represent the sources of error in an essay assessment.

162 Breland et al., *Assessing Writing Skill* 47. Table 7.6 (47) presents a factor structure extension model based on the six topics in the study (two narrative, two expository, and two persuasive).

163 Ruth and Murphy, *Designing Writing Tasks for the Assessment of Writing* 82.

164 Liz Hamp-Lyons and William Condon, *Assessing the Portfolio: Principles for Practice, Theory, and Research* (Creskill, NJ: Hampton P, 2000) 135.

165 Hamp-Lyons and Condon, *Assessing the Portfolio* 175–176.

166 Jennifer L. Kobrin, *Forecasting the Predictive Validity of the New SAT I Writing Section* (New York: College Board, 2004). 23 Jan 2005 <http://www.collegeboard.com>.

167 Brian A. Huot, "Toward a New Discourse of Assessment for the College Writing Classroom," *College English* 65.2 (2002): 177. The essay was released shortly before the publication of *(Re)Articulating Writing Assessment for Teaching and Learning* (Logan: Utah State UP, 2002).

168 Brian A. Huot, "The Literature of Direct Writing Assessment: Major Concerns and Prevailing Trends," *Review of Educational Research* 60.2 (1990) 237–263.

169 Michael M. Williamson and Brian A. Huot, eds., *Validating Holistic Scoring for Writing Assessment: Theoretical and Empirical Foundations* (Cresskill, NJ: Hampton P, 1993).

170 Richard Rorty wrote the following: "Orwell was successful because he wrote exactly the right books at exactly the right time. His description of a particular historical contingency was, it turned out, just what was required to make a difference to the future of liberal politics. He broke the power of what Nabokov enjoyed calling 'Bolshevik propaganda' over the minds of liberal intellectuals in England and America." *Contingency, Irony, and Solidarity* (Cambridge: Cambridge UP, 1989) 170.

171 It is significant that in 2003, *Technical Communication Quarterly* hosted a special issue on the assessment of technical communication. Margaret Hundleby, Marjorie Rush Hovde, and Jo Allen wrote the following: "Justification of the existence of assessment in technical communication is not sought by either the editors or authors represented in this issue, even though assessment's challenges disturb the deliberations of many campuses. Rather, we support the stance that a valuable, faculty owned process of looking at coursework, program goals, and student learning is possible and essential. Assessment, when well designed and carefully implemented, supplies the kinds of information that educators need to provide evidence of their impact and effectiveness and to guide decisions at both curricular and course levels" ("Guest Editor's Column" [12.1]: 6). Clearly, such language reflected the values expressed in Huot's book.

172 Huot, *(Re)Articulating Writing Assessment for Teaching and Learning* 191. As the present book was going to press, Patricia Lynne demonstrated that she had taken up Huot's challenge. In *Coming to Terms: Theorizing Writing Assessment in Composition Studies* (Logan: Utah State UP, 2004), Lynne depicts the tensions surrounding a clash between "the objectivist paradigm dominant in educational measurement theory and the social constructionist paradigm of composition studies"

(6). Terms such as reliability and validity, she argues, are a normal part of the language of educational assessment but are not "indigenous" to composition studies (12). She suggests separatism. In challenging the objectivist assessment paradigm, Lynne encourages the adoption of a framework that is, at once, "meaningful" and "ethical" (116). Within this new framework, meaningful relationships—among the participants, their writing products, and the purposes of the assessment—would develop due to a celebration of contextual richness. In following the ethical paradigms of critical theorists such as Jürgen Habermas and Seyla Benhabib, Lynne proposes an assessment practice that is responsive to the political and social issues surrounding assessment and that provides principles for understanding evaluative procedures and the agents who enact them. Answers that arise to questions of purpose, substance, community, and process thus become theoretical tools capable of rendering assessment an integral, integrating force in composition studies.

The corporate educational measurement community (embodying the objectivist paradigm) and the college composition research community (embodying the social constructivist paradigm) were in full force at the 2005 Fifty-Sixth Annual Convention of the Conference on College Composition and Communication. On March 12, 2005, approximately 330,000 students "gripped their pencils a little tighter" and filed in to take the new SAT, as the *New York Times* put it (Corey Kilgannon, "Warming Up to a New SAT, but Nail-Biting the Usual Way," 13 Mar. 2005: 37). In the opening address ("Who Owns Writing?) Douglas Hesse pointed out that the newest report of the National Commission on Writing (*Writing: A Ticket to Work...or A Ticket Out: A Survey of Business Leaders*) "did not square" with the "CCCC Position Statement on Teaching, Learning, and Assessing Writing in Digital Environments." In a session later that day entitled "The New SAT Writing Section: Perils and Possibilities," tensions emerged between the two communities. Kathleen Blake Yancey chaired as Arthur VanderVeen of the College Board fielded criticisms by Edward M. White (who would have welcomed the new SAT if it had only been the 1970s), Liz Hamp-Lyons (who called attention to the impact of topic design on diverse student populations), and Dennis Baron (who, after raising the question of *cui bono*, warned that the new SAT would not serve as an equalizer of opportunity).

Chapter 7
Lagniappe

Handbag high, I always tagged along with my grandmother and mother when they went to make groceries in my New Orleans home. After they placed the red beans and rice into the basket, they went to the butcher, telling him what they had bought. From overhead came the white wrapper, a piece of salt pork inside. That was the lagniappe. If you bought something, you received a little something in return, to use, or not, as you pleased.

While writing this history, I read Roy Jenkins' biography of Winston Churchill. Because so many of us were reading it along with Rudolph Giuliani, the book was hard to come by where I worked. After seeing the smoke that striking September morning, we all needed to find our way. My wife, a nurse, waited for the injured to come to her hospital, but there were none. In Newark we watched as the New York City skyline changed forever, one great northern city watching another fall, the roller coaster cars lurching forward suddenly.

Jenkins' biography ends with a single sentence: "I now put Churchill, with all of his idiosyncrasies, his indulgences, and his occasional childishness, but also his genius, his tenacity, and his persistent ability, right or wrong, successful or unsuccessful, to be larger than life, as the greatest human being ever to occupy 10 Downing Street."[1] Before that September morning, I would have ended this book with a similar grand flourish and disappeared off stage: "I put the collaborative assessment of writing ability as central to the profession of English, and the study of assessment must be understood to be of fundamental importance if we are to understand our heritage and our future." Yet there is room these days, I think, for just a little more, for something on why I wrote the book the way that I did, for a reflection on what I found while writing it, for information that may be used, or not, as you please. After all, America has changed now, and it may no longer be possible (perhaps it never was) to ask the travelers to ignore that man behind the curtain.

Historiography: The Dangers of Hegel, the Seduction of Judgment

For Hegel, history was a reflection of the emergence of Spirit. Within that reflection, Oriental civilization was culture's childhood, Greek its adolescence, Roman its manhood, and German its noble old age. Within each age, contradictions were resolved within dialectic, and a new age issued forth. For Hegel, there were World Historical Heroes, agents of the Spirit who drove civilization forward toward maturity so that, in the remains of the day, it could be said that we had erected a building constructed from our own inner sun, something we would esteem more highly than the original external Sun, for we would stand in conscious, free relation to our Spirit.

Kenneth Burke was having none of it. Timothy W. Crusius is correct in reminding us what Burke clearly realized: while we may be doomed to dialectic because we are creatures using language as a symbolic act, we do not have to be confined by any one version of it. For Burke, as Crusius points out, dialectic was not lurking either above or below, was not waiting for us to witness it as a reflection of any Spirit's agenda.[2] Burke's project was directed *ad bellum purificandum*, and the purification of war that he sought would be accomplished by encouraging tolerance through speculation. By 1945, when Burke published *A Grammar of Motives*, it was clear that the Alexanders and Caesars and Napoleons of this earth had caused enough damage by believing that, ever close to the fountainhead of Spirit, they were acting as agents during a ripe time. So Burke offered, as Crusius points out, a kind of praxis philosophy, language-centered in nature, that would allow us to identify a relative permanence that was, all contingencies considered, good enough. Burke's philosophical plan was, he hoped, an aid to help us "take delight in the Human Barnyard, with its addiction to the Scramble, an area that would cause us great unhappiness could we not transcend it by appreciation, classifying and tracing back to their beginnings in Edenic simplicity those modes of suasion that often seem little better than malice and lie." If we study our acts, he believed, we should be able to "see our own lives as a kind of rough first draft that lends itself at least somewhat to revision, as we may hope at last to temper the extreme rawness of our ambitions, once we become aware of the ways in which we are the victims of our own and one another's magic."[3] That, he believed, was the best we can hope for if we are to avoid the dissipation that is content to take whatever opportunities are handy and if we are to resist the fanaticism that would impose a singular terminology upon the whole world.

As should we all be. Now that the remorseless certainty of the great analytic systems—and the rhetorical methods that allowed their construction and deconstruction—are gone, the most appropriate action is, following Burke, to embrace systems that help us call the plays (or at least understand which plays are being called). For my salt pork part, I would think that, *ad bellum purificandum*, we would all be better off to seek relative permanence by identifying those language features that let us know when useful systems have existed in the past, how they are working out in the present, and what the chances are that similar systems may be secured in the future. What else can I do? With C. S. Lewis, I am the product of long corridors, empty sunlit rooms, and indoor silences. Also, of endless books. The similarity, of course, ends there: blessings and isolation fall differently to each across culture and class. A laboring father, doting mother, adoring grandparents, the Immaculate Heart nuns of the Roman Catholic grammar school and the Sacred Heart brothers and uniformed soldiers of the private high school—all made my success their desire as the tests (so many of them!) measured the loving support given in my home (rather than my borderline intelligence) and allowed a seat in college.

Perspective: Documenting the Scenes

As a postPhilosophical writer, I was in a dilemma as I wrote this history. My laptop was surrounded by voices, and hypervigilance was the order of the day. In the stack to my left were the theory texts. Hayden White's *The Content of the Form: Narrative Discourse and Historical Representation* was here, warning that rendering narrative is no simple task. Underneath were the new historicists, reminding, as Stephen Greenblatt believes, that we must abandon a stable, mimetic theory of art and attempt to formulate an interpretative model that will reveal "the hidden places of negotiation and change."[4] Articles taking the pulse of theory—such as W. T. J. Mitchell and Wang Ning's "The Ends of Theory: The Beijing Symposium on Critical Inquiry"—were also at hand. In the first pile, then, was a heap of information that suggested that, if not careful, I might well get on my horse and ride off in all directions at once. In the stack in front of me were volumes by those who have chosen to apply the ideas of the theorists to the specific job of writing histories of rhetoric. Here I have placed texts such as *Writing Histories of Rhetoric*, edited by Victor J. Vitanza. The advice is copious:

recognize that "*all uses of language exact a price and trying to avoid paying the price may be very expensive indeed*" (Hans Kellner), make lack of assurance a constructive partner (John Schilb), and wage war against representative anecdotes, against dialectic, and against The Truth and Author/ity (Vitanza).[5] The material in the second stack made me long for the traditional historiography of Herodotus: it may have been deeply flawed, but at least it allowed a basic narrative to emerge. Clearly, Roy Jenkins didn't sweat this stuff. And neither did James Berlin, who realized, with Burke, that one's terministic screens were a part of one's epistemology and that smart readers could identify the blind spots.[6] Which leads to the third stack, to my right, where I set the actual histories, books such as Arthur N. Applebee's *Tradition and Reform in the Teaching of English: A History*, James A. Berlin's *Writing Instruction in Nineteenth-Century American Colleges* and *Rhetoric and Reality: Writing Instruction in American Colleges, 1900–1985* (and, tucked into the first volume, Robert J. Connors' review accusing Berlin of cooking history in order to make polemical points), Mary Trachsel's *Institutionalizing Literacy: The Historical Role of College Entrance Examinations in English*, and David R. Russell's *Writing in the Academic Disciplines*. Here nearby was John C. Brereton's invaluable documentary history, *The Origins of Composition Studies in the American College, 1875-1925*. I also had in this pile of books the essays in David R. Shumway and Craig Dionne's *Disciplining English: Alternative Histories, Critical Perspectives*. Here, too, were the books that remind us of the impact of instruction, important books such as Marilyn S. Sternglass' *Time to Know Them: A Longitudinal Study of Writing and Learning at the College Level* and Deborah Brandt's *Literacy in American Lives*. (And, at a safe distance, was Louis Menand's *The Metaphysical Club: A Story of Ideas in America*, a book with the power to transform writers into readers.) And, of course, at my back were the primary texts themselves, calling out with the loudest voices of all to be heard: metal filing cabinets with hundreds upon hundreds of photocopied primary texts, borrowed and interlibrary loan books with the due dates swiftly passing, taped interviews waiting to be transcribed. After all, whatever was in these documents is the reason I developed an interest in the subject twenty years ago after Miriam Levin, senior examiner at the Educational Testing Service, tactfully suggested that my talents might be better used in the Brigham Library.

To quell the voices and get on with the business of writing, I adopted, finally, an attitude toward the subject rather than a strategy of action. I recognized that any rhetorical position (including my own) had true costs, but I also wanted to avoid grand systems of interpretative categorization. I did not want to advance an argument but, rather, wanted to document those historic occasions in which communities met to investigate writing ability. I wanted to write such a history for the reasons given by Kellner—to serve the past with a sense of gratitude and to rectify the neglect of past exclusions. Following Plutarch, I wanted to write lives; and with Santayana, I wanted to avoid the doom that forever accompanies forgetfulness. Yet whether we believe we are witnessing the manifestation of Spirit, the march of capitalism, the failure of communication, or the end of days does not make much difference if our primary interest rests in advancing an argument. If we are more interested in proposing rather than understanding, then something or other is going to get badly nuanced. So I tried to keep my interpretive urges out of the narrative and, following Edmund Husserl's lead, bracketed out all first impulses. I thought about Richard E. Palmer's thirty theses on interpretation, reminders that truth is never total or unambiguous and that the phenomenon, not the method, should lead. I wrote with the belief that thinking about association is far better than quibbling about cause-and-effect relationships. I slavishly documented primary texts so that others could recover and investigate for themselves the details that I uncovered, but I confined to the footnotes the voices of those who had dealt with the texts I was investigating simply because their own interpretive voice interrupted the narrative I was working to preserve. I realized that basic chronology was essential and that, unless I were going to post a website of scanned documents with computer-generated animation that rotated the links, I needed to establish periodization. (I may have been in love with Heraclites, but I was nevertheless seriously attracted to Aristotle when it came to assembling chapters.) I wrote with an enormous respect for my reader, who could figure out what I had done wrong, sniff out my agendas, and see the documents I ushered forth for their own worth.

What naïveté, people will say, to assume that an entire book could have been written as if interpretation were not present with each word choice, within each event selected! My response is simple: again, any rhetorical position has true costs. But to document with an argument in mind obscures, and to have written solely to present an interpretation would have badly interrupted the process of bringing forth the very events I sought to capture. As Robert Coles reminds us in *Doing Documentary Work*, the noun *document* is derived from the Latin *docere*, to teach. As is the case with all the classroom work I have ever done, I knew the risks in presenting ideas, in offering evidence, and in resolving tensions. But I wanted to write something honest and genuine in honor of a field which had been so kind to me. I just couldn't help myself.

The Nature of Association

In that I wanted to assemble rather than argue, to follow in my grandfather's and father's tradition of the *bricoleur* (the carpenter and factory worker, the skilled Jack-of-all-trades) producing a *bricolage* (furniture and machinery, a set of representations fitted to situations), I used the following table to help me keep track of the events I identified in the history of collaborative writing assessment. Burke's Dramatic Pentad, the famous system of placement that permits us to appreciate the scope and complexity of a subject, granted a framework through which I could establish associations and produce a narrative.

Burke had started to define his system with the notion of writing a theory of comedy applied to the foibles and antics of the modern world. The more appreciation and less excoriation the better, he imagined. He began with basic set of generative forms of thought that could be embodied, trivially or profoundly, in order to answer a basic question: What is involved when we say what people are doing and why they are doing it? He set five terms: scene (the background of the act, the situation in which it occurred), act (what took place in thought or deed), agent (what person, or kind of person, performed the act), purpose (the elusive aspect of motivation), and agency (the means or instruments employed in the Human Barnyard). But the project became complex. There was a rhetorical side to the project, a you and me aspect; and there was a symbolic side as well in the matter of appeal. The groundwork kept extending its claim until the few hundred words Burke had written to establish the theory had spun into the nearly 200,000 words of *A Grammar of Motives*. What had begun as a set of terms that could be understood at a glance was completed at the Institute for Advanced Study with the support of J. Robert Oppenheimer. Burke was, or course, characteristically clear. His was not an empirical treatment, a study at one with the high development of technological specialization or with its attendant involvement with the rationale of accountancy. Rather, his was a philosophical project.

Employing Burke's philosophical project as best I could, I have documented the major formal investigations in the history of writing assessment on pages 317–336. The impulse to assemble the circumstances surrounding each event led to the need for placing each in its social context. The groundwork indeed kept extending its claim. I was not naïve enough to think that the cultural object of study was completely accessible within a particular event, but I do believe that I have identified areas of shared meaning within certain historical contexts. [7] There remains much to learn.[8]

A History of Writing Assessment: Investigations

Scene (The Background of the Act)	Act (What Took Place)	Agent (Who Performed the Act)	Purpose (The Motives Behind the Act)	Agency (The Means Used)
1874	For the first time, every applicant for admission to Harvard was required to submit an English composition on topics from specific literary works.	Harvard University	It was hoped that the student would require a taste for good reading, would adopt better methods of thought and forms of expression, would be led to seek subjects for composition in the books named, and would pay closer attention to errors.	"To bring himself below the line of failure and success, a writer had to commit several serious faults; and even if he did commit such faults, he was allowed to pass if he offset them by tolerably good work in the rest of his book." In June 1879, of the 316 candidates taking the examination, 157 failed to pass (Hill, "An Answer" 49).
1901	Uniform college entrance requirements were established in English.	College Entrance Examination Board	The requirements were an attempt to introduce "law and order into an educational anarchy which towards the close of the nineteenth-century had become exasperating, indeed, almost intolerable, to schoolmasters" (Fuess 3).	Because the passing mark for the smaller colleges was 50 (and for some of the larger universities was 60), any paper falling in these ranges was re-read by one or more readers before a permanent rating was given. Because prizes were given for any paper marked over 90, those papers were also re-read. Papers between 60 and 90 were never re-read (L. T. Hopkins 13).

A History of Writing Assessment: Investigations

Scene (The Background of the Act)	Act (What Took Place)	Agent (Who Performed the Act)	Purpose (The Motives Behind the Act)	Agency (The Means Used)
1911	The Scale for Merit in English writing by young people was developed.	Edward L. Thorndike, Milo Hillegas, and Marion R. Trabue at Teachers College, Columbia University	The researchers worked to develop a scale of writing ability. "Such a scale would obviously be of great value to teachers, civil service examiners, college entrance boards, scientific students of education and others who need to measure the merit of specimens of English writing in order to estimate the abilities of individuals or changes in such abilities as the result of mental maturity, educational effort and other causes" (Thorndike, "A Scale for Merit in English Writing by Young People" 361); "No attempt has been made in this scale to define merit. The term as here used means just that quality which competent persons commonly consider as merit, and the scale measures just this quality" (Hillegas 9).	"The scale is composed of sample English compositions, the qualities of which have been determined by more than four hundred competent judges" (Hillegas 9).

A History of Writing Assessment: Investigations

Scene (The Back-ground of the Act)	Act (What Took Place)	Agent (Who Performed the Act)	Purpose (The Motives Behind the Act)	Agency (The Means Used)
1918	Psychological examinations were given in the United States Army during World War I. Literacy tests were given before the psychological examinations to separate literate from illiterate recruits.	Robert M. Yerkes and colleagues	The psychological examiners in the Army used literacy tests in order to separate literate from illiterate recruits.	The use of the Thorndike Reading Scale, Kelley Literacy Test, and the Devens Literacy Test yielded results in which 30% of recruits (386,196) were identified as illiterate (Yerkes, *Psychological Examining* 745).
1926	The Scholastic Aptitude Test was first given on June 23.	Carl Campbell Brigham for the College Entrance Examination Board	The test items were seen as symbols of error. Detailed information concerning error provided the means to eradicate them. "From this point of view, therefore, test findings would not be constructed as necessarily revealing unalterable psychological characteristics of the individual, but merely as exposing what is happening to the individual in his culture" (Brigham, *A Study of Error* 46).	In 1926, nine sections were included on the SAT: definitions; arithmetical problems; classification; artificial language; antonyms; number series completion; analogies; logical inference; paragraph reading.

A History of Writing Assessment: Investigations

Scene (The Back-ground of the Act)	Act (What Took Place)	Agent (Who Performed the Act)	Purpose (The Motives Behind the Act)	Agency (The Means Used)
1934	A study of the Comprehensive Examinations in English from 1929 to 1933 was published.	Carl Campbell Brigham for the College Entrance Examination Board	"The purpose of this document is to set forth publicly the 'inside' information which first caused the change [in the evaluation process for scoring the Comprehensive Examination] and to report in detail the results of the investigations of the 1933 readings which have been proceeding continuously for the last five months" (Brigham, *The Reading of the Comprehensive Examination in English* 1).	Both inter-reader agreement and correlations varied from 1929 to 1932. The 1933 reading was designed to eliminate sources of error, but the correlations between the first and second reading of the questions asked on the Comprehensive Examination (.52, .56, .56, .48, and .49, on the six examination questions,) were too unreliable to be reported (26). As a solution, Brigham stressed better reader selection: "If one were able to select only those readers whose judgment correlated higher than .60 with the group judgment on questions one, three, and four, and higher than .50 with the group judgment on questions five and six, the general reliability of the reading would be greatly increased. A selection of superior readers only would give a more homogeneous and consistent group against which the reliability of a single reader could be tested" (30).

A History of Writing Assessment: Investigations

Scene (The Background of the Act)	Act (What Took Place)	Agent (Who Performed the Act)	Purpose (The Motives Behind the Act)	Agency (The Means Used)
1938	The *Report on the English Examination of June 1937* demonstrated effective examination procedures.	Edward S. Noyes and John M. Stalnaker for the College Entrance Examination Board	"The purpose of this Bulletin is to describe in detail the methods of preparing, holding, and reading the comprehensive English examinations of 1937"(5).	Improved scoring methods led to a correlation of .84 on all six questions of the Comprehensive Examination. (The theme reliability was .68.) While the overall .84 correlation was "somewhat lower than that obtained in other subjects," reliabilities as high as .84 were considered "rare." "It is hoped that the new method of reading will, when it is perfected, yield reader reliabilities approximating those in other subjects" (50).
1943	The Qualifying Test for Civilians was given to approximately 316,000 high-school and college-age men on April 2.	John M. Stalnaker and Henry Chauncey for the College Entrance Examination Board	The Qualifying Test was given to institute a nation-wide screening program that would measure and assess students for the Navy College Training Program.	150 multiple-choice questions were used to test verbal, scientific, reading, and mathematical ability (Stuit 109).

A History of Writing Assessment: Investigations				
Scene (The Back-ground of the Act)	**Act (What Took Place)**	**Agent (Who Performed the Act)**	**Purpose (The Motives Behind the Act)**	**Agency (The Means Used)**
1945	"When, under wartime conditions, the acceleration of college courses forced the abandonment of the old June sessions of three-hour comprehensive examinations, the series of aptitude and achievement tests offered as a substitute was at first entirely objective in type [in 1942]" (5). In 1943, an essay test alone was introduced. The 1945 *Report on the First Six Tests in English Composition* noted problems with examination procedures.	Edward S. Noyes, William Merritt Sale, Jr., and John M. Stalnaker for the College Entrance Examination Board	In 1943 the Board included a one-hour test in English composition. The report was written so that "teachers and administrators in school and college understand the special problems presented by a one-hour test in composition" and the efforts being made toward solutions (5).	Procedures established to read the essay alone produced correlations ranging from .58 to .83 in the six examination periods, with an average reliability of .67. "Reliabilities of reading should be of the order of .85 or higher before the reading can be deemed satisfactory" (67).

A History of Writing Assessment: Investigations

Scene (The Background of the Act)	Act (What Took Place)	Agent (Who Performed the Act)	Purpose (The Motives Behind the Act)	Agency (The Means Used)
1948	Formal investigation into the ability to write was initiated at the newly formed Educational Testing Service (ETS), chartered January 1, 1948, for the College Entrance Examination Board	Edith Huddleston at ETS for the College Entrance Examination Board from 1947 to 1954	A series of studies was designed to answer two questions: What is the ability to write? How can that ability be measured? (Huddleston, "Recent Studies of the English Composition Test." 45).	A series of correlation studies was designed with the criterion variables identified as instructor's ratings of students and English course grades (Huddleston, "Measurement of Writing Ability at the College-Entrance Level" 190–191). Correlations such as .76 and .77 between the SAT and the respective criterion measures led Huddleston to conclude that writing ability is "no more than verbal ability" that is best measured by multiple-choice tests (204). Inter-reader reliability for three essays was estimated at .78 and interpreted as "low" (179–180), leading Huddleston to conclude that there was "a stone wall blocking future progress" on the use of valid and reliable essay examinations (204).

A History of Writing Assessment: Investigations

Scene (The Background of the Act)	Act (What Took Place)	Agent (Who Performed the Act)	Purpose (The Motives Behind the Act)	Agency (The Means Used)
1950	The College Entrance Examination Board invited its member colleges to construct and administer "a composition test which would be, in fact, a composition test, but which would be graded in a way designed to reduce the hazards of reader unreliability" (*Fiftieth Annual Report of the Director* 3).	Earle G. Eley for the College Entrance Examination Board from 1950 to 1956	The College Entrance Examination Board responded to lobbying from its 115 member colleges to create tests "which require that the candidate write a composition which would be judged on both technical and literary standards." The direct tests were seen as different from Huddleston's "symptomatic tests," which judged students on "technical standards" alone (3).	The General Composition Test was designed to minimize subject matter differences by giving students reading passages. Essays were scored on five qualities and produced inter-reader reliability scores of .88. However, in 1955 the process of resolving discrepant readings was debated (a failure of reliability), and the General Composition Test did not correlate as well as the SAT with teachers' judgments of their students (a failure of validity). The test was dropped in 1956.

A History of Writing Assessment: Investigations

Scene (The Background of the Act)	Act (What Took Place)	Agent (Who Performed the Act)	Purpose (The Motives Behind the Act)	Agency (The Means Used)
1951	The Selective Service College Qualifying Test was given to 330,042 candidates during the four 1951 testing dates.	ETS	Deferment from the draft to ensure an educated pool of scientists and engineers was initiated on March 31, 1951, by President Truman.	Candidates were told that the test "examines your ability to read with an understanding and to solve new problems by using your general knowledge" (from SSCQT, *Bulletin of Information*). Questions based on reading comprehension, verbal relations, arithmetic reasoning, and data interpretation yielded a 64% pass rate in the first series and a 58% pass rate in the second series.
1952	The Tests of Developed Ability were designed at ETS.	William E. Coffman at ETS for the College Entrance Examination Board	The emerging emphasis on general education in colleges would, the College Board believed in 1949, lead to new tests for college admissions.	A panel of content-area experts designed both objective and essay questions to evaluate the "expected outcomes" of instruction (Coffman, "Development of the Tests" 7). High correlations with the SAT suggested the Tests of Developed Abilities were duplicative of the SAT. The Tests of Developed Abilities were abandoned in 1957.

A History of Writing Assessment: Investigations

Scene (The Background of the Act)	Act (What Took Place)	Agent (Who Performed the Act)	Purpose (The Motives Behind the Act)	Agency (The Means Used)
1954	The Advanced Placement Program was added to the list of tests offered by the College Board.	Originally sponsored by the Ford Foundation's Fund for the Advancement of Education, the articulation between high-school and college courses was begun as the Kenyon Plan by Kenyon College's president, Gordon Keith Chalmers.	The 1952 publication of *The Republic and the Person* revealed that more could be done to advance talented students in their transition from high school to college. By 1954 the *College Board Review* formulated the program's purpose: "to encourage superior preparation of college candidates in the secondary schools by providing a method whereby able students with superior training can demonstrate their proficiency and quality for advanced placement" (2).	The development of written examinations linked to courses in areas such as English involved 532 candidates from eighteen schools in the spring of 1954.

A History of Writing Assessment: Investigations				
Scene (The Back-ground of the Act)	**Act (What Took Place)**	**Agent (Who Performed the Act)**	**Purpose (The Motives Behind the Act)**	**Agency (The Means Used)**
1961	A study of judgments that readers make when evaluating student essays was published.	Paul B. Diederich, John W. French, and Sydell T. Carlton at ETS; research supported by funding from the Carnegie Corporation	"The purpose of this study was to serve as a stepping stone toward closer agreement among judges of student writing at the point of admission to college by revealing common causes of disagreement" (Abstract). After the failure of the General Composition Test, it was agreed within ETS that "further progress in grading essays must wait upon a factor analysis of the judgments of a diverse group of competent readers in an unstructured situation, where each could grade as he liked" (3).	The study employed factor analysis techniques and identified five "schools of thought" in the judgment of essays written by college freshmen: ideas, form, flavor, mechanics, and wording (French, "Schools of Thought in Judging Excellence of English Themes" 6).

A History of Writing Assessment: Investigations

Scene (The Background of the Act)	Act (What Took Place)	Agent (Who Performed the Act)	Purpose (The Motives Behind the Act)	Agency (The Means Used)
1966	"This study was an attempt to compare the validities of item types commonly used in the English Composition Test of the College Entrance Examination Board" ("A Study of the English Composition Tests" 1). The research was completed in 1961. The final report, *The Measurement of Writing Ability*, was published in 1966.	Fred I. Godshalk, Frances Swineford, and William E. Coffman at ETS for the College Entrance Examination Board	The experiment, conducted among eleventh- and twelfth-grade students in twenty-four secondary schools, was to become something more than "just another" validity study in that the item types were to be "related to a logically sound criterion of writing performance, consisting of five 'work samples' of free writing" (Swineford and Godshalk, "Memorandum for All Concerned" 2).	The criterion of writing performance was to be evaluated by papers read holistically. The reliability of the reading ranged from .758 to .777. A study of correlations was prepared of the various measures used in the study. Inclusion of the essays increased the multiple correlations among the item types with the essays "from .756 to .767 for seniors and from .733 to .796 among juniors" who had been classified according to performance criteria (34). The researchers concluded that there was strong evidence that a 20-minute essay would not only maintain the current high validity of the English Composition Test as a measure of writing ability but would probably increase such validity when used with objective questions ("A Study of the English Composition Tests" 36).

A History of Writing Assessment: Investigations				
Scene (The Back-ground of the Act)	**Act (What Took Place)**	**Agent (Who Performed the Act)**	**Purpose (The Motives Behind the Act)**	**Agency (The Means Used)**
1973	On May 12, 1973, the California State University Freshman Equivalence Examination was administered to 4,071 students.	Edward M. White and colleagues from the California State University English Departments	In 1971 White and his colleagues defeated an administrative attempt to institute a multiple-choice test that would yield scores revealing if entering freshmen students could receive credit for freshman composition.	After successful political resistance, the California State University system implemented a faculty-designed Freshman Equivalence Examination that included both multiple-choice and direct assessment techniques.
1974	Writing samples were scored by both holistic and primary trait methods for The National Assessment of Educational Progress (NAEP), a Congressionally mandated, continuing national assessment designed to measure educational performance of elementary-, middle-, and high-school students.	Richard Lloyd-Jones and colleagues for the National Assessment of Educational Progress	"NAEP designed the writing tasks to reflect the differing purposes for which people write at home, at school, and in the community" (Applebee, et al., *Writing Trends Across the Decade*, 1974-84 5).	Primary trait scoring was developed to isolate particular features of writing essential to accomplishing the task; holistic scoring was used to provide an estimate of relative fluency. From 1974 to 1984, the inter-reader correlations were reported from .73 to .95; the holistic score inter-reader correlations were reported from .71 to .94 (67–69).

A History of Writing Assessment: Investigations

Scene (The Background of the Act)	Act (What Took Place)	Agent (Who Performed the Act)	Purpose (The Motives Behind the Act)	Agency (The Means Used)
1981	The first international writing study examined the teaching and learning of written composition in the schools of 14 countries: Chile, England, Finland, Federal Republic of Germany (Hamburg), Hungary, Indonesia, Italy, The Netherlands, New Zealand, Nigeria, Sweden, Thailand, the United States, and Wales (3).	Alan C. Purves and colleagues for the International Association for the Evaluation of Educational Achievement (IEA)	The IEA International Study of Written Composition was designed to contribute to the conceptualization of the domain of writing, to develop an internationally appropriate set of writing tasks, to describe recent development in written composition, and to identify factors which explain differences and patterns in performance (Gorman, Purves, Degenhart 8). Writing scripts were obtained from 116,597 students.	Fourteen writing tasks were constructed: six pragmatic tasks addressed to a known audience; four common learning tasks (e.g., summarizing, paraphrasing, description of an object, describing a process); two tasks in which students had to organize and generate their own view of externally observable and internally experienced reality; and two tasks in which students persuaded the reader (30–31). The complex analytic scoring technique worked well in the national comparisons, producing correlation coefficients between .83 and .91 (69), but the international comparison proved complex because of the use of different scoring scales. Female students were found to be successful as academic writers, and home culture influenced writing performance.

A History of Writing Assessment: Investigations

Scene (The Background of the Act)	Act (What Took Place)	Agent (Who Performed the Act)	Purpose (The Motives Behind the Act)	Agency (The Means Used)
1982	Task structure was investigated as a basis for understanding test performance.	Edys S. Quellmalz and colleagues at the Center for the Study of Evaluation, University of California, Los Angeles	The study addressed "two salient measurement issues concerned with the structure of competency-based writing assessment tasks and resulting performance" (241). The first issue addressed whether alternative discourse aims of writing tasks "tap different cognitive skills and produce different levels of performance." The second issue was "whether the indirect (recognition) and direct (production) response modes are task features that elicit different strategies and yield different profiles of writing competence" (241–242).	"The generalizability coefficients across rater and topics for the [five] subscales [used to rate the essays] ranged from .70 to .84. Considering the rater pairs separately, the median generalizability coefficients for the two rater pairs were .61 and .83" (246). Lower ratings were assigned to narrative essays on all five subscales and total scores (248). The relationship between indirect and direct response modes was affected by which response mode was included in the analysis. "In summary, the study highlights the importance of precision in designing, analyzing and reporting writing assessment data" (256).
1982	A writing portfolio project was proposed at ETS.	Roberta Camp for the Educational Testing Service	The project was intended to provide a comprehensive measure of writing ability for secondary-school students, to improve curricula, and to facilitate the transition from secondary to postsecondary institutions.	The project was structured to field test tasks for portfolio design and to determine appropriate scales and methods of scoring.

A History of Writing Assessment: Investigations				
Scene (The Back-ground of the Act)	**Act (What Took Place)**	**Agent (Who Performed the Act)**	**Purpose (The Motives Behind the Act)**	**Agency (The Means Used)**
1983	Writing portfolio experiments were begun at SUNY Stony Brook.	Peter Elbow and Pat Belanoff at SUNY Stony Brook	"In retrospect, what was striking was an urgent and growing pressure for assessment, assessment, assessment; test everyone and everything again and again; give everything and everyone a score; don't trust teachers." The events at Stony Brook "were a paradigm of the times. The faculty senate had decided several years earlier not to trust the grades given by first year writing teachers" and therefore mandated a proficiency exam. Because Elbow and Belanoff resisted the system, they were "driven to find an alternative" (Elbow and Belanoff, "Reflections" 22–23).	A process of collaboration and negotiation was introduced in the freshman English curriculum. Instructors evaluated three revised pieces of writing and one in-class essay on a pass or fail basis. A second reading occurred only in cases in which the instructor disagreed with the evaluation. "What was central to our experiment was to move portfolios outside the individual classroom so that they would be read by someone else in addition to the classroom teacher" (24).

A History of Writing Assessment: Investigations				
Scene (The Back-ground of the Act)	**Act (What Took Place)**	**Agent (Who Performed the Act)**	**Purpose (The Motives Behind the Act)**	**Agency (The Means Used)**
1987	A replication was undertaken of the Godshalk, Swineford, and Coffman study.	Hunter M. Breland and colleagues at ETS for the College Board	The study was an "attempt to determine the most effective method for assessing the kind of writing skill needed in college courses in English composition" (*Assessing Writing Skill* vii).	Two hundred and sixty-seven students were asked to write six essays each in narrative, expository, and persuasive modes. Six multiple-choice test scores were also collected for each student. The reliability estimate for a single essay read twice was .53 (60). A procedure used to estimate the analysis of variance for various sources of error yielded an estimate of .876 (26). The study confirmed and extended the Quellmalz study but also found that specific topics within specific aims related to different factors of ability. The results confirmed the Godshalk study in that the use of a multiple-choice test with an essay assessment yielded a multiple correlation of .71 (59). Thus, "the best estimates of students' writing abilities are obtained through tests that combine essay assessments and multiple choice assessments" (61).

A History of Writing Assessment: Investigations

Scene (The Back-ground of the Act)	Act (What Took Place)	Agent (Who Performed the Act)	Purpose (The Motives Behind the Act)	Agency (The Means Used)
1987	Susan McLeod began a first-year composition portfolio examination, similar to Pat Belanoff and Peter Elbow's system [begun in 1983] at SUNY Stony Brook (Haswell 207).	Richard Haswell, Richard Law, Susan McLeod, William Condon, and colleagues at Washington State University	To address perceived lack of writing competence of undergraduates, the university initiated a writing program with a qualifying examination (207).	The portfolio assessment is embedded within a university-wide writing program with a Writing Center, Writing Assessment, and Writing Across the Curriculum.
1998	A prototype for automated scoring systems was developed based on features of writing as specified in holistic rubrics.	Jill Burstein and colleagues for the Educational Testing Service	"This study was conducted to explore the extent to which essays could be automatically rated using features that reflected the 6-point holistic rubrics used by human raters to assign scores to essays" (Burstein, et al., 4).	An electronic program, e-rater, was designed to score argumentative and issue-related essay responses to the GMAT Analytic Writing Assessments. The program achieved a 93% agreement with human rater scores and demonstrated the ability to generate diagnostic and instructional information.

A History of Writing Assessment: Investigations

Scene (The Background of the Act)	Act (What Took Place)	Agent (Who Performed the Act)	Purpose (The Motives Behind the Act)	Agency (The Means Used)
2002	The College Board announced plans to redesign the SAT to include a handwritten short essay.	The College Board	"The changes we are making now will improve the alignment of the SAT to curriculum and instructional practices in high schools and colleges" (College Board, "New SAT 2005").	In response to criticism from the University of California and others that the SAT did not reflect classroom practice, the College Board announced a revamping of the test to include a handwritten short essay and multiple-choice writing questions. (Lewin).
2004	The *New SAT Writing Prompt Study: Analyses of Group Impact and Reliability* was published.	Hunter Breland and colleagues at ETS for the College Board	To investigate the impact on ethnic, language, and gender groups of a new kind of essay prompt type intended for use with the SAT: Reasoning Test in 2005.	The study investigated the impact of essay prompt types for the new 2005 SAT. Two prompt types were used: prompts from the SAT II: Writing Subject Tests; and modification of these prompts that provided more information on the topic and encouraged persuasive writing. Results of the impact analyses revealed no significant prompt type effects for ethnic, gender, or language groups. The study also revealed that students should expect that their scores may change appreciably if they take the same kind of essay test again within a few months.

A History of Writing Assessment: Investigations

Scene (The Back-ground of the Act)	Act (What Took Place)	Agent (Who Performed the Act)	Purpose (The Motives Behind the Act)	Agency (The Means Used)
2005	The College Board launched the new SAT I Writing Section.	Wayne Camara, Brian Bremen, and colleagues for the College Board	"The changes in the SAT —especially the inclusion of an writing section with an essay—are part of a commitment by the College Board to play a leading role in this 'Writing Revolution'" (*A Guide to the New SAT® Essay*)	The new SAT writing section was designed to include both multiple-choice items (35 minutes) and a student-written essay (25 minutes).The multiple-choice writing questions were designed to measure a student's ability to improve sentences and paragraphs and identify errors (such as diction, grammar, sentence construction, subject-verb agreement, proper word usage, and wordiness). The short essay was designed to measure a student's ability to organize and express ideas clearly, develop and support a main idea, and use appropriate word choice and sentence structure.

And so, of course, the table is not complete. Much more historical investigation into writing assessment deserves to be undertaken. And so, as with Laurence Sterne in *Tristram Shandy*, I invite readers to insert their own findings here in order to establish other important investigations. (That failing, descriptions of the Widow Wadman's beauty are welcome.)

Key Moments in the History of Writing Assessment: In Which the Reader Furthers the Documentary Effort				
Scene (The Background of the Act)	**Act (What Took Place)**	**Agent (Who Performed the Act)**	**Purpose (The Motives Behind the Act)**	**Agency (The Means Used)**

If following Plutarch, Santayana, or Kellner speaks to your condition, there is much to be done. And don't worry too much about your agenda: your reader will, if you do your job, be as interested in looking at the primary documents as in nailing down your ideologies. Readers really are terribly smart.

An Interpretation of Association: Context

By now, it should be clear that I believe that the history of writing assessment is best understood, in Burke's terms, as an agent-agency ratio occurring within a specified scene. In that the ratios are principles of determination for Burke, I would argue that the best way to look at this history is within the context of individuals and influences. Within these scenes, I believe that the following is generally true regarding the synchronic history of writing assessment as it is embedded within the scene of American education: that at the close of the nineteenth century Americans engineered a new society in which the College Entrance Examination Board and its tests became integral to the educational mission of that society, and that this period of societal engineering lasted well into the 1950s; that the 1960s witnessed a rhythm of rebellion that questioned the impact of all that engineering, and that this radical shift of perspective is evident in the strategy of Godshalk and his colleagues in their design of an experiment in which student writing itself, individual acts of a formerly disenfranchised group (so much *parole*) became the criterion against which other assessment forms were to be evaluated; that the 1970s marked a period in which rebellion ushered in reform, in which the gains of civil disobedience were made permanent through legislation, in which mandates such as the National Assessment of Educational Progress were established to evaluate and potentially ensure the literacy gains of a nation's schools; that the 1980s operationalized that legislation, often in ways—such as the demand for accountability witnessed by Peter Elbow and Pat Belanoff at their university—that obscured the very freedoms gained in the previous twenty years; and that the period from 1990 through 2005 led to new reforms which, in turn, led to broader interpretations of educational outcomes such as those found in the 1999 *Standards for Educational and Psychological Testing* regarding the validity and reliability of portfolio assessment.

But, at the very same time, I also know that there are specific truths in each period that falsify each of these general truths. An interpretation of emerging, informed progress implied by the general truths is not at all valid. In 2002, for example, Herbert J. Walberg, university scholar at the University of Illinois at Chicago, advocated the fairness and defensibility of machine-scored, multiple-choice tests with a passion that would have made Edith Huddleston of ETS blush.[9] The volume, *School Accountability: An Assessment by the Koret Task Force on K–12 Education*, contains Walberg's essay and others—all products of the Hoover Institution at Stanford University—and serves as a reminder that Peter Elbow's 1994 statement—that the composition community has "seriously discredited multiple-choice tests of writing" and has "convinced institutions, the public, and significant portions of the professional testing community to take portfolios seriously"—is open to debate: we may know the direction of the road, but getting to the end is another matter.[10]

There are many examples that serve to undermine myths of universal progress. Informed voices, for example, were present from the beginning. When scales were all the rage, the University of Illinois' Edward William Dolch, Jr., established in 1922 a critique of general excellence in writing that would easily answer Bob Broad's 2003 call for the profession to advance beyond rubrics in teaching and assessing writing. And Fred Newton Scott's 1912 presidential address before the 1912 National Council of Teachers of English is as lucid and compelling in its caution regarding measurement—"we ought to encourage Professor Thorndike and Dr. Hillegas in their attempts to provide us with a scale for the measurement of English compositions, but then when the scale is ready, we had better refrain from using it"—as the (re)articulation of writing assessment that would be advanced by Brian Huot ninety years later.[11] Agents advocating informed writing assessment methods were there from the beginning, and conservative forces remain present in full force on the contemporary scene.

As well, a look at the enduring nature of conflicting metaphors used in the assessment process does not allow an interpretation of progress. The mechanistic view of perception offered by Fullerton and Cattell in 1892 was adopted by Hillegas in the early twentieth century and endured through Braddock's chemical metaphor of 1963.[12] By 1986, Hillocks argued that such analogies were inappropriate. Researchers were not expected to discover laws, he assured his readers, but they may be able to predict the effects of certain practices with some accuracy. The mechanistic view of writing and its accompanying metaphors, drawn from the physical sciences, appeared to be safely dead. Yet in 1990 Edward M. White could easily validate that the reflex arc systems of understanding, informed by the same views of perception found in the work of Fullerton and Cattell, remained in full force. As White reminded his readers, the language of the educational assessment community was persistent in defining writing as a skill resting on component parts and expressed in measurable products. In the early twenty-first century world of the No Child Left Behind Act, for each writing assessment researcher who rejects mechanistic metaphor, an accountability advocate supplies a replacement by calling for increased gains through more testing. Two emblematic, conceptual epistemologies—those of Fullerton and Cattell's 1892 experimental apparatus and of Linda Flower's 1994 model of discourse construction—are always and everywhere before us.[13]

Such identification of pattern and notation of exception leads to the conclusion that in writing assessment, context is critical. The nation's wars, for example, are important to our understanding of the social history of writing assessment. America's entrance into World War I had an impact on Carl Campbell Brigham, and his work with the Canadian Military Hospitals Commission, at Camp Dix, and later with the Federal Board for Vocational Education led him to gain great familiarity with massive assessment systems. When Brigham returned to Princeton University in 1920, he simply had more assessment field experience than he ever would have had if America had not entered the war. His writing assessment work with the College Board demonstrated his great familiarity with large-scale assessment and his attempts to bring scientific practice to the new world of American educational accountability. America's entrance into World War II ushered in the rise of an efficiency movement in writing assessment. While English teachers protested, the power behind multiple-choice assessments, now scored by machine and correlated with multiple criterion measures, grew. America's entry into the Korean War, at a time in which the Educational Testing Service came into national prominence as the nation's leader in measurement, strengthened the impulse to efficient assessment. During the early 1960s, an era of war anxiety and protest, the complexities of direct assessment were re-introduced as the nation sought to problematize its complexities in the hope of a more democratized future. In writing assessment, the result of such creative tension led to the use of writing samples as a criterion measure (such sassiness!) and the invention of holistic scoring methods to evaluate those samples (so liberal!).

Individuals in each period—John Stalnaker during World War II, Paul B. Diederich during the Korean War, Fred Godshalk and William Coffman during the Vietnam War—were involved in institutions deeply committed to a national agenda of assessment. From the Great War to the Era of Protest, these individuals went into offices in which government work and educational work were carried on concurrently. As associate secretary of the College Board, Stalnaker served as general director of the Army-Navy Testing Program in 1944, coordinating the work of the young Henry Chauncey, the associate director of the Army-Navy Testing Program, while working with Edward Noyes and William Sale to report on the first six tests of English composition. Diederich wrote memos in 1951 to Henry Chauncey, now president of the Educational Testing Service, about the Selective Service College Qualifying Test, closed that folder, and opened another on educational evaluation. William Coffman's work records efforts both to design the Tests of Developed Ability in 1957 and to offer a proposal for the systematic study of cultural differences in SAT performance in 1962. And with them all was Frances Swineford, one of the longest-serving staff members at ETS, writing the statistical reports. All were individuals working within a national context, learning how to do things with assessment. As America moved through the turbulent twentieth century, these researchers carried writing assessment along with them.

Within such a synchronic context—from Harvard University's call for a written composition in 1874 to the College Board's addition of an essay section to the SAT in 2005—I have identified three master tropes in a diachronic perspective: the impulse for accountability, the struggle for methodological design, and the construction of literacy. Each deserves attention.

The Impulse for Accountability: The Rhetoric of Disenfranchisement

The desire to establish public accountability in education was emerging in 1874. The oral world of recitation, present in the Harvard University catalogue in 1873, was receding: reading aloud from *Vicar of Wakefield*, noted as a requirement in that catalogue, was gone. No more prizes were to be awarded for performance. In place was the silent, written proof of mastery: the essay. As Harvard University's new president in 1869, Charles Eliot had ushered in a new agenda for the unity of literature and science. Both fields, Eliot declared, promoted the material welfare of mankind. This material welfare was to be ensured, in the case of English composition, by means of instruction and writing. In 1879 Adams Sherman Hill documented, as would Charles F. Adams in 1892, the poor writing ability of entering students during the period before Eliot's reform. "Children who learned their ABC's under the old system could call the letters in a word by name, but were often unable to pronounce the same word, or to understand its meaning," he wrote. Students who were able to talk glibly about parts of speech "could not explain the sentences they took to pieces, or write grammatical sentences of their own." And as for the reading of essays,

> Those of us who have been doomed to read manuscript written in an examination room—whether at a grammar school, high school, or a college—have found the work of even good scholars disfigured by bad spelling, confusing punctuation, ungrammatical, obscure, ambiguous, or inelegant expressions. Every one who has had much to do with the graduating classes of our best colleges has known men who could not write a letter describing their own commencement without making blunders which would disgrace a boy of twelve years old.[14]

At first, other colleges developed different methods, a situation Wilson Farrand described as "extremely annoying" in his inaugural address as the new president of the Schoolmasters' Association of New York and Vicinity. His speech, "The Reform of College Requirements," called for uniform entrance requirements and for entrance examinations that were to be administered accurately, fairly, and wisely. To achieve these goals, he called for agitation and for legislation. Through the efforts of Eliot at Harvard University, Nicholas Murray Butler of Columbia University, and Farrand himself of Newark Academy, uniformity was achieved by May 12, 1900, the adoption date of the statement of subjects to be examined by the newly formed College Entrance Examination Board. By November 17, the Board had its first official meeting. By June 1901, 978 students had been examined.

The accountability movement in education had been concretized. With it, the collaborative assessment of literacy had also been established. Yet, instead of a balanced appraisal of the discoveries that such accountability yielded, only censure appeared. Whatever abilities existed were overshadowed by the students' failure to achieve excellence. In that distribution was required—student scores had to be distributed across a scale according to the Gaussian (normal) distribution—it was logically impossible for the majority of students to achieve scores at the very highest ends of the scale. Yet distribution mattered little: only the top of the scale mattered. In a rhetoric designed to disenfranchise students, accountability and censure were, from the first, interwoven.

Remarkably, the pattern endures today. On January 3, 2003, the *Chronicle of Higher Education*—alluding to the famous December 8, 1975, *Newsweek* story[15]—released "Why Johnny Can't Write, Even Though He Went to Princeton." Within the article were observations that students at Princeton University, Duke University, Columbia University, Brown University, Bowdoin College, and Harvard University lacked basic composition skills. "We've been hearing from faculty members that students are having trouble with their writing," complained a dean at Brown. What kind of trouble? "Professors cite a host of writing-related shortcomings among students, most often their inability to construct the sort of lengthy, sophisticated research papers required in upper-division courses."[16] In April of that year, the National Commission on Writing in America's Schools and Colleges published *The Neglected "R": The Need for a Writing Revolution*, a report sponsored by the College Board that documents the lack of writing ability on a national scale. Here were the latest findings from the National Assessment of Educational Progress, "the nation's report card," the authors remind us. The 1998 NAEP findings indicate, we are told, that about four out of five students in grades 4, 8, and 12 are at or above a basic level of writing. However, only about one-quarter of the students at each grade level are at or above the level of proficiency. Even more telling, only one in one hundred is thought to be writing at an advanced level. The NAEP data reveal that students can write and that they know language. That is, however, not enough. Students cannot, we are told, produce writing at the mature levels of skill and sophistication required in a complex, modern economy. While their grammar, spelling, and punctuation are not an utter disaster, the report's authors conclude, students cannot create precise, engaging, and coherent prose.

"Common as such shames were," Hill had written 124 years earlier, "they went on, not indeed without protest, but without criticism loud enough to disturb those through whom reform, if reform was to be, must come." For Hill, reform had to come from the schools that had produced such shameful students. For the National Commission on Writing and its readers, reform would result, in part, from the impact of the 2005 SAT essay. Hill had his goals, his "desirable objects": that the student would become familiar with works holding a high place in literature, that the student would acquire a taste for good reading, that the student would insensibly adopt better methods of thought and expression, that teachers would ask students to write about the books noted in the examination, and that teachers would attend to errors in elementary matters. The College Board, as well, had its goals: that the changes to the SAT would align the test to curriculum and instructional practices in high school and college, that predictive validity would be increased, that the new writing section would reinforce the importance of writing skills throughout a student's career, and that the new writing section would support the improvement of the academic preparation of all students, thus bolstering their chances of academic success.

In 1879, Hill had his results before him: there was change for the better, he believed, that had come from the 1874 examination. More work was done in the schools; greater proficiency was demanded for admission; the Harvard faculty had begun to accept the requirements in English as important; and many of the college instructors had begun to take account of student-written expression.

For the twenty-first century College Board, the results are yet to come. Perhaps we should prepare ourselves for an interpretation similar to Hill's regarding his Harvard students and wait for the shame to fall. Or perhaps the response will resemble that of the National Commission on Writing in America's Schools and Colleges regarding the NAEP data in which the earned proficiency of four out of five students was not good enough. Perhaps there will even be, as was the case with Adams' report of the Committee on Composition and Rhetoric, facsimile specimens. The new scoring process will, after all, use scanned samples posted to secure websites that will certainly be vulnerable to those seeking to download low-scoring essays—their error-ridden existence certain, media-ready proof of our failed educational system. Indeed, if the study of history offers lessons in prediction, we should brace ourselves for nightly news conclusions such as those drawn in 1892:

> What is the result? That result can be studied in the papers and facsimiles submitted as part of this report. There are eight printed papers and forty-two facsimiles,—the facsimiles being nearly ten per cent. of the whole number of papers handed in. In the judgment of your Committee the writer of not one of those forty-two facsimiles had received adequate, or even respectable preparatory training in a branch of instruction undeniably elementary, and one accordingly in which a fair degree of excellence should be a necessary requisite to a college course.[17]

But, of course, there will be solutions, just as there were in 1892 when "the remedy [was] within easy reach. At present a large corps of teachers have to be engaged and paid from the College treasury to do that which should have been done before the student presented himself for admission.

While teaching these so-called students to write their mother-tongue, these instructors pass years correcting papers a mere glance at which shows that the present preparatory training is grossly inadequate."[18] We have only to wait and to listen for the rhetoric of disenfranchisement to appear again.

The Struggle for Methodological Design: A Matter of Context

The ability to measure writing has been inextricably linked to inter-reader reliability, yet that very reliability was often identified as insufficient when correlations were obtained. In a circle that has been ever vicious, research regarding inter-reader reliability was undertaken, the correlations were found to be too low, and further inter-reader reliability research was begun that would be seen, again, as too low when the correlations were studied.

Consider the various inter-reader correlations noted in the table on pages 317–336. The College Board had been evaluating essay papers for thirty-three years when Brigham found that the correlations, ranging from .48 to .52, were too unreliable to yield accurate scores. Brigham set the goal of a correlation of .5 for the essay to increase the reliability of the reading. When Noyes and Stalnaker identified a theme reliability of .68 in 1938—higher than that set by Brigham—they were pleased and hopeful. In 1945, however, when there was only a theme to be read because of wartime constraints—the brief written answers had been replaced by objective-type questions—the inter-reader reliability average correlation of .67 was found to be unreliable. The essay had become a one-item test. With no other higher correlations to offset the essay correlations, .67 was found insufficient, and a new correlation was established by Noyes, Sale, and Stalnaker, one based on observed reliabilities for other Board tests, for sufficient inter-reader reliability: .85. (Recall that, as early as 1937, Stalnaker himself had noted in *School and Society* that other examinations—biology, chemistry, German, history, Latin, mathematics, physics, and Spanish—were read with reliabilities of over .98, so a .67 was quite far from the mark.) Edith Huddleston's research was filled with literature demonstrating that essays could not be read reliably, a fact confirmed in her own 1952 study in which correlations ranging from .47 to .67 were seen as low. The very process of resolving discrepant scores was called into question in the General Composition Test of 1950: the inter-reader correlations of .88 were discredited, and the test was abandoned in 1956 when it failed to correlate with other criterion-related measures such as the SAT and teachers' judgments of student ability. The 1961 study of the Godshalk team reported reader reliabilities from .739 to .777, and the essay itself correlated well with other measures of writing—a sense of criterion-related validity that had not appeared in the General Composition Test. As a result, Noyes himself declared that the reliability problem had been solved by the new method: holistic scoring. Yet Noyes himself had established .85 in 1945 as the standard, and the Godshalk study had failed to meet that correlation. The 1974 NAEP studies of holistic scoring reliabilities were as low as .71, yet readings were not invalidated, the scores continued to be reported, and policy decisions were made on the reports. Purves' IEA study, began in 1981, reported analytic scoring reliabilities between .83 and .91, yet the 1982 Quellmalz study on prompt design reported inter-reader reliabilities as low as .61 without apology. And the 1987 replication of the Godshalk study by Hunter Breland and his colleagues reported estimates of inter-reader reliability as .53—lower than that reported by the original 1961 study and almost as low as the Brigham study that raised the reliability issue in the first place fifty-three years earlier.

In the final decade of the twentieth century, the struggle for reliability remained evident. In the first issue of *Assessing Writing* in 1994, Grant Wiggins warned against sacrificing validity to reliability. While reliability of scoring may be achieved in assessment programs such as the NAEP, he noted that readers were being asked to judge only a crude story-telling format instead of looking for characteristics of a psychologically astute study. Yes, he acknowledged, reliability could be obtained; it was just that it wasn't worth much compared to the validity of the scoring procedures that were being sacrificed. In their 1999 analysis of reliability issues in holistic assessment, Roger D. Cherry and Paul R. Meyer wrote that "most psychometricians would be very uncomfortable about using a test with an instrument reliability of only .5 for making decisions about individuals." (After all, as Stalnaker reminded us decades before of a similar situation yielding a .5 correlation, how confident would any of us be in predicting someone's height if all we knew was their weight?) A correlation of .5, they find, is acceptable for making decisions between or among groups, but assessments about an individual writer should be higher than .5. "How high should instrument reliabilities be, then? In our view," they write, "a definitive answer to this question is not possible at this time. We need additional research on instrument reliability in different assessment situations before we begin to answer the question with any confidence." Indeed, even the practice of adjudication between discrepant scores is termed "a kind of fraud," a practice that "should be discontinued altogether in research and evaluation."[19]

Has everything that has been done in the ninety-eight years since the College Board's first assessment—all the national and state and local assessments, all the experimental work—been undertaken in conditions of such uncertainty? Is the assessment community so obsessed by reliability that its achievement remained, even in 1999, a subject still under debate? And if all we are able to muster is a list of differing reliability coefficients, what about all those lives that were being changed, all those students who found themselves on one side or the other of a cut score? What lives have been irrevocably altered under assessment conditions that were unreliable? Who makes the apologies, and who awards the reparations?

In writing this book, I have paid close attention to the reliability coefficients and have come to the only conclusion that can be reached: Where writing assessment is concerned, the assessment context must be understood as a unique event. This sense of context is not a goal for the future, something Brian Huot and Patricia Lynne correctly desire; rather, it is a demonstrated fact of the past. Sometimes, the inter-reader reliability event is understood to be so troubled that further measures are taken, such as Brigham's 1934 orders to have the essays related to a common frequency curve which related the marks in English to the Board's past experience in giving marks. Other times, one measure of reliability is offset by others, such as the 1938 reliability coefficient that Noyes and Stalnaker found as acceptable when related to other coefficients but unacceptable when standing alone. Still other times, the inter-reader correlation is itself not the ultimate measure, as Breland demonstrated in 1987 when he introduced a brilliant model of reliability that took into consideration scores as determined by the various sources of error present. In our most modern assessment research, such as that undertaken by Jill Burstein in the development of e-rater, the agreement criterion was established as a match of 87 percent of exact plus adjacent scores, yet that standard was set only for the Graduate Management Admissions Test.

If, then, reliability is contextual—if there is no standard that can be identified across time and circumstance—does it then follow that all writing assessment has historically been contextual? If the fundamental measurement aspect of reliability is program specific, does this mean, in turn, that writing assessment itself is one series of case studies, linked inextricably to individual program developers and unique design circumstances? For that answer, we must turn to the interpretation of literacy itself.

The Construction of Literacy: Implementing Variance

The assumption, of course, is that definitions of literacy are established before programs are begun and research is designed, yet this history of writing assessment demonstrates that such is not at all the case. Frank H. Bowles's 1951 statement regarding the construct validity of the General Composition Test, made after the test had been administered, is illustrative: "Assuming that a test per se is a good test, what then does it test, and how can the results be used?"[20] How could the test have been termed good in the first place, we wonder, if the very developers didn't know what it was measuring? It was not until attention was turned to the writing task itself in the early 1980s, as Peter Cooper's ETS report documents, that the possession of writing ability was thought to be anything other than a commonplace occurrence in American education. Surely, it was assumed by educational researchers, good students could write on any topic.

At Harvard in 1874, the construct of literacy was based on the ability to interpret set texts, an educational goal that continued through the Restrictive Examinations of the College Board until they were dropped in 1934, though the goal was challenged as early as 1915 when the Board began offering Comprehensive Examinations designed not to prescribe curriculum but, rather, to test general ability. Within the SAT—from its first administration on June 23, 1926, when "verbal aptitude" was assessed through analogies, through the deletion of these analogies in 2005—the assessment centered on verbal reasoning. Within other contexts—the NAEP, for example—students were asked to compose in response to narrative or informative or persuasive "tasks" (if the test designers were more influenced by Dewey's organic circle of co-ordination) or "prompts" (if the designers followed the reflex arc's stimulus-response model). Within university settings, the assessment may be made on the basis of various types of academic writing contained between portfolio covers; for the 2003 National Assessment of Adult Literacy, the assessment was made on a construct of literacy in which printed and written information—a bus schedule, for example—was used to measure an ability to function in society, to achieve goals, and to develop potential.

There is only one conclusion that can be drawn: the validity of literacy, and the reliability calculations used to assess it, vary according to context. The history of writing assessment is a series of case studies, linked inextricably to individual program developers and unique design circumstances. It appears, after all, to be more about identified context than about systematized meta-paradigms. As is the case with intelligence assessment, there are multiple variables at play. Sometimes we can get at them; often we can't. We should not, therefore, be talking about a behavioral aggregate called writing ability any more than we should be talking about general intelligence. History will not be kind to us if we allow the present course to persist.

Our culture, however, does not function on the basis of situational discovery. The presence of literacy is like the presence of virtue. If evident, both are the subject of restrained praise; if absent, both are the object of scandal. The professors who cited "a host of writing-related shortcomings among students, most often their inability to construct the sort of lengthy, sophisticated research papers required in upper-division courses" to the *Chronicle of Higher Education* in 2003 didn't appear to have given a thought to who might be responsible for such advanced instruction. They weren't concerned about the complex construct of writing ability; it was easier to be scandalized. Surely, as Adams Sherman Hill had declared in 1879, all this was someone else's problem.

The Persistence of Pattern: A Matter of Power

Thus far, I have identified three master diachronic tropes in the history of writing assessment: an impulse for accountability recorded as student disenfranchisement, a struggle for methodological design resulting in a series of case studies, and a construction of literacy that varies across time and circumstance. Each trope, we may now be tempted to conclude, is accompanied by the demonstration of failure, the assignment of blame, the acceptance of guilt, and the enforcement of additional accountability.

Outcomes are desired, we may conclude, yet there are always more shortcomings than successes when the spreadsheets are analyzed. Design is tied to reliability, yet evidence of reliability is so contingent upon context that the modern composition program administrator would, according to the field's own contemporary leaders, have difficulty citing sources from the writing assessment literature that agree upon a reliability standard needed to make placement decisions. And the construct of literacy? Performance is linked to task design, the sole question that the student writer was answering in the first place. As the most contemporary research demonstrates, while there may be little difference in essays written to address either a brief prompt encouraging discussion or a more extensive prompt encouraging persuasion, there are significant differences in mean scores on essay-writing performance for ethnic and gender groups. When Hunter

Breland, one of the premier researchers in the field, wrote in 2004 that "there has been no previous research on the comparative impact of prompt types on ethnic, gender, or language groups," he confirmed a fact that was established fourteen years earlier by Brian Huot.[21] In that essay assessments are known to be less reliable—that is, less stable—than most traditional educational assessments, and because we know so little about the comparative impact of prompt types on groups that have been the previous targets of discrimination, we would expect a demonstrable amount of humility in claims about our capabilities to measure writing, more cautions about the use of the results. Instead, we too often encounter language that tells us little about limitations and a lot about basic achievements that are, while not an utter disaster, just not good enough. We must, we are told, do better.

Why has the language of failure emerged with such regularity around issues of accountability, reliability, and validity—even when it is clear to researchers that the limitations of the methods themselves suggest that qualified conclusions about the uses of these tests are more appropriate than witch hunts undertaken to establish blame?

We might answer in the following way: the history of writing assessment reflects the presence of power. The emergence of a modern sense of literacy—a sense of reading and writing that is fastened to later-nineteenth-century utilitarian systematization instead of associated with seventeenth- and eighteenth-century ideals of community service—coincides with the development of American capitalism. The history of the assessment of writing ability from 1874 to the present is tied to the history of modern technology: humans, along with their literacy, are, as Martin Heidegger warned, standing reserves to be exploited in the service of modern technological life.[22] As an asset, literacy must always and everywhere be harnessed in the most efficient ways. Writing as a vehicle used to express appreciation through mastery of literary texts—the last appearance of the link between God and man at Harvard—was eroded by the 1915 advent of the Comprehensive Examinations, a new assessment system designed to capture and foster more useful thinking skills that could be harnessed in the new economy of Fordism. (Recall Antonio Gramsci's observation in his *Prison Notebooks* that "Americanism and Fordism derive from an inherent necessity to achieve the organization of a planned economy," a transition from the older "economic individualism."[23]) While the economic link between writing and thinking existed for most of the twentieth century, by the early twenty-first century the demand for even higher levels of writing—the ability to offer a reasoned opinion, to extend one's utility beyond mere reflection—is congruent with advanced models of production, with a nation in which manufacturing has disappeared, as William Julius Wilson has claimed, and a new information-based economy has emerged.[24] (It would be false to claim that most students cannot write, the National Commission on Writing acknowledged in 2003. It is just that they cannot write well enough to meet the demands they will face in higher education and in the workplace.) Within this system, it is important that writing ability not be allowed to dissipate itself in pleasurable pursuits such as narrative or imaginative writing; the very modes of discourse associated with identity are denied. Exposition and argument are the desired forms of discourse, types of writing that are favored in the schools because they serve the new economy.

In order to maintain a focused, utilitarian sense of literacy, American society constantly castigates itself about its literacy failings. Found guilty, educators thus create their own forms of self-governance that are maintained through routine accounts of failure. Low scores are the result of assessment designs so limited in scope (how very little can ever be exhibited in twenty-five minutes!) that only basic levels of ability could possibly emerge, levels that can readily be called into criticism, thus sealing the cycle of self-governance. Establishing an economic model for the early twenty-first century does not require the obvious tactics of Fordism, the prevalent command and control methods of the early twentieth century: the new capitalism of postmodernism—what David Harvey has called flexible accumulation[25]—can be achieved by self-governance. In declaring that no child can be left behind and subsequently assessing knowledge by methods that record only minimal achievement, all children—and their teachers—remain oppressed. A similar strategy of oppression is executed by privileging exposition and argument while ignoring transactional discourse, a type of writing designed to accomplish marketplace, organizational ends. By declaring that only certain types of academic discourse are needed and concurrently failing to provide instruction in needed non-academic methods (courses such as technical writing, designed to teach transactional writing, are unknown in the school curriculum and shunned as service courses in the university), all remain oppressed.

An educational system found inferior—as is the case with identified inadequacies of gender, race, and English-language abilities in American society itself—ensures docility. From Hill's lament in 1879 to the Report of the National Commission on Writing in America's Schools and Colleges in 2003, the discourse interpreting the results of assessment holds up well because it is easy to uphold. The educational culture engineered by Charles

Eliot created a machinery that manufactured inferiority through calls for excellence. The somber tests always say no. The uniform apparatus, the logic of censorship, the insistence of the rule—each results in the cycle of prohibition that holds both student and teacher captive between legislative power on one side and public censure on the other. Obedience is assured. The sheer power of the system is exercised from innumerable points, from children who find themselves on a conveyor belt of exit exams designed by compromised educational researchers, from parents who have learned to be hypervigilant about the documented success of their children on that belt, from school principals who must answer to superintendents who must answer to legislators who are put into office by the voting parents who are too paralyzed with fear about their children's future to do anything but maintain the system. The power relations surrounding the assessment of writing ability are, thus, not found in exteriority (there is no need for the melting-pot graduation ceremony of the Ford Motor Company's English School)[26] but are immanent in each and every relationship. Obedience is assured within every act, in the very moment in which the student, asked to produce evidence of writing ability, lifts the pencil as the proctor announces that only twenty-five minutes will be allowed. The tactical polyvalence of power is densely ever present and, thus, is stunningly more efficient than law. To dissent is to be deemed hysterical; to assent is to become party to the Malthusian model of socialization.

The Persistence of Pattern: The Problem of Power

If such an analysis sounds familiar, it is because it directly follows Michel Foucault's treatment of power relations.[27] The argument and the language itself are Foucault's own, wrapped into an analysis of the history of writing assessment. Is such an analysis an accurate representation of the history I have presented in this book?

The analysis is, of course, compelling—especially to those of us who have designed enough assessment systems to realize their overwhelming impact upon individual students. Who, for example, cannot shudder when recalling Sternglass' recollection of Chandra? An entering college student who tried to produce her best work, Chandra drafted her placement essay, ran out of time in completing the final copy, and failed the test. "That Chandra was penalized by the time constraints for trying to produce a rough draft before a final draft," Sternglass writes, "seems an incredible irony in a field in which revision is so highly valued."[28] There is, no doubt, a rhetoric of disenfranchisement surrounding writing assessment, and the powerlessness that results can be palpable within a community: the heartbreaking tears of the third-grader who fails a competency test, the confused rage of the college student who passes the composition course but fails the exit examination. If one does not bring forward an analysis informed by Foucault's theories of the history of writing assessment, one has no heart.

Yet if one offers only such responses in reflecting about the history of writing assessment, one has no head. The three master tropes—the contingencies of accountability, design, and literacy—exist in a web of complex power relations. The drive for accountability leads to an efficiently designed assessment that, in turn, leads to a construct of literacy that is reified from the design—a solipsistic nightmare. The combined use of limited-response testing and direct assessment that the Godshalk research team identified in 1966 as "the most efficient predictor of a reliable direct measure of writing ability" remains with us. Interpretations of major rhetorical theories that inform writing instruction—say, the objective, subjective, and transactional paradigms offered by James Berlin—are not considered in the assessment design because such theories embody constructs of literacy that are not going to be captured in a twenty-five minute draft. The more we problematize the construct of literacy, the more the goal of efficient assessment recedes into the distance; the more we seek efficiency, the more our construct of literacy deteriorates into a postcard's worth of crude common sense. To imagine that power relations do not exist as the tropes are manifested within specific scenes—the school and the testing agency and the sponsoring state system—is naïve.

Yet it is equally naïve to construct the individual assessment situations that constitute the history of writing assessment solely as a tale of power manifested, as somehow different, for example, from similar struggles that exist in American culture among the injection drug user, the city health department, and the state legislature regarding needle exchange programs. Defining the regime of power and knowledge, Foucault's great intellectual contribution, is necessary but not sufficient to an understanding of the history of writing assessment. Indeed, it is positively blinding if used as the singular terministic screen of analysis.

And So

I return to Burke's method, to looking at agent-agency interactions within specific scenes, to identifying diachronic patterns for explication, to inviting others to craft more informed matrices for more subtle analysis.

I do not want to be thought of as blind to the terrible misinterpretation that Carl Campbell Brigham introduced to readers in *A Study of American Intelligence* and that others, humanists among them, have introduced regarding the assessment of writing ability. In 1923 Brigham was a follower of eugenics, who, nevertheless, established a legacy of language use—that language is a window to the culture and the individual within—that allowed more informed constructs of writing to emerge and be evaluated by less elementalist methods. As a child, I realized that the same laboring ushers I saw at Sunday mass got in their cars at night and drove to Klan meetings; and in the university I later learned that educated people also do terrible things. The College Board listed *The Merchant of Venice* as recommended reading each year from 1901 to 1925 for its examinations, yet when we realize that Brigham felt at ease concluding that the high standard deviation of intelligence scores of Jews suggested that "Jewish immigrants have a low average intelligence but a higher variability"—thus lending to the conclusion that the "able Jew is popularly recognized not only because of his ability, but because he is able and a Jew"—the heart sickens at what might have been taught in those classes about the nature of Shylock.[29] Yet I also learned, both at home and in school, that if we do not look deeply into the methods of complex individuals such as Brigham, we stand to let similar injustices pass unexamined. Brigham's conclusions were based on a deeply flawed understanding of literacy—so many African American soldiers, judged as illiterate, standing in line for the beta test—and if we do not recognize the damage that flawed views of literacy can do, we will not truly understand why inequalities continue to exist in those whose writing we assess.

The lesson to be learned from Brigham's 1923 book is not that he was a man of his time. Three contemporaries offered views more informed that same year. Stanford University's Percy E. Davidson reminded readers of the *Scientific Monthly* that no one knew what anyone was capable of achieving, and in the *New Republic*, E. G. Boring, a former captain in the School of Military Psychology, cautioned readers about the limits of tests. In "A Defense of Education," columnist Walter Lippmann called attention to the sheer injustice of the Army's tests.[30] Rather, the lesson to be learned is that we continue to make similar errors, continue to make claims that cannot be supported. The modification of Thorndike's Reading Scale, the Kelley Literacy Test and the Devens Literacy Test captured a badly flawed educational system thirty-six years before George C. E. Hayes, Thurgood Marshall, and James Nabrit, Jr., argued against segregation before the Supreme Court. Those tests did not capture literacy; they reflected the contexts in which a kind of literacy did or did not emerge that could be captured by those deeply flawed, academically oriented instruments.[31]

Today, we continue to capture what exists in context. We see in our assessment programs the contexts in which a kind of writing ability does or does not emerge that can or cannot be captured by our own limited instruments. Even the portfolios at Washington State University—perhaps the most sophisticated assessment system we now have to serve its intended purpose—do not tell us if the students will be able to write proposals and user's manuals, if they will be able to post and evaluate corporate websites for their usability, all skills necessary for success in the new flexible capitalism of postmodernism. We do what we can within known contexts, and the claims that we make that extend beyond these contexts put all of us at risk. If we shudder at those who claim to have assessed intelligence, we should also shudder at our claims that we are assessing writing ability.

The key to our future, then, is not to abandon our systems but to make them better, to improve them and to provide more information about the limits of our findings to those who will use the tests. I do not believe that the College Board and the Educational Testing Service are part of an axis of evil, the distorted outcome of a military-industrial culture of capitalism begun with Charles Eliot and concretized by Henry Chauncey. Rather, I believe that the College Board and ETS have been two of the great educational institutions of the twentieth century, agencies that will continue to provide informed leadership in the twenty-first century. The flaws that we may identify in their history are flaws that exist in the history of all modern organizations. There are cases of heavy-handed self-assurances, consequences of myopic urges for systematization. Yet when I read John Stalnaker's 1943 statement—"Eventually, it is hoped, sufficient evidence will be accumulated to outlaw forever the 'write-a-theme-on...' type of examination"[32]—I know that I would have written the same. Had I reviewed the first six tests in English composition with Edward S. Noyes and William M. Sale, Jr., I know I, too, would have concluded that the essays were not being read reliably and were not serving to predict grades in freshman English. The Scholastic Aptitude Test was doing a better job. Stalnaker did not know the answer; he only knew that students were not being well served. It is not that Stalnaker embodied a shallow positivism and sought to find proof in the self-referential correlations of the SAT, a test that was creating a world that was a reflection of itself. It was, more simply, that Stalnaker could not support a writing sample that could not be read reliably and did not correlate with the identified criterion measures.

The flaws are not solely in the tests that we design but rather in the ways the tests are used. To draw a conclusion about an individual's writing ability based on a single assessment given on a single day is an error. To make a high-stakes decision about that individual based on the single assessment is a tragedy. We who design assessment programs should know better. We know about the mind-bending complexities of participants and processes and texts from the work of Leo Ruth and Sandra Murphy. We know, from Sara Cushing Weigle, that every assessment context is different and that maximizing elements of reliability, construct validity, authenticity, interactiveness, impact, and practicality is, in fact, a trade-off in which overall usefulness is gained as each element is simultaneously diminished. We know the dedicated work of teachers, as documented most recently by George Hillocks, Jr., in *The Testing Trap*, and we know that we fail to trust or support them.

We know, as did Voltaire, that this is not the best of all possible worlds. It is we who know better and need to do better. We are, after all, a long way from that Harvard catalogue of 1874. The distant world of Carl Brigham and the contemporary world of Paul Ramsey are part of a history that we should embrace in all its complexities and try, as best we can, to understand how it is that we came to be victims of our own and each other's magic.

As for Katherine

She is a postmodern indulgence, someone who helped me think about how we can be less cruel to each other. Richard Rorty is correct in *Contingency, Irony, and Solidarity* when he tells us that there are books that are relevant to our relations with others, characters within those books who help us to notice the effects our actions have.[33] In seeking solidarity—not a recognition of a core self, but, as Rorty defines it, a sense of recognition of a human essence, a way to see differences as irrelevant when compared to similarities such as suffering—I thought of other characters that have been and will be with us as we assess writing.

Tom Buchanan is here, the resonant voice that exists to exclude, to smash up people's lives and retreat behind privilege, letting others clean up the mess. So is Willy Loman, believing that promises made across desks secure the future, that there is a way to get past the gatekeepers, that there is a real world in which the street smarts of Biff will, every day, put him five times ahead of drudges such as Bernard. Richard Sumner and Bunny Watson are there, too. He forgets himself, keeps secrets, thinks he knows; she cleverly knows better. Both are just as limited by their views of each other as they are visionary in their understanding of those limits. And there is Richard Atkinson's granddaughter, the bright child who will succeed no matter what plans grand-père has for her. In her, irony abounds.

And there is Katherine. She looks at the students and their teachers—at all those found wanting—and yells across the lawn to them that they're worth the whole damn bunch put together.

For writing assessment, like writing itself, is a sad business filled with irony, work that you can't get right no matter how hard you try. In such a situation, you had better know your limits and had better see things for what they really are. And you had better be determined. Because it is all so very hard. And it takes so long. Katherine, I think, will always know that.

Endnotes

1 Roy Jenkins, *Churchill: A Biography* (New York: Farrar, 2001) 912.

2 Burke disputes, Crusius writes, "the Philosophical conviction that 'the dialectic' is lurking, waiting to be discovered somewhere 'underneath' or 'above' its multiplicity of uses" (186). Timothy W. Crusius, *Kenneth Burke and the Conversation after Philosophy* (Carbondale: Southern Illinois UP, 1999).

3 Kenneth Burke, *A Grammar of Motives* (1945; Berkeley: U of California P, 1962) 442.

4 Stephen Greenblatt, "Towards a Poetics of Culture," *The New Historicism*, ed. H. Aram Veeser (New York: Routledge, 1989) 13.

5 Hans Kellner, "After the Fall," *Writing Histories of Rhetoric*, ed. Victor J. Vitanza (Carbondale: Southern Illinois UP, 1994) 30; John Schilb, "Future Historiographies of Rhetoric and the Present Age of Anxiety," *Writing Histories of Rhetoric* 138; Victor J. Vitanza, "An After/Word: Preparing to Meet the Faces That 'We' Will Have Met," *Writing Histories of Rhetoric* 250. See also Thomas P. Miller and Joseph G. Jones, "Review: Working Out Our History," rev of *The Selected Essays of Robert J. Connors*, ed. by Lisa Ede and Andrea Lunsford, *Writing in the Academic Disciplines: A Curricular History*, by David R. Russell, *Imagining Rhetoric: Composing Women of the Early United States*, by Janet Carey Eldred and Peter Mortensen, and *Gender and Rhetorical Space in American Life, 1866–1910*, *College English* 67.4 (2005): 421–439.

6 "Finally," Berlin wrote in "Revisionary Histories of Rhetoric," his chapter in Vitanza's *Writing Histories of Rhetoric*, "I would like to say a last word about the complex relation between the past and present in writing the contextualized history I am recommending. As I have suggested repeatedly, objectivity is out of the question" (121).

7 I also kept in mind the web of relationships offered by the environmental historian Carolyn Merchant. Merchant has argued that writers keep in mind the ecological core of a particular event by examining the interactions of production, reproduction, and consciousness. Bringing forth the nature of such relationships was an ever-present goal of the book. See "The Theoretical Structure of Ecological Revolutions," *Environmental Review* 11.4 (1987): 265–274.

8 Deborah Brandt's definition of the sponsors of literacy was significant in helping me to identify sponsors of writing assessment, the individual and institutional agents identified in *Literacy in American Lives* (Cambridge: Cambridge UP, 2001): "Sponsors, as I have come to think of them, are any agents, local or distant, concrete or abstract, who enable, support, teach, and model, as well as recruit, regulate, suppress, or withhold, literacy—and gain advantage by it in some way" (19).

9 *School Accountability: An Assessment by the Koret Task Force on K–12 Education*, ed. Williamson M. Evers and Herbert J. Walberg (Stanford: Hoover Institution P, 2002). See especially Walberg's chapter, "Principles for Accountability Designs" 155–183.

10 Peter Elbow, "Will the Virtues of Portfolios Blind Us to Their Potential Dangers?" *New Directions in Portfolio Assessment: Reflective Practice, Critical Theory, and Large-Scale Scoring*, ed. Laurel Black et al. (Portsmouth, NH: Boynton/Cook, 1994) 47–48.

11 Fred Newton Scott, "Our Problems," *English Journal* 2.1 (1913): 5.

12 In his introduction to Hillocks' *Research on Written Composition* (Urbana: NCTE, 1986) Richard Lloyd-Jones attributes the chemical metaphor to Richard Braddock. Lloyd-Jones writes, "In 1963 I was not sure I shared Braddock's hope that we are emerging from an age of alchemy, and I still think of lore and other forms of experiential knowledge as essential to our crafts; but Hillocks has demonstrated here how much empirical studies have to offer, and he provides useful counsel for those who wish to conduct such studies" (xiv).

13 It is with much fear and trembling that one compares Purves' 1975 *Common Sense and Testing in English* with both CCCC's 1995 "Writing Assessment: A Position Statement" and the 2004 "CCCC Position Statement on Teaching, Learning, and Assessing Writing in Digital Environments." While it is clear that gains have been made, it is difficult not to empathize with Huot's reaction of surprise and dismay in finding that almost half of the respondents from his 1991 survey of English Chairpersons reported using some indirect method for placing students in writing courses ("A Survey of College and University Writing Placement Practices," *WPA: Writing Program Administration* 17.3 [1994]: 54). It is hard not to think of the work of the writing assessment community as beating on against the current, born back ceaselessly into the past.

14 Adams Sherman Hill, "An Answer to the Cry for More English," (1879) *Twenty Years of School and College English* (Cambridge: Harvard University, 1896) 6.

15 Merrill Sheils, "Why Johnny Can't Write," *Newsweek* 8 Dec. 1975: 58–65.

16 Thomas Bartlett, "Why Johnny Can't Write, Even Though He Went to Princeton," *Chronicle of Higher Education* 3 Jan. 2003: A39.

17 Adams, Charles Francis, Edwin Lawrence Godkin, and Josiah Quincy, *Report of the Committee on Composition and Rhetoric* (Cambridge: Harvard University, 1892) 156.

18 Adams, Godkin, and Quincy, *Report of the Committee on Composition and Rhetoric* 156.

19 Roger D. Cherry and Paul R. Meyer, "Reliability Issues in Holistic Assessment," *Validating Holistic Scoring for Writing Assessment: Theoretical and Empirical Foundations*, eds. Michael M. Williamson and Brian A. Huot (Creskill, NJ: Hampton P, 1993) 134–136.

20 *Fifty-First Annual Report of the Director* (New York: College Entrance Examination Board, 1951) 9.

21 Hunter M. Breland et al., *New SAT Writing Prompt Study: Analysis of Group Impact and Reliability*, RR 2004.1 (New York: College Board, 2004) 1. For Huot's review, see "The Literature of Direct Writing Assessment: Major Concerns and Prevailing Trends," *Review of Educational Research* 60.2 (1990) 240–245. As Huot wrote, "It is safe to say at this point that many features of the relationship between writing task and the score assigned to written compositions are basically unknown. Because this is a relatively new area and the results of recent studies are inconclusive, topic development and task selection are areas that should see much activity in the next few years" (246). In that fourteen years later this call for needed research has not been answered—and in that these tests have so impacted various ethnic, gender, and language groups—it is hard not to recall Paul Ramsey's conclusion: "Sure evidence of racism is neither in our tests nor in our classrooms but in our ignorance." See "Minorities and Standardized Tests," *Consensus and Dissent: Teaching English Past, Present, and Future*, ed. Marjorie N. Farmer (Urbana: NCTE, 1986) 90.

22 Martin Heidegger, "The Question Concerning Technology," *Basic Writings*, ed. David Farrell Krell (New York: Harper, 1977) 287–317.

23 Antonio Gramsci, "Americanism and Fordism," *Selections from the Prison Notebooks,* eds. and trans. Quintin Hoare and Geoffrey Nowell Smith (New York: International Publishers, 1971) 279.

24 William Julius Wilson, *When Work Disappears: The World of the New Urban Poor* (New York: Knopf, 1996).

25 David Harvey, *The Condition of Postmodernity: An Inquiry into the Origins of Cultural Change* (Cambridge: Basil Blackwell, 1989). For an analysis of the implications of Harvey's theory of flexible accumulation to the profession of English, see Richard

Ohmann, *The Politics of Knowledge: The Commercialization of the University, the Professions, and Print Culture* (Middletown: Wesleyan UP, 2003) 28–41.

26 "On the stage was represented an immigrant ship. In front of it was a huge melting pot. Down the gang plank came the members of the class dressed in their national garb and carrying luggage such as they carried when they landed in this country. Down they poured into the Ford melting pot and disappeared. Then the teachers began to stir the contents of the pot with long ladles. Presently the pot began to boil over and out came the men dressed in their best American clothes and waving American flags." Qtd. in Oliver Zunz, *The Changing Face of Inequality* (Chicago: U of Chicago P, 1982) 312.

27 Michel Foucault, *The History of Sexuality: An Introduction* (New York: Vintage, 1990).

28 Marilyn S. Sternglass, *Time to Know Them: A Longitudinal Study of Writing and Learning at the College Level* (Mahwah: Lawrence Erlbaum, 1997) 146.

29 Carl Campbell Brigham, *A Study of American Intelligence* (Princeton: Princeton UP, 1923) 190. The listing for *The Merchant of Venice* is found in the College Entrance Examination Board's *Entrance English Questions Set by the College Entrance Examination Board, 1901–1923* (Boston: Ginn, 1924) xii. The 1902 question is listed as follows: "Discuss Shylock's position as one of a persecuted race and as a money lender, and show its effect upon his character" (15).

30 Percy E. Davidson, "The Social Significance of the Army Intelligence Findings," *Scientific Monthly* 16.2 (1923): 184–193; E. G. Boring, "Intelligence as the Tests Test It," *New Republic*, 6 June 1923: 35–37; Walter Lippmann, "A Defense of Education," *Century Magazine* 106 (1923): 95–103, Disability History Museum. 23 Jan. 2005 <http://www.disabilitymuseum.org>.

31 No matter how flawed the definition of illiteracy used in early literacy reports—the government defined illiteracy as the inability to read or write in any language—the recorded rates of illiteracy suggest that the army tests captured little more than existing disparities. Among "Black and other" groups in 1910, the percentage of persons fourteen and over who were illiterate was 30.5 percent and in 1920 the rate was recorded at 23 percent. In 1910, the percentage of "Foreign born, White" illiterates was 12.7 and in 1920 had risen to 13.1. In contrast, the percentage of "Native, White," illiterates in 1910 was 3.0 and in 1920 was 2.0. See Thomas N. Snyder, ed., *120 Years of American Education: A Statistical Portrait* (Washington: National Center for Educational Statistics, 1993) Table 6, 21.

32 *Forty-Third Annual Report of the Executive Secretary* (New York: College Entrance Examination Board, 1943) 24.

33 Richard Rorty, *Contingency, Irony, and Solidarity* (Cambridge: Cambridge UP, 1989) 141, 192.

Epilogue: Katherine, December 2004

I should copy down the URL for the scoring guide, Katherine thought, but so many of them don't have computers at home. I could print the guide out and pin copies to the wall. But then she remembered that these were high-school juniors, not the elementary-school children she was used to teaching. Her students were nearly as tall as she and far too sophisticated to stand up and read. So she hauled the LCD projector she had purchased with her own money out of the closet. She would download the information from the site to her laptop and project the versions of the six-point scale on the wall. She hadn't been able to pull the screen down all year and had gotten tired of asking for someone to fix it for her. Then she remembered that the published guide had sample essays to match the six-point scale, so she would scan those with the scanner (purchased, again, with her own money) and show those, as well.

I could take one of their essays in hand, read it to the class, and then compare it to the scale. The students could then look at the wall and try to judge the merit of their individual essays to the projected ones. The scoring guide would be, she thought, the center of attention in class for at least ten minutes and might break up the deadening silence. That time in elementary school was not badly spent after all. Her work with younger children had allowed her to learn more techniques than her dull, rule-driven male colleagues would ever be able to implement in their dreadful classes. Indeed, it would be nice to have the students work in groups, to talk together about their essays and how they compared to the samples. But they probably wouldn't. They had seen so many of these guides over the years from other teachers, from their grade-school classes through middle school. How many timed essays had they written? The yearly examinations for the state, for the national standards studies—it would be just more of the same. Portfolios? Who had the time to score warehouses full of binders only to find five paragraphs that had been written in half an hour's time? So much effort, so many still left behind. (She smiled. School reform had been on her mind when the Republican Convention had come to town in late August, but the Sunday afternoons had led her away from Madison Square Garden. She had visited The Pierogi 2000 gallery in Brooklyn and saw Rachel Mason's sculpture *Kissing President Bush* but did not buy a T-shirt there to benefit John Kerry's campaign. Her friend had called the gallery a chamber of horrors. On another Sunday, this time alone, she had gone to the Metropolitan Museum of Art to see the Childe Hassam exhibit of American impressionism. In Gallery 7 she found *Parc Monceau*, and its garden path captured her heart. She wanted a chance to see where those curved lines led.)

Some of her students would be motivated enough to learn how to write to the criteria explained in the scales. Some, at least, had told her that they wanted to be admitted to college. Maybe she could hook them, encourage them to move beyond what could be expressed in a twenty-five-minute essay. Maybe.

After class she would walk to West 120th Street. She had just been accepted into the graduate program at Teachers College, and she used the journals in the library there to give her ideas about teaching. Maybe she would find research there that would help her to get the students writing, to shake off their cynicism. Last week had been unsettling. While trying yet another time to pull down the screen, she had just finished telling them about the importance of writing in order to learn and was about to fire up the laptop when a muffled voice said, "No, it's really writing to please, KKKKaty."

But she had learned never, ever to show weakness. In the classroom, there were lessons for all.

It was 2004, and Katherine knew what there was to know when she slung her laptop and projector over her shoulder and headed for the door.

Works Cited

Adams, Charles Francis, Edwin Lawrence Godkin, and Josiah Quincy. *Report of the Committee on Composition and Rhetoric to the Board of Overseers of Harvard College*. Cambridge: Harvard University, 1892. 117–163.

Alderfer, Jane B., and Gary D. Zaredzky. "History." *Navy Papers Inventory*. Princeton: ETS Archives, 1971.

Allan, Roy A. *A History of the Personal Computer: The People and the Technology*. London: Allan Publishing, 2001.

American Educational Research Association; American Psychological Association; and National Council on Measurement in Education. *Standards for Educational and Psychological Testing*. Washington: American Psychological Association, 1985.

———. *Standards for Educational and Psychological Testing*. Washington: American Psychological Association, 1999.

American Psychological Association; American Educational Research Association; and National Council on Measurement Used in Education. *Technical Recommendations for Psychological Tests and Diagnostic Techniques*. Washington: American Psychological Association, 1954.

Anderson, Melville B. "English at Stanford University." *The Dial* 16 Mar. 1894: 167–170.

Applebee, Arthur N. *Tradition and Reform in the Teaching of English: A History*. Urbana: NCTE, 1974.

———, Judith A. Langer, and Ina V. S. Mullins. *Writing Trends Across the Decade, 1974–84*. ETS Report No. 15-W-01. Princeton: ETS, 1985.

Ashburn, Frank D. "Progress Report—Committee on English Testing." *College Board Review* 11 (1950) 140–141.

———. "Recommendations for Achievement Testing." *College Board Review* 18 (1952) 314.

"Assessment." Def. 5b. *Oxford English Dictionary*. 2nd ed. 1989.

Atkinson, Richard C. "AERA Public Service Award Address." 14 Apr. 2004. San Diego: American Education Research Association.

———. "Standardized Tests and Access to American Universities." The 2001 Robert H. Atwell Distinguished Lecture, 83rd Annual Meeting of the American Council on

Education. Washington: Marriott Wardman Park Hotel. 18 Feb. 2001.Washington. 23 Jan. 2005 <http://www.ucop.edu/welcome1.html>.

Bartlett, Thomas. "Why Johnny Can't Write, Even Though He Went to Princeton." *Chronicle of Higher Education* 3 Jan. 2003: A39.

Bartnik, Robert B., and William W. Turnbull. "A Revolutionary Change in Test Scoring." *College Board Review* 40 (1960): 21–23.

Barzun, Jacques. Foreword. *The Tyranny of Testing*. By Banesh Hoffman. New York: Collier, 1952. 7–11.

Basic Aims Committee. "Basic Aims for English Instruction in American Schools." *English Journal* 31.1 (1942): 40–55.

Beaven, Mary H. "Individualized Goal Setting, Self-Evaluation, and Peer Evaluation." *Evaluating Writing: Describing, Measuring, Judging*. Ed. Cooper and Odell. 135–153.

Beaver, Daniel R. *Newton D. Baker and the American War Effort, 1917–1919*. Lincoln: U of Nebraska P, 1966.

Becker, Samuel L. "A Methodological Review." Rev. of *The Measurement of Writing Ability*, by Fred I. Godshalk, William E. Coffman, and Frances I. Swineford. *Research in the Teaching of English* 1.1 (1967): 76–79.

Belanoff, Pat, and Marcia Dickinson. *Portfolios: Process and Product*. Portsmouth, NH: Boynton/Cook, 1991.

Berlin, James A. "Revisionary Histories of Rhetoric: Power, Politics, and Plurality." *Writing Histories of Rhetoric*. Ed. Vitanza. 112–138.

———. *Rhetoric and Reality: Writing Instruction in American Colleges, 1900–1985*. Carbondale: Southern Illinois UP, 1987.

———. *Writing Instruction in Nineteenth-Century American Colleges*. Carbondale: Southern Illinois UP, 1984.

Billington, Ray Allen. *Frederick Jackson Turner: Historian, Scholar, Teacher*. New York: Oxford UP, 1973.

Black, Laurel, et al., eds. *New Directions in Portfolio Assessment*. Portsmouth, NH: Boynton/Cook, 1994.

Blackmer, Alan R. "The Three School, Three College Plan." *College Board Review* 18 (1952): 300–304.

Boring, Edwin G. *A History of Experimental Psychology*. 2nd ed. New York: Appleton, 1950.

———. "Intelligence as the Tests Test It." *New Republic* 6 June 1923: 35–37.

———. "The Marking System in Theory." *Pedagogical Seminary* 21 (1914): 269–277.

Braddock, Richard, Richard Lloyd-Jones, and Lowell Schoer. *Research in Written Composition*. Urbana: NCTE, 1963.

Brandt, Deborah. *Literacy in American Lives*. Cambridge: Cambridge UP, 2001.

Braun, Robert J. "Educator Faults Whitman College Plan." *Star-Ledger* 23 Mar. 1994: 1.

———. "Remediation Helps Boost Return on Investment." *Star-Ledger* 26 Jan. 1992: 52.

Breland, Hunter M. "Computer-Assisted Writing Assessment: The Politics of Science versus the Humanities." *Assessment of Writing: Politics, Policies, Practices*. Ed. Edward M. White, William D. Lutz, and Sandra Kamusikiri. 249–256.

———. *The Direct Assessment of Writing Skill: A Measurement Review*. College Board Report No. 83-6, ETS Research Report No. 83-32. New York: College Board, 1983.

Breland, Hunter M., et al. *Assessing Writing Skill*. Research Monograph No. 11. New York: College Board, 1987.

Breland, Hunter M., et al. *Factors in Performance on Brief, Impromptu Essay Examinations*. College Board Report No. 95-4, ETS Research Report 95-41. New York: College Board, 1996.

Breland, Hunter M., et al. *New SAT Writing Prompt Study: Analyses of Group Impact and Reliability*. College Board Research Report No. 2004-1, ETS RR-04-03. New York: College Board, 2004.

Bremen, Brian. Telephone interview. 6 Apr. 2004.

Bremmer, Cornelius Daniel. "American Bank Failures." Diss. Columbia U, 1935.

Brereton, John C., ed. *The Origins of Composition Studies in the American College, 1875–1925*. Pittsburgh: U of Pittsburgh P, 1995.

———. *Traditions of Inquiry*. New York: Oxford UP, 1985.

Briggs, Le Baron Russell. "The Correction of Bad English, as a Requirement for Admission to Harvard College." 1890. *Twenty Years of School and College* 33–43.

———. "The Harvard Admission Examination in English." 1888. *Twenty Years of School and College English*. 17–32.

Brigham, Carl Campbell. "Intelligence Tests of Immigrant Groups." *Psychological Review* 38 (1930): 158–165.

———. "The Place of Research in a Testing Organization." *School and Society* 11 Dec. 1937: 756–759.

———. *Preliminary Report of a Study of the Entrance Examination System at Cooper Union*. Princeton: Princeton U, 1923.

———. *The Reading of the Comprehensive Examination in English: An Analysis of the Procedures Followed During the Five Reading Periods from 1929–1933*. Princeton: Princeton UP, 1934.

———. *A Study of American Intelligence*. Princeton: Princeton UP, 1923.

———. *A Study of Error*. New York: College Entrance Examination Board, 1932.

Broad, Bob. *What We Really Value: Beyond Rubrics in Teaching and Assessing Writing*. Logan: Utah State UP, 2003.

Brooks, Cleanth. *The Well Wrought Urn: Studies in the Structure of Poetry*. New York: Dennis Dobson, 1949.

Brossell, Gordon. "Current Research and Unanswered Questions in Writing Assessment." *Writing Assessment: Issues and Strategies*. Ed. Greenberg, Wiener, and Donovan. 168–182.

Burchard, John E. "Science Education and the Liberal Arts." *College Board Review* 33 (1957): 13–18.

Burke, Kenneth. *A Grammar of Motives*. 1945. Berkeley: U of California P, 1962.

Burnham, Chris. "Portfolio Evaluation: Room to Breathe and Grow." *Training the New Teacher of College Composition*. Ed. Charles W. Bridges. Urbana: NCTE, 1986. 125–138.

Burns, Stewart. *Social Movements of the 1960s: Searching for Democracy*. Boston: Twayne, 1990.

Burstein, Jill. Personal interview. 17 May 2004.

Burstein, Jill, et al. "Computer Analysis of Essay Content for Automated Score Prediction: A Prototype Automated Scoring System for GMAT Analytical Writing Assessment Essays." ETS Research Report 98-15. Princeton: ETS, 1998.

Burt, Forrest D., and Sylvia King, eds. *Equivalency Testing: A Major Issue for College English*. Urbana: NCTE, 1974.

Camara, Wayne. Telephone interview. 4 May 2004.

Camp, Roberta. "The ETS Writing Portfolio: A New Kind of Assessment." Conf. on Coll. Composition and Communication. Detroit. 17 Mar. 1983.

———. "New Views of Measurement and New Models for Writing Assessment." *Assessment of Writing: Politics, Policies, and Practices*. Ed. White, Lutz, and Kamusikiri. 135–157.

———. "Proposal for Writing Portfolio Project, Phases I and II and Progress Report for Writing Portfolio Project, Phase I." 15 Jan. 1982. Princeton: ETS.

Campbell, George. *The Philosophy of Rhetoric*. 1776. Ed. Lloyd F. Bitzer. Carbondale: Southern Illinois UP, 1963.

Carlson, Sybil B. *Survey of ETS Writing Activities*. Princeton: ETS, 1982.

Carmichael, Stokley. "What We Want." *New York Review of Books* 22 Sept. 1966: 5+.

Chalmers, Gordon K. *The Republic and the Person: A Discussion of Necessities in Modern American Education*. Chicago: Regnery, 1952.

Channing, Edward T. *Lectures Read to the Seniors in Harvard College*. 1856. Carbondale: Southern Illinois UP, 1968.

Chase, Alan. *The Legacy of Malthus: The Social Costs of the New Scientific Racism*. New York: Knopf, 1977.

Chauncey, Henry. "The College Entrance Examination Board: Origins and Current Trends." *College Board Review* 1.5 (1948): 63–67.

———. "ETS—Major Problems in Effecting the Merger of Constituent Agencies." 12 Dec. 1947. Chauncey Merger File. Princeton: ETS Archives.

———. Interview. Part Six. 8 Nov. 1977. Princeton: ETS Archives Oral History Program 11.

———. Memorandum for the Board of Trustees. 20 Apr. 1951. Chauncey Merger File. Princeton: ETS Archives.

———. Note. Apr. 1951. Chauncey Merger File. Princeton: ETS Archives.

———. Public Opinion News Service. 27–28 May 1951. Chauncey Merger File. Princeton: ETS Archives.

———. "Testing Offices of the Three Organizations Merge." *College Board Review* 1.3 (1947): 36–37.

Cherry, Roger D., and Paul R. Meyer. "Reliability Issues in Holistic Assessment." *Validating Holistic Scoring for Writing Assessment: Theoretical and Empirical Foundations*. Ed. Michael M. Williamson and Brian A. Huot. Cresskill, NJ: Hampton P, 1993. 134–136.

Christensen, Francis. *The Christensen Rhetoric Program*. New York: Harper, 1968.

Claggert, Fran. "Integrating Reading and Writing in Large Scale Assessment." *Evaluating Writing: The Role of Teachers' Knowledge about Text, Learning, and Culture*. Ed. Cooper and Odell. 344–365.

Cochran, Thomas C. *The Great Depression and World War II: 1929–1945*. Glenview, IL: Scott, Foresman, 1968.

Coffman, William E. Annual Service Recognition Dinner, 27 Apr. 1968. Princeton: ETS Archives.

———. "Development of the Tests." *College Board Review* 31 (1957): 6–10.

———. "Essay Examinations." In *Educational Measurement*. 2nd ed. Ed. Robert L. Thorndike. Washington: American Council on Education, 1971. 271–302.

———. On the Reliability of Ratings of Essay Examinations in English." *Research in the Teaching of English* 5.1 (1971): 24–36.

———. "Teacher Morale and Curriculum Development: A Statistical Analysis of Responses to a Reaction Survey." Diss., Teachers College, Columbia U, 1949.

Coleman, James S. et al. *Equality of Educational Opportunity*. Washington: GPO, 1996.

College Board. *A Guide to the New SAT® Essay*. New York: The College Board, 2004.

———. "The New SAT 2005." 23 Jan. 2005 <http://www.collegeboard.com/newsat/index.html>

College Entrance Examination Board. *Entrance English Questions Set by the College Entrance Examination Board, 1901–1923*. Boston: Ginn, 1924.

———. *Plan of Organization of the College Entrance Examination Board for the Middle States and Maryland and a Statement of Subjects in Which Examinations Are Proposed*. New York: College Entrance Examination Board, 1900.

———. *Questions Set at the Examinations, June 16–21, 1913*. Boston: Ginn, 1913.

———. *The Work of the College Entrance Examination Board, 1901–1925*. New York: Ginn, 1926.

———. *First Annual Report of the Secretary*. New York: College Entrance Examination Board, 1901.

———. *Nineteenth Annual Report of the Secretary*. New York: College Entrance Examination Board, 1919.

———. *Twentieth Annual Report of the Secretary*. New York: College Entrance Examination Board, 1920.

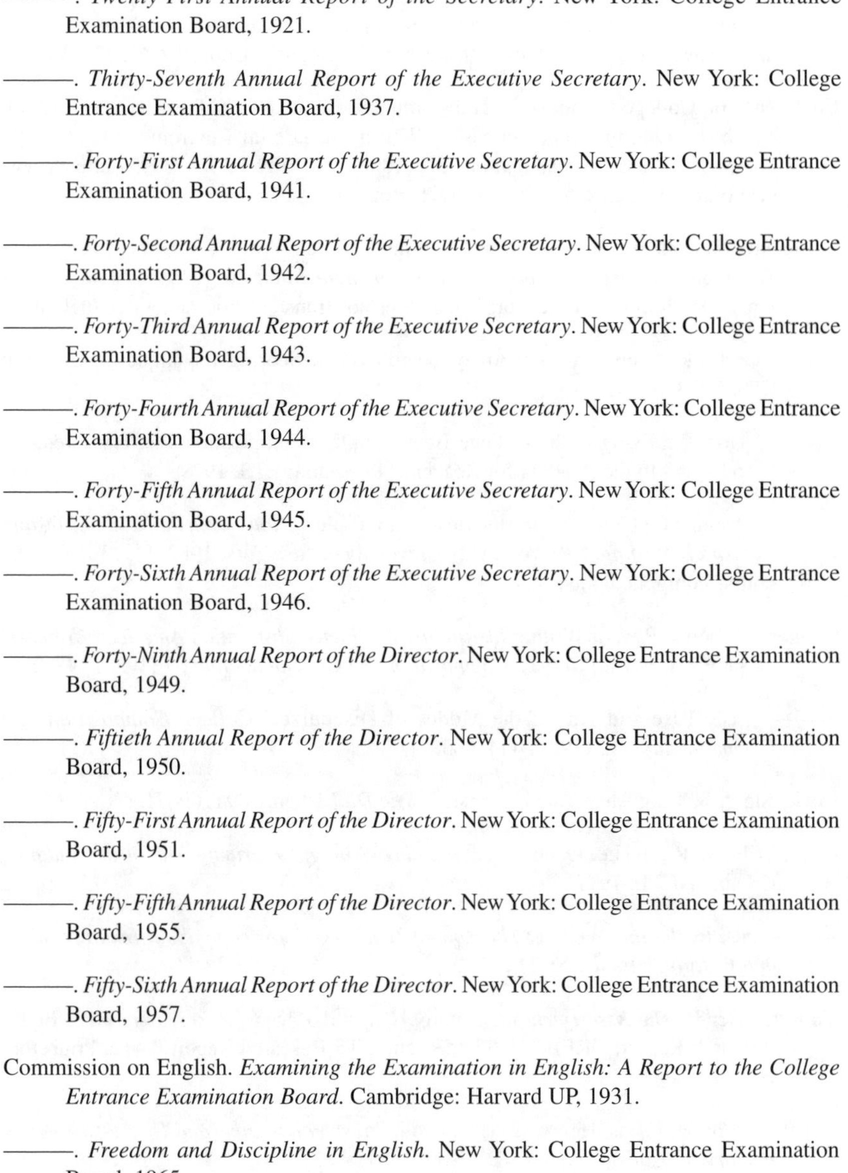

———. *Twenty-First Annual Report of the Secretary*. New York: College Entrance Examination Board, 1921.

———. *Thirty-Seventh Annual Report of the Executive Secretary*. New York: College Entrance Examination Board, 1937.

———. *Forty-First Annual Report of the Executive Secretary*. New York: College Entrance Examination Board, 1941.

———. *Forty-Second Annual Report of the Executive Secretary*. New York: College Entrance Examination Board, 1942.

———. *Forty-Third Annual Report of the Executive Secretary*. New York: College Entrance Examination Board, 1943.

———. *Forty-Fourth Annual Report of the Executive Secretary*. New York: College Entrance Examination Board, 1944.

———. *Forty-Fifth Annual Report of the Executive Secretary*. New York: College Entrance Examination Board, 1945.

———. *Forty-Sixth Annual Report of the Executive Secretary*. New York: College Entrance Examination Board, 1946.

———. *Forty-Ninth Annual Report of the Director*. New York: College Entrance Examination Board, 1949.

———. *Fiftieth Annual Report of the Director*. New York: College Entrance Examination Board, 1950.

———. *Fifty-First Annual Report of the Director*. New York: College Entrance Examination Board, 1951.

———. *Fifty-Fifth Annual Report of the Director*. New York: College Entrance Examination Board, 1955.

———. *Fifty-Sixth Annual Report of the Director*. New York: College Entrance Examination Board, 1957.

Commission on English. *Examining the Examination in English: A Report to the College Entrance Examination Board*. Cambridge: Harvard UP, 1931.

———. *Freedom and Discipline in English*. New York: College Entrance Examination Board, 1965.

Commission on New Possibilities for the Admission Testing Program. *Beyond Prediction*. New York: College Board, 1990.

Condon, William, and Liz Hamp-Lyons. "Maintaining a Portfolio-Based Writing Assessment: Research That Informs Program Development." *New Directions in Portfolio Assessment*. Ed. Black, et al. Portsmouth, NH: Boynton/Cook, 1994. 277–285.

Conference on College Composition and Communication. "CCCC Position Statement on Teaching, Learning, and Assessing Writing in Digital Environments." *College Composition and Communication* 55.4 (2004): 785–789. 23 Jan. 2005 <http://www.ncte.org/groups/cccc/positions/115775.htm>

Conference on College Composition and Communication. "Writing Assessment: A Position Statement." *College Composition and Communication* 46.3 (1995): 430–437. 23 Jan. 2005 <http://www.ncte.org/about/over/positions/category/assess/107610.htm>

Conlan, Gertrude. "Comparison of Analytic and Holistic Scoring Techniques." Princeton: ETS, 1978.

———. "How the Essay in the College Board English Composition Test Is Scored. An Introduction to the Reading for Readers." Princeton: ETS, 1978.

———. "Panning for Gold: Finding the Best Essay Topics." *Notes from the National Testing Network in Writing*. New York: City University of New York, 1982. 11. 23 Jan. 2005. <http://comppile.tamucc.edu>.

Connors, Robert J. Rev. of *Writing Instruction in Nineteenth-Century American Colleges*, by James A. Berlin. *College Composition and Communication* 37 (1986) 247–249.

———. "The Rise and Fall of the Modes of Discourse." *College Composition and Communication* 32 (1981) 444–463.

Cook, Albert S. "English at Yale University." *The Dial* 1 Feb. 1894: 69–71.

Cooper, Charles R., and Lee Odell, eds. *Evaluating Writing: Describing, Measuring, Judging*. Urbana: NCTE, 1977.

———, eds. *Evaluating Writing: The Role of Teachers' Knowledge about Text, Learning, and Culture*. Urbana: NCTE, 1999.

Cooper, Peter L. *The Assessment of Writing Ability: A Review of Research*. GRE Board Research Report, GREB No. 82-15R, and ETS Research Report 84-12. Princeton: ETS, 1984.

Copeland. Charles T., and Henry Milner Rideout. *Freshman English and Theme-Correcting in Harvard College*. New York: Silver, 1901.

Corson, Hiram. "English Literature at Cornell University." *The Dial* 1 Apr. 1894: 201–202.

Courtis, Stuart A. "Forty Years of Educational Measurement: An Appraisal and a Prophecy." *National Elementary Principal* 25 (1946): 19–22.

Cremin, Lawrence A. *The Transformation of the School: Progressivism in American Education, 1876–1957*. New York: Knopf, 1961.

Crusius, Timothy W. *Kenneth Burke and the Conversation after Philosophy*. Carbondale: Southern Illinois UP, 1999.

Cuban, Carry. *How Teachers Taught: Constancy and Change in American Classrooms, 1880–1990*. 2nd ed. New York: Teachers College P, 1993.

Davidson, Percy E. "The Social Significance of the Army Intelligence Findings." *Scientific Monthly* 16.2 (1923): 184–193. JSTOR 23 Jan. 2005 <http://www.jstor.org/search>.

Dedication Ceremony: Carl Campbell Brigham Library, Educational Testing Service, November 12, 1961. Princeton: ETS Archives, 1961.

Dewey, John. "The Reflex Arc Concept in Psychology." *The Early Works, 1882–1898*. Ed. Jo Ann Boydston. Vol. 5. Carbondale: Southern Illinois UP, 1972. 99–106.

Diederich, Paul B. "Innovations in English Teaching." *Needed Research in the Teaching of English: Proceedings, English Research Conference, 5–7 May 1962*. Princeton: ETS Archives. 72–78.

———. *Measuring Growth in English*. Urbana: NCTE, 1974.

———. Memo for Mr. Dobbin: The CEEB General Composition Test. 3 Oct. 1951. Paul B. Diederich Papers. Princeton: ETS Archives.

———. Memorandum to Henry Chauncey. 16 May 1951. Chauncey Merger File. Princeton: ETS Archives.

———. "Readers, Aides, and Technicians." *Harvard Graduate School of Education Association Bulletin* 6.1 (1961): 5–7.

———. To All My Friends and Well-Wishers. 6 Mar. 1966. Diederich Papers. Princeton: ETS Archives.

Diederich, Paul B., John W. French, and Sydell T. Carlton. *Factors in Judgments of Writing Ability*. RB-61-15. Princeton: ETS, 1961.

Divine, Robert A. *American Immigration Policy, 1924–1952*. New Haven: Yale UP, 1957.

Dolch, Edward William, Jr. "More Accurate Use of Composition Scales." *English Journal* 11 (1922): 536–544.

Donlon, Thomas F. "Brigham's Book." *College Board Review* 113 (1979): 24–30.

Douglass, Wallace. "Barrett Wendell." *Traditions of Inquiry*. Ed. Brereton. New York: Oxford UP, 1985. 3–25.

Downey, Matthew T. *Carl Campbell Brigham: Scientist and Educator*. Princeton: ETS, 1961.

Dudley, David A. "The Beginnings of the Advanced Placement Program." Dec. 1963. Princeton: ETS Archives.

Dunning, John. *On the Air: An Encyclopedia of Old Time Radio.* New York: Oxford UP, 1998.

Dyer, Henry S. "The Tests of Developed Ability." *College Board Review* 31 (1957): 5–6.

Eaton, Arthur Wentworth. *College Requirements in English Examinations*. Boston: Ginn, 1900.

Edel, Leon. *Henry James: A Life*. New York: Harper, 1985.

Effectiveness of Remedial Programs in New Jersey Public Colleges and Universities, Fall 1987–Spring 1989. Trenton: Department of Higher Education, 1992.

Eisenhower, Dwight. D. "Military-Industrial Complex Speech." *Public Papers of the Presidents of the United States*. Washington: Federal Register Division, National Archives and Records Service, General Services Administration, 1961. 1035–1040. 23 Jan. 2005 <http://www.yale.edu/lawweb/avalon/>.

Elbow, Peter. "Opinion: The Cultures of Literature and Composition: What Could Each Learn from the Other?" *College English* 64.5 (2002): 533–546.

Elbow, Peter, and Pat Belanoff. "Reflections on an Explosion: Portfolios in the '90s and Beyond." In *Situating Portfolios: Four Perspectives*. Ed. Kathleen Blake Yancey and Irwin Weiser. Logan: Utah State UP, 1997. 21–42.

Elbow, Peter. "State University of New York, Stony Brook: Portfolio-Based Evaluation Program." *New Methods in College Writing Programs: Theory into Practice*. Ed. Paul Connolly and Teresa Vilardi. New York: MLA, 1986. 95–105.

———. *Writing Without Teachers*. New York: Oxford UP, 1973.

———. "Will the Virtues of Portfolios Blind Us to Their Potential Dangers?" *New Directions in Portfolio Assessment*. Ed. Black, et al. Portsmouth, NH: Boynton/Cook, 1994. 40–55.

Eley, Earle G. "An Analysis of Writing Competence." Diss. U of Chicago, 1953.

Eley, Earle G. "The Experiment in General Composition." *College Board Review* 15 (1951): 217–221.

———. "The Test Satisfies an Educational Need." *College Board Review* 25 (1955) 9–13.

Eliot, Charles William. "President Eliot's Inaugural Address." *The Development of Harvard University.* Ed. Morison. lvix–lxxviii.

Elledge, Scott. "For the Board's English Tests: An Old Era Ends, What Lies Ahead?" *College Board Review* 71 (1969): 22.

Emig, Janet. *The Composing Process of Twelfth Graders*. Research Report 13. Urbana: NCTE, 1971.

Encyclopedia of American Immigration. Ed. James Ciment. 4 vols. Armonk, NY: M. E. Sharpe, 2001.

Evers, Williamson M., and Herbert J. Walberg. *School Accountability: An Assessment by the Koret Task Force on K–12 Education*. Stanford: Hoover Institution P, 2002.

Faigley, Lester; Stephen P. Witte; James Kinneavy; and John Daily. "The Writing Project Assessment Project." *Notes from the National Testing Network in Writing*. New York: The City University of New York, 1982. 5. CompPile 23 Jan. 2005 <http://comppile.tamucc.edu/>.

Farrand, Wilson. "Are College Entrance Requirements Too Great in Quantity?" *Educational Review.* Jan. 1906: 1–17.

———. *The Reform of College Entrance Requirements. Inaugural Address*. Newark: Wm. A. Baker, Printer, 1895.

Findley, Warren G. "Carl C. Brigham Revisited." *College Board Review* 119 (1981): 6–9.

Finn, Patrick J. "Computer-Aided Descriptions of Mature Word Choices in Writing." *Evaluating Writing: Describing, Measuring, Judging*. Ed. Cooper and Odell. 69–90.

Fitzgerald, F. Scott. *The Great Gatsby*. 1925. New York: Collier, 1986.

Flesch, Rudolph. *Why Johnny Can't Read—And What You Can Do About It*. New York: Harper, 1955.

Flower, Linda S., and John R. Hayes. "The Cognition of Discovery: Defining a Rhetorical Problem." *College Composition and Communication* 31 (1980): 21–32.

———. "A Cognitive Process Theory of Writing." *College Composition and Communication* 32 (1981): 365–387.

———. "The Pregnant Pause: An Inquiry into the Nature of Planning." *Research in the Teaching of English* 15 (1981) 229–244.

Flynn, George Q. *Conscription and Democracy: The Draft in France, Great Britain, and the United States*. Westport: Greenwood P, 2001.

———. *The Draft, 1940–1973*. Lawrence: UP of Kansas, 1993.

Foucault, Michel. *The History of Sexuality: An Introduction*. New York: Vintage, 1990.

French, John C. *A History of the University Founded by Johns Hopkins.* Baltimore: Johns Hopkins UP, 1946.

French, John W. "Schools of Thought in Judging Excellence of English Themes." Proc. of Invitational Conference on Testing Procedures, 1961. ETS Reprint. Princeton: ETS, 1962.

———. "What Is Factor Analysis?" *College Board Review* 10 (1950): 129–131.

Frisch-Kowalski, Sue. *The SAT®: A Timeline of Changes*. New York: College Entrance Examination Board, 2003. 23 Jan. 2005 < http://www.collegeboard.com/prod_downloads/sat/techhandbook/chapter4.pdf>

Frusciano, Thomas J. "Student Deferment and the Selective Service College Qualifying Test, 1951–1967." *Research Memorandum* RM-83-1. Princeton: ETS, 1980.

Frye, Brian N. "Restrictive Legislation." *Encyclopedia of American Immigration*. 150–155.

Fuess, Claude M. *The College Board: Its First Fifty Years*. New York: Columbia UP, 1950.

Fullerton, George Stuart, and James McKeen Cattell. *On the Perception of Small Differences, with Special Reference to the Extent, Force, and Time of Movement*. Philadelphia: U of Pennsylvania P, 1892.

"The GCT Experiment: Final Report." *College Board Review* 29 (1956): 31–32.

Galton, Francis. "Eugenics: Its Definition, Scope, and Aims." *American Journal of Sociology* 10.1 (1904) 1–24. JSTOR 23 Jan. 2005 <http://www.jstor.org/search>.

———. *Hereditary Genius: An Inquiry into Its Laws and Consequences*. London: Macmillan, 1869.

———. *Natural Inheritance*. London: Macmillan, 1889.

Gayley, Charles Mills. "English at the University of California," *The Dial* 16 July 1894: 28–32.

Geiser, Saul, and Roger Studley. *UC and the SAT: Predictive Validity and Differential Impact of the SAT I and the SAT II at the University of California*. Berkeley: Office of the President, Oct. 29, 2001. 23 Jan. 2005 <http://www.ucop.edu/welcome1.html>.

Geissler, Suzanne. *A Widening Sphere of Usefulness: Newark Academy, 1744–1993*. West Kennebunk: Phoenix Publishing, 1993.

Genung, John Franklin. "English at Amherst College." *The Dial* 1 Aug. 1894: 54–56.

Gere, Anne Ruggles. "Empirical Research in Composition." *Perspectives on Research and Scholarship in Composition*. Ed. Ben W. McClelland and Timothy R. Donovan. New York: MLA, 1985. 110–124.

Gibson, John M. *Physician to the World: The Life of General William C. Gorgas*. Durham: Duke UP, 1950.

Gilman, Daniel Coit. *The Benefits Which Society Derives from Universities: An Address*. Baltimore: Johns Hopkins UP, 1885.

———. *Inaugural Address*. San Francisco: John H. Carmany, 1872.

Godshalk, Fred I. "A Reply to the Critics." Rev. of *The Measurement of Writing Ability*, by Fred I. Godshalk, William E. Coffman, and Frances I. Swineford. *Research in the Teaching of English* 1.1 (1967): 84–88.

———. "Testing the English Composition Test." School and College Conf. on English. Barnard College, New York. 16 and 17 Feb. 1962. Green File, Roll 13. Princeton: ETS Archives.

———, Frances Swineford, and William E. Coffman. *The Measurement of Writing Ability*. New York: College Entrance Examination Board, 1966.

———, Frances Swineford, and William E. Coffman. "A Study of the English Composition Tests of the College Entrance Examination Board as Predictors of an Essay Criterion." Green File, Roll 13. Princeton: ETS Archives, 1961.

Gorman, T. P., Alan C. Purves, and R. Elaine Degenhart, eds. *The IEA Study of Written Composition I: The International Writing Tasks and Scoring Scales*. Oxford: Pergamon P, 1988.

Goswami, Dixie, Janice C. Redish, et al. *Writing in the Professions: A Course Guide and Instructional Materials for Advanced Composition*. Washington: American Institutes for Research, 1981. ERIC ED 220 860.

Gould, Stephen J. *The Mismeasure of Man*. New York: Norton, 1981.

Gramsci, Antonio. "Americanism and Fordism." *Selections from the Prison Notebooks*. Ed. and trans. Quintin Hoare and Geoffrey Nowell Smith. New York: International Publishers, 1971. 279–318.

Grandgent, Charles H. "The Modern Languages, 1869–1929." *The Development of Harvard University*. Ed. Morison. 65–105.

Greenberg, Karen. *The Effects of Essay Questions on the Writing of CUNY Freshmen*. New York: City University of New York Instructional Research Center, 1981.

Greenberg, Karen, Harvey S. Weiner, and Richard A. Donovan, eds. *Notes from the National Testing Network in Writing*. New York: The City University of New York, 1982. CompPile 23 Jan. 2004 <http://comppile.tamucc.edu/>.

Greenblatt, Stephen. "Towards a Poetic of Culture." *The New Historicism*. Ed. H. Aram Veeser. New York: Routledge, 1989. 1–14.

Grey, James, and Leo Ruth. *Properties of Writing Tasks: A Study of Alternative Procedures for Holistic Writing Assessment.* Final Report NIE-G-80-0034. Berkeley: U of California Graduate School of Education, Bay Area Writing Project, 1982. ERIC ED 230 576.

Guilford, J. P. "New Standards for Test Evaluation." *Educational and Psychological Measurement* 6 (1946): 427–438.

Hale, Edward E., Jr. "English at the State University of Iowa." *The Dial* 1 June 1894: 328–329.

Hamilton, A. E. "Eugenics." *Pedagogical Seminary* 21 (1914): 28–61.

Hamp-Lyons, Liz. "Writing Assessment in the World." *Assessing Writing* 9.1 (2004) 1–3.

Hamp-Lyons, Liz, and William Condon. *Assessing the Portfolio: Principles for Practice, Theory, and Research.* Cresskill, NJ: Hampton P, 2000.

Hampel, Robert L. "The Origins of the Educational Testing Service." *A Faithful Mirror: Reflections on the College Board and Education in America.* Ed. Michael C. Johanek. New York: College Board, 2001. 247–270.

Harkin, Patricia. "Child's Ballads: Narrating Histories of Composition and Literary Studies." *Disciplining English.* Ed. Shumway and Dionne. 17–37.

Hart, James Morgan. *German Universities: A Narrative of Personal Experience.* New York: G. P. Putnam's Sons, 1878.

The Harvard University Catalogue, 1872–73. Cambridge: Charles W. Sever, 1873.

The Harvard University Catalogue, 1873–74. Cambridge: Charles W. Sever, 1874.

Harvey, David. *The Condition of Postmodernity: An Inquiry into the Origins of Cultural Change.* Cambridge: Basil Blackwell, 1989.

Haswell, Richard H., ed. *Beyond Outcomes: Assessment and Instruction Within a University Writing Program.* Westport: Ablex, 2001.

Hawkins, Hugh. *Banding Together: The Rise of National Associations in American Higher Education, 1887–1950.* Baltimore: Johns Hopkins UP, 1992.

Hayakawa, S. I. *Language in Thought and Action.* 2nd ed. New York: Harcourt, 1941.

Heidegger, Martin. "The Question Concerning Technology." *Basic Writings.* Ed. David Farrell Krell. New York: Harper, 1977. 287–317.

Hesse, Douglas. "Who Owns Writing?" Chair's Address. Conf. on Coll. Composition and Communication Convention. Moscone Center, San Francisco. 17 Mar. 2005.

Heyman, Neil M. *World War I.* Westport: Greenwood P, 1997.

Higham, John. *Send These to Me: Immigrants in Urban America*. Baltimore: Johns Hopkins UP, 1984.

Hill, Adams Sherman. "An Answer to the Cry for More English." 1879. *Twenty Years of School and College English*. 6–16.

———. *The Principles of Rhetoric and Their Application*. New York: Harper, 1878.

Hillegas, Milo B. "A Scale for the Measurement of Quality in English Composition by Young People." *Teachers College Record* 13.4 (1912): 1–55.

Hillocks, George, Jr. *Research on Written Composition: New Directions for Teaching*. Urbana: NCTE, 1986.

———. *The Testing Trap: How State Writing Assessments Control Learning*. New York: Teachers College P, 2002.

Hoffmann, Banesh. *The Tyranny of Testing*. New York: Collier, 1962.

Hogan, Robert F. Foreword to *Measuring Growth in English*. Urbana: NCTE, 1974. ii–iv.

Hollis, Martin. *The Philosophy of Social Science: An Introduction*. Cambridge: Cambridge UP, 1994.

Hopkins, L. Thomas. *The Marking System of the College Entrance Examination Board*. Studies in Educational Psychology and Educational Measurement. Series 1, No. 2. Cambridge: Harvard Graduate School of Education, 1921.

Howe, M. A. deWolfe, ed. *Barrett Wendell and His Letters*. Boston: Atlantic Monthly P, 1924.

Huddleston, Earle. "The Effect of Objective Standards upon Composition Teachers' Judgments." *Journal of Educational Research* 12.5 (1925): 329–340.

Huddleston, Edith M. "Measurement of Writing Ability at the College-Entrance Level: Objective vs. Subjective Testing Techniques." *Journal of Experimental Education* 22.3 (1954): 165–213.

———. "Recent Studies of the English Composition Test." *College Board Review* 1.4 (1948): 45+.

Hundleby, Margaret, Marjorie Rush Hovde, and Jo Allen. "Guest Editor's Column." *Technical Communication Quarterly* 12.1 (2003): 5–6.

Huot, Brian. "Editorial: An Introduction to *Assessing Writing*." *Assessing Writing* 1.1 (1994) 1–9.

———. "The Literature of Direct Writing Assessment: Major Concerns and Prevailing Trends." *Review of Educational Research* 60.2 (1990): 237–263.

———. *(Re)Articulating Writing Assessment for Teaching and Learning*. Logan: Utah State UP, 2002.

———. "A Survey of College and University Writing Placement Practices." *WPA: Writing Program Administration* 17.3 (1994): 49–65.

———. "Toward a New Discourse of Assessment for the College Writing Classroom." *College English* 65.2 (2002): 163–180.

Ittenback, Richard F., Irvin G. Estes, and Howard Wainer. "The History of Test Development." *Contemporary Intellectual Assessment: Theories, Tests, and Issues*. Ed. Dawn P. Flanagan, Judy L. Genshaft, and Patti L. Harrison. New York: Guilford P, 1997. 17–31.

James, Henry. *Charles W. Eliot: President of Harvard University, 1869–1909*. 2 vols. London: Constable and Company, 1930.

James, Henry. *Letters: 1843–1875*. Ed. Leon Edel. Vol. 1. Cambridge: Harvard UP, 1974–1984.

Jamieson, Amie, Andrea Curry, and Gladys Martinez. *Current Population Reports: School Enrollment in the United States—Social and Economic Characteristics of Students, October 1999*. Washington: US Census Bureau, 2001. 23 Jan. 2005 < http://www.census.gov/prod/2001pubs/p20-533.pdf>

Jenkins, Roy. *Churchill: A Biography*. New York: Farrar, 2001.

Johnson, Eugene G., and Rebecca Zwick. *Focusing the New Design: The 1988 NAEP Technical Report*. ED 325 496. Princeton: ETS Technical Report, 1988.

Johnson, Lyndon B. "Memorandum to Major General Lewis B. Hershey." 13 June 1951. Chauncey Merger File. Princeton: ETS Archives.

Johnson, Nan. *Nineteenth-Century Rhetoric in North America*. Carbondale: Southern Illinois UP, 1968.

Joncich, Geraldine M. *The Sane Positivist: A Biography of Edward L. Thorndike*. Middletown: Wesleyan UP, 1968.

Kamphaus, R. W., Martha D. Petoskey, and Anna Walters Morgan. "A History of Intelligence Interpretation." *Contemporary Intellectual Assessment: Theories, Tests, and Issues*. Ed. Dawn P. Flanagan, Judy L. Genshaft, and Patti L. Harrison. New York: Guilford P, 1997. 32–47.

Kayfetz, Isidore. "A Critical Study of the Hillegas Composition Scale." *Pedagogical Seminary* 21 (1914): 559–577.

Kellner, Hans. "After the Fall." *Writing Histories of Rhetoric*. Ed. Vitanza. Carbondale: Southern Illinois UP, 1994. 20–37.

Kelley, Truman Lee. *Interpretation of Educational Measurement.* Chicago: World Book, 1927.

Kelly-Riley, Diane. "Whither? Some Questions, Some Answers." *Beyond Outcomes.* Ed. Haswell. 191–192.

Kevles, Daniel J. *In the Name of Eugenics: Genetics and the Uses of Human Heredity.* New York: Knopf, 1985.

———. "Testing the Army's Intelligence: Psychologists and the Military in World War I." *Journal of American History* 55.3 (1968): 565–581.

Kilgannon, Corey. "Warming Up to a New SAT, but Nail-Biting the Usual Way." *New York Times* 13 Mar. 2005: 37+.

Kliebard, Herbert M. *The Struggle for the American Curriculum, 1893–1958.* 2nd ed. New York: Routledge, 1995.

Kobrin, Jennifer L. *Forecasting the Predictive Validity of the New SAT I Writing Section.* New York: College Board, 2004. 23 Jan. 2005 <http://www.collegeboard.com>.

Kuder, G. F., and M. W. Richardson. "The Theory of the Estimation of Test Reliability." *Psychometrika* 2 (1937): 151–160.

Lagemann, Ellen Condliffe. *Private Power for the Public Good: A History of the Carnegie Foundation for the Advancement of Teaching.* Middletown: Wesleyan UP, 1983.

Law, Richard. "The Continuing Program: A Retrospective View." *Beyond Outcomes.* Ed. Haswell. 3–12.

Lawrence, Ida. M., et al. *A Historical Perspective on the Content of the SAT.* College Board Research Report No. 2003-3, ETS-RR-03-10. New York: College Entrance Examination Board, 2003.

Lederman, Marie Jean. "Evolution of an Instructional Resource Center: The CUNY Experience." *ADE Bulletin* 82 (1985): 43–47. 23 Jan 2005 <http://www.mla.org/ade/bulletin/N082/082043.htm>

Lehrer, Jim. "The SAT Debate." *NewsHour.* 30 Mar. 2001. 23 Jan. 2005. <http://www.pbs.org>.

Leighton, R. F. *Harvard Examination Papers.* 9th ed. Boston: Ginn, Heath, and Co., 1883.

Lemann, Nicholas. *The Big Test: The Secret History of the American Meritocracy.* New York: Farrar, 1999.

———. "What Do These Two Men Have in Common?" *Time.* 4 Mar. 2001. 23 Jan. 2005 <http://www.time.com/time/nation/article/0,8599,101322,00.html>.

Leonhardy, Galen, and William Condon. "Exploring the Difficult Cases: In the Cracks of Writing Assessment." *Beyond Outcomes.* Ed. Haswell. 65–79.

Lewin, Tamar. "College Board to Revise SAT after Criticism by University." *New York Times* 23 Mar. 2002, late ed.: A10.

Lippmann, Walter. "A Defense of Education." *Century Magazine* May 1923: 95–103. *Disability History Museum.* 23 Jan. 2005 <http://www.disabilitymuseum.org>.

Liu, Jinghua; Miriam Feigenbaum; and Linda Cook. *A Simulation Study to Explore Configuring the New SAT Critical Reading Section Without Analogy Items.* College Board Research Report No. 2004-2, ETS RR-04-01. New York: College Board, 2004.

Lloyd-Jones, Richard. "Primary Trait Scoring." *Evaluating Writing: Describing, Measuring, Judging*. Ed. Cooper and Odell. 32–66.

———. "Richard Braddock." *Traditions of Inquiry*. Ed. Brereton. 153–170.

———. "Skepticism About Test Scores." *Notes from the National Testing Network in Writing.* New York: The City University of New York, 1982. 3, 9. CompPile 23 Jan. 2005 <http://comppile.tamucc.edu/>.

Lord, Frederick M. *Applications of Item Response Theory to Practical Testing Problems.* Hillsdale, NJ: Erlbaum, 1980.

Lowell, Abbot Lawrence. "The Art of Examination." 1926: *The Work of the College Entrance Examination Board, 1901–1925.* New York: Ginn, 1926. 31–43.

Lutkus, Anthony D., Robert E. Lynch, and Paul A. Ramsey. "Three Major Issues in Large Scale Essay Assessment." *Notes from the National Testing Network in Writing* 9. New York: The City University of New York, 1990. 14. CompPile 23 Jan. 2005 <http://comppile.tamucc.edu/>.

Lyman, Rollo L. *Summary of Investigations Relating to Grammar, Language, and Composition.* Chicago: U of Chicago P, 1929.

Lynch, Robert E. Interview. *Composition Chronicle* 5.6 (1992): 3.

———. Personal Interview 19 Nov. 2003.

———. "Testimony Before New Jersey Board of Higher Education." 12 May 1994.

Lynne, Patricia. *Coming to Terms: Theorizing Writing Assessment in Composition Studies.* Logan: Utah State UP, 2004.

MacLean, George E. "The University of Minnesota." *English in American Universities*. Ed. Payne. 155–161.

Marcus, Alan I., and Howard P. Segal. *Technology in America: A Brief History*. 2nd ed. New York: Wadsworth, 1999.

Marx, Leo. *The Machine in the Garden: Technology and the Pastoral Ideal in America.* 1970. New York: Oxford UP, 2000.

McCleary, Bill. "New Jersey Study Finds Remedial Writing Courses Successful for College Students Who Pass Them." *Composition Chronicle* 5.6 (1992) 1–3, 11.

McGrath, Charles. "Writing to the Test." *New York Times* (Education Supplement) 7 Nov. 2004: 24+.

McSeveney, Sam. "Immigrants, the Literacy Test, and Quotas: Selected American History College Textbooks' Coverage of the Congressional Restriction of European Immigrants, 1917–1929." *History Teacher* 21.1 (1987): 41–51.

Menand, Louis. *The Metaphysical Club: A Story of Ideas in America.* New York: Farrar, 2001.

Merchant, Carolyn. "The Theoretical Structure of Ecological Revolutions." *Environmental Review* 11.4 (1987): 265–274.

Miller, Arthur. *Death of a Salesman: Certain Private Conversations in Two Acts and a Requiem.* New York: Viking, 1949.

Miller, Thomas P., and Joseph G. Jones. "Review: Working Out Our History." Rev of *The Selected Essays of Robert J. Connors*, ed. by Lisa Ede and Andrea Lunsford, *Writing in the Academic Disciplines: A Curricular History*, by David R. Russell, *Imagining Rhetoric: Composing Women of the Early United States*, by Janet Carey Eldred and Peter Mortensen, and *Gender and Rhetorical Space in American Life, 1866–1910. College English* 67.4 (2005): 421–439.

Mitchell, W. J. T., and Wang Ning. "The Ends of Theory: The Beijing Symposium on Critical Inquiry." *Critical Inquiry* 31.2 (2005): 265–270.

Mizell, Linda Kay. "Major Shifts in Writing Assessment for College Admission, 1874–1964." Diss., East Texas State U, 1994.

Moffett, James. *Active Voice: A Writing Program Across the Curriculum.* Montclair: Boynton/Cook, 1981.

Morison, Samuel Eliot, ed. *The Development of Harvard University Since the Inauguration of President Eliot, 1869–1929.* Cambridge: Harvard UP, 1930.

Moss, Pamela. "Testing the Test: A Response to 'Multiple Inquiry in the Validation of Writing Tests.'" *Assessing Writing* 5.1 (1998): 111–122.

Münsterberg, Hugo. *American Traits from the Point of View of a German.* New York: Houghton, 1901.

Murchison, Carl, ed. "Edward Lee Thorndike." *A History of Psychology in Autobiography.* Vol. 3. Worcester: Clark UP, 1930. 263–270.

———. "Robert Mearns Yerkes." *A History of Psychology in Autobiography*. Vol. 2. Worcester: Clark UP, 1930. 381–407.

Myers, Miles. *A Procedure for Writing Assessment and Holistic Scoring*. Urbana: NCTE, 1980.

Nairn, Allen. *The Reign of ETS: The Corporation That Makes Up Minds*. New Jersey: Nairn and Associates. 1980.

National Center for Education Statistics. *Projections of Education Statistics to 2013*. Washington: National Center for Education Statistics, 2003. 23 Jan. 2005 <http://nces.ed.gov/pubsearch/>.

National Commission on Writing for America's Families, Schools, and Colleges. *Writing: A Ticket to Work…Or a Ticket Out: A Survey of Business Leaders*. New York: College Board, 2004. 23 Jan. 2005 < http://www.writingcommission.org/>

National Commission on Writing in America's Schools and Colleges. *The Neglected "R": The Need for a Writing Revolution*. New York: College Board, 2003. 23 Jan. 2005 <http://www.writingcommission.org/>

National Education Association of the United States. *Report of the Committee of Ten on Secondary School Studies, with the Reports of the Conferences Arranged by the Committee*. New York: American Book Company, 1894.

New Jersey College Basic Skills Placement Testing, Fall 1991. Trenton: Department of Higher Education, 1991.

Niebuhr, Reinhold. Introduction. *The Varieties of Religious Experience*. By William James. 1902. New York: Collier, 1961. 5–8.

No Child Left Behind Act of 2001. Pub. L. 107–110. 8 Jan. 2002. Stat. 115.1425.

Noyes, Edward Simpson. Introduction. *The Measurement of Writing Ability—A Significant Breakthrough*. By Fred I. Godshalk, Frances Swineford, and William E. Coffman. New York: College Entrance Examination Board, 1966. iv–vi.

———. "The New Type of Tests in Composition." *English Leaflet* 44.392 (1945): 49–58. Reel No. 5, Green File. Princeton: ETS Archives.

———. "Teaching and Testing of English." *College Composition and Communication* 12.1 (1961): 33–38.

Noyes, Edward Simpson, and John Marshall Stalnaker. *Report on the English Examination of June 1937: A Description of the Procedures Used in Preparing and Reading the Examination in English and an Analysis of the Results of the Reading*. New York: College Entrance Examination Board, 1938.

Noyes, Edward Simpson, William Merritt Sale, Jr., and John Marshall Stalnaker. *Report on the First Six Tests in English Composition, with Sample Answers from the Tests of April and June, 1944*. New York: College Entrance Examination Board, 1945.

"Objective Tests in Literature." Editorial. *English Journal* 17.3 (1928): 251–252.

Odell, Lee. "Defining and Assessing Competence in Writing." *The Nature and Measurement of Competency in English*. Ed. Charles R. Cooper. Urbana: NCTE, 1981. 95–138.

———. "Measuring the Effect of Instruction in Pre-Writing." *Research in the Teaching of English* 8.2 (1974): 228–241.

———. "New Questions for Evaluators of Writing." *Notes from the National Testing Network in Writing*. New York: The City University of New York, 1982. 10–13. CompPile 23 Jan. 2005 <http://comppile.tamucc.edu/>.

———. "Piaget, Problem-Solving, and Freshman Composition." *College Composition and Communication* 24.1 (1973): 36–42.

———. Telephone interview. 12 Apr. 2004.

Odell, Lee, and Dixie Goswami, eds. *Writing in Nonacademic Settings*. New York: Guilford P, 1986.

Ogden, C. K., and I. A. Richards. *The Meaning of Meaning: A Study of the Influence of Language upon Thought and of the Science of Symbolism*. New York: Harcourt, 1922.

Oh, Hyeon-Jo, and Michael Walker. *The Effects of Essay Placement and Prompt Type of Performance of the New SAT*. ETS Statistical Report ST-2003-72. Princeton: ETS, 2003.

Ohmann, Richard. *Politics of Knowledge: The Commercialization of the University, the Professions, and Print Culture*. Middletown: Wesleyan UP, 2003.

Page, Ellis B. "The Imminence of Grading Essays by Computer." *Phi Delta Kappan* 47 (1966): 238–243.

Palmer, Orville. "Sixty Years of English Testing." *College Board Review* 42 (1960): 8–14.

Payne, William Morton, ed. "College and University English: A Summary." *The Dial* 1 Nov. 1894: 242–251.

———. *English in American Universities*. Boston: Heath, 1895.

Pearson, Karl. *The Life, Letters and Labors of Francis Galton*. Vol. 1. Cambridge: Cambridge UP, 1914.

———. *The Life, Letters and Labors of Francis Galton: Researches of Middle Life*. Vol. 2. Cambridge: Cambridge UP, 1924.

Pearson, Richard. "The Test Fails as an Entrance Examination." *College Board Review* 25 (1955): 2–9.

Persky, Hilary R., Mary C. Daane, Ying Jin. *The Nation's Report Card: Writing 2002.* Washington: U.S. Department of Education, Institute of Education Sciences, and National Center for Education Statistics, 2003. 23 Jan. 2005 <http://nces.ed.gov/nationsreportcard/pdf/main2002/2003529.pdf>

Perl, Sondra. "The Composing Process of Unskilled College Writers." *Research in the Teaching of English* 13 (1979): 317–336.

Perry, Ralph Barton. "Psychology, 1876–1929." *The Development of Harvard University.* Ed. Morison. 216–230.

Porter, Theodore M. *The Rise of Statistical Thinking, 1820–1900.* Princeton: Princeton UP, 1986.

Powers, Donald E., et al. *Stumping E-Rater: Challenging the Validity of Automated Essay Scoring.* GRE Board Professional Report No. 98-08bP and ETS Research Report 01-3. Princeton: ETS, 2001.

Purves, Alan. C., et al. *Common Sense and Testing in English.* Urbana: NCTE, 1975.

Purves, Alan C. "Designing the Board's New Literature Achievement Test." *College Board Review* 67 (1968) 16–20.

———, ed. *The IEA Study of Written Composition II: Education and Performance in Fourteen Countries.* Oxford: Pergamon P, 1992.

———. "Implications of the IEA Studies in Reading and Literature for College English Departments." *ADE Bulletin* 72 (Summer 1982) 1–3. 26 Aug. 2004 <http://mla/org.ade>.

———. *The Web of Text and the Web of God: An Essay on the Third Information Transformation.* New York: Guilford, 1998.

Purves, Alan C., A. Söter, Sauli Takala, and Anneli Vähäpassi. "Towards a Domain-Referenced System for Classifying Composition Assignments." *Research in the Teaching of English* 18.4 (1984): 385–406.

Quellmalz, Edys S., Frank J. Cappel, and Chih-Ping Chou. "Effects of Discourse and Response Mode on the Measurement of Writing Competence." *Journal of Educational Measurement* 19.4 (1982): 241–258.

Ramsey, Paul A. "Are There Equity Implications in High-Stakes Teacher Testing?" Keynote Address, Standards-Based Teacher Education Project Conference, 11 June 2001, Washington. 23 Jan. 2005 <http://www.c-b-e.org>.

———. “Minorities and Standardized Tests.” *Consensus and Dissent: Teaching English Past, Present, and Future*. Ed. Marjorie N. Farmer. Urbana: NCTE, 1986. 88–94.

———. “Teaching the Teachers to Teach Black-Dialect Writers.” *College English* 41.2 (1979): 197–201.

———. Telephone interview. 25 Nov. 2004.

Ravitch, Diane. “Testing and Accountability, Historically Considered.” *School Accountability: An Assessment by the Koret Task Force on K–12 Education*.” Ed. Williamson M. Evers and Herbert J. Walberg. Stanford: Hoover Institution P, 2002. 9–21.

“Reading Conference.” *College Board Review* 19 (1953): 324–326.

“Reliability.” Def. 2. *Oxford English Dictionary*. 2nd ed. 1989.

Remondino, C. “A Factorial Analysis of the Evaluation of Scholastic Compositions in the Mother Tongue.” *The British Journal of Educational Psychology* 29 (1959): 242–251.

Reynolds, Terry S. *75 Years of Progress: A History of the American Institute of Chemical Engineers*. New York: AIChE, 1983.

Rice, Joseph Mayer. *The Public-School System in the United States*. 1893. New York: Arno P, 1969.

———. *Scientific Management in Education*. 1914. New York: Arno P, 1969.

Rickover, Hyman George. *Education and Freedom*. New York: Dutton, 1959.

Rorty, Richard. *Contingency, Irony, and Solidarity*. Cambridge: Cambridge UP, 1989.

Rosenblatt, Louise M. Rosenblatt, *Literature as Exploration*. New York: Appleton, 1938.

Rudolph, Frederick. *The American College and University: A History*. New York: Vintage, 1962.

Russell, David R. *Writing in the Academic Disciplines: A Curricular History*. 2nd ed. Carbondale: Southern Illinois UP, 2002.

Ruth, Leo, and Catharine Keech. “Designing Prompts for Holistic Writing Assessments: Knowledge from Theory, Research, and Practice.” *Properties of Writing Tasks*. Grey and Ruth. 32–259.

Ruth, Leo, and Sandra Murphy. *Designing Writing Tasks for the Assessment of Writing*. Norwood, NJ: Ablex, 1988.

Sampson, Martin W. “The University of Indiana.” *The Dial* 1 July 1894: 5–7.

Santayana, George. *Character and Opinion in the United States, with Reminiscences of William James and Josiah Royce and Academic Life in America*. New York: Scribner's, 1920.

Saretzky, Gary D. "Carl Campbell Brigham, the Native Intelligence Hypothesis, and the Scholastic Aptitude Test." *Research Memorandum* RM-82-4. Princeton: ETS, 1982.

Sattelmeyer, Robert. "The Remaking of Walden." *Writing the American Classics*. Ed. James Barbour and Tom Quirk. Chapel Hill: U of North Carolina P, 1990. 53–78.

———. *Thoreau's Reading: A Study in Intellectual History with Bibliographic Catalogue*. Princeton: Princeton UP, 1988.

"Scale." Def. 5c. *Oxford English Dictionary*. 2nd ed. 1989.

Scardamalia, Marlene. "How Children Cope with the Cognitive Demands of Writing." In *Writing: Process, Development, and Communication*. Vol. 2. Ed. Carl H. Frederiksen and Joseph F. Dominic. Hillsdale, NJ: Erlbaum, 1981.

———. *The Psychology of Written Composition*. Hillsdale, NJ: Erlbaum, 1987.

Scardamalia, Marlene, Carl Bereiter, and Bryant Fillion. *Writing for Results: A Sourcebook of Consequential Composing Activities*. Toronto: Ontario Institute for Studies in Education, 1981.

Schelling, Felix F. "The University of Pennsylvania." *The Dial* 16 Sept. 1894: 146–147.

Schilb, John. "Future Historiographies of Rhetoric and the Present Age of Anxiety." *Writing Histories of Rhetoric*. Ed. Vitanza. 128–138.

Sciara, Frank J., and Richard K. Jantz, eds. *Accountability in American Education*. Boston: Allyn and Bacon, 1972.

Scott, Fred Newton. "English at the University of Michigan." *The Dial* 16 Aug. 1894: 82–84.

———. "Our Problems." *English Journal* 2.1 (1913): 1–10.

Selective Service College Qualifying Test. *Bulletin of Information*. Mar.–June 1951. Princeton: ETS Archives.

Self, Robert T. *Barrett Wendell*. Boston: Twayne, 1975.

Shaughnessy, Mina P. *Errors and Expectations: A Guide for the Teacher of Basic Writing*. New York: Oxford UP, 1977.

Sheils, Merrill."Why Johnny Can't Write." *Newsweek* 8 Dec. 1975: 58–65.

Shermis, Mark D., and Jill Burstein, eds. *Automated Essay Scoring: A Cross-Disciplinary Perspective*. Hillsdale, NJ: Erlbaum, 2003.

"Should the General Composition Test Be Continued?" *College Board Review* 25 (1955): 2.

Shugrue, Michael F. *English in a Decade of Change*. New York: Pegasus, 1968.

Shumway, David R., and Craig Dionne. *Disciplining English: Alternative Histories, Critical Perspectives*. State U of New York P, 2002.

Smyth, Herbert Weir. "The Classics: 1867–1929." *The Development of Harvard University*. Ed. Morison. 33–64.

Snyder, Thomas D., ed. *120 Years of American Education: A Statistical Portrait*. Washington: National Center for Educational Statistics, 1993.

Spearman, Charles. *The Abilities of Man: Their Nature and Measurement*. New York: Macmillan, 1927.

———. "'General Intelligence,' Objectively Determined and Measured." *American Journal of Psychology* 15 (1904): 201–293.

———. "The Proof and Measurement of Association Between Two Things." *American Journal of Psychology* 15 (1904): 72–101.

Spencer, Herbert. *Education: Intellectual, Moral, and Physical*. New York: Appleton, 1860.

———. *Philosophy of Style: An Essay*. New York: Appleton, 1933.

———. *Social Statics, or the Conditions Essential to Human Happiness Specified, and the First of Them Developed*. London: John Chapman, 1851.

Spring, Joel. *Conflicts of Interest: The Politics of American Education*. New York: McGraw-Hill, 1997.

Stalnaker, John Marshall. "Essay and Objective Writing Tests." *English Journal* (College Edition) 22.3 (1933): 217–222. Microfilm Roll No. 10 (Green Files). Princeton: ETS Archives.

———. "Essay Examinations Reliably Read." *School and Society* 46 (1937): 671–672.

———. Interview. *ETS Archives Oral History Program*. 12 June 1985. Princeton: ETS Archives, 1985.

———. "Question VI—The Essay." *English Journal* (College Edition) 26.2 (1937): 133–140. Microfilm Roll No. 10 (Green Files). Princeton: ETS Archives.

Stalnaker, John Marshall, and Ruth C. Stalnaker. "Reliable Reading of Essay Tests." *School Review* 42.8 (1934) 599–605. JSTOR 23 Jan. 2005 <http://www.jstor.org/search>.

Standardized Testing. S.5200-A. Senate Assembly of the State of New York. 26 April 1979.

Starch, Daniel, and Edward C. Elliott. "Reliability of the Grading of High-School Work in English." *School Review* 20 (1912): 442–457.

Steinmann, Martin, Jr. "A Conceptual Review." Rev. of *The Measurement of Writing Ability*, by Fred I. Godshalk, William E. Coffman, and Frances I. Swineford. *Research in the Teaching of English* 1.1 (1967): 79–84.

Sternglass, Marilyn. *Time to Know Them: A Longitudinal Study of Writing and Learning at the College Level*. Mahwah: Lawrence Erlbaum: 1997.

Stewart, Donald C. "Fred Newton Scott." *Traditions of Inquiry*. 26–49.

Stigler, Stephen M. *The History of Statistics: The Measurement of Uncertainty Before 1900*. Cambridge: Harvard UP, 1986

Stout, Dale, and Sue Stuart. "E. G. Boring's Review of Brigham's *A Study of American Intelligence*: A Case Study in the Politics of Reviews." *Social Studies of Science* 21 (1991): 133–142.

Stroud, James B., et al. "Educational Measurements." *Review of Educational Research* 26.3 (1956): 268–291.

Stuit, Dewey B., ed. *Personnel Research and Test Development in the Bureau of Naval Personnel*. Princeton: Princeton UP, 1947.

Swineford, Frances. "The Effect of Motivation on Scores on a Grammar Test." *The School Review* 44.6 (1936): 434–444.

———. "Factor Analysis in Educational and Vocational Guidance." *The School Review* 46.10 (1938): 760–762.

———. Interview. *ETS Oral History Program*. Princeton: ETS Archives, 1992.

———. "Test Analysis of College Entrance Examination Board Advanced Placement Tests." Sept. 1956. SR-56-28. Princeton: ETS Archives.

Swineford, Frances, and Fred I. Godshalk. "Memorandum for All Concerned; Subject: CEEB Research Proposal—Validity of the Interlinear." 2 Oct. 1961. Princeton: ETS Archives.

Swineford, Frances, and John Landis. "Questioning the Questions." *College Board Review* 11 (1950): 142–147.

Terman, Lewis M. "Letter to Don Marquis." 24 Sept. 1948. Lewis Terman Papers. SC038/ Box 15/Folder 5. Stanford University.

Thomas, Charles Swain. "The Examinations in English." *English Journal* 21.6 (1932): 441–452.

Thomson, Godfrey H., and Stella Bailes. "The Reliability of Essay Marks." *Forum of Education* 4.2 (1926): 85–91.

Thoreau, Henry David. *Walden*. 1854. Ed. J. Lyndon Shanley. Princeton: Princeton UP, 2004.

Thorndike, Edward L. "A Constant Error in Psychological Ratings." *Journal of Applied Psychology* 4.1 (1920): 25–29.

———. *Educational Psychology*. New York: Lemcke and Buechner, 1903.

———. "An Empirical Study of College Entrance Examinations." *Science* 1 June 1906: 839–845. JSTOR 23 Jan. 2005 <http://www.jstor.org/search>.

———. "The Future of the College Entrance Examination Board." *Educational Review* 31 (1906): 470–483.

———. *Handwriting*. New York: Teachers College, 1917.

———. "A Scale for Merit in English Writing by Young People." *Journal of Educational Psychology* 2 (1911): 361–368.

———. "Notes on the Significance and Use of the Hillegas Scale for Measuring the Quality of English Composition." *English Journal* 2.9 (1913): 551–561.

Tichenor, Daniel J. *Dividing Lines: The Politics of Immigration Control in America*. Princeton: Princeton UP, 2002.

Tolman, Albert H. "English at the University of Chicago." *The Dial* 16 June 1894: 356–357.

Trabue, Marion R. "Supplementing the Hillegas Scale." *Teachers College Record* 18 (1917): 51–84.

Trachsel, Mary. *Institutionalizing Literacy: The Historical Role of College Entrance Examinations in English*. Carbondale: Southern Illinois UP, 1992.

Troyka, Lynn Quitman. "Looking Back and Moving Forward." *Notes from the National Testing Network in Writing*. New York: The City University of New York, 1982. 3, 9. CompPile 23 Jan. 2005 <http://comppile.tamucc.edu/>.

Truman, Harry S. "Statement by the President." June 27, 1950. Truman Presidential Museum and Library. 23 Jan. 2005 <http://www.trumanlibrary.org>.

Tucker, Ledyard R. "A Note on the Estimation of Test Reliability by the Kuder-Richardson Formula (20)." *Psychometrika* 15 (1949): 117–119.

Turnbull, William W. "How Can We Make Testing More Relevant?" *College Board Review* 67 (1968): 5–10.

Turner, Frederick Jackson. "Crossing the Continent." *The Dial* 1 Feb. 1894: 80–82.

———. *History, Frontier, and Section: Three Essays.* Albuquerque: U of New Mexico P, 1993.

Twenty Years of School and College English. Cambridge: Harvard University, 1896.

Valentine, John A. *The College Board and the School Curriculum: A History of the College Board's Influence on the Substance and Standards of American Education, 1900–1980*. New York: College Board, 1987.

"Validate." Def. 2b. *Oxford English Dictionary*. 2nd ed. 1989.

Van Hise, Charles R. *Principles of North American Pre-Cambrian Geology*. Washington: GPO, 1896.

Van Wagenen, M. J. *Educational Diagnosis and the Measurement of School Achievement*. New York: Macmillan, 1926.

Vitanza, Victor J. "An After/Word: Preparing to Meet the Faces That 'We' Will Have Met." *Writing Histories of Rhetoric*. Ed. Vitanza. 217–257.

———, ed. *Writing Histories of Rhetoric*. Carbondale: Southern Illinois UP, 1994.

Wagner, Charles A. *Harvard: Four Centuries and Freedoms*. New York: Dutton, 1950.

Walberg, Herbert J. "Principles for Accountability Designs." In *School Accountability: An Assessment by the Koret Task Force on K–12 Education* Ed. Williamson M. Evers and Herbert J. Walberg. Stanford, CA: Hoover Institution P, 2002. 155–183.

Walker, Helen M. *Studies in the History of Statistical Method, with Special Reference to Certain Educational Problems*. Baltimore: Williams and Wilkins, 1929.

Washington State University. "WSU Writing Programs: Junior Writing Portfolio Final Rating Categories." 23 Jan. 2005 <http://www.wsu.edu>.

Weidlein, Edward R. "College-Level Equivalency Exams in English Draw Fire." *Chronicle of Higher Education* 12 Mar 1973: 1+.

Weigle, Sara Cushing. *Assessing Writing*. New York: Cambridge UP, 2002.

———. "Integrating Reading and Writing in a Competency Test for Non-Native Speakers of English." *Assessing Writing* 9.1 (2004): 27–55.

Wendell, Barrett. "English at Harvard." *The Dial* 1 Mar. 1894: 131–133.

———. *English Composition: Eight Lectures Given at the Lowell Institute*. New York: Scribner's, 1891.

Wesdorp, Hildo, Barbara A. Bauer, and Alan C. Purves. "Toward a Conceptualization of the Scoring of Written Composition." *Evaluation in Education* 5.3 (1982): 299–315.

Whately, Richard. *Elements of Rhetoric*. 1828. Delmar, NY: Scholars' Facsimile Imprints, 1991.

White, Edward M., ed. *Comparison and Contrast: The 1973 California State University and Colleges Freshman English Equivalency Examination*. ERIC ED 114825.

———, ed. *Comparison and Contrast: The 1980 and 1981 California State University and Colleges Freshman English Equivalency Examination*. ERIC ED 227511.

———. "Holisticism." *College Composition and Communication* 35.4 (1984): 400–409.

———. "Jane Austen and the Art of Parody." Diss. Harvard U, 1960.

———. "Language and Reality in Writing Assessment." *College Composition and Communication* 41.2 (1990): 187–200.

———. "The Opening of the Modern Era of Writing Assessment: A Narrative." *College English* 63.3 (2001): 306–320.

———. "Some Issues in the Testing of Writing." *Notes from the National Testing Network in Writing*. New York: City University of New York, 1982. 17. 23 Jan. 2005 <http://compppile.tamucc.edu>.

———. *Teaching and Assessing Writing: Recent Advances in Understanding, Evaluating, and Improving Student Performance*. San Francisco: Jossey-Bass, 1985.

White, Edward M., William D. Lutz, and Sandra Kamusikiri, eds. *Assessment of Writing: Politics, Policies, Practices*. New York: Modern Language Association, 1996.

White, Edward M., and Leon L. Thomas. "Racial Minorities and Writing Skills Assessment in the California State University and Colleges." *College English* 43.3 (1981): 276–283.

"Why a Commission on Tests?" *College Board Review* 65 (1967): 14.

Wiggins, Grant. *Assessing Student Performance: Exploring the Purpose and Limits of Testing*. San Francisco: Jossey-Bass, 1993.

———. "The Constant Danger of Sacrificing Validity to Reliability: Making Writing Assessment Serve Writers." *Assessing Writing* 1.1 (1994): 129–139.

Wilhelms, Fred T. *Evaluation as Feedback and Guide*. Washington: Association for Supervision and Curriculum Development, 1967.

Williamson, Michael M., and Brian A. Huot, eds. *Validating Holistic Scoring for Writing Assessment: Theoretical and Empirical Foundations*. Cresskill, NJ: Hampton P, 1993.

Wilson, William Julius. *When Work Disappears: The World of the New Urban Poor*. New York: Knopf, 1996.

Wilson, Woodrow. *The Papers of Woodrow Wilson*. Ed. Arthur S. Link. Vol. 27. Princeton: Princeton UP, 1978.

Witte, Stephen, and Lester Faigley. *Evaluating College Writing Programs*. Carbondale: Southern Illinois UP, 1983.

Woodlief, Annette M. "The Influences of Theories of Rhetoric on Thoreau." *Thoreau Journal Quarterly* 7 (Jan. 1975) 13–22. *American Transcendentalism Web*. 23 Jan. 2005 <http://www.vcu.edu/engweb/transcendentalism/>.

Yancey, Katheen Blake. "A Brief History of Writing Assessment in the Late Twentieth Century: The Writer Comes Center Stage." *History, Reflection, and Narrative: The Professionalization of Composition, 1963–1983*. Eds. Mary Rosner, Beth Boehm, and Debra Journet. Greenwich, CT: Ablex, 1999. 115–128.

———. "Looking Back and We Look Forward: Historicizing Writing Assessment." *College Composition and Communication* 50.3 (1999): 483–503.

Yancey, Kathleen Blake, and Irwin Weiser, eds. *Situating Portfolios: Four Perspectives*. Logan: Utah State UP, 1997.

Yerkes, Robert Mearns. Foreword. *A Study of American Intelligence*. By Carl Campbell Brigham. Princeton: Princeton UP, 1923. v–vii.

———. "Measuring the Mental Strength of an Army." *Proceedings of the National Academy of Sciences* 4.10 (1918): 295–297.

———. "A Point Scale for Measuring Mental Ability." *Proceedings of the National Academy of Science* 1.2 (1915): 117–119.

———, ed. *Psychological Examining in the United States Army*. Memoirs of the National Academy of Sciences. Vol. 15. Washington: GPO, 1921.

Young, Richard E., Alton L. Becker, and Kenneth L. Pike. *Rhetoric: Discovery and Change*. New York: Harcourt, 1970.

Younglove, William A. "A Look at Behavioristic Measurement of English Composition in United States Public Schools, 1901–1941." California Educational Research Association. 17–18 Nov. 1983. ERIC ED 246 109.

Zunz, Oliver. *The Changing Face of Inequality*. Chicago: U of Chicago P, 1982.

Index

C

D

E

F

G

H

I

J

N

O

P

Q

R

S

Y

Z

Studies in Composition and Rhetoric

Edited by Leonard A. Podis

This series welcomes both single-author and essay collections. Titles may refer to case studies but should consistently deal with larger theoretical issues. At the moment, we are especially interested in books that might be used for graduate courses in one or more of the following subjects: cultural studies and the teaching of writing; feminist perspectives on composition and rhetoric; values and ideologies in the teaching or writing; postmodernism and composition/rhetoric; and the composition as a site of knowledge production and research. At the same time, we also seek proposals in the following areas: the influence of social context on composing; the relationship of composition and rhetoric to various disciplines and schools of thought; new ways of conceiving discourse analysis, the composition classroom and the writing process, or the history of rhetoric; analyses of research methods, such as ethnography and textual hermeneutics; the relationship of theory and practice; and current and potential roles for composition and rhetoric in the academy.

For additional information about this series or for the submission of manuscripts, please contact:

Peter Lang Publishing, Inc.
Acquisitions Department
275 7th Avenue, 28th Floor
New York, NY 10001

To order other books in this series, please contact our Customer Service Department at:

(800) 770-LANG (within the U.S.)
(212) 647-7706 (outside the U.S.)
(212) 647-7707 FAX

or browse online by series at:

WWW.PETERLANGUSA.COM